VIZ GRAPHIC NOVEL

ANGEL OF CHAOS

A BATTLE ANGEL ALITA™ GRAPHIC NOVEL

STORY AND ART BY

YUKITO KISHIRO

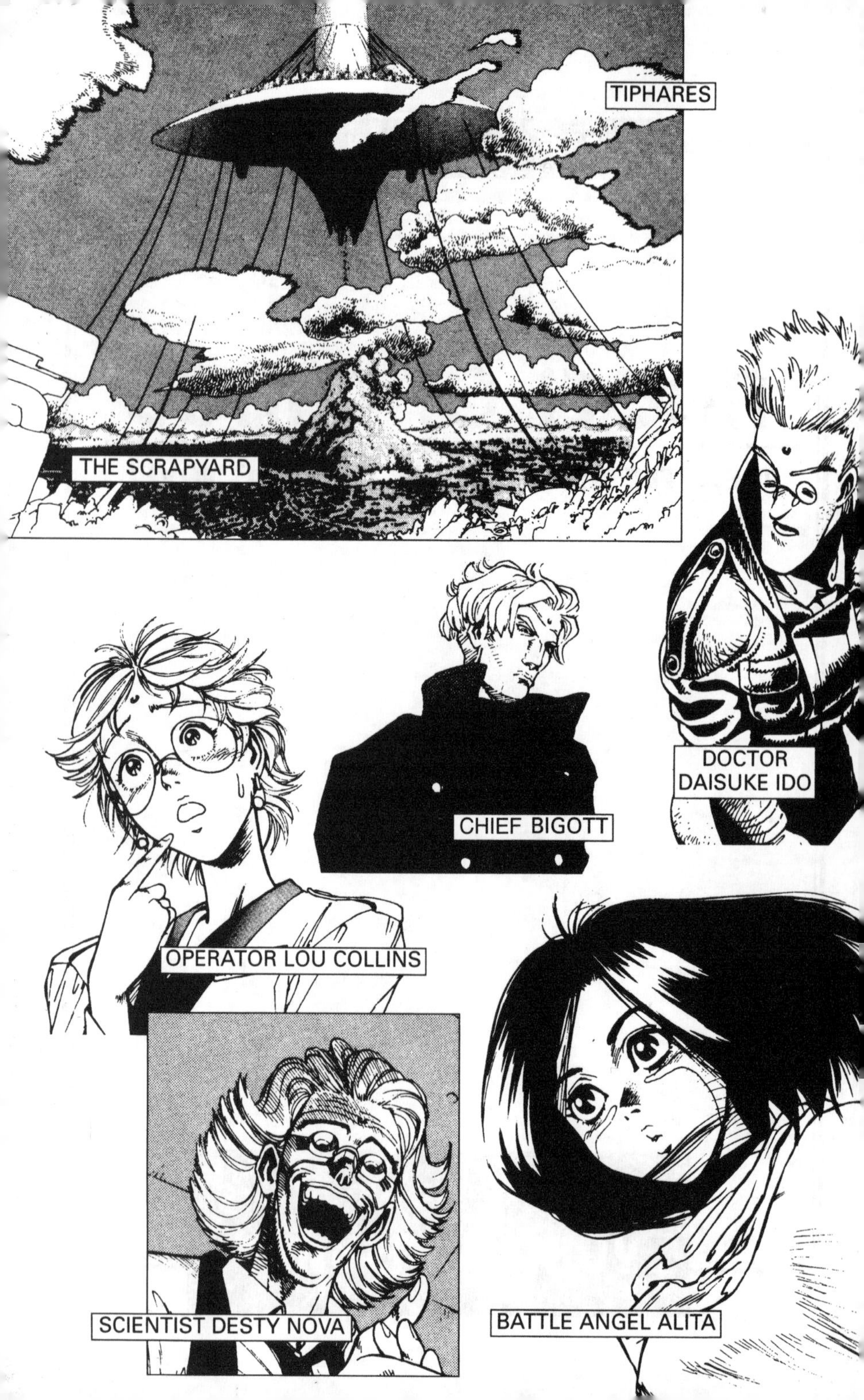
TIPHARES
THE SCRAPYARD
DOCTOR DAISUKE IDO
CHIEF BIGOTT
OPERATOR LOU COLLINS
SCIENTIST DESTY NOVA
BATTLE ANGEL ALITA

THE STORY THUS FAR...

When Doc Ido, a talented cyborg physician, found Alita, she had lost all memory of her past life. But when he reconstructed her, she discovered her body still instinctively remembered the *Panzer Kunst*, the most powerful cyborg fighting technique ever known!

Alita's second lease on life hasn't been easy. Her heart was broken when she fell in love with Hugo, a young man who dreamed of moving to Tiphares, the utopian city which floats tantalizingly above their bleak world of the Scrapyard. For a time, Alita gained some solace from her work as a Hunter-Warrior, a bounty hunter for the Factory (the giant corporation that governs the Scrapyard), and as a champion in Motorball, a life-and-death sport.

Then Alita committed a capital offense—firing a hand gun. She did it to save the Scrapyard from annihilation, but the Factory was unforgiving, and Alita was sentenced to death! Then, in the eleventh hour, she was granted a reprieve—if she agreed to become a member of the "Tuned," the elite force of Tiphares, her life would be spared.

Alita has served Tiphares well, under the control of her eager-to-please "operator" Lou Collins. Her first assignment: protect a nuclear-powered train from the infamous brigands known as Barjack. En route, she managed to catch the eye of a brash, handsome mercenary, despite her intimidating nickname "Angel of Death." Unfortunately, Barjack, led by their ruthless centaur leader Den, succeeded in stealing the train she was bound to protect.

Now Alita is on a quest to find her surrogate father, Doc Ido. Mad scientist Desty Nova was responsible for his death, and has promised to resurrect him. But Den and his followers stand in her way....

BARJACK LEADER DEN

FURY

DEEJAY KAOS

KOYOMI

CONTENTS

INHERIT THE SKIES

BARD OF THE BADLANDS

PANZER BRIDE

DEN OF BARJACK

FORK IN THE ROAD

SWEET FRUIT OF LIFE

This volume contains BATTLE ANGEL ALITA PART SIX in its entirety.

STORY AND ART BY YUKITO KISHIRO

**ENGLISH ADAPTATION BY
FRED BURKE & TOSHIFUMI YOSHIDA**

Touch-Up Art & Lettering/Wayne Truman
Cover Design/Viz Graphics
Editor/Annette Roman
Assistant Editor/Toshifumi Yoshida

Senior Editor/Trish Ledoux
Editor-in-Chief/Satoru Fujii
Publisher/Seiji Horibuchi

First published as *Gunnm* by Shueisha, Inc. in Japan

Printed in Canada

Published by Viz Communications, Inc.
P.O. Box 77010 • San Francisco, CA 94107

10 9 8 7 6 5 4 3 2 1
First printing, March 1997

Vizit
us at our World Wide Web site at **http://www.viz.com**
and
our new Internet magazine **J-pop.com** at **http://www.J-pop.com**!

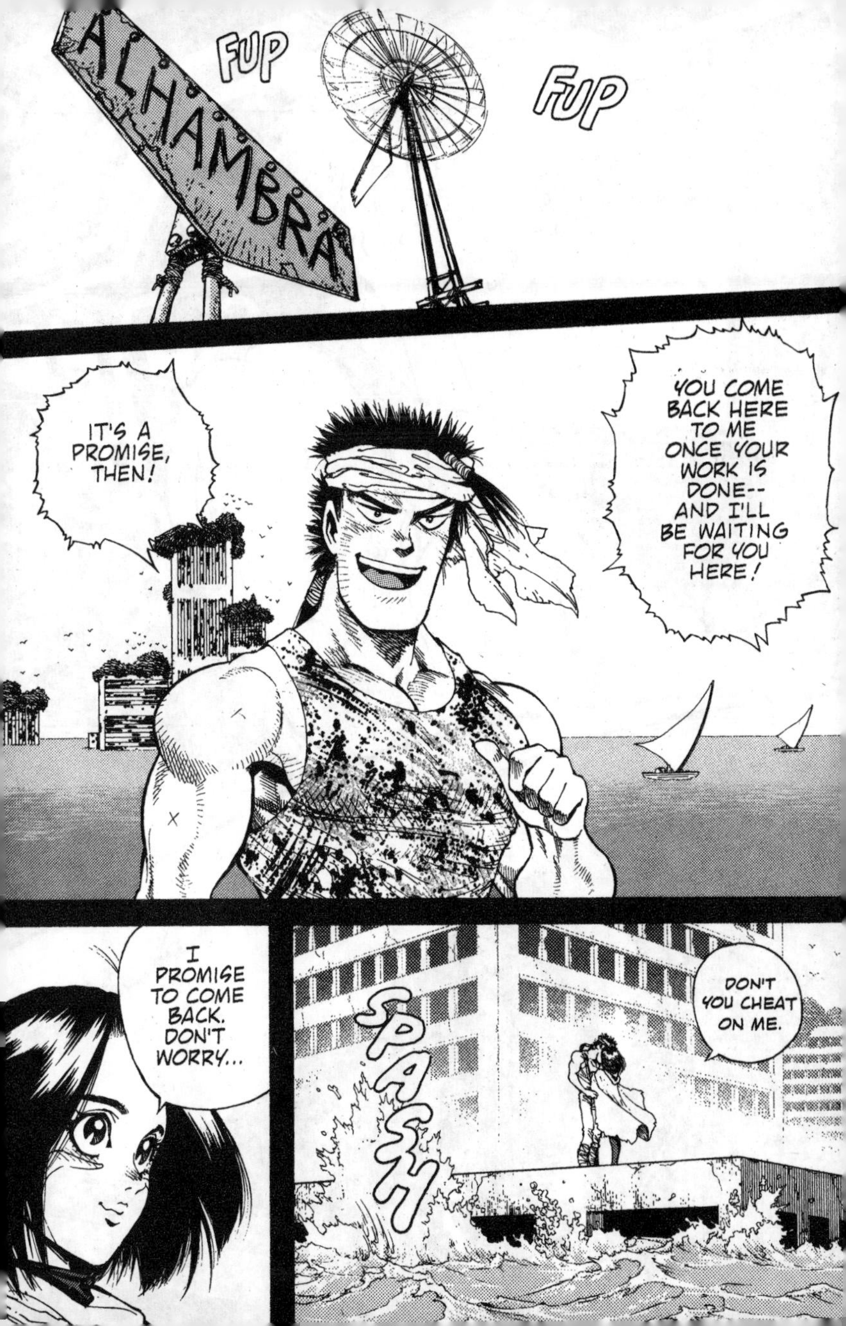
ALHAMBRA
FUP
FUP
IT'S A PROMISE, THEN!
YOU COME BACK HERE TO ME ONCE YOUR WORK IS DONE-- AND I'LL BE WAITING FOR YOU HERE!
I PROMISE TO COME BACK. DON'T WORRY...
SPASH
DON'T YOU CHEAT ON ME.

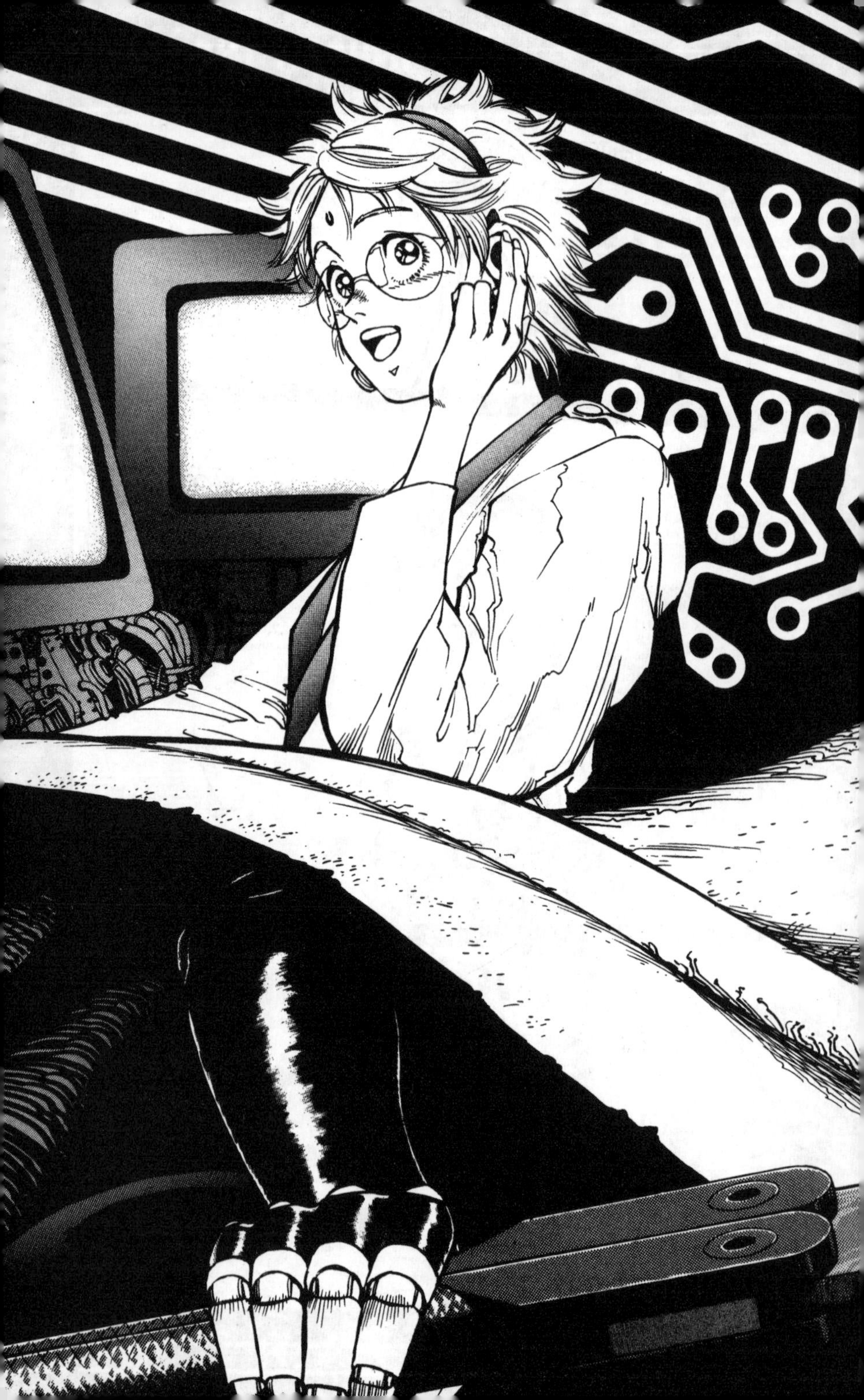

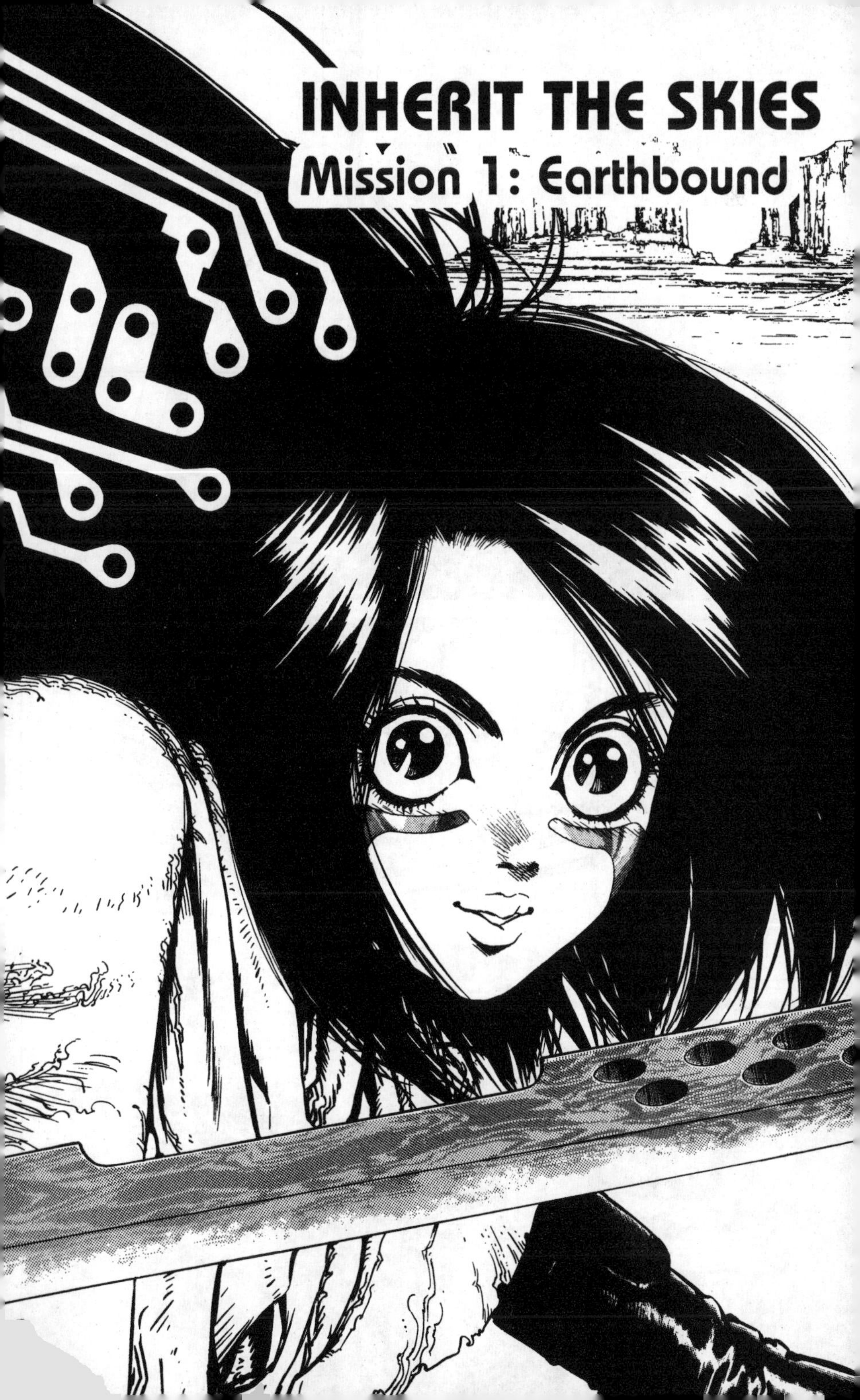

INHERIT THE SKIES
Mission 1: Earthbound

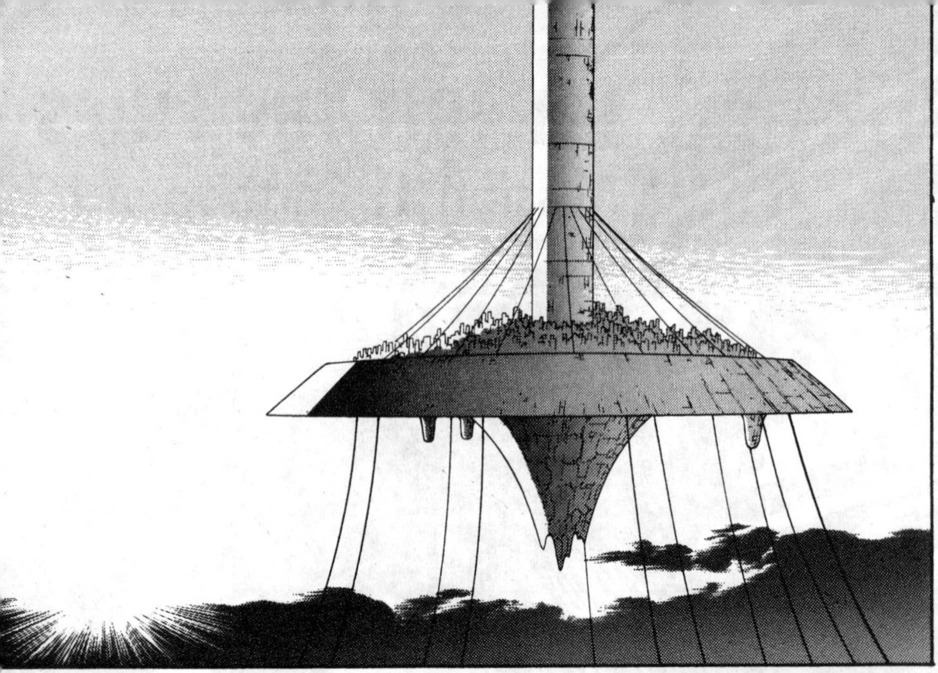
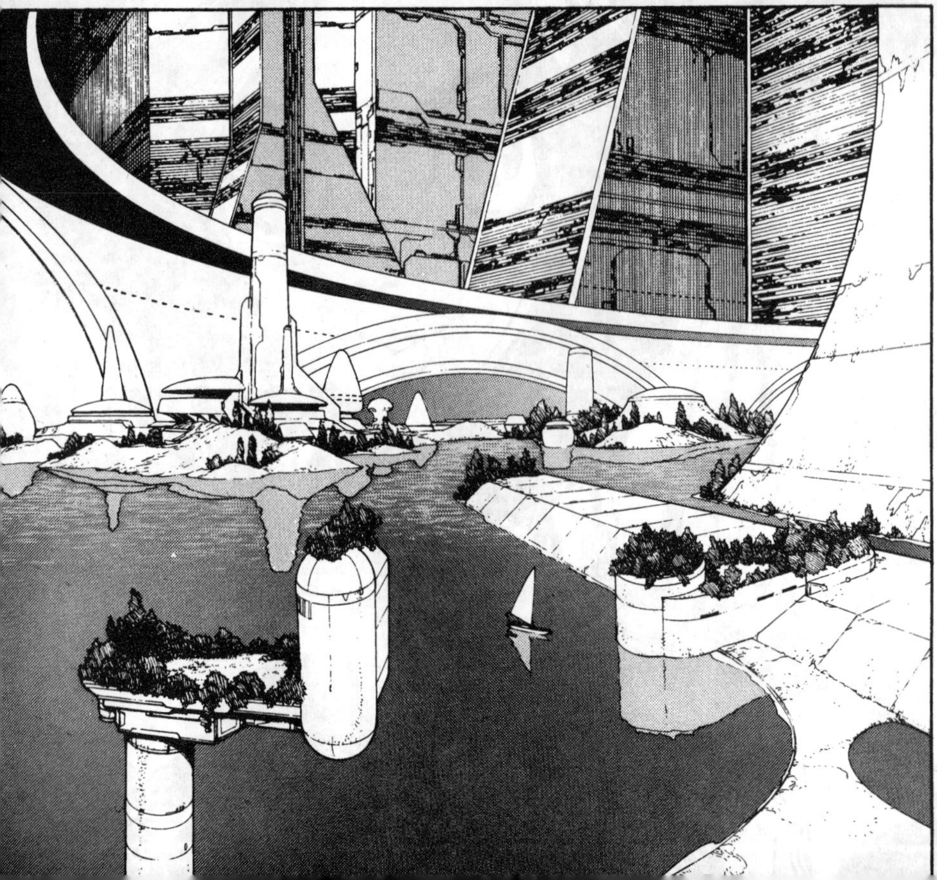

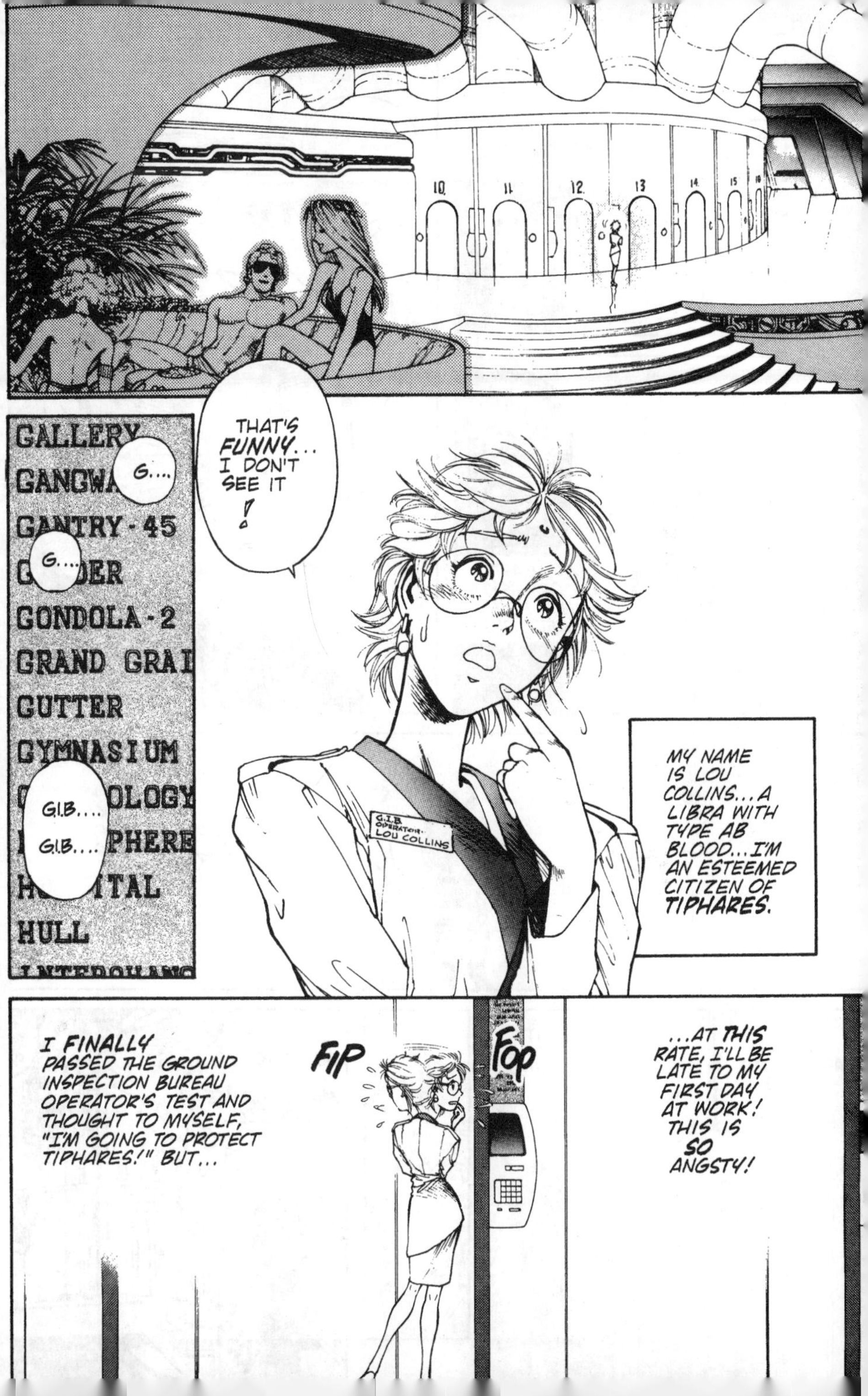

10.
11
12.
13
14.
15
16
GALLERY
GANTRY-45
GONDOLA-2
GUTTER
GYMNASIUM
HULL
G....
G....
G.I.B....
G.I.B....
THAT'S FUNNY... I DON'T SEE IT !
G.I.B. OPERATOR: LOU COLLINS
MY NAME IS LOU COLLINS... A LIBRA WITH TYPE AB BLOOD... I'M AN ESTEEMED CITIZEN OF TIPHARES.
I FINALLY PASSED THE GROUND INSPECTION BUREAU OPERATOR'S TEST AND THOUGHT TO MYSELF, "I'M GOING TO PROTECT TIPHARES!" BUT...
FIP
FOP
...AT THIS RATE, I'LL BE LATE TO MY FIRST DAY AT WORK! THIS IS SO ANGSTY!

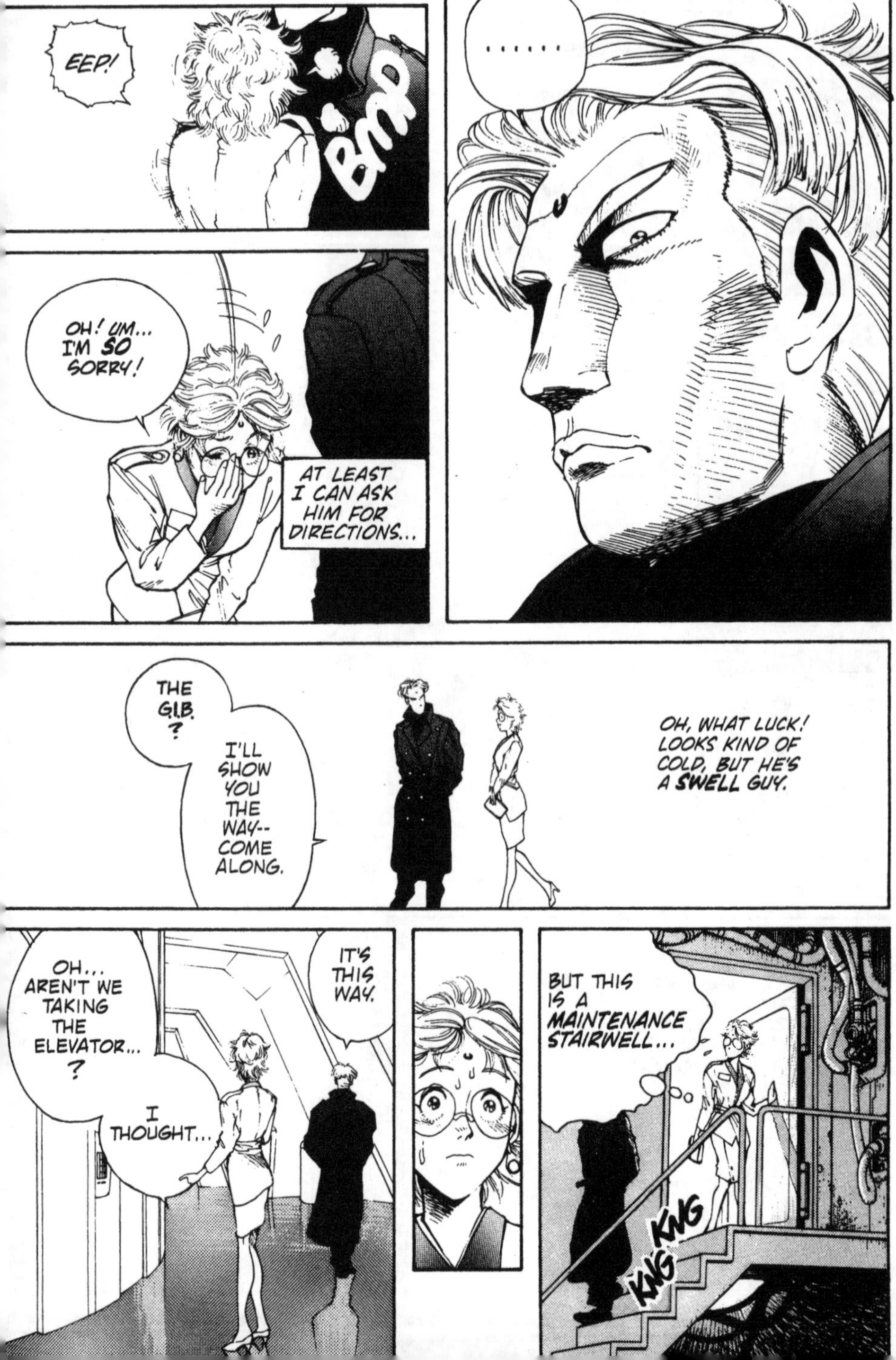
EEP!
BMP
OH! UM... I'M SO SORRY!
AT LEAST I CAN ASK HIM FOR DIRECTIONS...
......
THE G.I.B. ?
I'LL SHOW YOU THE WAY-- COME ALONG.
OH, WHAT LUCK! LOOKS KIND OF COLD, BUT HE'S A SWELL GUY.
OH... AREN'T WE TAKING THE ELEVATOR... ?
I THOUGHT...
IT'S THIS WAY.
BUT THIS IS A MAINTENANCE STAIRWELL...
KNG KNG

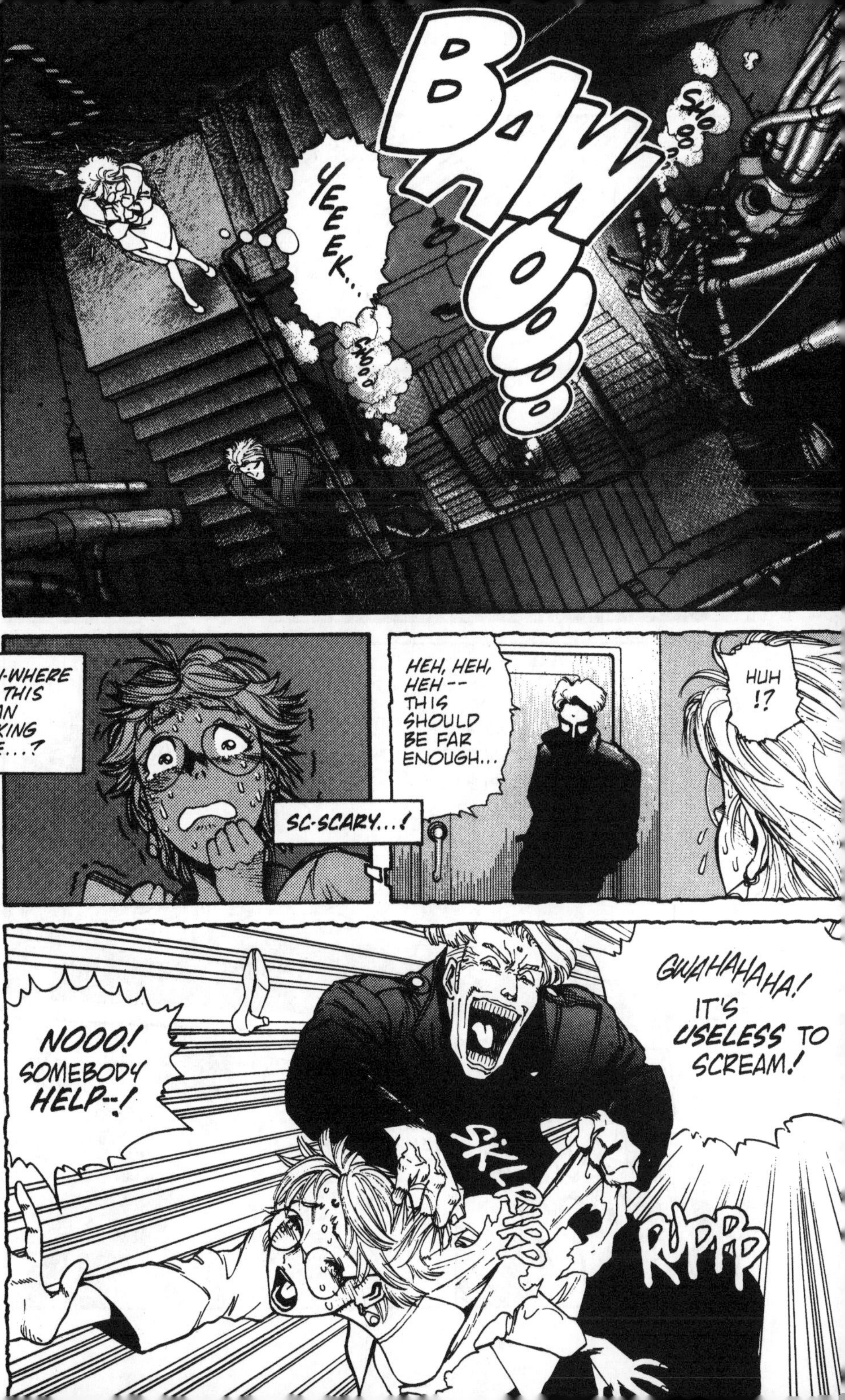
YEEEEK...
BAWOOOOO
SHOOO
SHOOO
H-WHERE S THIS AN AKING E...?
SC-SCARY...!
HEH, HEH, HEH -- THIS SHOULD BE FAR ENOUGH...
HUH !?
NOOO! SOMEBODY HELP--!
GWAHAHAHA! IT'S USELESS TO SCREAM!
SKLRIPP
RIPPP

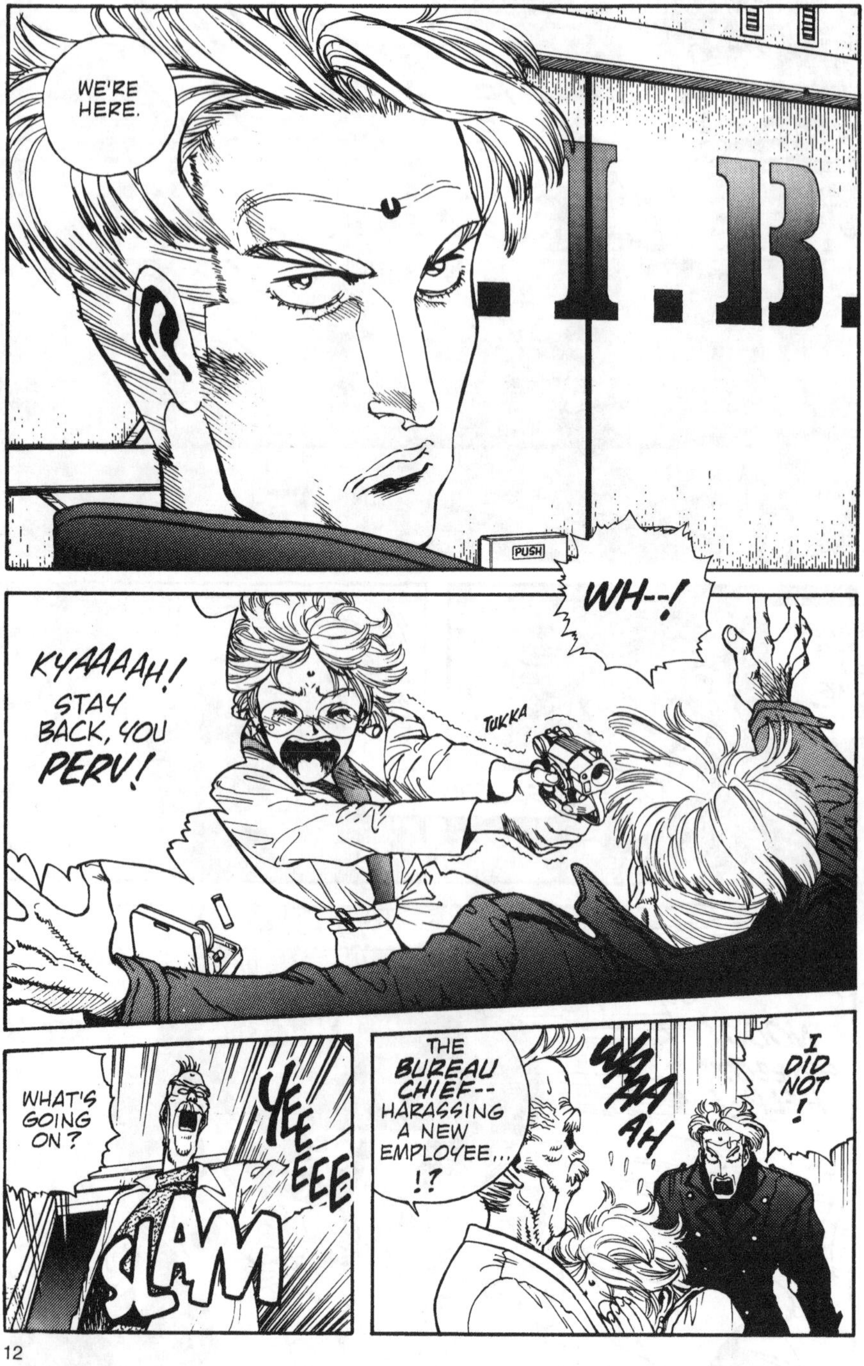

WE'RE HERE.
I.B.
PUSH
WH--!
KYAAAAH! STAY BACK, YOU PERV!
TUKKA
WHAT'S GOING ON?
YEEEEE
SLAM
THE BUREAU CHIEF-- HARASSING A NEW EMPLOYEE...!?
WAAAAAH
I DID NOT!

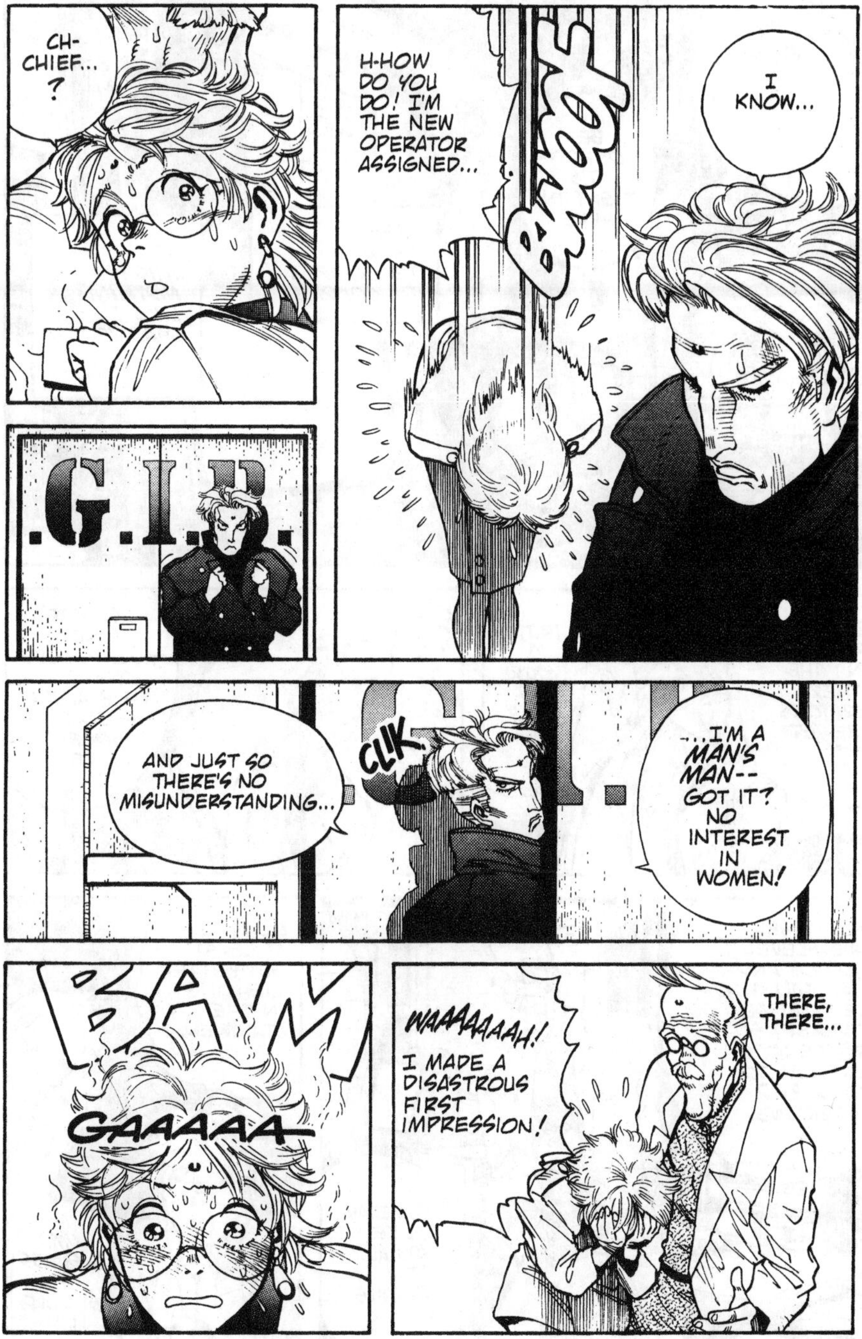

CH-CHIEF...?
H-HOW DO YOU DO! I'M THE NEW OPERATOR ASSIGNED...
I KNOW...
AND JUST SO THERE'S NO MISUNDERSTANDING...
CLIK
...I'M A MAN'S MAN-- GOT IT? NO INTEREST IN WOMEN!
BAM
GAAAAA
WAAAAAAAH!
I MADE A DISASTROUS FIRST IMPRESSION!
THERE, THERE...

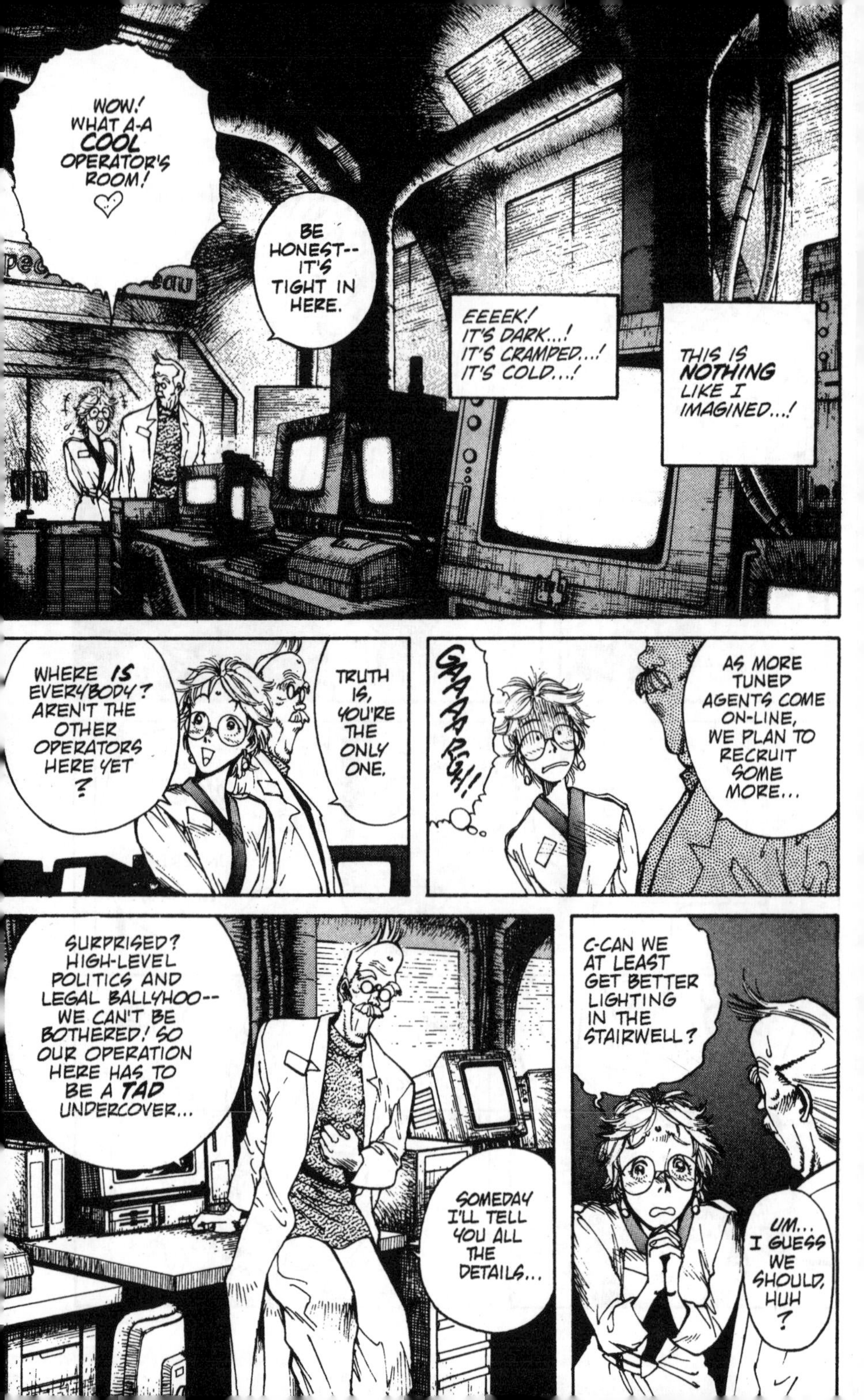
WOW! WHAT A-A **COOL** OPERATOR'S ROOM! ♡
BE HONEST-- IT'S TIGHT IN HERE.
EEEEK! IT'S DARK...! IT'S CRAMPED...! IT'S COLD...!
THIS IS **NOTHING** LIKE I IMAGINED...!
WHERE ***IS*** EVERYBODY? AREN'T THE OTHER OPERATORS HERE YET?
TRUTH IS, YOU'RE THE ONLY ONE.
AS MORE TUNED AGENTS COME ON-LINE, WE PLAN TO RECRUIT SOME MORE...
SURPRISED? HIGH-LEVEL POLITICS AND LEGAL BALLYHOO-- WE CAN'T BE BOTHERED! SO OUR OPERATION HERE HAS TO BE A ***TAD*** UNDERCOVER...
SOMEDAY I'LL TELL YOU ALL THE DETAILS...
C-CAN WE AT LEAST GET BETTER LIGHTING IN THE STAIRWELL?
UM... I GUESS WE SHOULD, HUH?

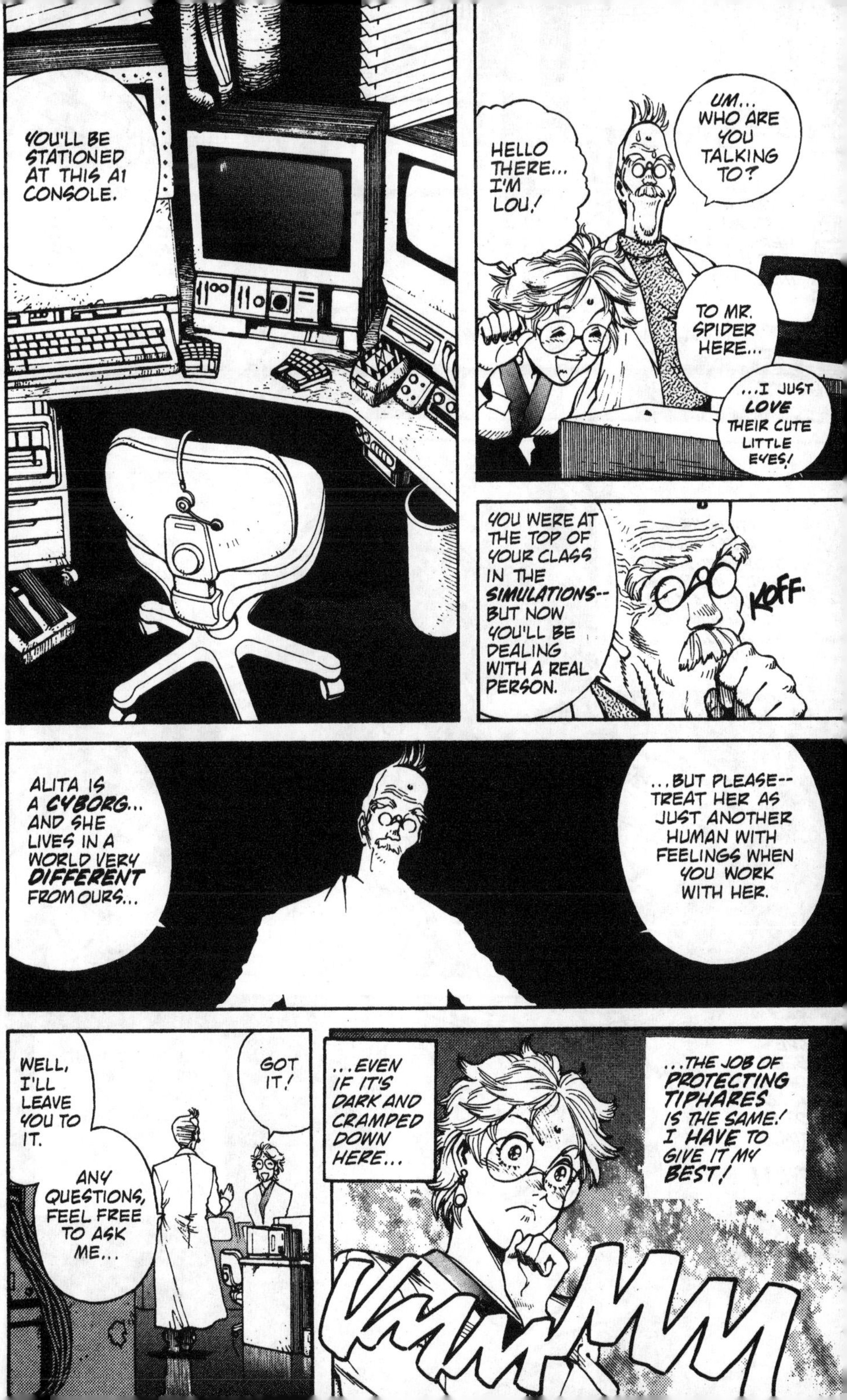
YOU'LL BE STATIONED AT THIS A1 CONSOLE.
HELLO THERE... I'M LOU!
UM... WHO ARE YOU TALKING TO?
TO MR. SPIDER HERE...
...I JUST LOVE THEIR CUTE LITTLE EYES!
YOU WERE AT THE TOP OF YOUR CLASS IN THE SIMULATIONS-- BUT NOW YOU'LL BE DEALING WITH A REAL PERSON.
KOFF
ALITA IS A CYBORG... AND SHE LIVES IN A WORLD VERY DIFFERENT FROM OURS...
...BUT PLEASE-- TREAT HER AS JUST ANOTHER HUMAN WITH FEELINGS WHEN YOU WORK WITH HER.
WELL, I'LL LEAVE YOU TO IT.
ANY QUESTIONS, FEEL FREE TO ASK ME...
GOT IT!
...EVEN IF IT'S DARK AND CRAMPED DOWN HERE...
...THE JOB OF PROTECTING TIPHARES IS THE SAME! I HAVE TO GIVE IT MY BEST!
UMMMM

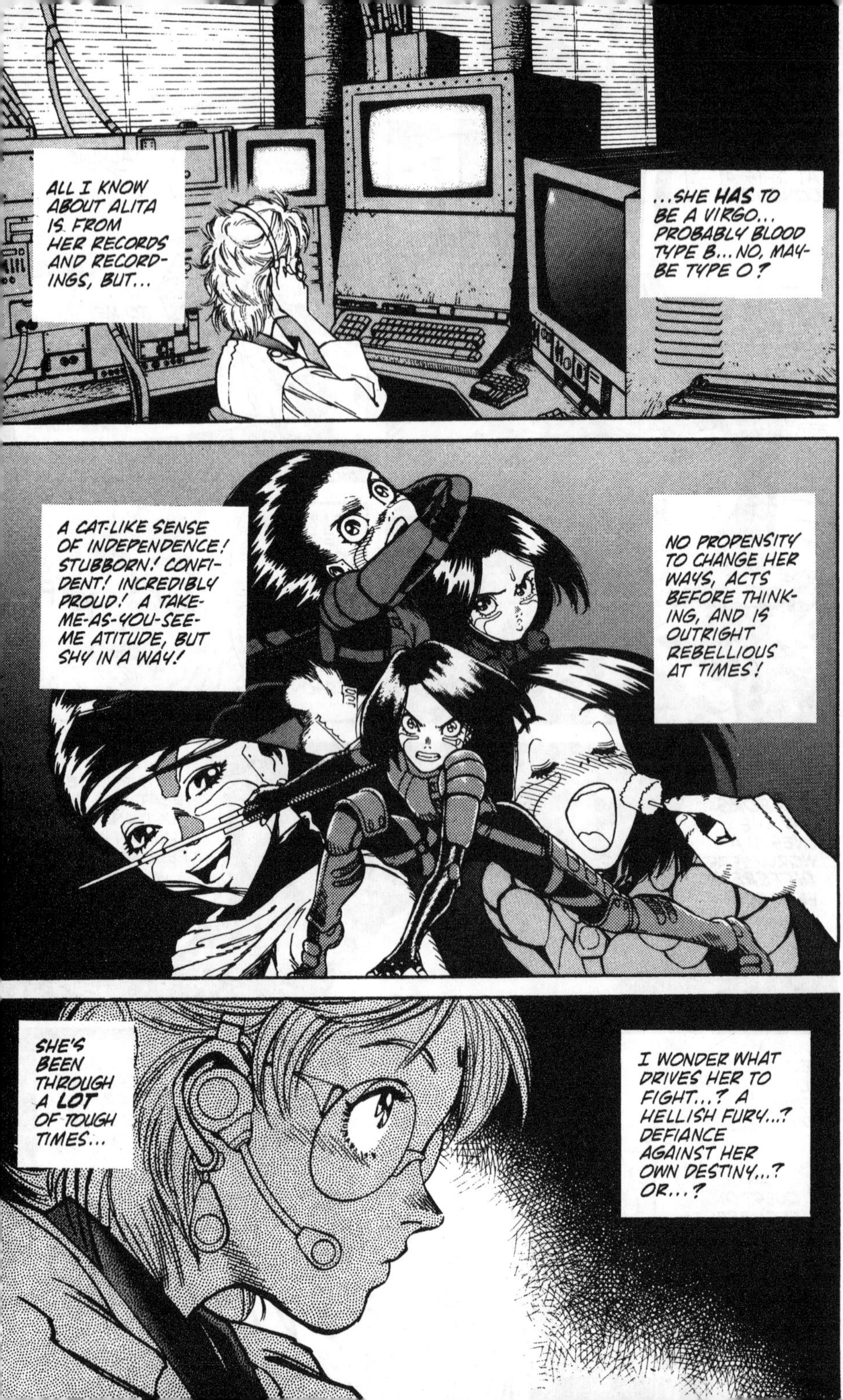
ALL I KNOW ABOUT ALITA IS FROM HER RECORDS AND RECORDINGS, BUT...
...SHE HAS TO BE A VIRGO... PROBABLY BLOOD TYPE B... NO, MAYBE TYPE O?
A CAT-LIKE SENSE OF INDEPENDENCE! STUBBORN! CONFIDENT! INCREDIBLY PROUD! A TAKE-ME-AS-YOU-SEE-ME ATITUDE, BUT SHY IN A WAY!
NO PROPENSITY TO CHANGE HER WAYS, ACTS BEFORE THINKING, AND IS OUTRIGHT REBELLIOUS AT TIMES!
SHE'S BEEN THROUGH A LOT OF TOUGH TIMES...
I WONDER WHAT DRIVES HER TO FIGHT...? A HELLISH FURY...? DEFIANCE AGAINST HER OWN DESTINY...? OR...?

THERE I GO AGAIN! WHY DOES MY IMAGINATION WANDER OFF SO MUCH?!

PMP PMP

OKAY, LOU! GET WITH IT!

IT'S NOT EXAGGERATING TOO MUCH TO SAY THAT THE FUTURE OF TIPHARES LIES IN THIS *FIRST* CONTACT!

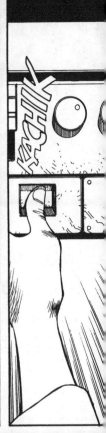

KACHIK

VWE EEEEN

HERE GOES...

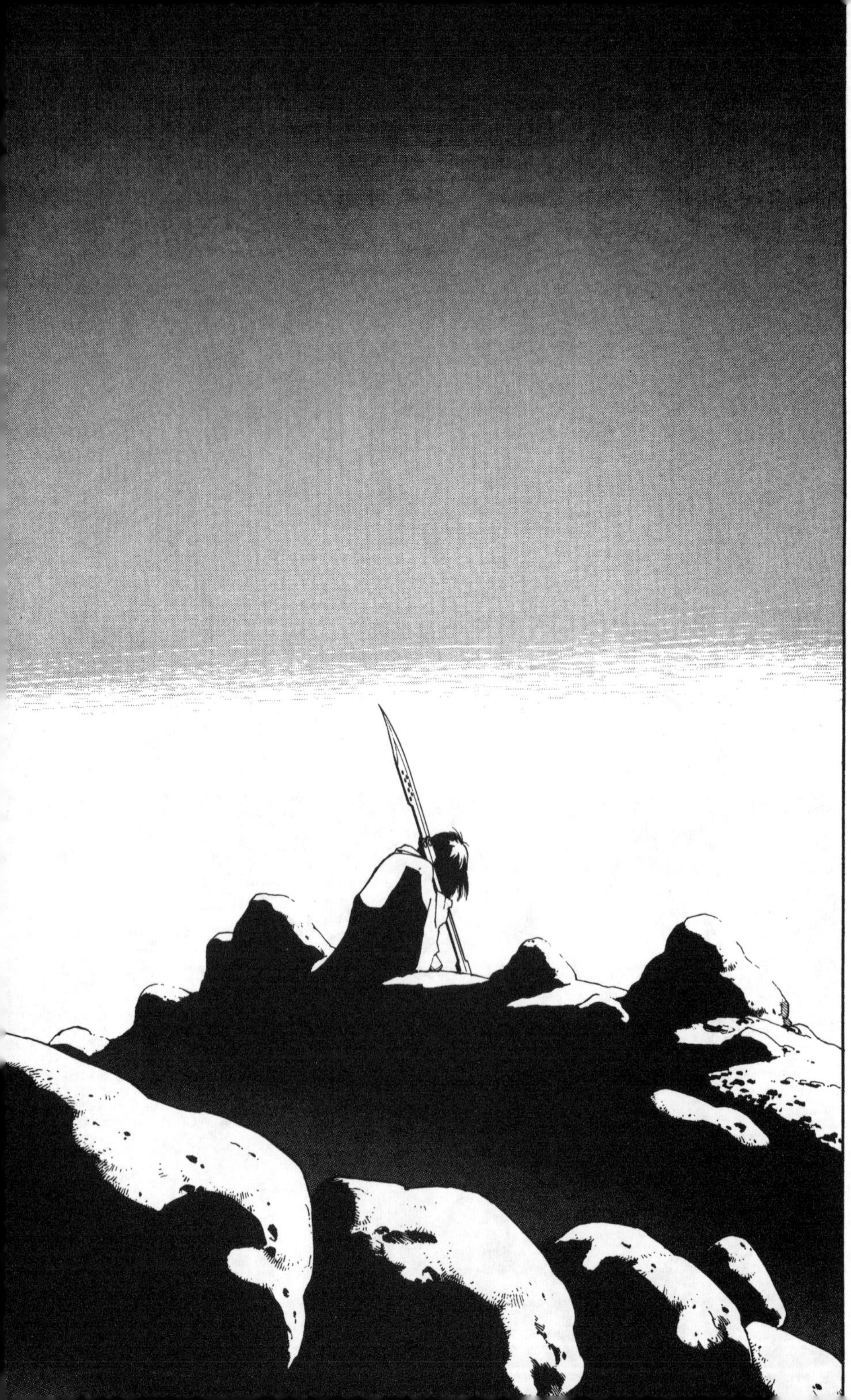

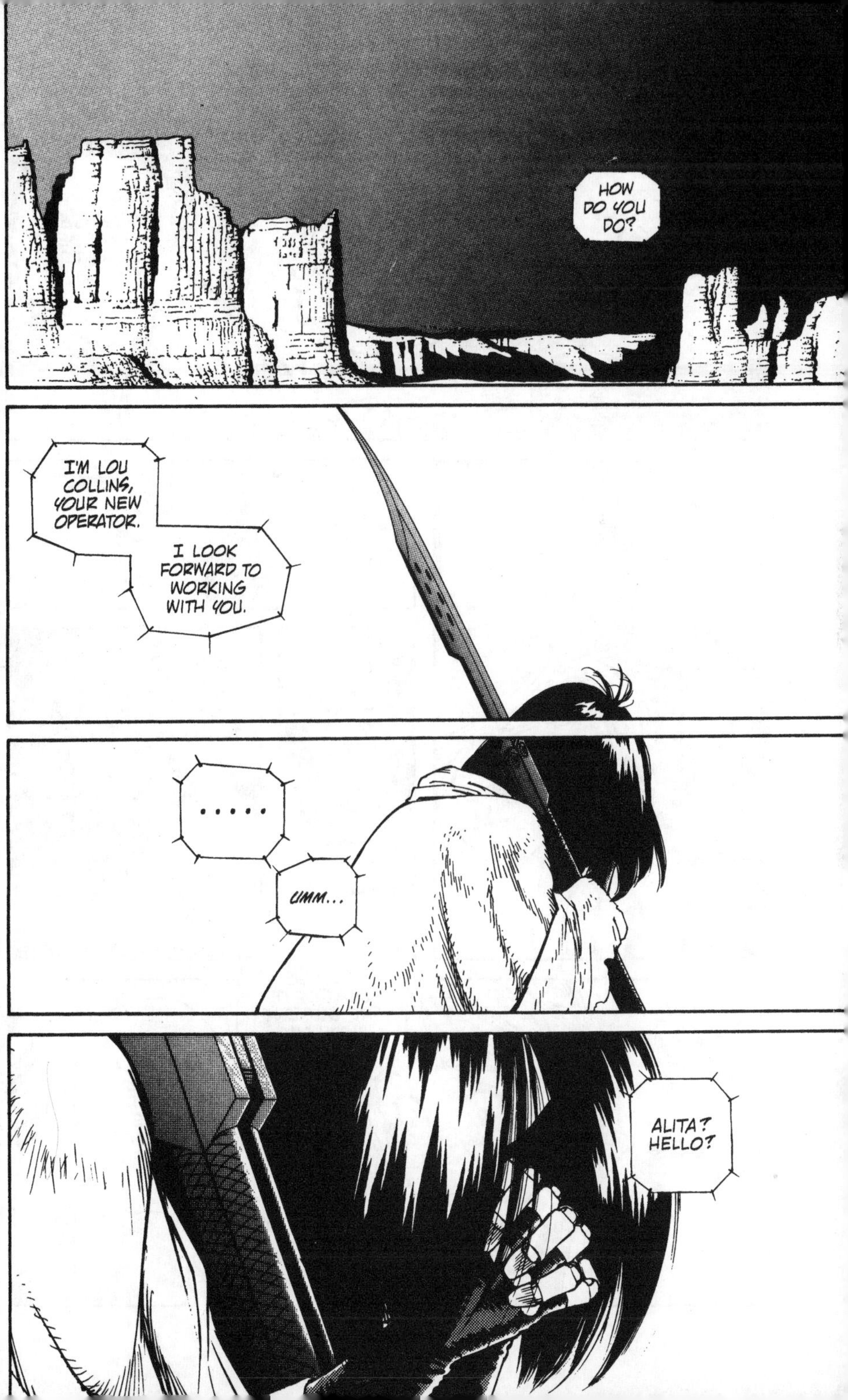
HOW DO YOU DO?
I'M LOU COLLINS, YOUR NEW OPERATOR.
I LOOK FORWARD TO WORKING WITH YOU.
.....
UMM...
ALITA? HELLO?

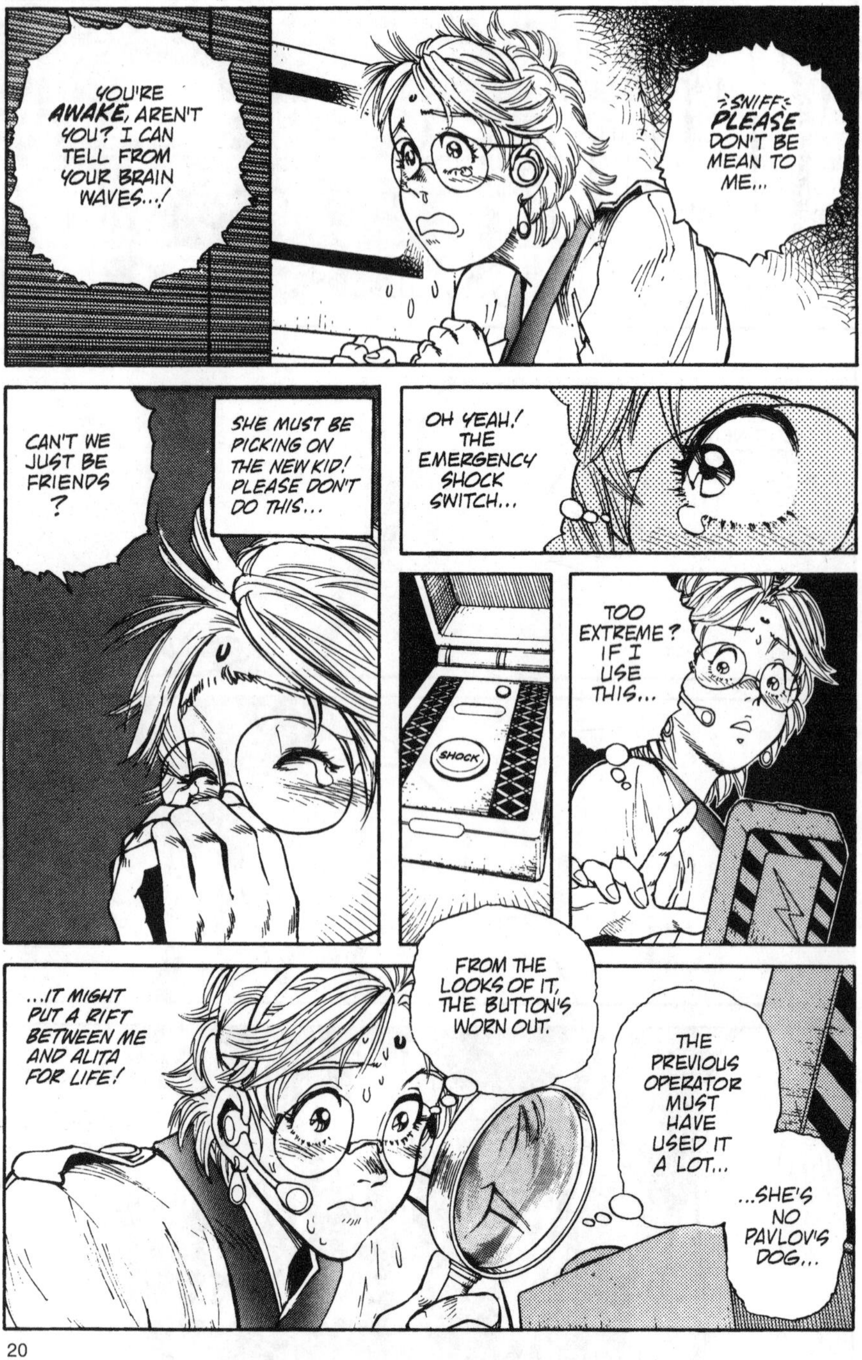
YOU'RE AWAKE, AREN'T YOU? I CAN TELL FROM YOUR BRAIN WAVES...!
=SNIFF= PLEASE DON'T BE MEAN TO ME...
CAN'T WE JUST BE FRIENDS?
SHE MUST BE PICKING ON THE NEW KID! PLEASE DON'T DO THIS...
OH YEAH! THE EMERGENCY SHOCK SWITCH...
SHOCK
TOO EXTREME? IF I USE THIS...
...IT MIGHT PUT A RIFT BETWEEN ME AND ALITA FOR LIFE!
FROM THE LOOKS OF IT, THE BUTTON'S WORN OUT.
THE PREVIOUS OPERATOR MUST HAVE USED IT A LOT...
...SHE'S NO PAVLOV'S DOG...

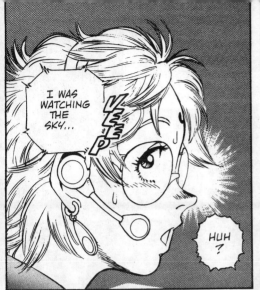

I WAS WATCHING THE SKY...

VEEP

HUH?

WHAT DID YOU SAY?

SINCE DAWN... I'VE BEEN WATCHING THE SKY TURN...

UM... OKAY!

...FROM THE DARKNESS OF NIGHT TO A DEEP BLUE I'VE NEVER SEEN SO CLEAR...

...TRANSFIXED BY THE BEAUTY OF THE ATMOSPHERE, PASSING THROUGH ITS INFINITE GRADATIONS OF COLOR...

THEN, LIKE MAGIC, THE BLUE FROM THE SKY FELL UPON ME.

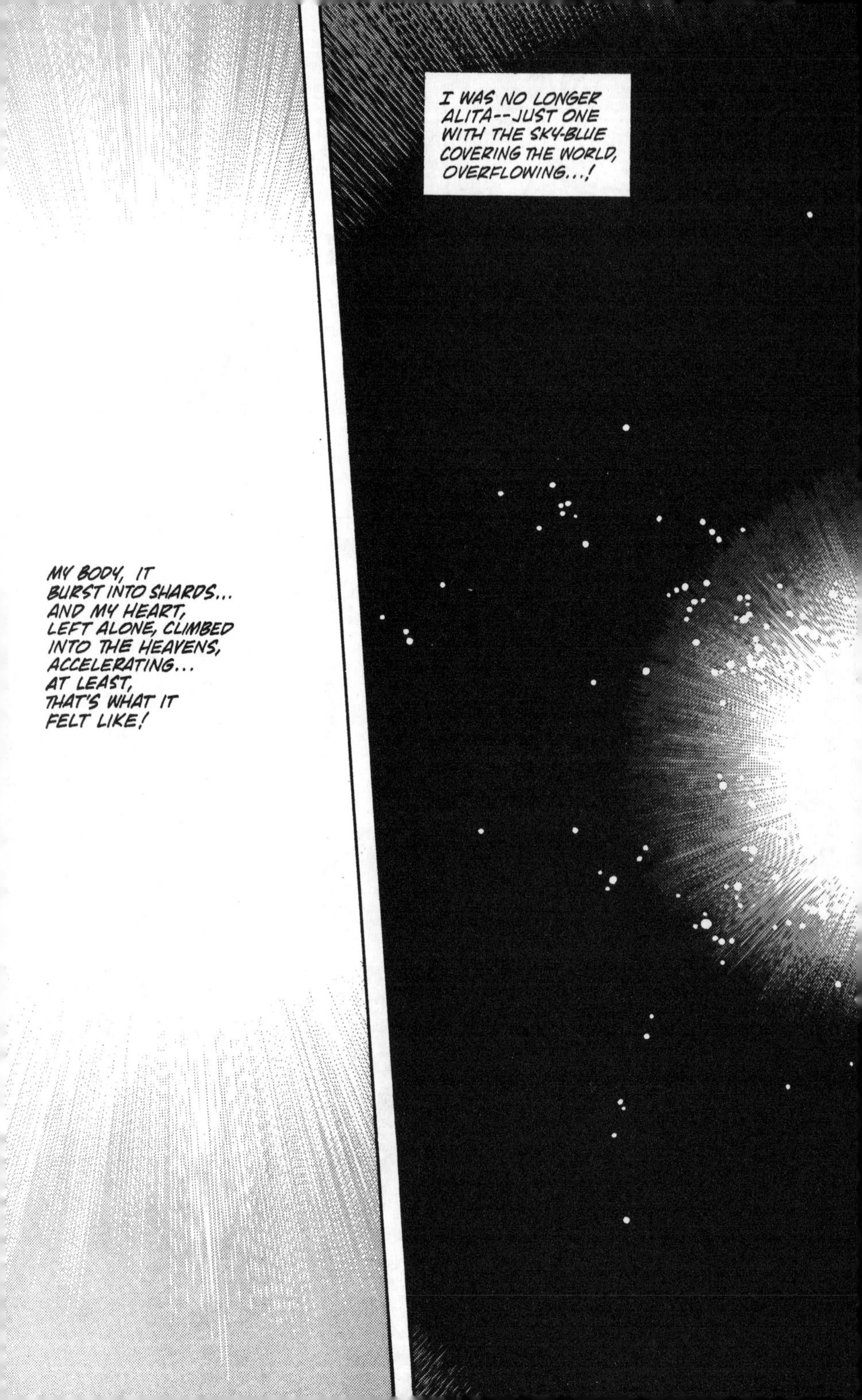
MY BODY, IT BURST INTO SHARDS... AND MY HEART, LEFT ALONE, CLIMBED INTO THE HEAVENS, ACCELERATING... AT LEAST, THAT'S WHAT IT FELT LIKE!
I WAS NO LONGER ALITA--JUST ONE WITH THE SKY-BLUE COVERING THE WORLD, OVERFLOWING...!

I THINK MAYBE I UNDERSTAND NOW...
AND FOR A FEW SECONDS--OR HOURS...I DON'T KNOW--I EXPERIENCED SOMETHING... BIZARRE AND POWERFUL...
ALL THE PEOPLE I'VE MET, THE THINGS I'VE DONE...I COULD NEVER FULLY COMPREHEND IT BEFORE... THE SADNESS...BUT...

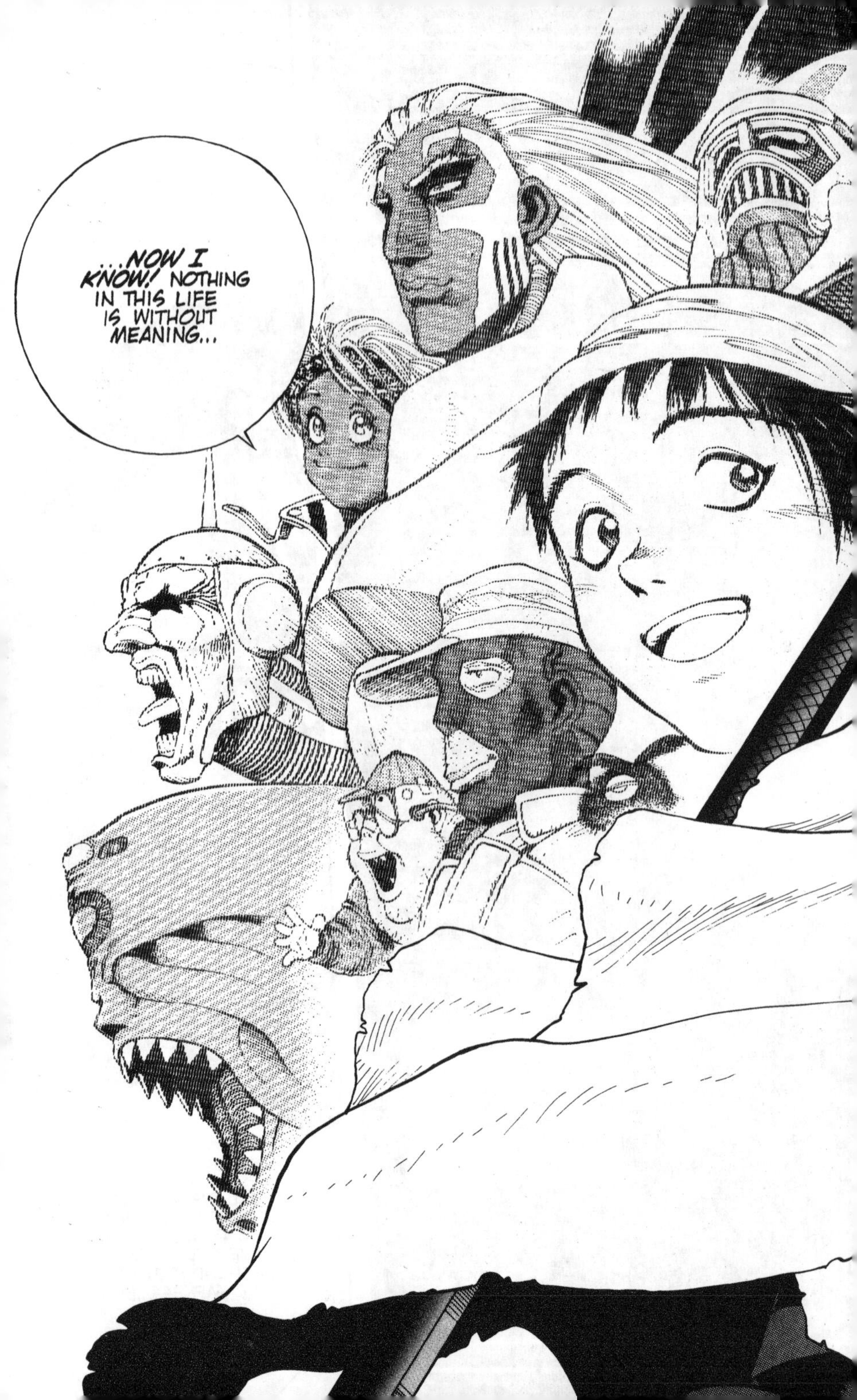
...NOW I KNOW! NOTHING IN THIS LIFE IS WITHOUT MEANING...

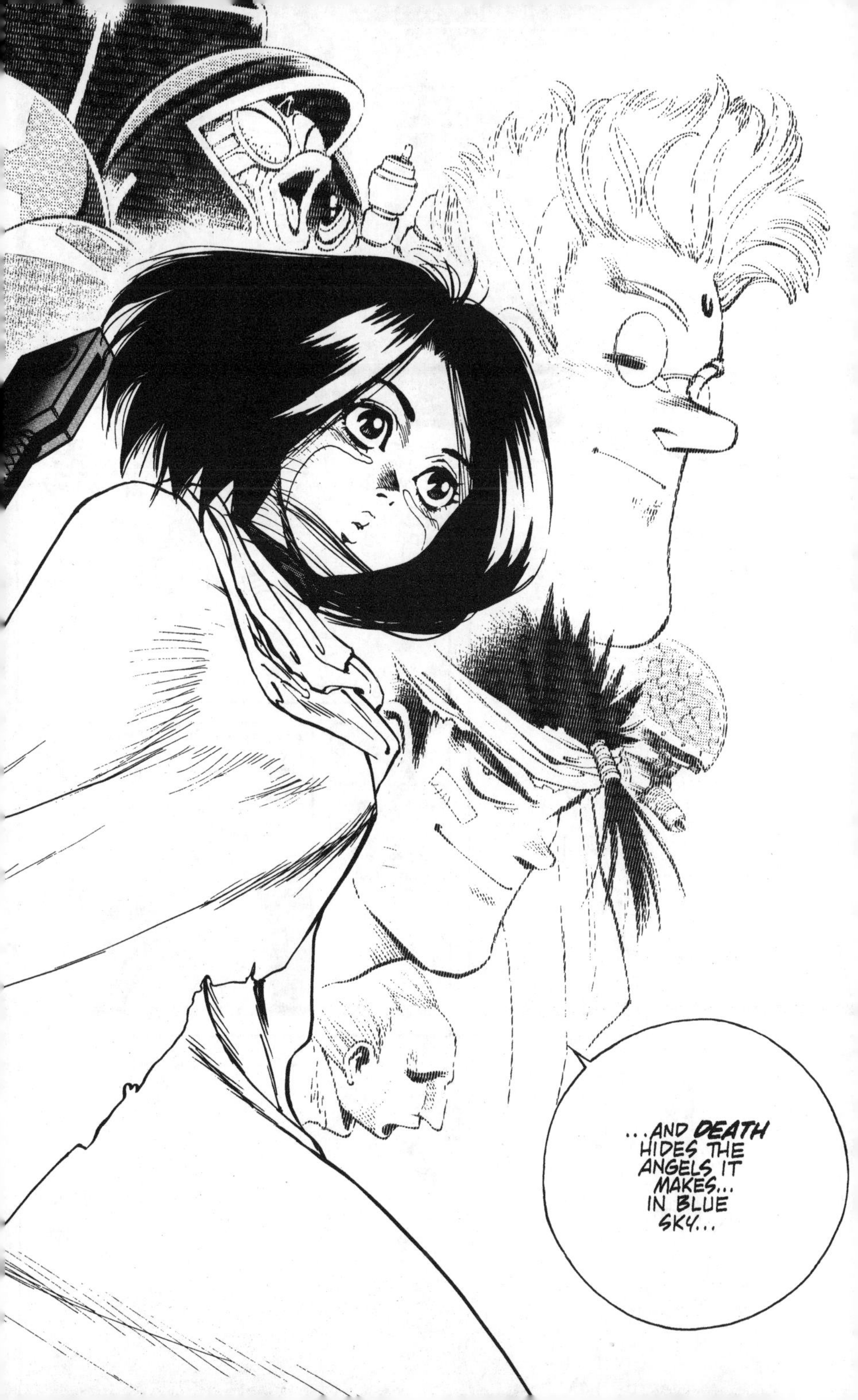
...AND DEATH HIDES THE ANGELS IT MAKES... IN BLUE SKY...

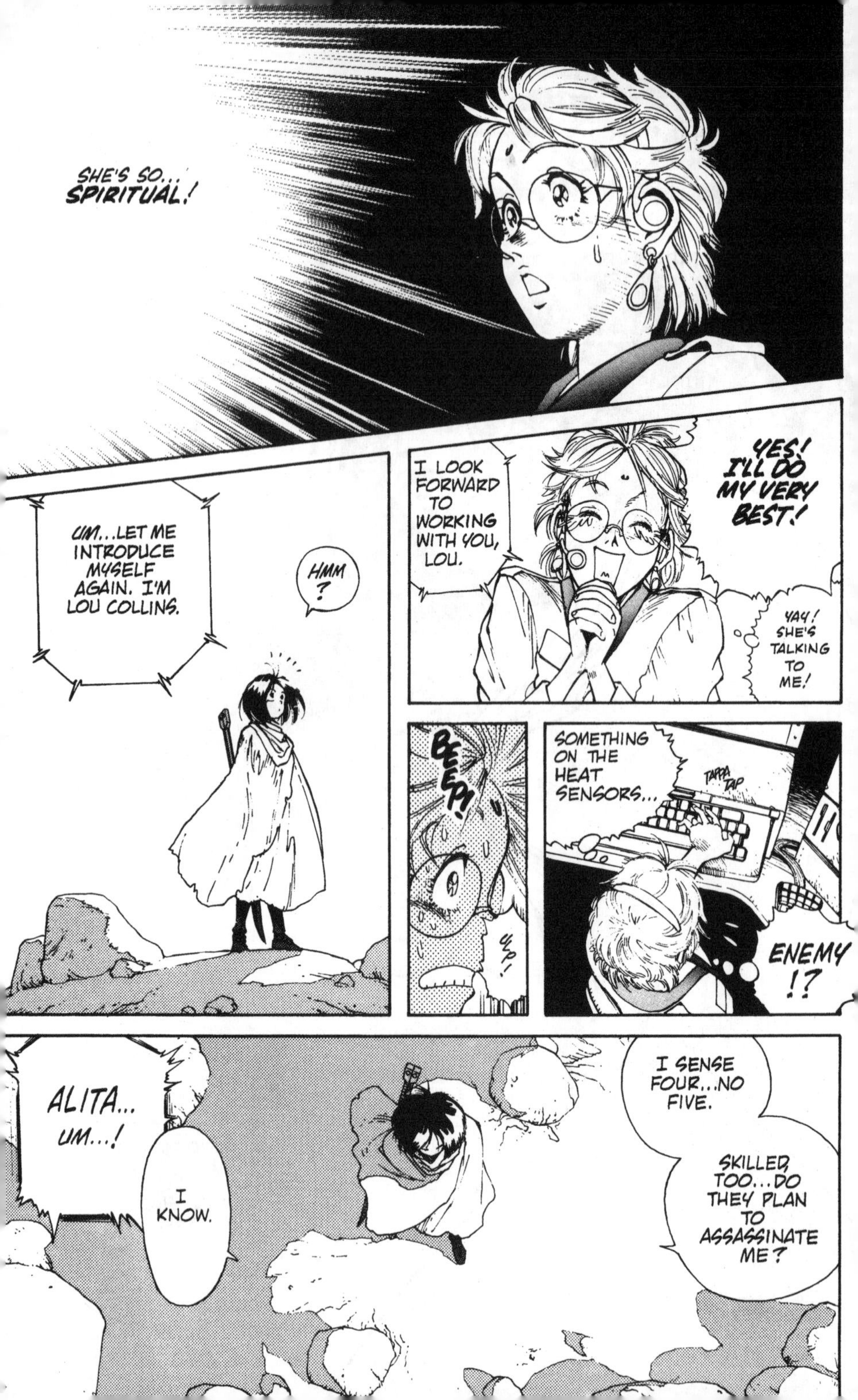
SHE'S SO... SPIRITUAL!
UM...LET ME INTRODUCE MYSELF AGAIN. I'M LOU COLLINS.
HMM?
I LOOK FORWARD TO WORKING WITH YOU, LOU.
YES! I'LL DO MY VERY BEST!
YAY! SHE'S TALKING TO ME!
BEEP!
URP!
SOMETHING ON THE HEAT SENSORS...
TAPPA TAP
ENEMY!?
ALITA... UM...!
I KNOW.
I SENSE FOUR...NO FIVE.
SKILLED, TOO...DO THEY PLAN TO ASSASSINATE ME?

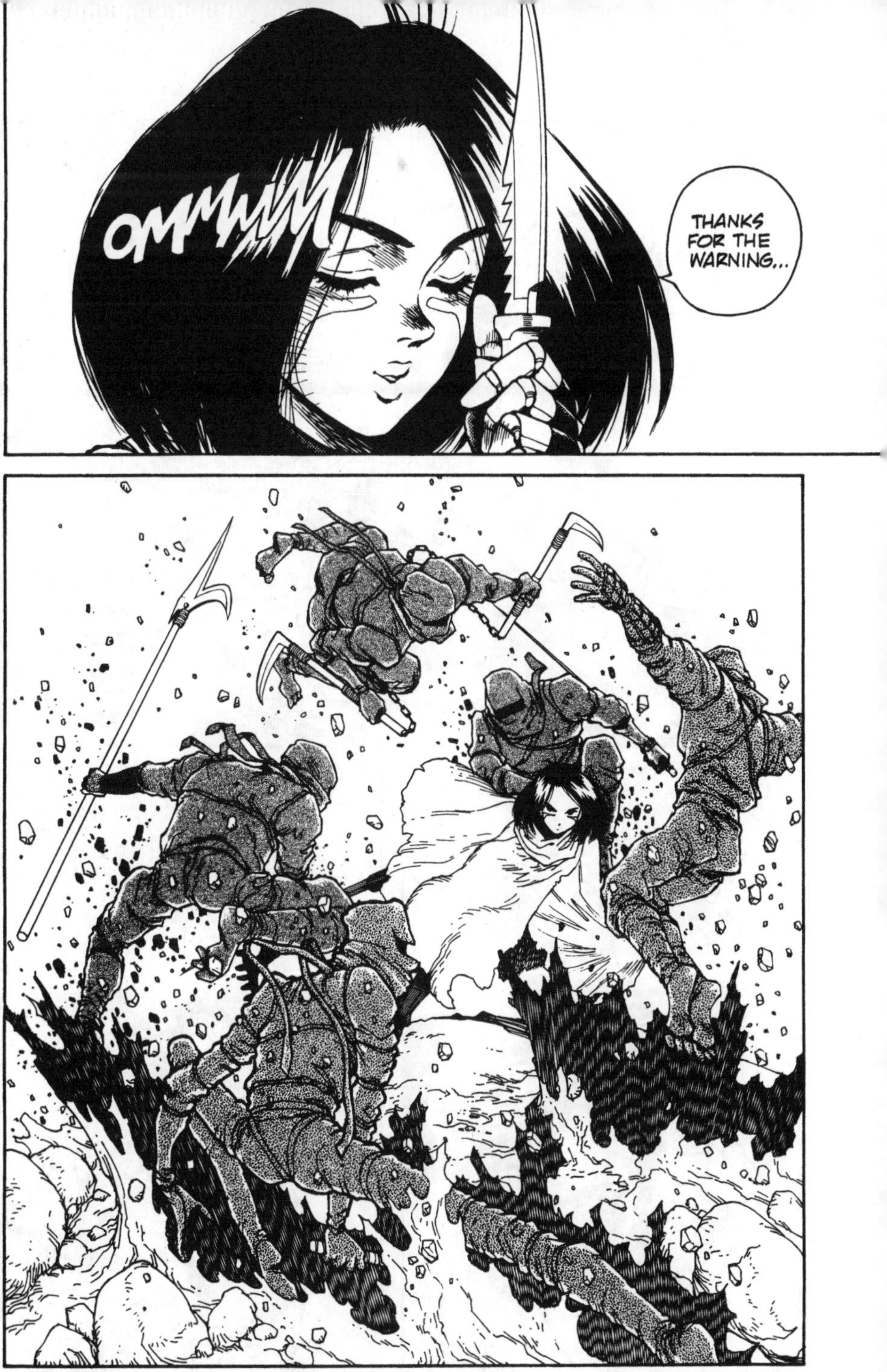
THANKS FOR THE WARNING...

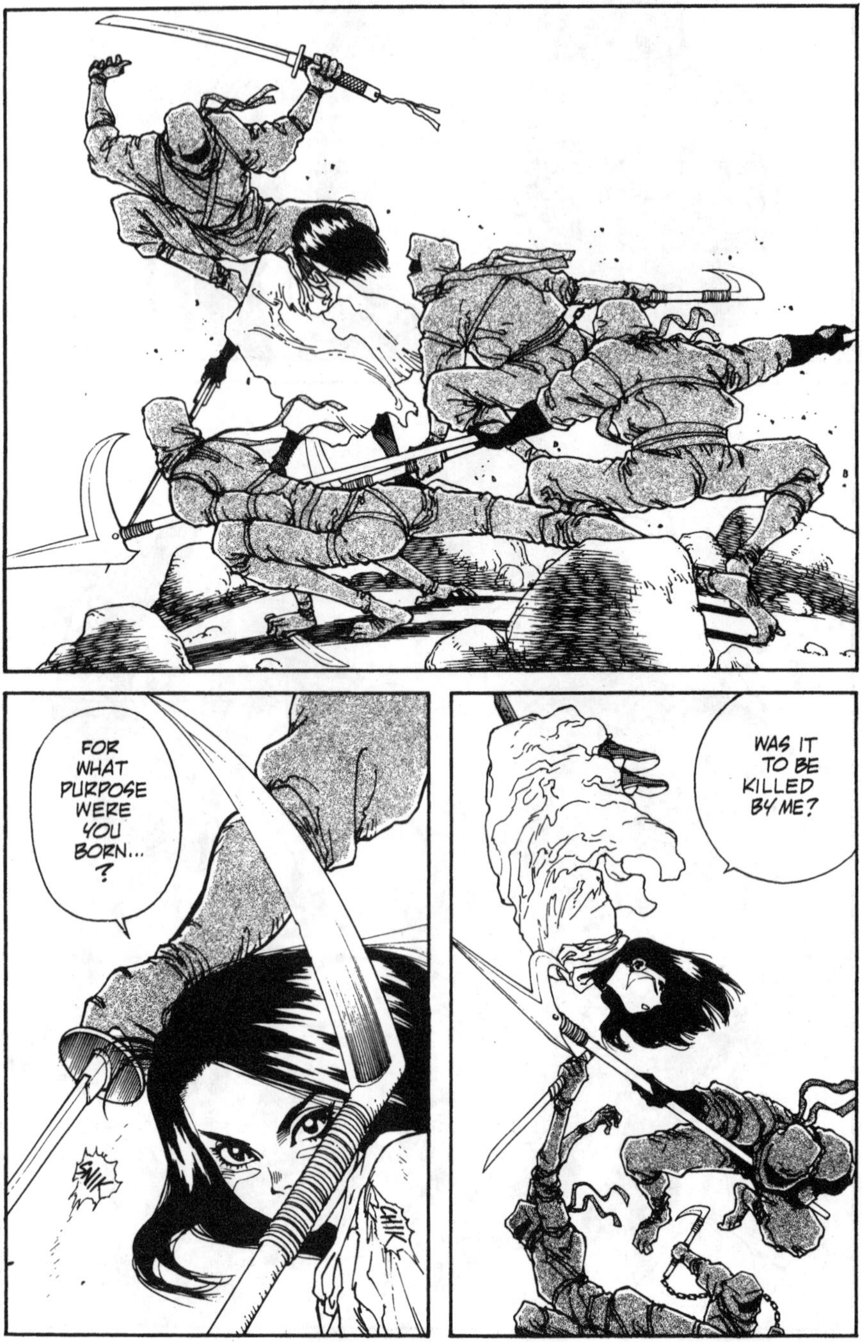
FOR WHAT PURPOSE WERE YOU BORN...?
SNIK
CHIK
WAS IT TO BE KILLED BY ME?

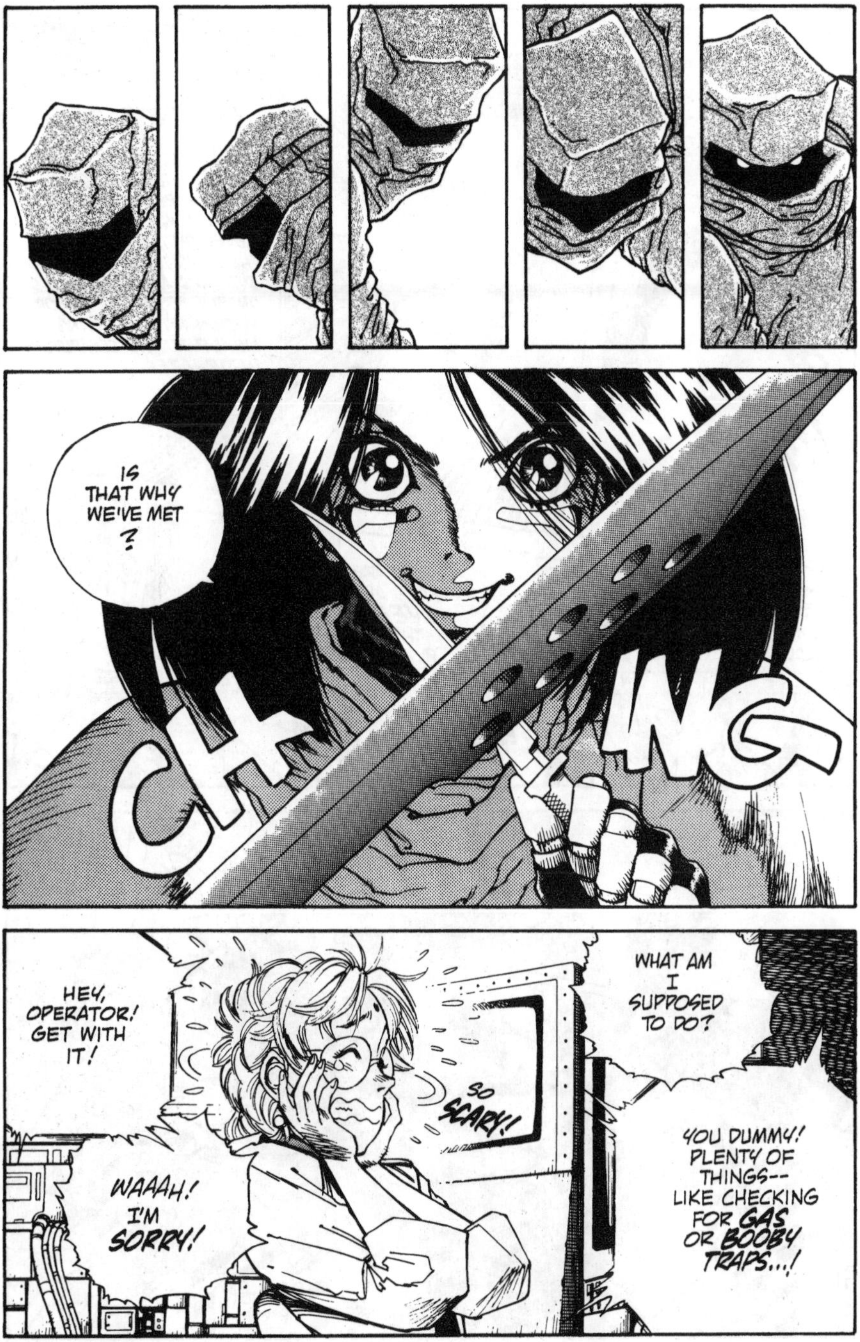
IS THAT WHY WE'VE MET ?
CH- -ING
HEY, OPERATOR! GET WITH IT!
WHAT AM I SUPPOSED TO DO?
SO SCARY!
WAAAH! I'M SORRY!
YOU DUMMY! PLENTY OF THINGS-- LIKE CHECKING FOR GAS OR BOOBY TRAPS...!

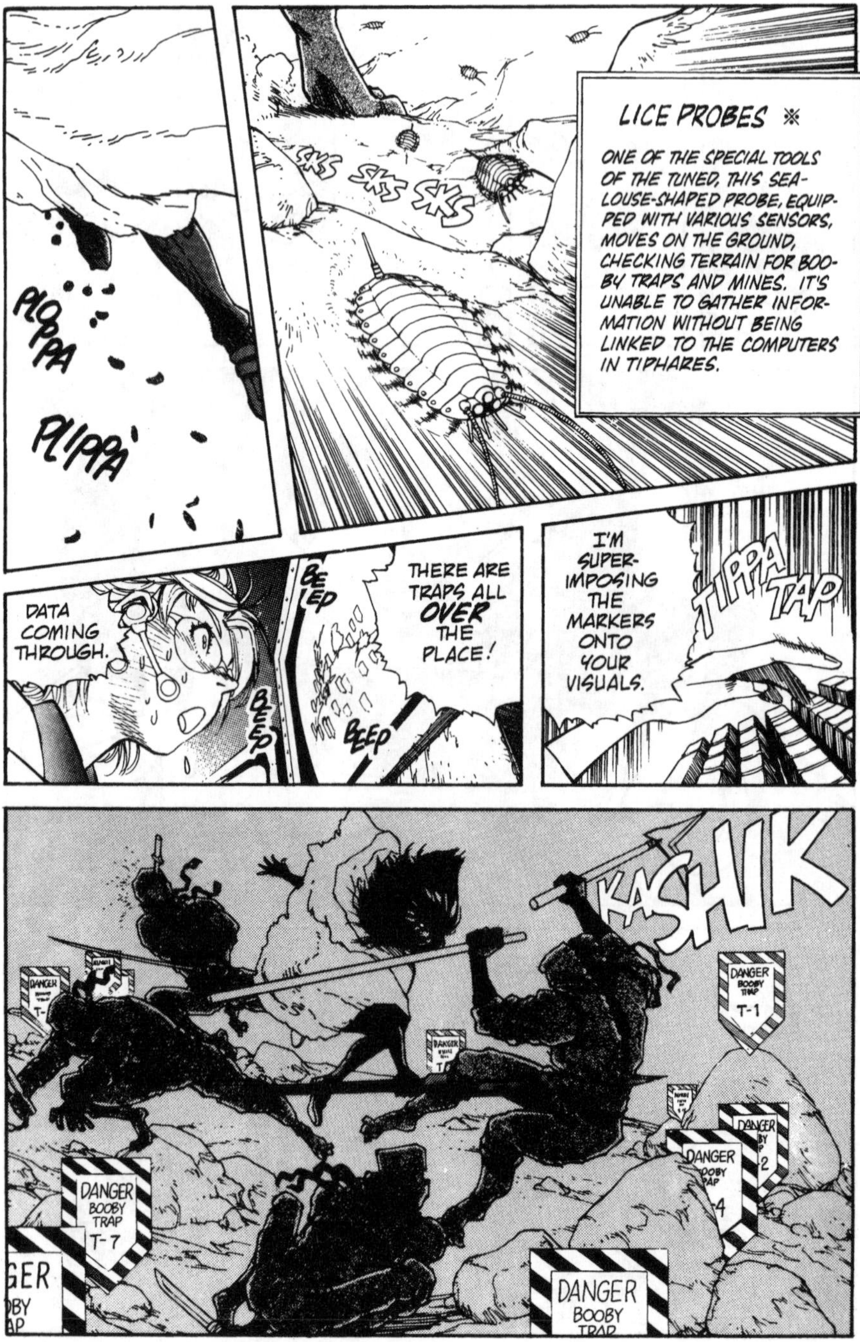
PLOPPA
PLIPPA
SKS SKS SKS
LICE PROBES ※
ONE OF THE SPECIAL TOOLS OF THE TUNED, THIS SEA-LOUSE-SHAPED PROBE, EQUIPPED WITH VARIOUS SENSORS, MOVES ON THE GROUND, CHECKING TERRAIN FOR BOOBY TRAPS AND MINES. IT'S UNABLE TO GATHER INFORMATION WITHOUT BEING LINKED TO THE COMPUTERS IN TIPHARES.
DATA COMING THROUGH.
BEEP
BEEP
THERE ARE TRAPS ALL OVER THE PLACE!
BEEP
I'M SUPERIMPOSING THE MARKERS ONTO YOUR VISUALS.
TIPPA TAP
KASHIK
DANGER BOOBY TRAP T-1
DANGER BOOBY TRAP T-7
DANGER BOOBY TRAP

SLAK

!?

THAT FELT **STRANGE**!

AH!

FOOM

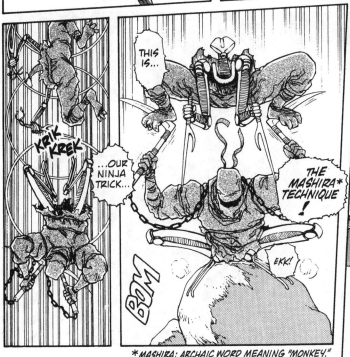

THIS IS...

...OUR NINJA TRICK...

KRIK KREK

THE MASHIRA* TECHNIQUE!

BOM

EKK!

NOT BAD...!

A CYBORG WITH INDEPENDENT UPPER AND LOWER BODIES!

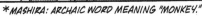

*MASHIRA: ARCHAIC WORD MEANING "MONKEY."

I'M GOING FOR THE ULTRASONICS! BACK ME UP, LOU!

FOFF

POFF

ROGER!

ACTIVATING TRANSDUCERS!

ULTRASONIC PULSE SET TO FIVE MEGAHERTZ.

RENDERING IMAGES!

TAPPA-TIP

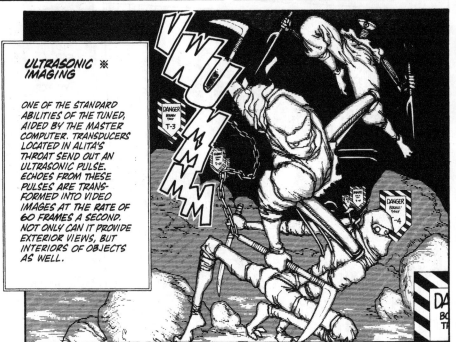

ULTRASONIC ※ IMAGING

ONE OF THE STANDARD ABILITIES OF THE TUNED, AIDED BY THE MASTER COMPUTER. TRANSDUCERS LOCATED IN ALITA'S THROAT SEND OUT AN ULTRASONIC PULSE. ECHOES FROM THESE PULSES ARE TRANSFORMED INTO VIDEO IMAGES AT THE RATE OF 60 FRAMES A SECOND. NOT ONLY CAN IT PROVIDE EXTERIOR VIEWS, BUT INTERIORS OF OBJECTS AS WELL.

VWUMMMM

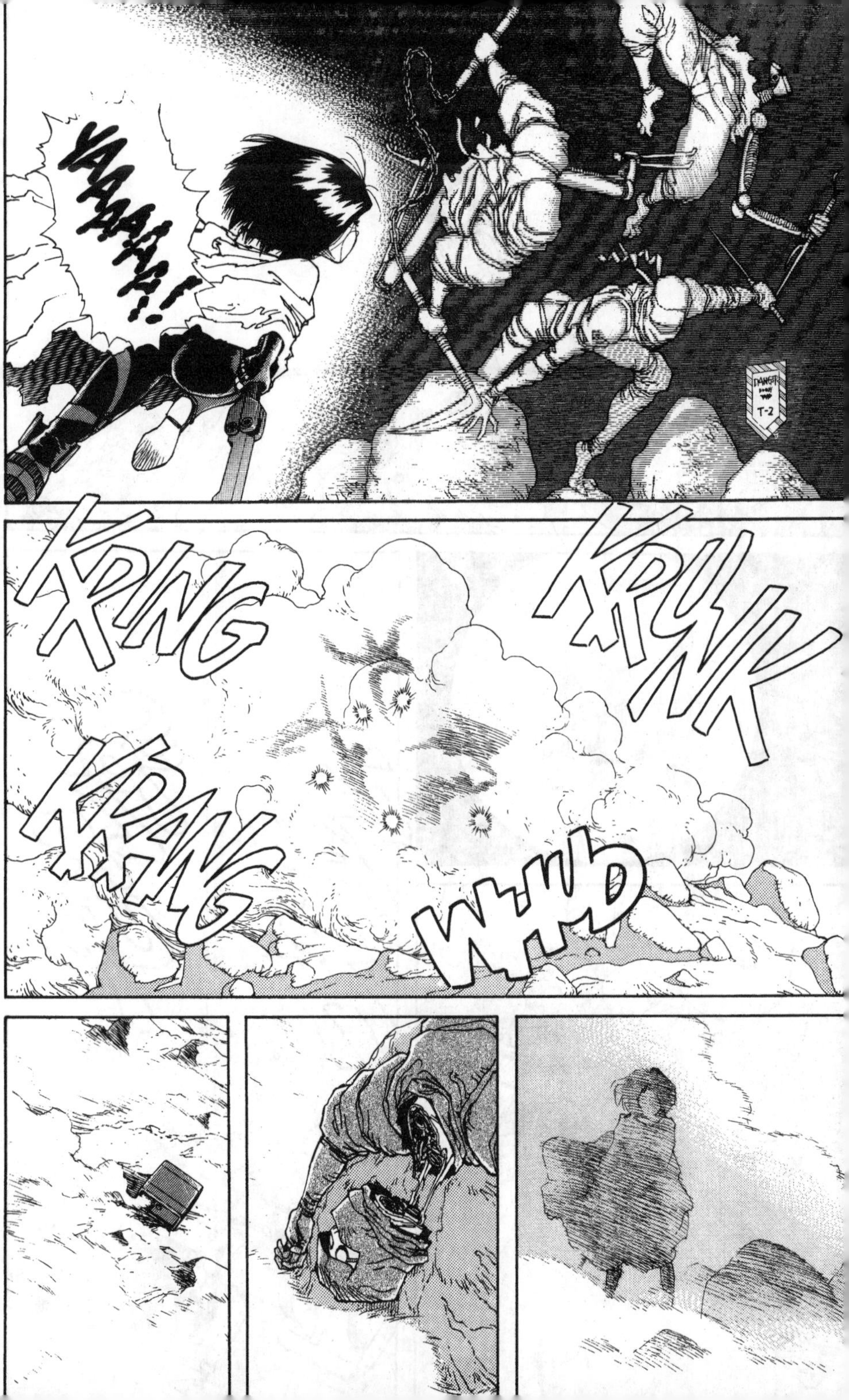
YAAAAAAH!!
DANGER
T-2
KRING
KRUNK
KRANG
WHUD

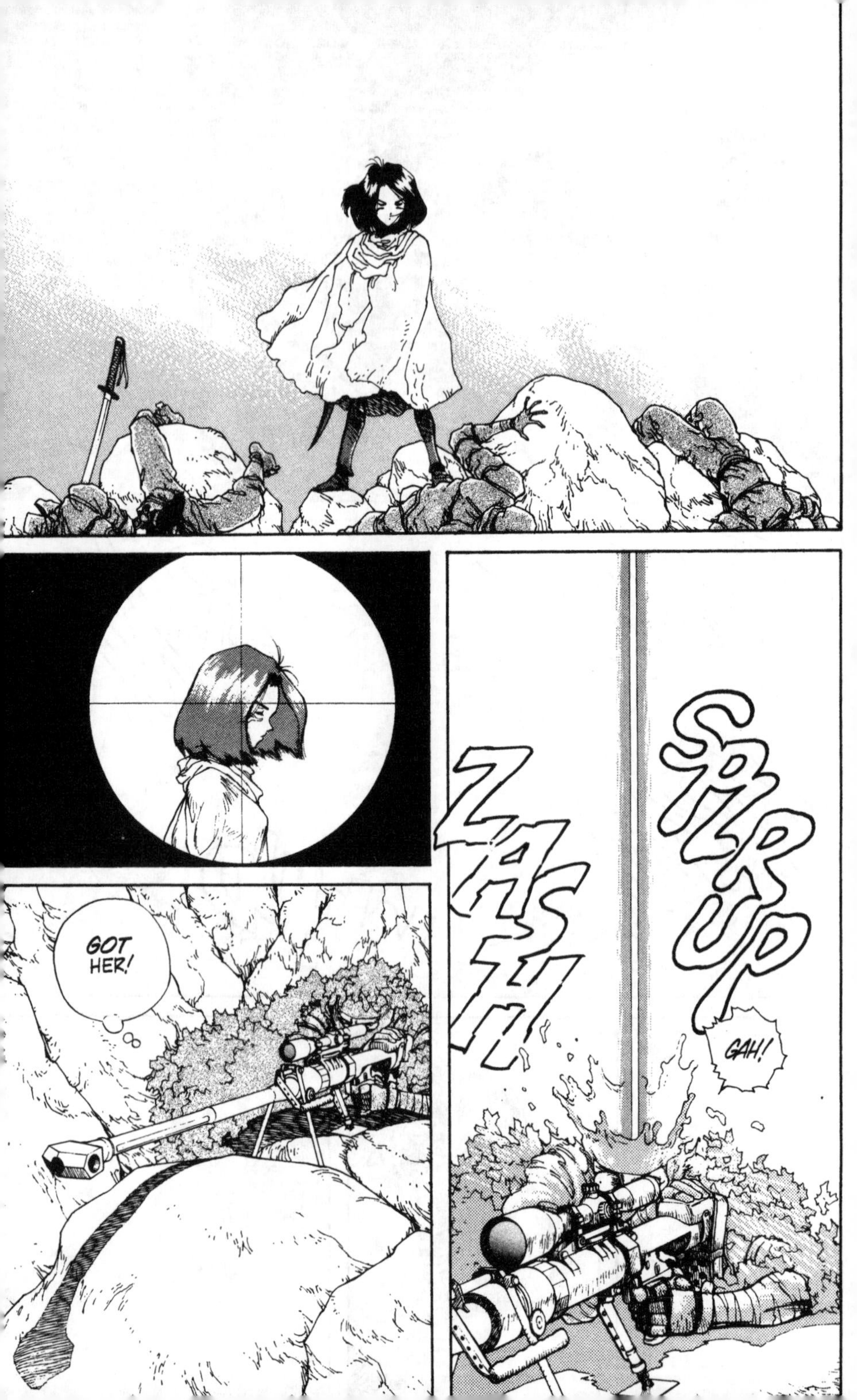
GOT HER!
ZASHH!
SPLURP
GAH!

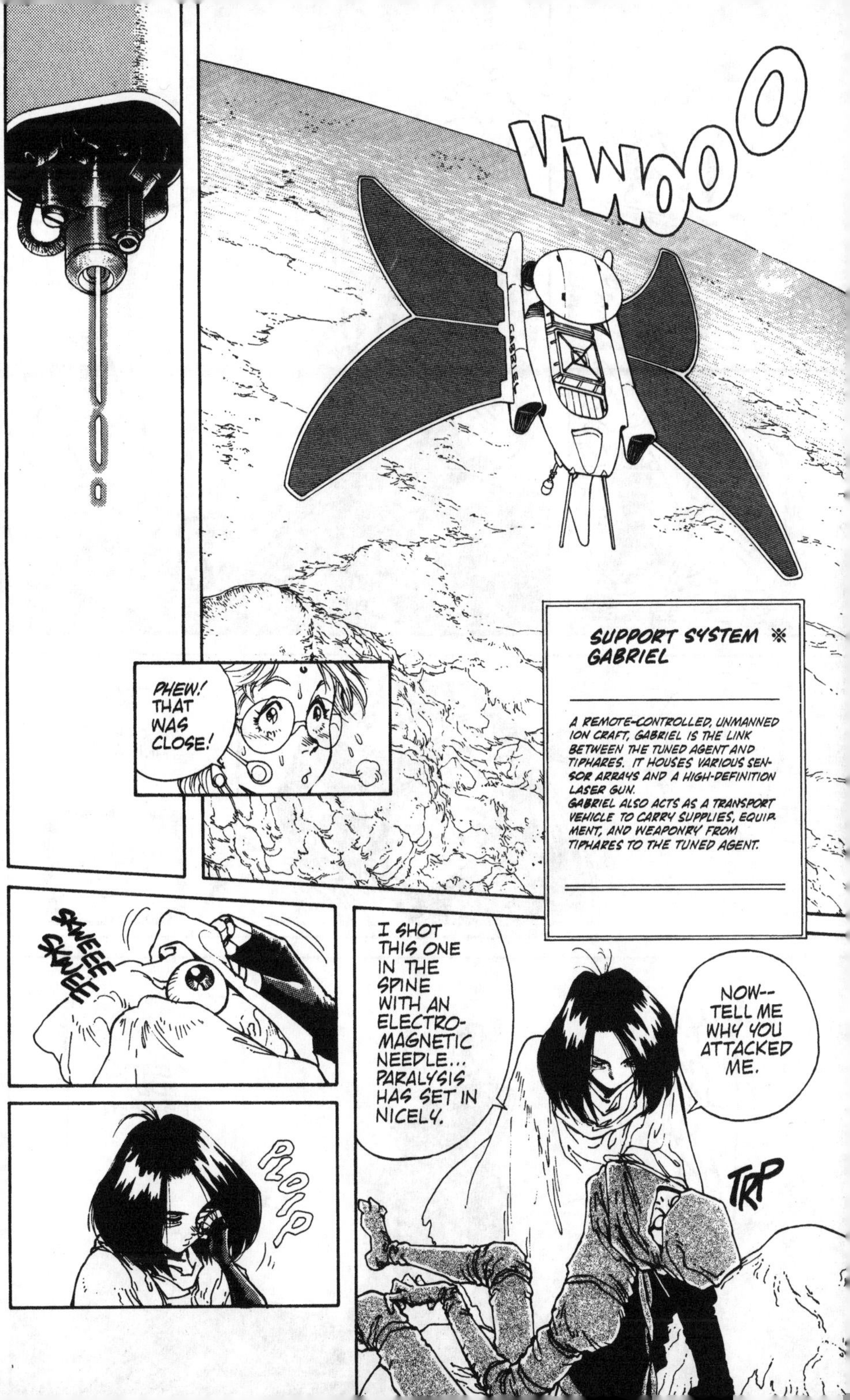
VWOOOO
GABRIEL
PHEW! THAT WAS CLOSE!
SUPPORT SYSTEM ※ GABRIEL
A REMOTE-CONTROLLED, UNMANNED ION CRAFT, GABRIEL IS THE LINK BETWEEN THE TUNED AGENT AND TIPHARES. IT HOUSES VARIOUS SENSOR ARRAYS AND A HIGH-DEFINITION LASER GUN.
GABRIEL ALSO ACTS AS A TRANSPORT VEHICLE TO CARRY SUPPLIES, EQUIPMENT, AND WEAPONRY FROM TIPHARES TO THE TUNED AGENT.
SKWEEE SKWEE
PLOIP
I SHOT THIS ONE IN THE SPINE WITH AN ELECTRO-MAGNETIC NEEDLE... PARALYSIS HAS SET IN NICELY.
NOW-- TELL ME WHY YOU ATTACKED ME.
TRP

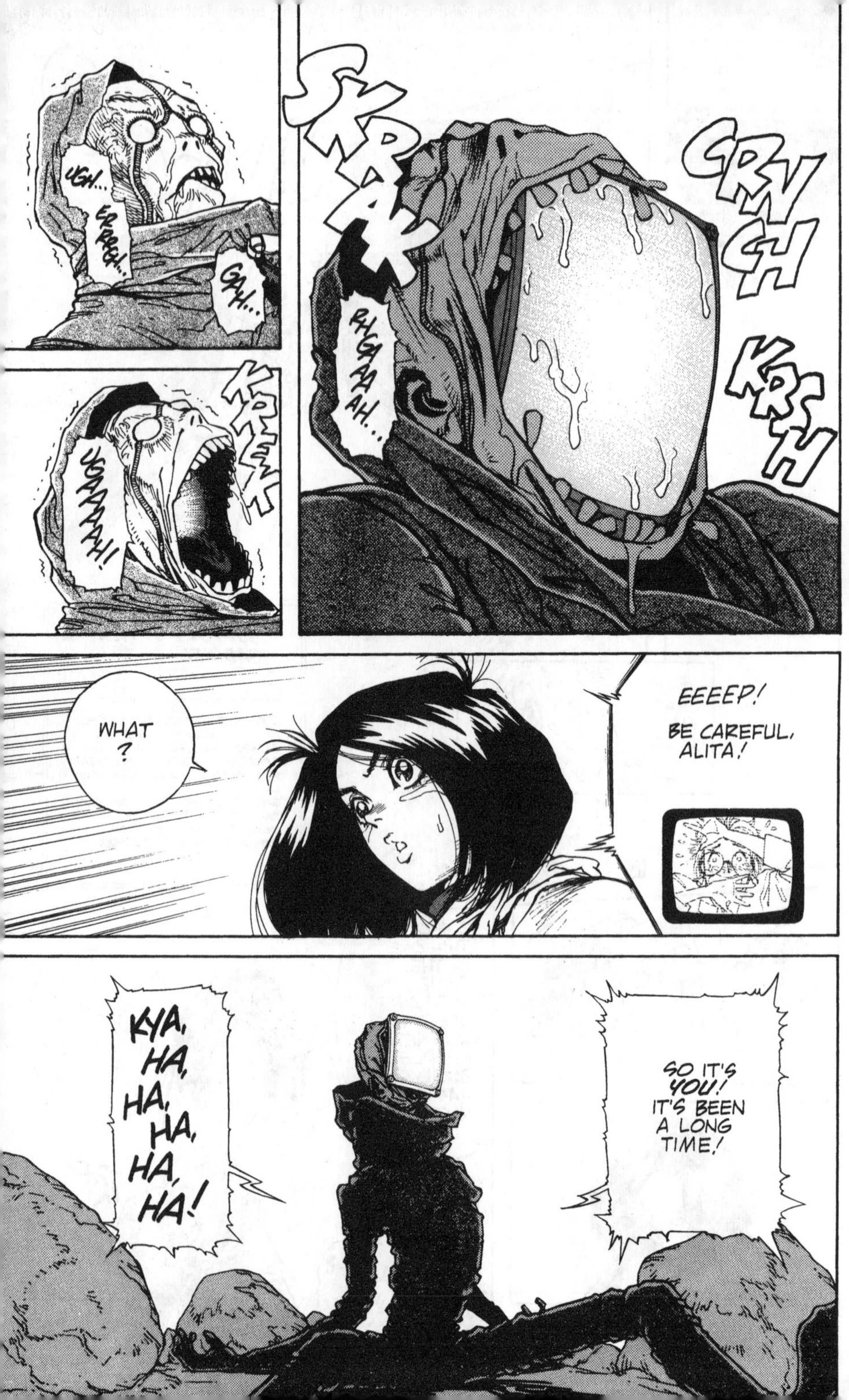
UGH...
ERRRGH...
GAH...
KREEENK
UGAAAAAH!
SKRAK
RHGAAAAAH...
CRUNCH
KRSH
WHAT?
EEEEP!
BE CAREFUL, ALITA!
KYA, HA, HA, HA, HA, HA!
SO IT'S YOU! IT'S BEEN A LONG TIME!

LET'S SEE... TEN YEARS, EIGHT MONTHS, AND SIXTEEN DAYS, I BELIEVE. HOW ARE YOU, ALITA?

OR SHOULD I SAY, "TUNED AGENT A1"?

DESTY NOVA!

SO THIS IS PROFESSOR NOVA!?

THIS ISN'T A RECORDING! IT'S A REAL-TIME BROADCAST VIDEO. I'M TRACING IT NOW!

I THOUGHT YOU DIED FIGHTING THE BERSERKER ALL THOSE YEARS AGO, BUT... MMM-MM...YOU ARE A TOUGH ONE, AREN'T YOU?

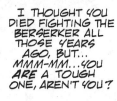

SKRSH

YOU PROMISED ME...

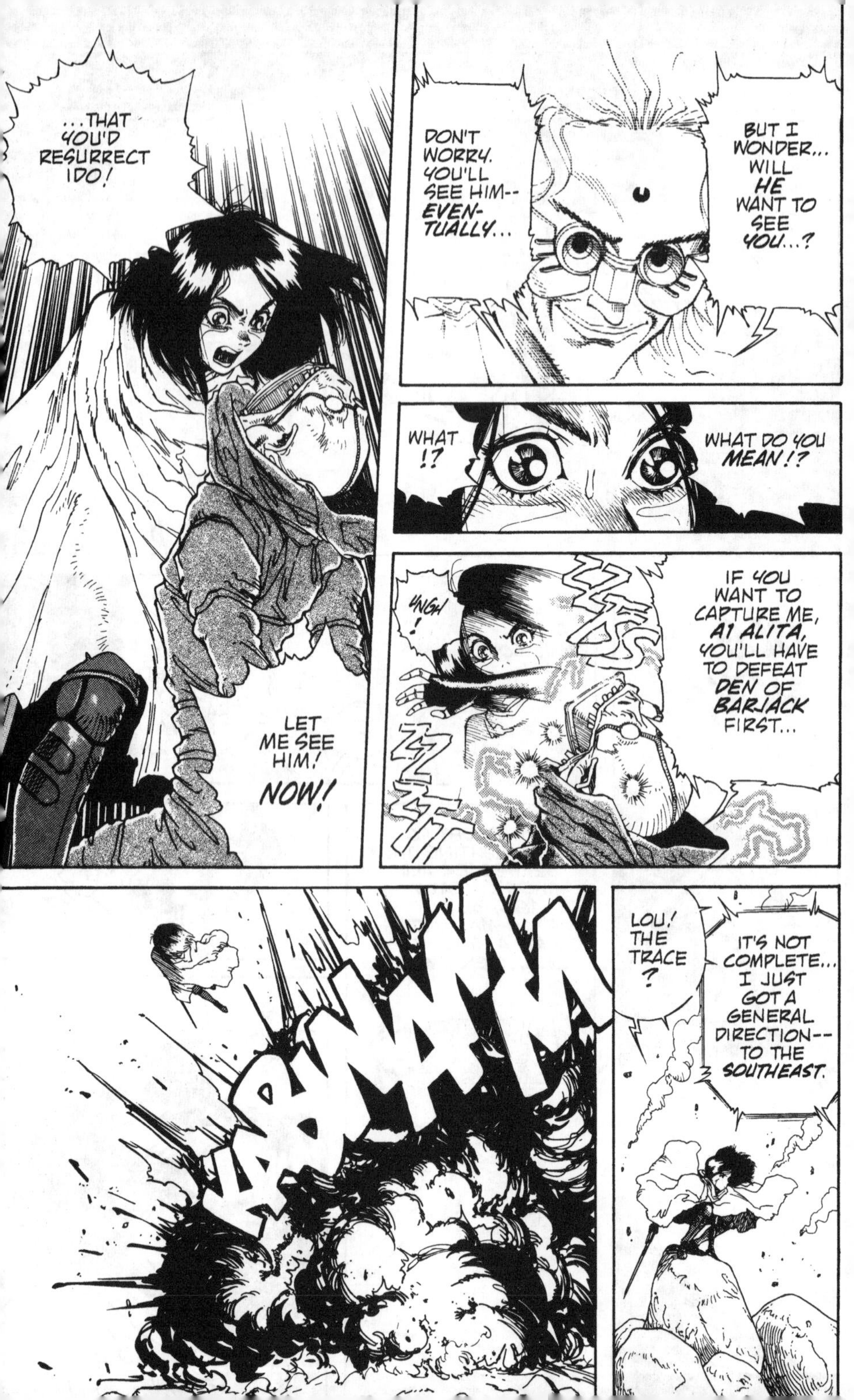
...THAT YOU'D RESURRECT IDO!
LET ME SEE HIM! NOW!
DON'T WORRY. YOU'LL SEE HIM-- EVEN-TUALLY...
BUT I WONDER... WILL HE WANT TO SEE YOU...?
WHAT !?
WHAT DO YOU MEAN!?
UNGH!
IF YOU WANT TO CAPTURE ME, A1 ALITA, YOU'LL HAVE TO DEFEAT DEN OF BARJACK FIRST...
KABLAAM
LOU! THE TRACE?
IT'S NOT COMPLETE... I JUST GOT A GENERAL DIRECTION-- TO THE SOUTHEAST.

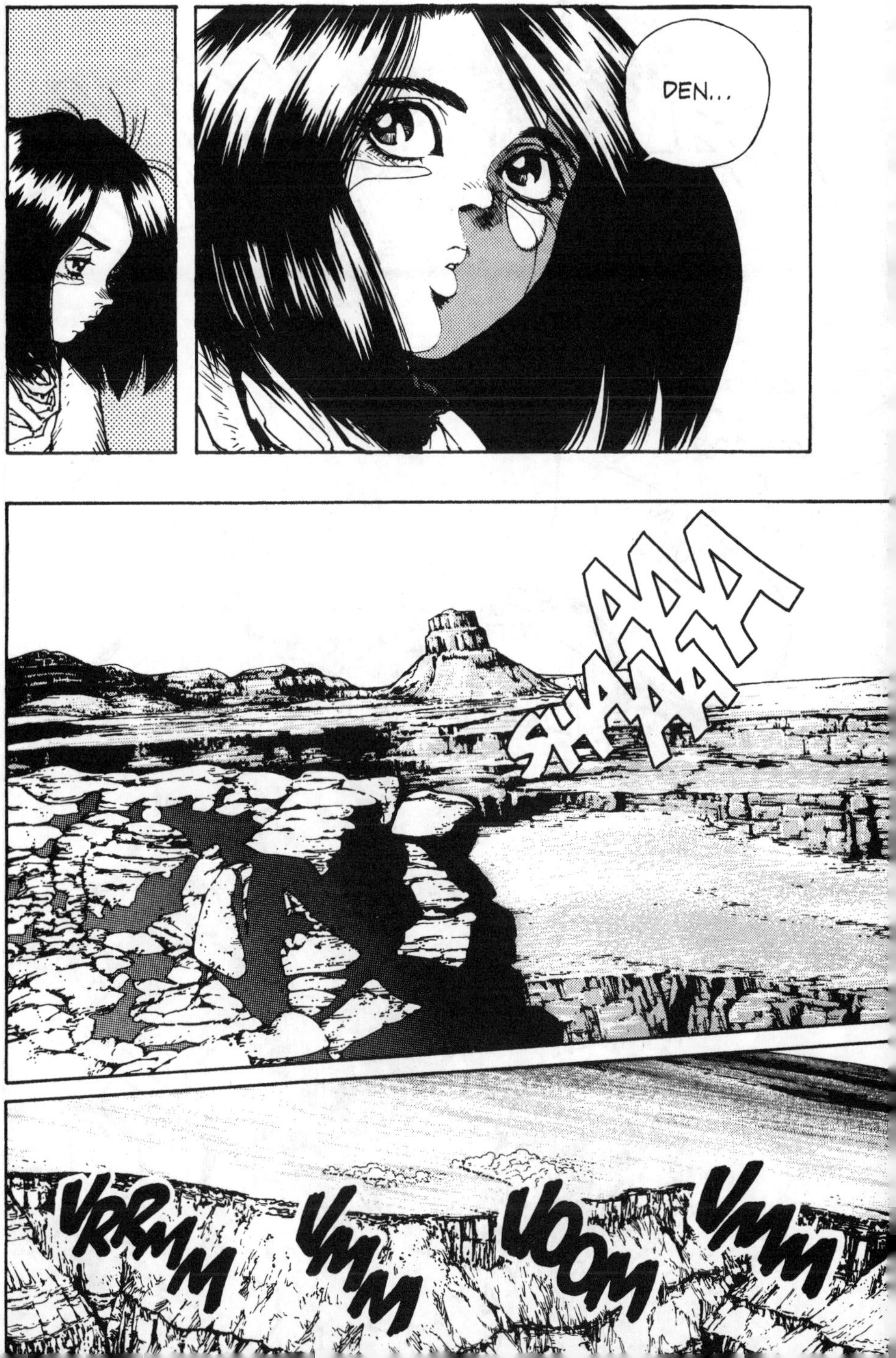
DEN...
SHAAAAAA
VRRMM
VMM
VOOM
VMM

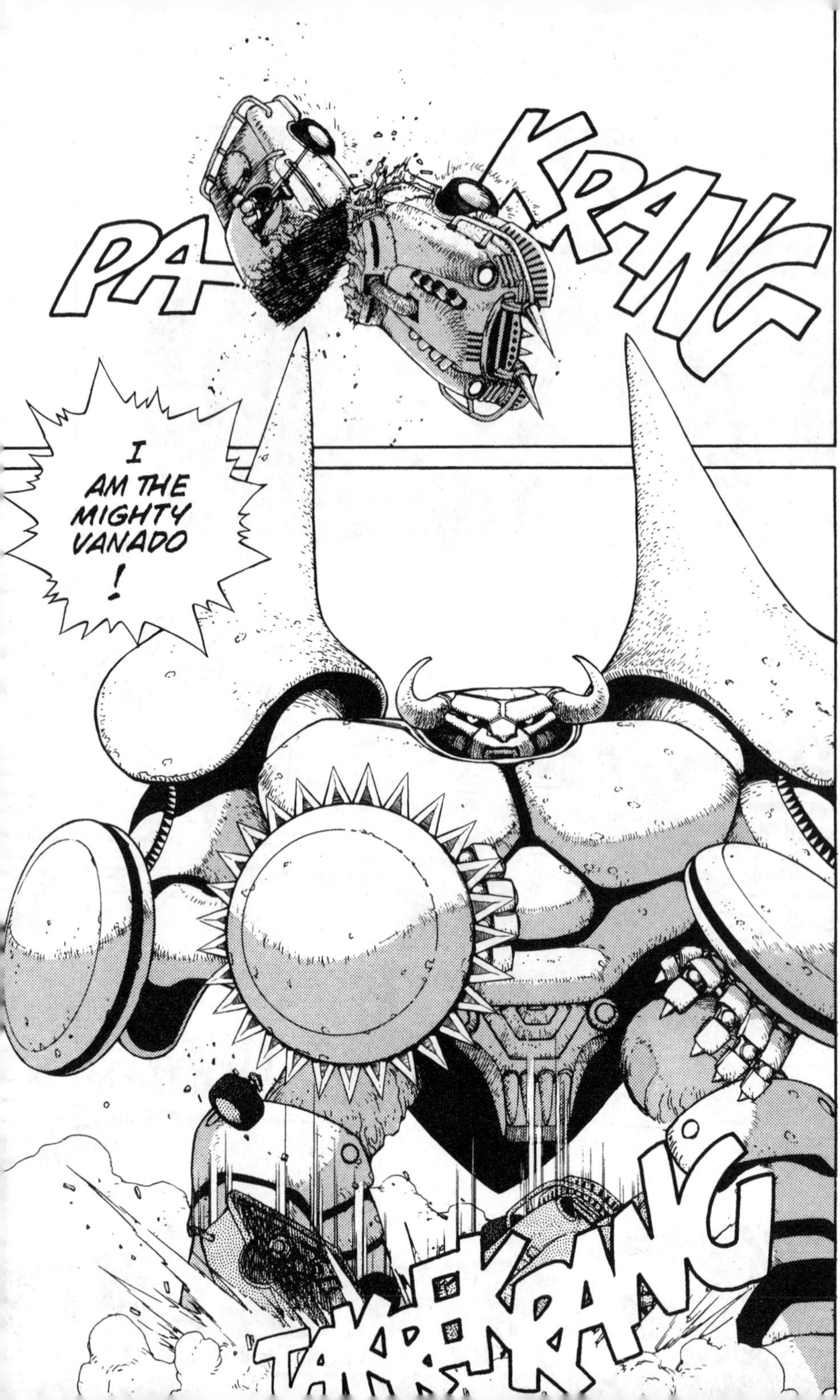
PA-KRANG
I AM THE MIGHTY VANADO !

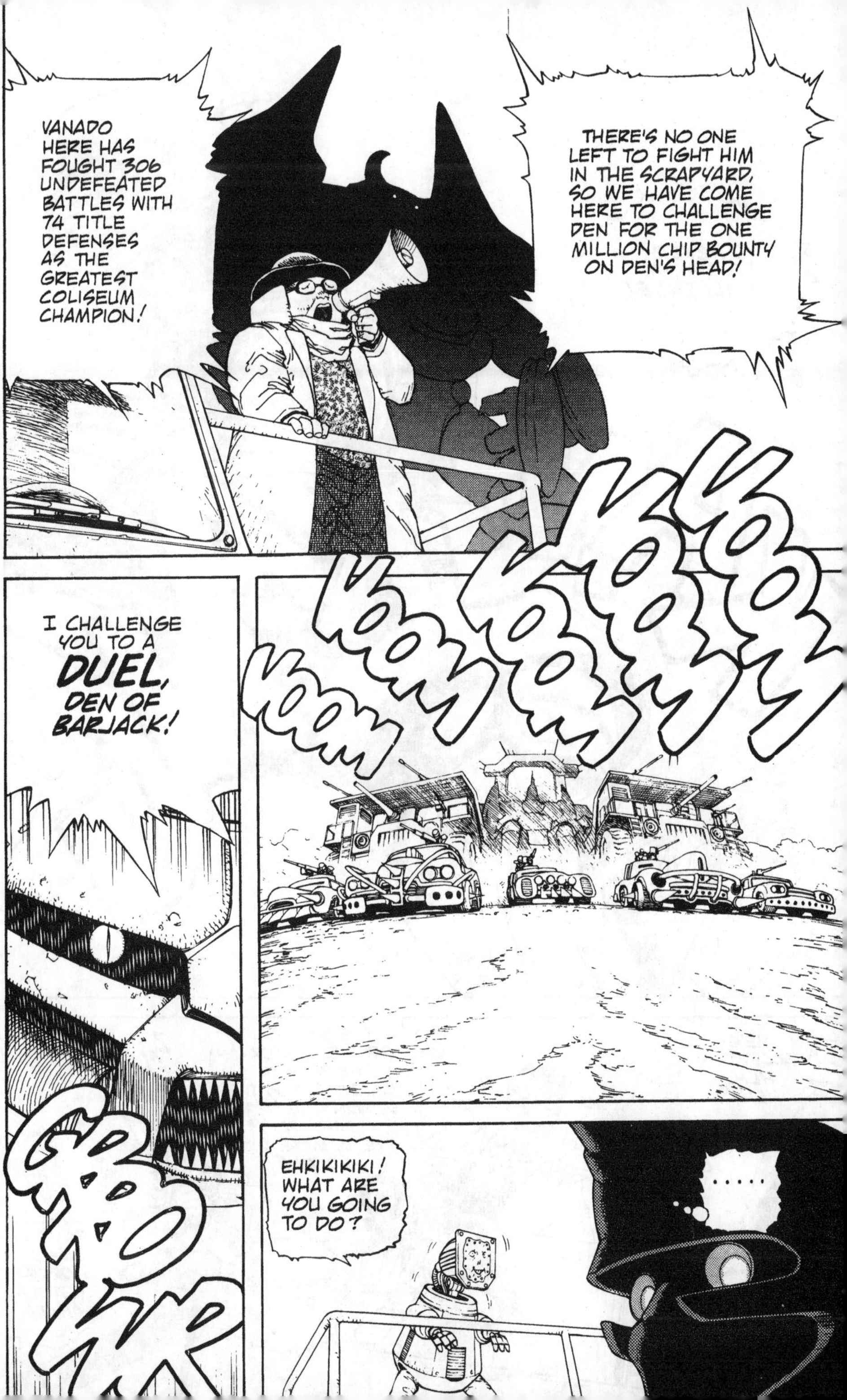
VANADO HERE HAS FOUGHT 306 UNDEFEATED BATTLES WITH 74 TITLE DEFENSES AS THE GREATEST COLISEUM CHAMPION!
THERE'S NO ONE LEFT TO FIGHT HIM IN THE SCRAPYARD, SO WE HAVE COME HERE TO CHALLENGE DEN FOR THE ONE MILLION CHIP BOUNTY ON DEN'S HEAD!
I CHALLENGE YOU TO A **DUEL,** DEN OF BARJACK!
EHKIKIKIKI! WHAT ARE YOU GOING TO DO?
.....

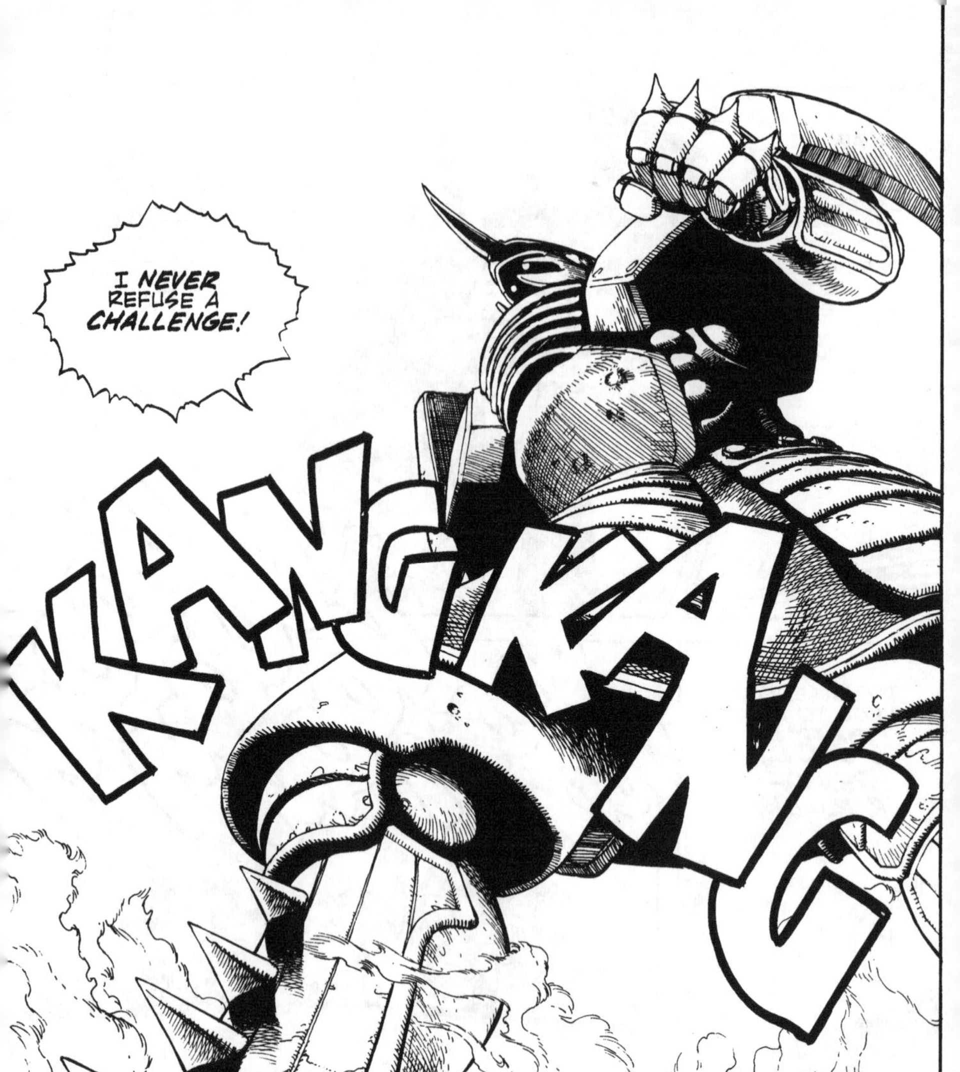
I NEVER REFUSE A CHALLENGE!
KANG KANG

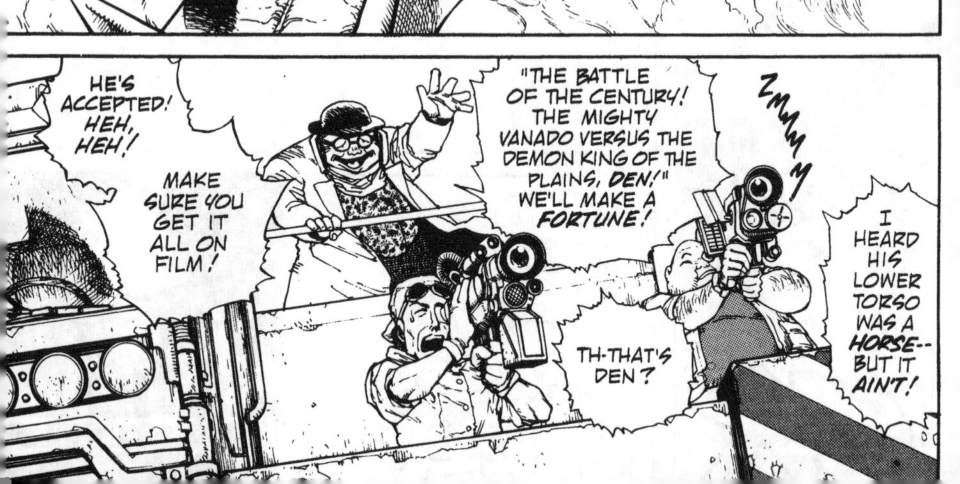
HE'S ACCEPTED! HEH, HEH!
MAKE SURE YOU GET IT ALL ON FILM!
"THE BATTLE OF THE CENTURY! THE MIGHTY VANADO VERSUS THE DEMON KING OF THE PLAINS, DEN!" WE'LL MAKE A FORTUNE!
ZMMMMM
TH-THAT'S DEN?
I HEARD HIS LOWER TORSO WAS A HORSE-- BUT IT AIN'T!

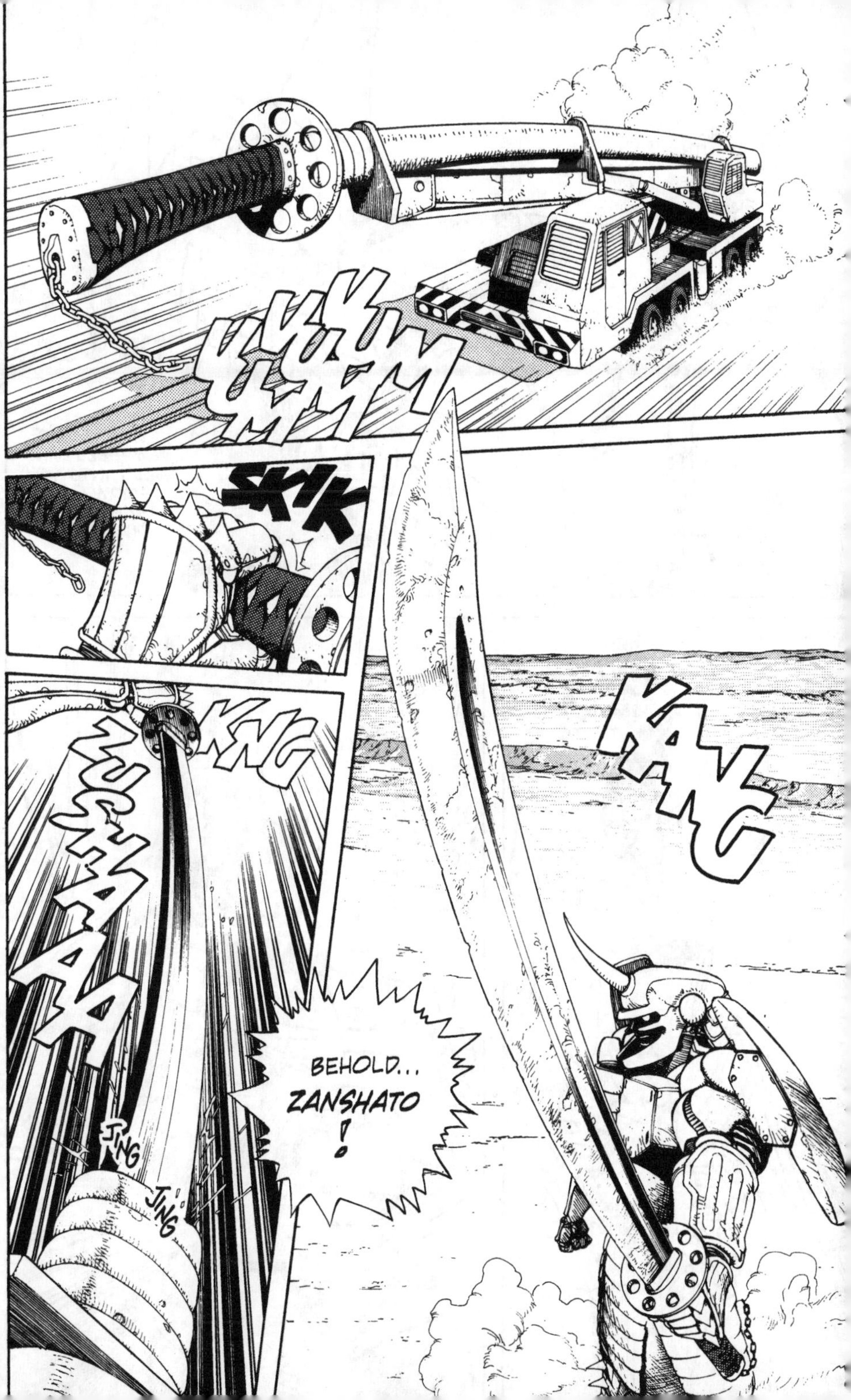
VWWWWMMM
SKIK
KNG
VUSHAAA
JING
JING
BEHOLD... ZANSHATO!
KANG

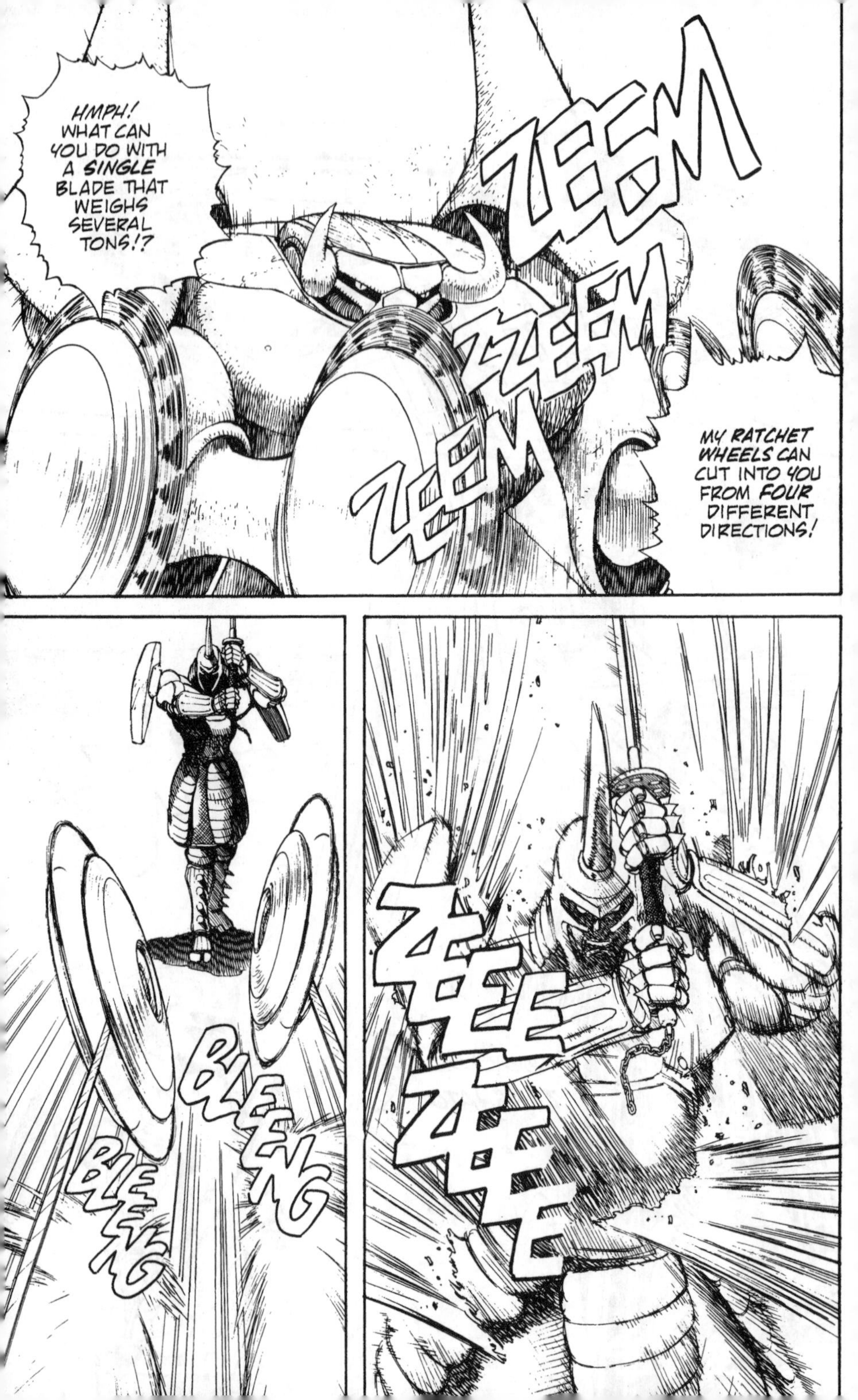

HMPH! WHAT CAN YOU DO WITH A SINGLE BLADE THAT WEIGHS SEVERAL TONS!?
ZEEM
ZEEM
ZEEM
MY RATCHET WHEELS CAN CUT INTO YOU FROM FOUR DIFFERENT DIRECTIONS!
BLEENG
BLEENG
ZEEE
ZEEE

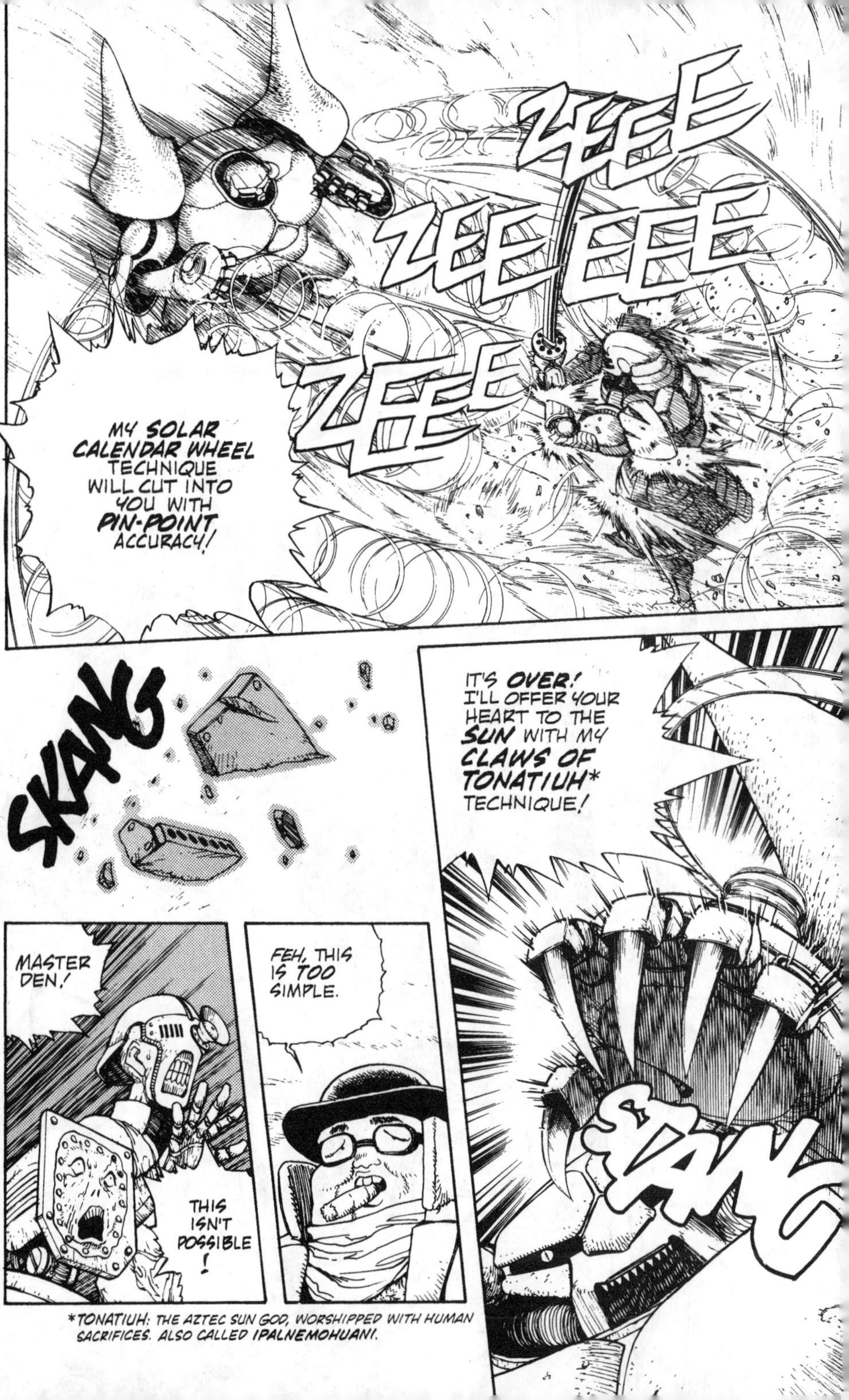
ZEEE
ZEE EEE
ZEEE
MY SOLAR CALENDAR WHEEL TECHNIQUE WILL CUT INTO YOU WITH PIN-POINT ACCURACY!
SKANG
MASTER DEN!
THIS ISN'T POSSIBLE!
FEH, THIS IS TOO SIMPLE.
IT'S OVER! I'LL OFFER YOUR HEART TO THE SUN WITH MY CLAWS OF TONATIUH* TECHNIQUE!
SKAN

*TONATIUH: THE AZTEC SUN GOD, WORSHIPPED WITH HUMAN SACRIFICES. ALSO CALLED IPALNEMOHUANI.

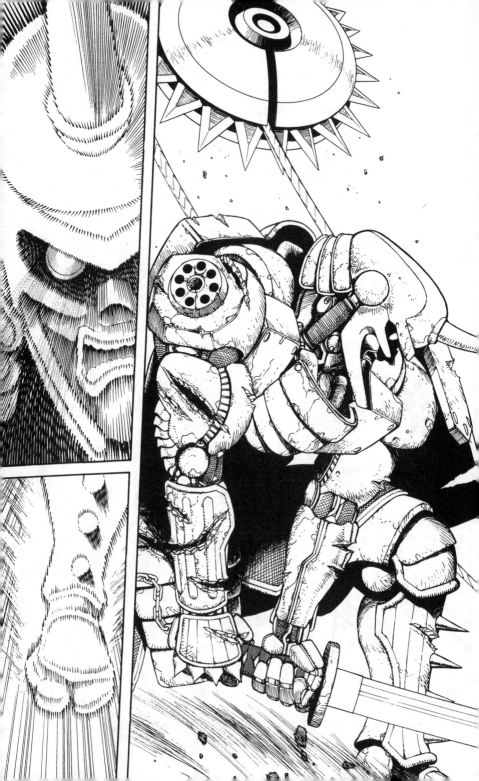

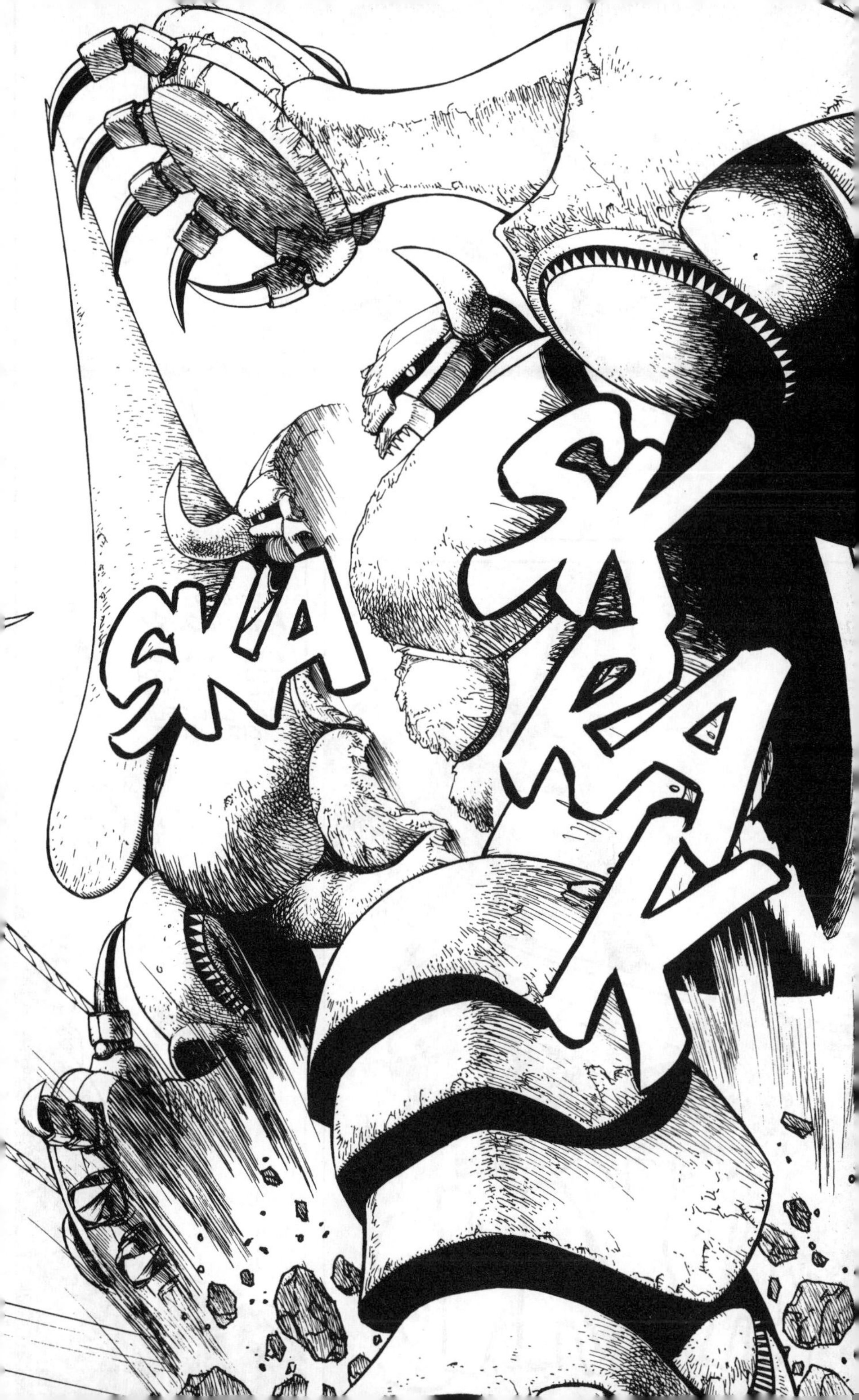
SKA
SKRAK

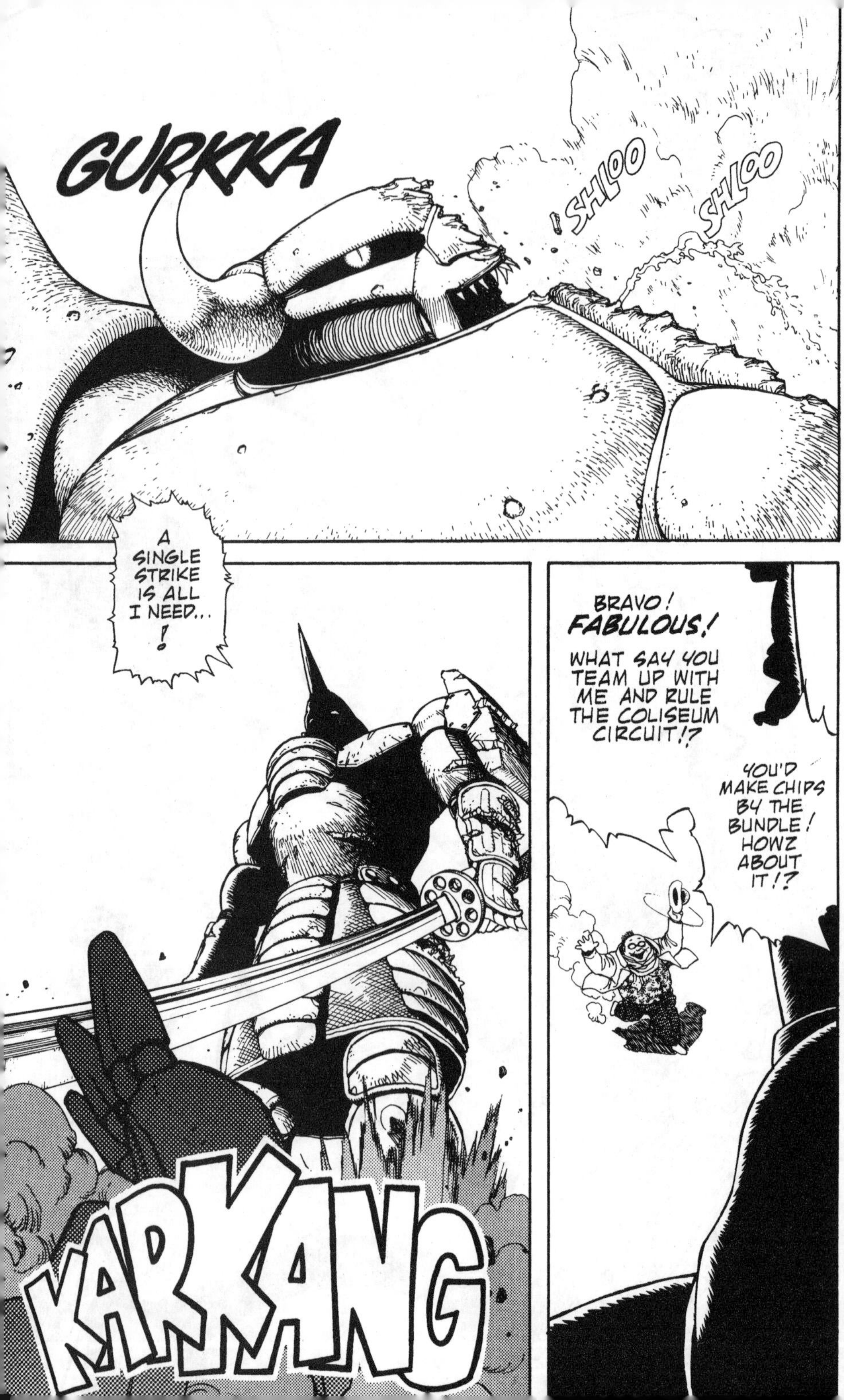
GURKKA
SHLOO
SHLOO
A SINGLE STRIKE IS ALL I NEED...!
KARKANG
BRAVO! FABULOUS!
WHAT SAY YOU TEAM UP WITH ME AND RULE THE COLISEUM CIRCUIT!?
YOU'D MAKE CHIPS BY THE BUNDLE! HOWZ ABOUT IT!?

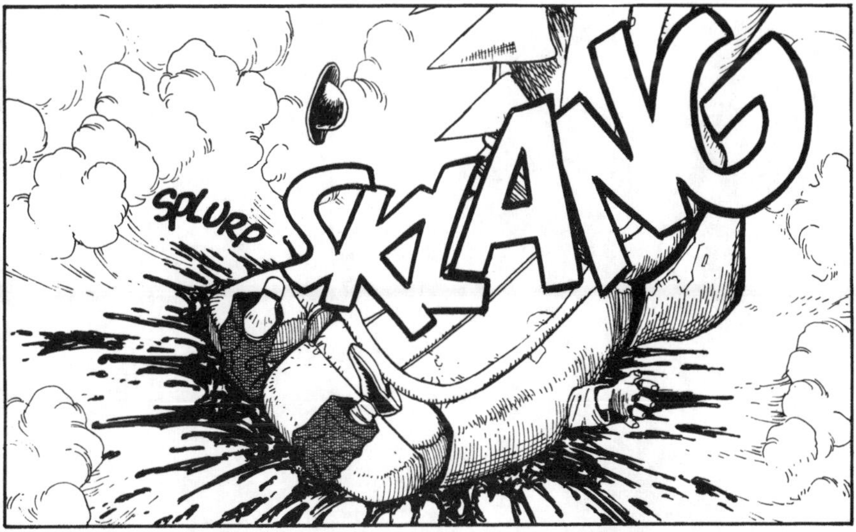
SPLURP
SKLANG
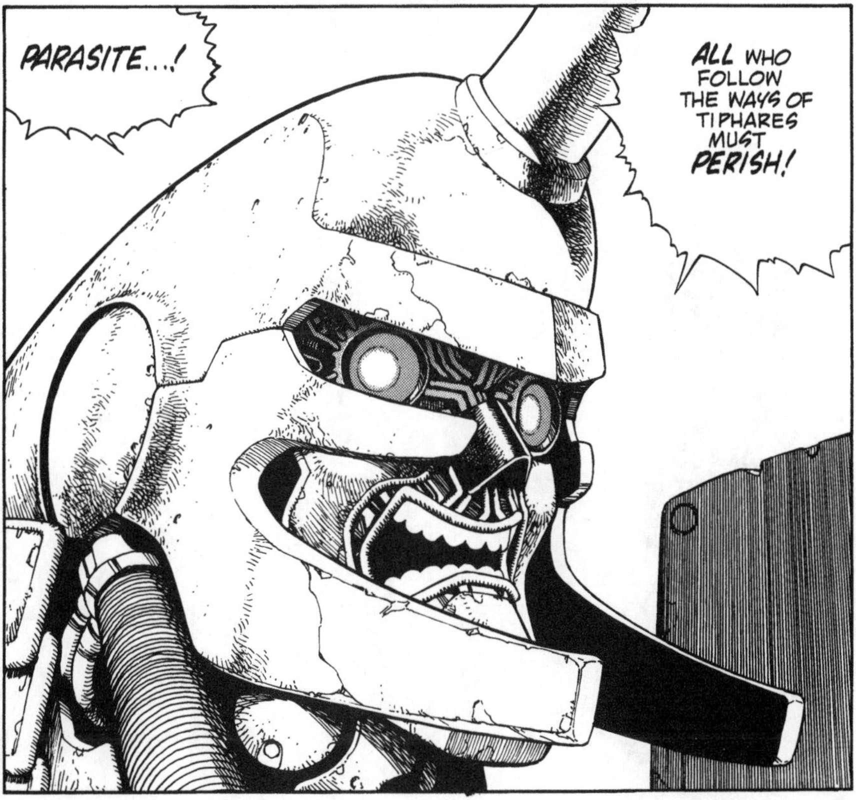
PARASITE...!
ALL WHO FOLLOW THE WAYS OF TIPHARES MUST PERISH!

BARD OF THE BADLANDS
Mission 2: Reunion

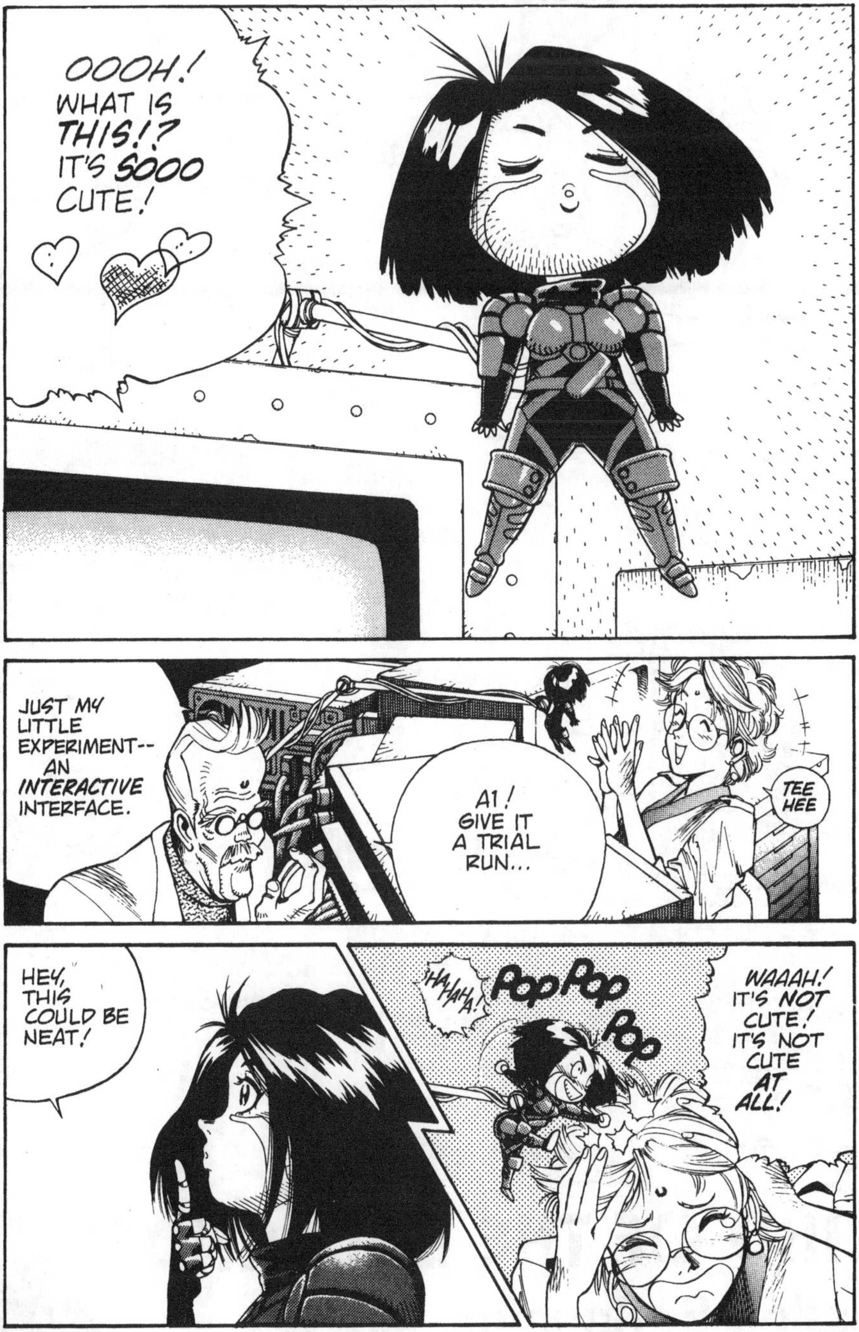
OOOH! WHAT IS THIS!? IT'S SOOO CUTE!
JUST MY LITTLE EXPERIMENT-- AN INTERACTIVE INTERFACE.
A1! GIVE IT A TRIAL RUN...
TEE HEE
HEY, THIS COULD BE NEAT!
HA HA HA!
POP POP POP
WAAAH! IT'S NOT CUTE! IT'S NOT CUTE AT ALL!

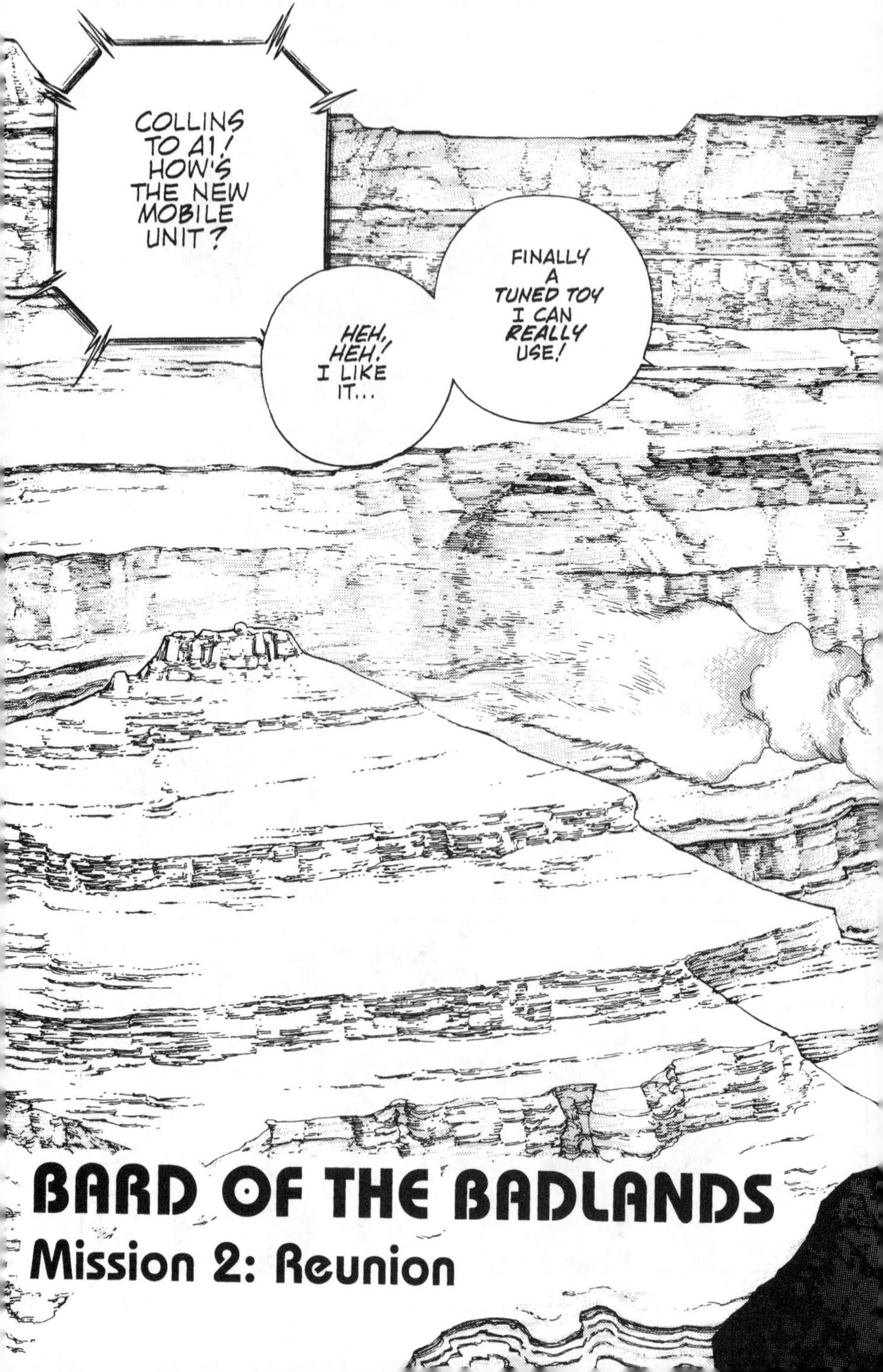
COLLINS TO A1! HOW'S THE NEW MOBILE UNIT?
HEH, HEH! I LIKE IT...
FINALLY A TUNED TOY I CAN REALLY USE!
BARD OF THE BADLANDS
Mission 2: Reunion

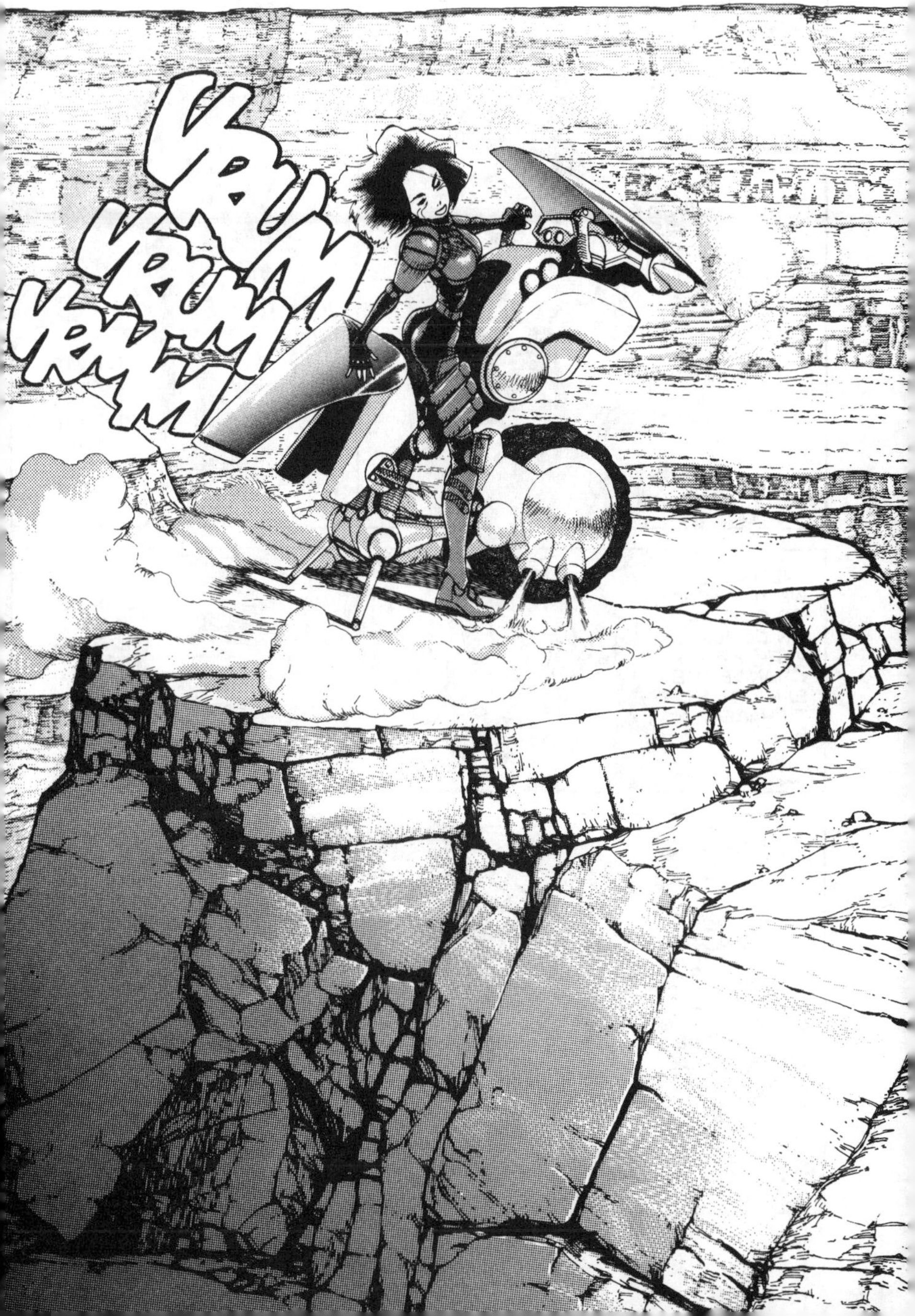
VRUM VRUM VRUMM

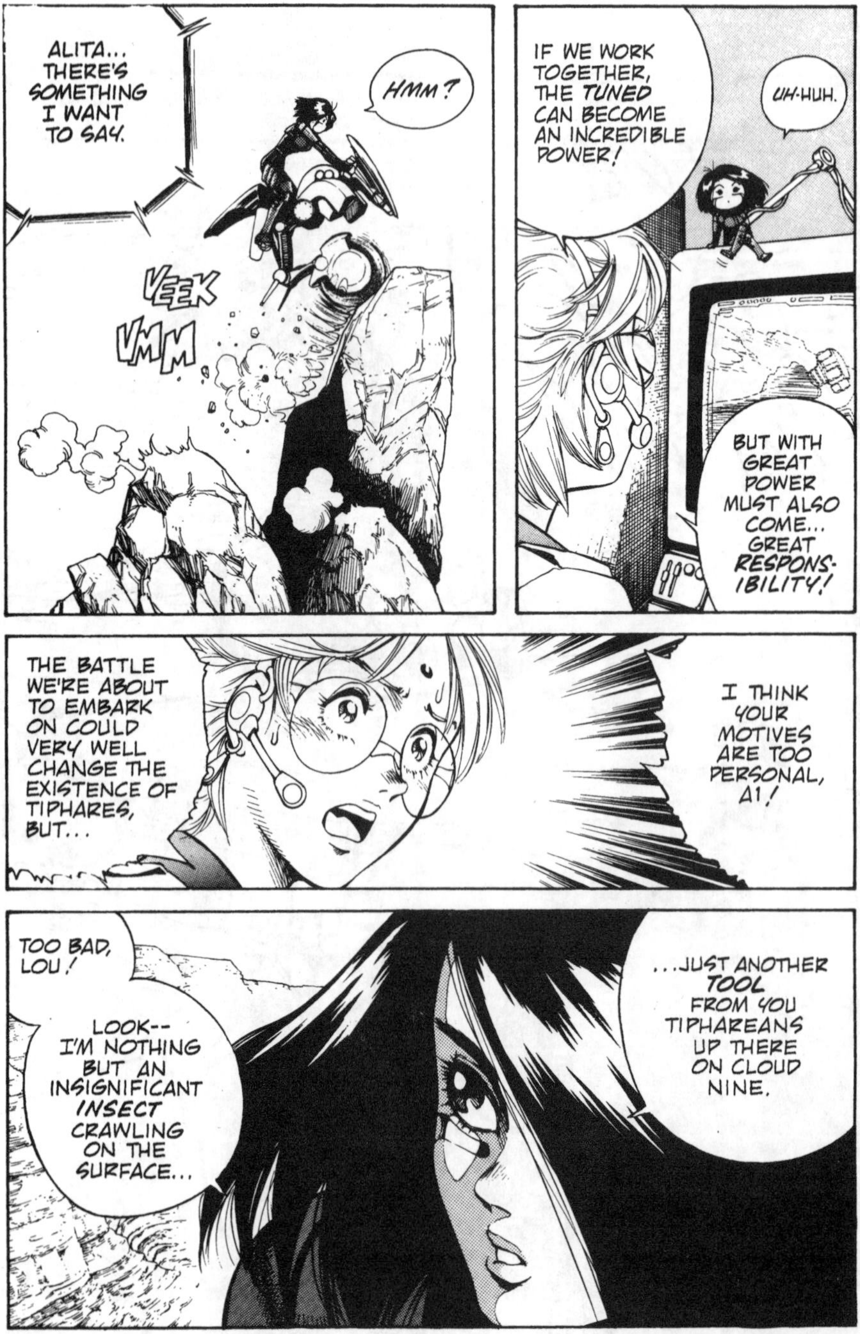
ALITA... THERE'S SOMETHING I WANT TO SAY.
HMM?
VEEK
VMMM
IF WE WORK TOGETHER, THE TUNED CAN BECOME AN INCREDIBLE POWER!
UH-HUH.
BUT WITH GREAT POWER MUST ALSO COME... GREAT RESPONS-IBILITY!
THE BATTLE WE'RE ABOUT TO EMBARK ON COULD VERY WELL CHANGE THE EXISTENCE OF TIPHARES, BUT...
I THINK YOUR MOTIVES ARE TOO PERSONAL, A1!
TOO BAD, LOU!
LOOK-- I'M NOTHING BUT AN INSIGNIFICANT INSECT CRAWLING ON THE SURFACE...
...JUST ANOTHER TOOL FROM YOU TIPHAREANS UP THERE ON CLOUD NINE.

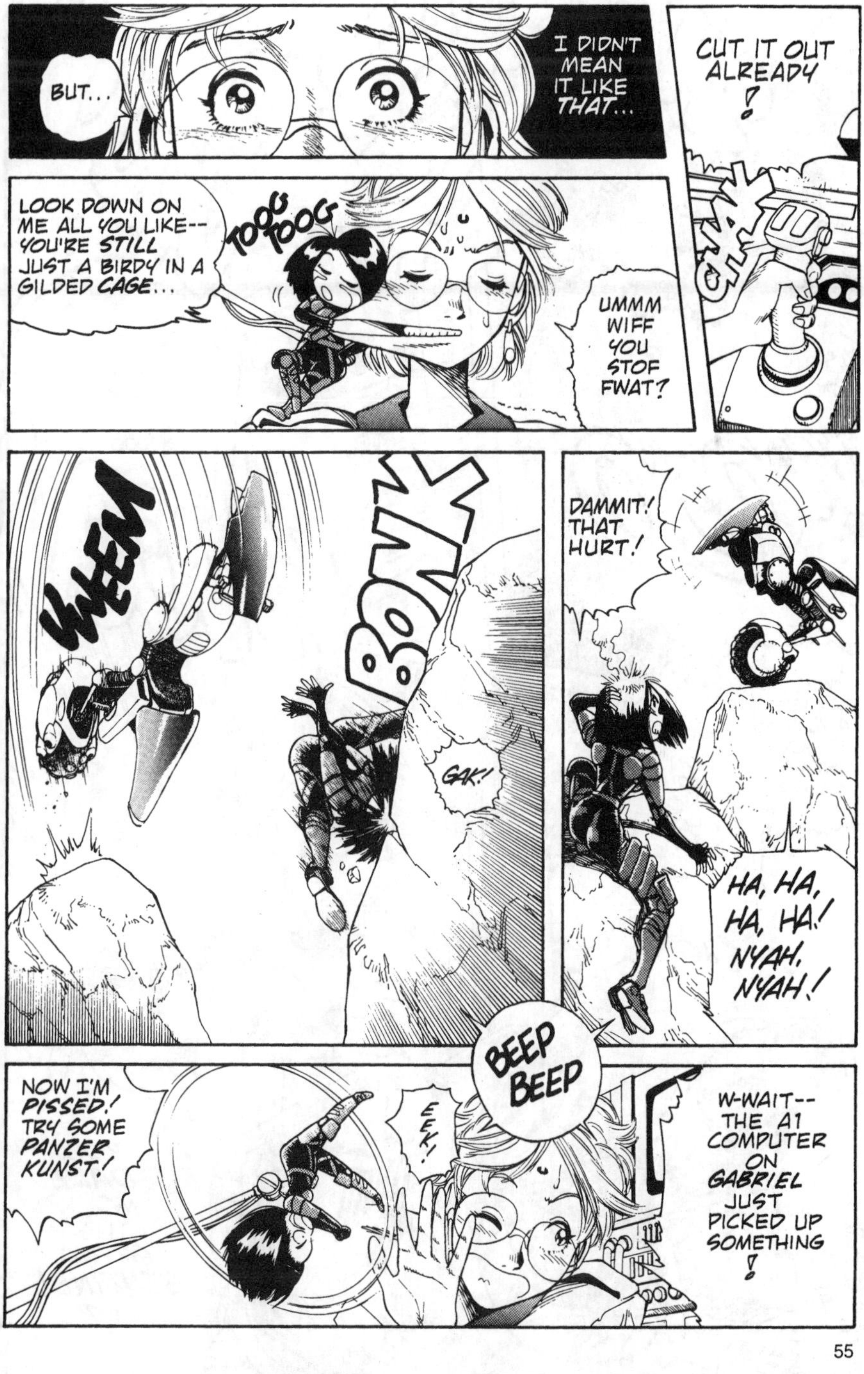
BUT...
I DIDN'T MEAN IT LIKE *THAT*...
CUT IT OUT ALREADY!
GAK
LOOK DOWN ON ME ALL YOU LIKE-- YOU'RE *STILL* JUST A BIRDY IN A GILDED *CAGE*...
TOOG TOOG
UMMM WIFF YOU STOF FWAT?
WEEEM
BONK
GAK!
DAMMIT! THAT HURT!
HA, HA, HA, HA! NYAH, NYAH!
NOW I'M *PISSED*! TRY SOME *PANZER KUNST*!
EEK!
BEEP BEEP
W-WAIT-- THE A1 COMPUTER ON *GABRIEL* JUST PICKED UP SOMETHING!

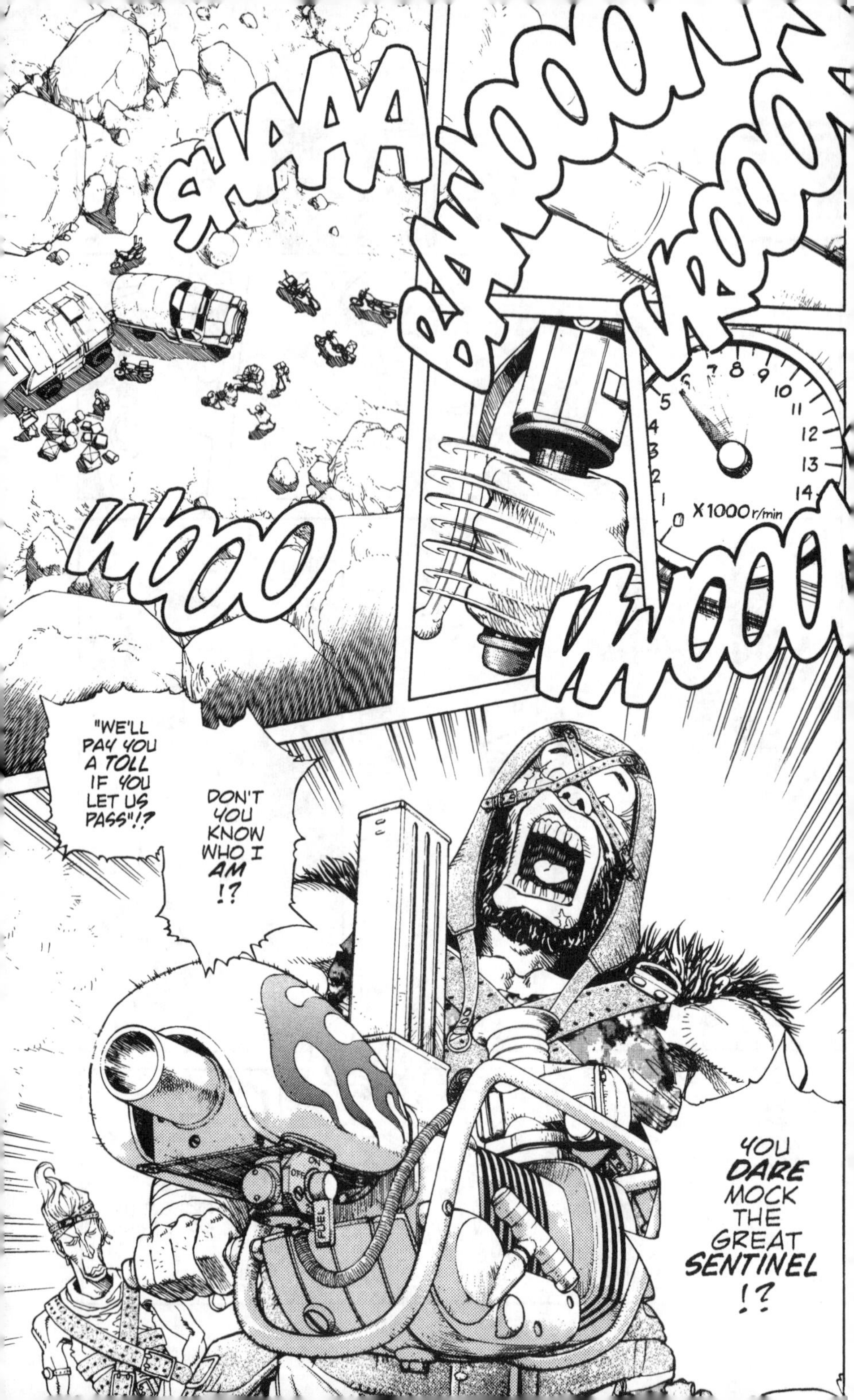
SHAAA
BAWOOON
VROOOM
WOOO
WOOO
X1000 r/min
"WE'LL PAY YOU A TOLL IF YOU LET US PASS"!?
DON'T YOU KNOW WHO I AM !?
YOU DARE MOCK THE GREAT SENTINEL !?

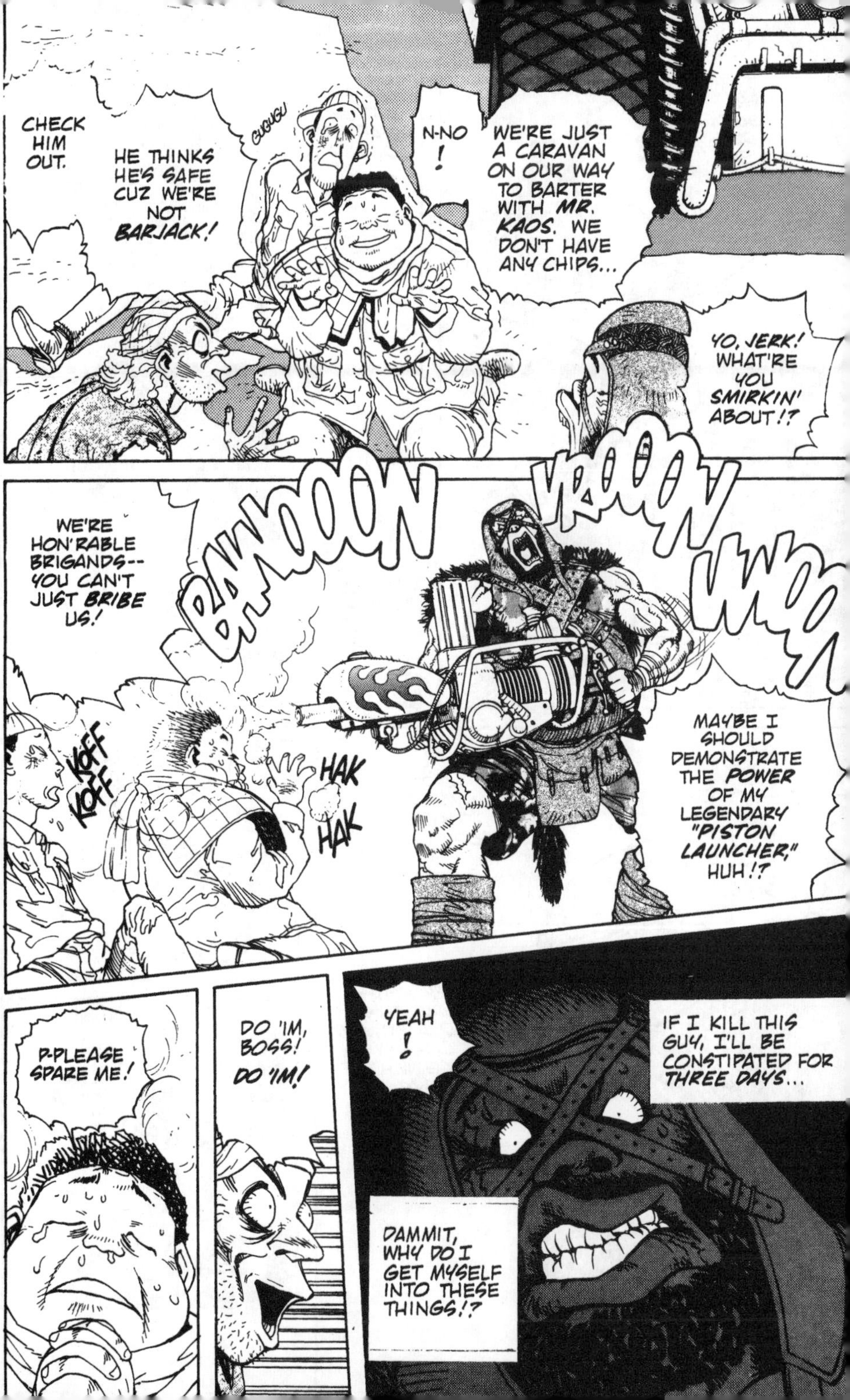
CHECK HIM OUT.
HE THINKS HE'S SAFE CUZ WE'RE NOT *BARJACK!*
GUGUGU
N-NO!
WE'RE JUST A CARAVAN ON OUR WAY TO BARTER WITH *MR. KAOS.* WE DON'T HAVE ANY CHIPS...
YO, JERK! WHAT'RE YOU *SMIRKIN'* ABOUT!?
WE'RE HON'RABLE BRIGANDS-- YOU CAN'T JUST *BRIBE* US!
KOFF KOFF
HAK HAK
MAYBE I SHOULD DEMONSTRATE THE *POWER* OF MY LEGENDARY *"PISTON LAUNCHER,"* HUH!?
P-PLEASE SPARE ME!
DO 'IM, BOSS! *DO 'IM!*
YEAH!
IF I KILL THIS GUY, I'LL BE CONSTIPATED FOR *THREE DAYS*...
DAMMIT, WHY DO I GET MYSELF INTO THESE THINGS!?

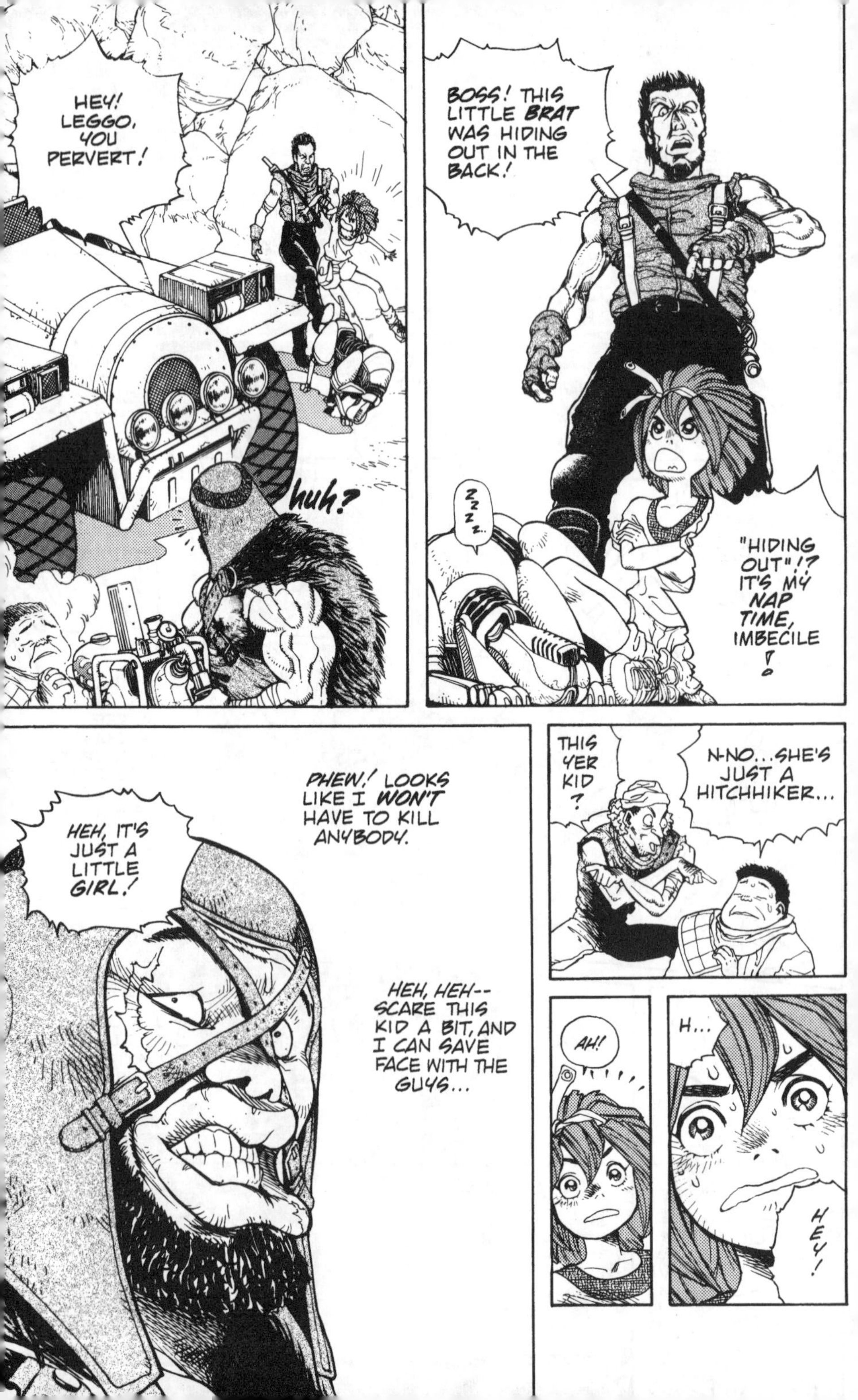
HEY! LEGGO, YOU PERVERT!
huh?
BOSS! THIS LITTLE BRAT WAS HIDING OUT IN THE BACK!
Z Z Z...
"HIDING OUT"!? IT'S MY NAP TIME, IMBECILE!
HEH, IT'S JUST A LITTLE GIRL!
PHEW! LOOKS LIKE I WON'T HAVE TO KILL ANYBODY.
HEH, HEH-- SCARE THIS KID A BIT, AND I CAN SAVE FACE WITH THE GUYS...
THIS YER KID?
N-NO...SHE'S JUST A HITCHHIKER...
AH!
H...
HEY!

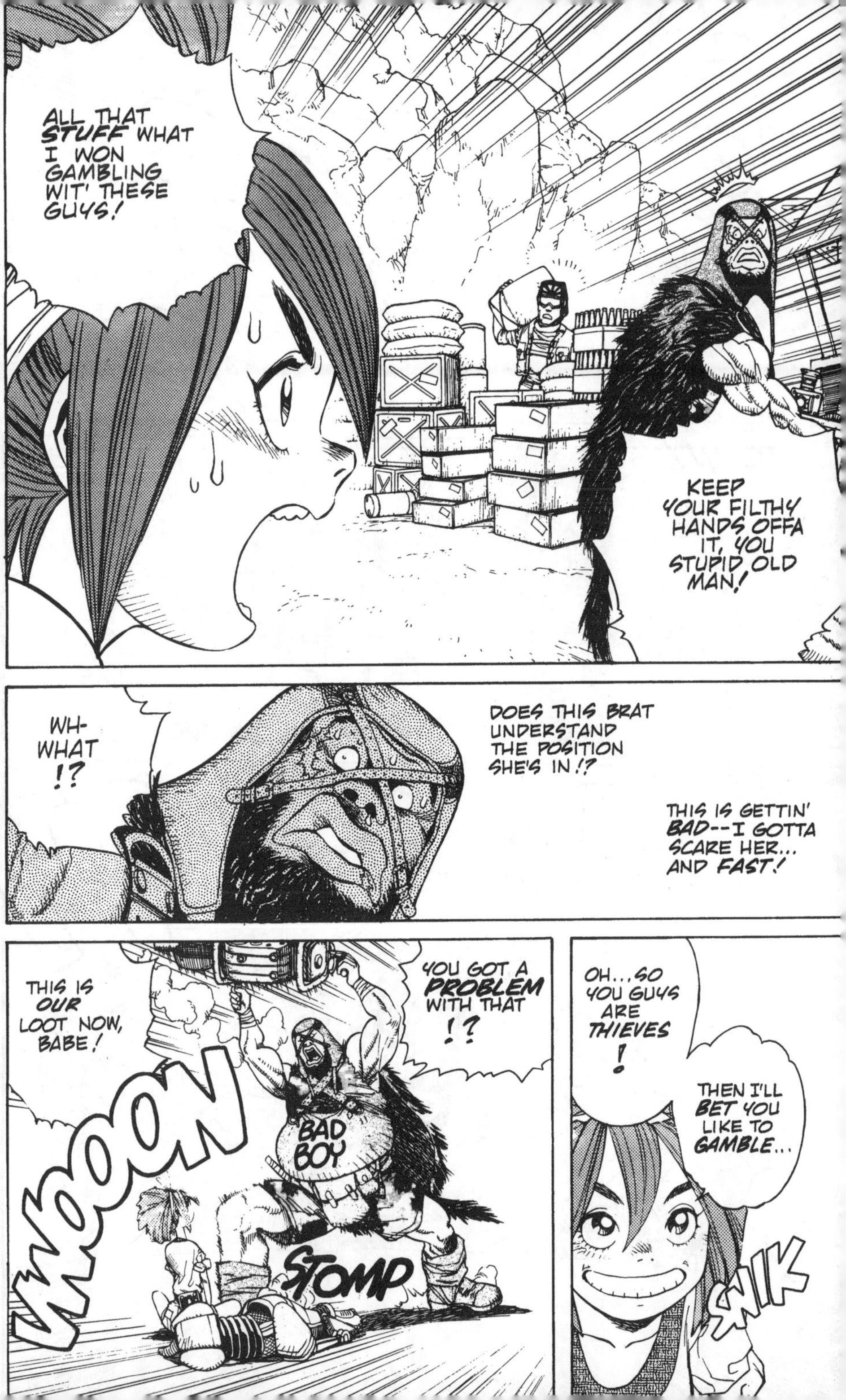
ALL THAT STUFF WHAT I WON GAMBLING WIT' THESE GUYS!
KEEP YOUR FILTHY HANDS OFFA IT, YOU STUPID OLD MAN!
WH-WHAT !?
DOES THIS BRAT UNDERSTAND THE POSITION SHE'S IN!?
THIS IS GETTIN' BAD--I GOTTA SCARE HER... AND FAST!
THIS IS OUR LOOT NOW, BABE!
YOU GOT A PROBLEM WITH THAT !?
WHOOON
BAD BOY
STOMP
OH...SO YOU GUYS ARE THIEVES !
THEN I'LL BET YOU LIKE TO GAMBLE...
SNIK

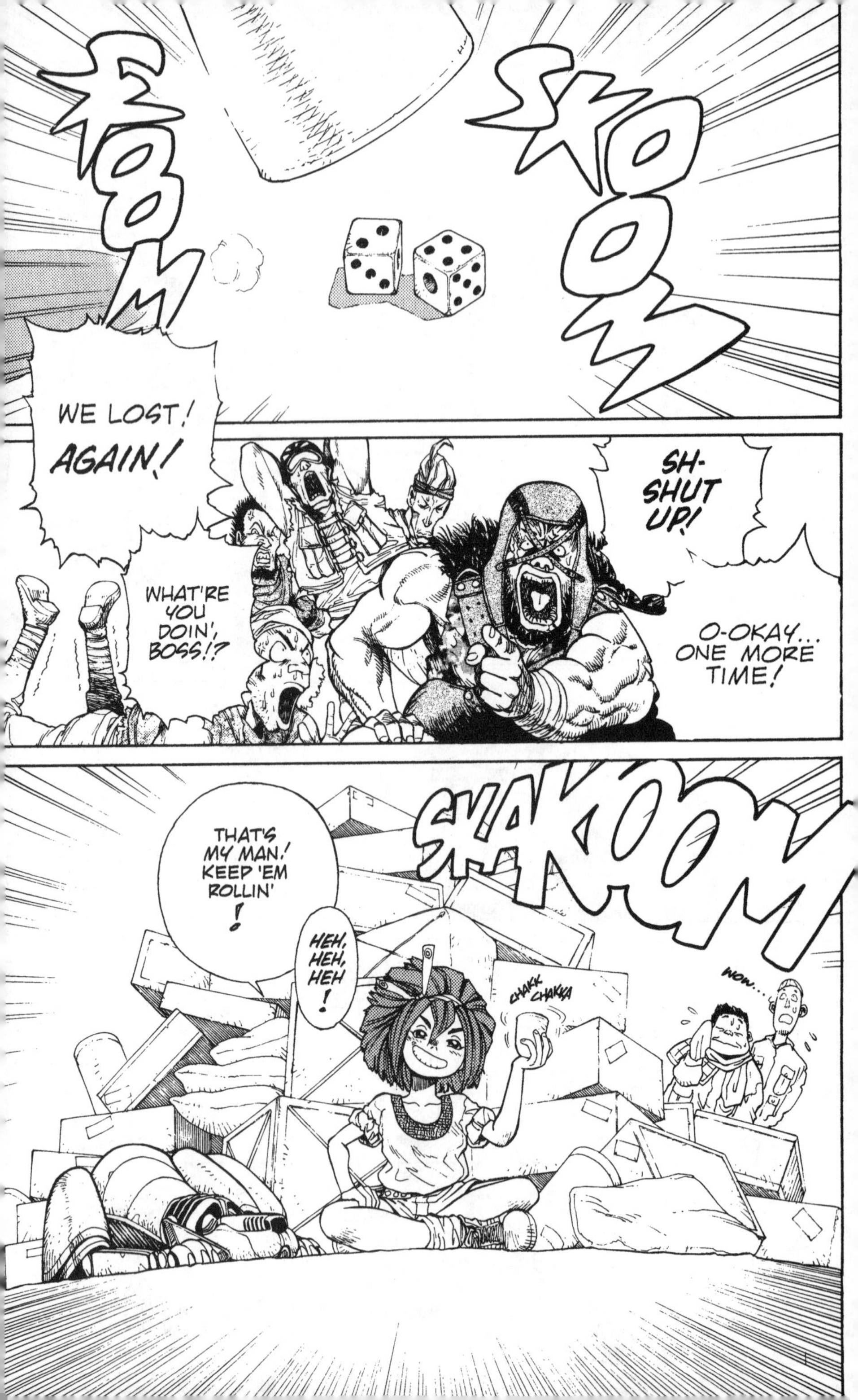
FROM
SKOOM
WE LOST! AGAIN!
WHAT'RE YOU DOIN', BOSS!?
SH-SHUT UP!
O-OKAY... ONE MORE TIME!
THAT'S MY MAN! KEEP 'EM ROLLIN'!
HEH, HEH, HEH!
SKAKOOM
CHAKK CHAKKA
WOW...

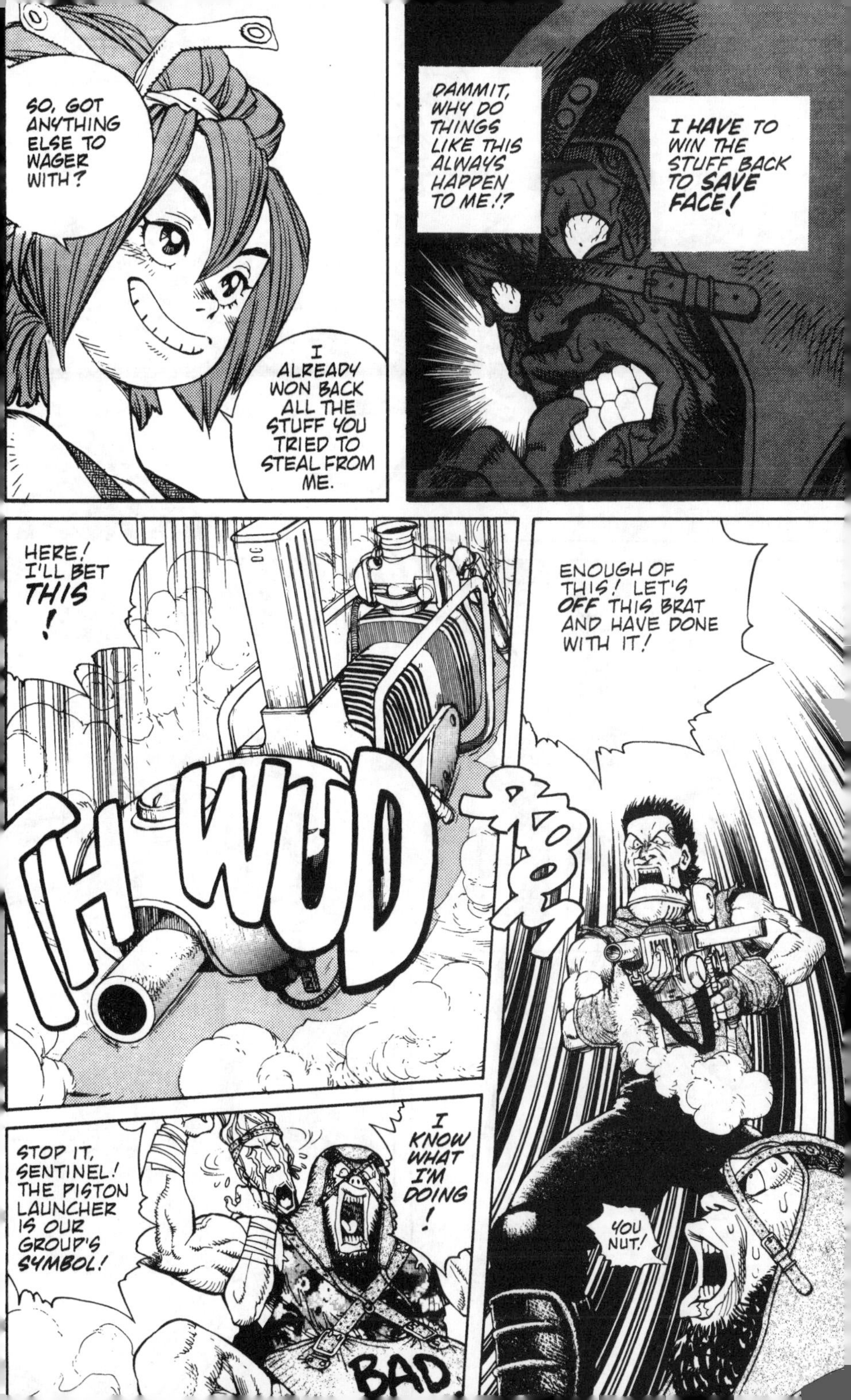
SO, GOT ANYTHING ELSE TO WAGER WITH?
I ALREADY WON BACK ALL THE STUFF YOU TRIED TO STEAL FROM ME.
DAMMIT, WHY DO THINGS LIKE THIS ALWAYS HAPPEN TO ME!?
I HAVE TO WIN THE STUFF BACK TO SAVE FACE!
HERE! I'LL BET THIS!
THWUD
ENOUGH OF THIS! LET'S OFF THIS BRAT AND HAVE DONE WITH IT!
STOP IT, SENTINEL! THE PISTON LAUNCHER IS OUR GROUP'S SYMBOL!
I KNOW WHAT I'M DOING!
YOU NUT!
BAD

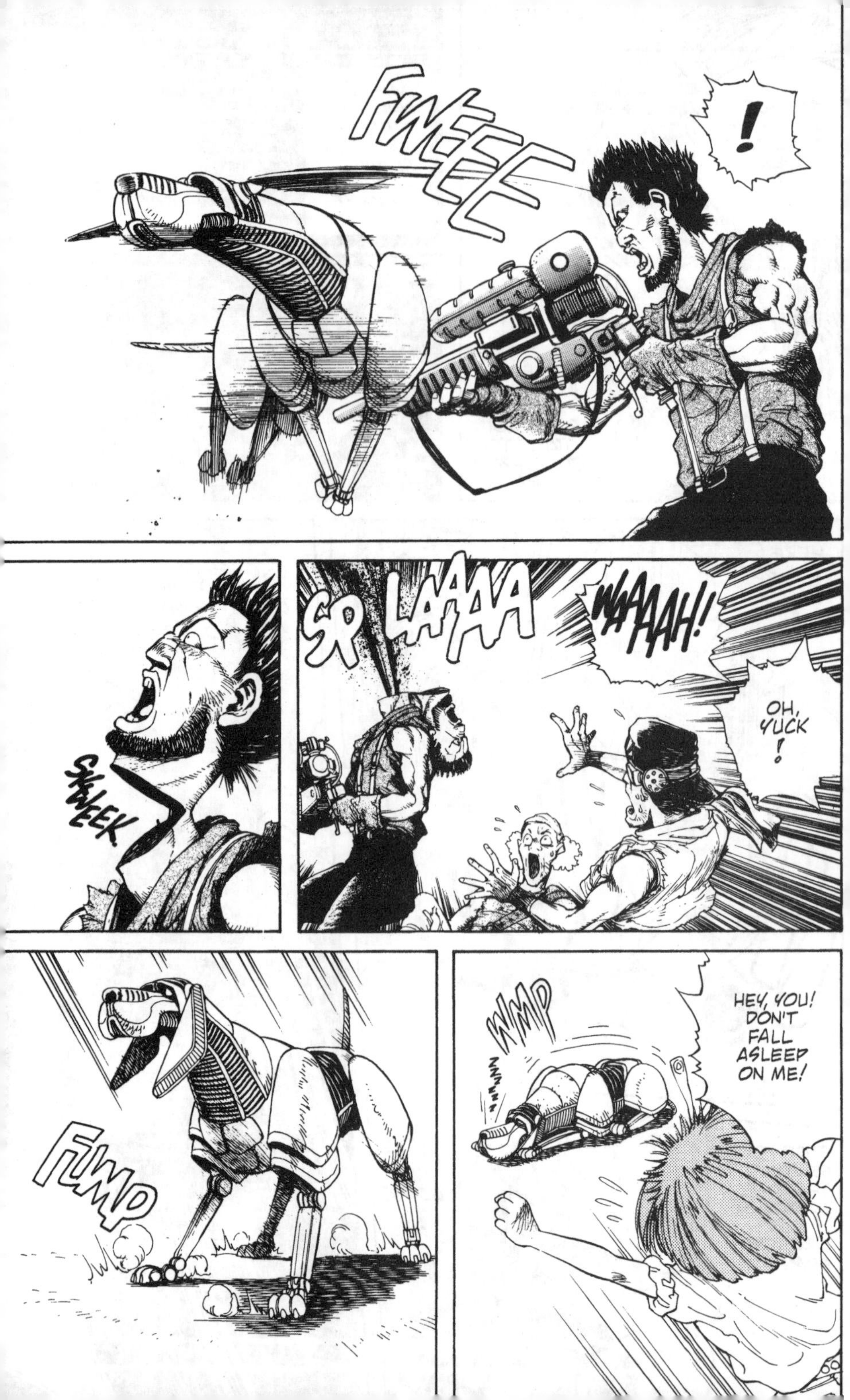

FWEEEE
!
SKWEEK
SPLAAAA
WAAAAH!
OH, YUCK!
FLUMP
WMP
HEY, YOU! DON'T FALL ASLEEP ON ME!

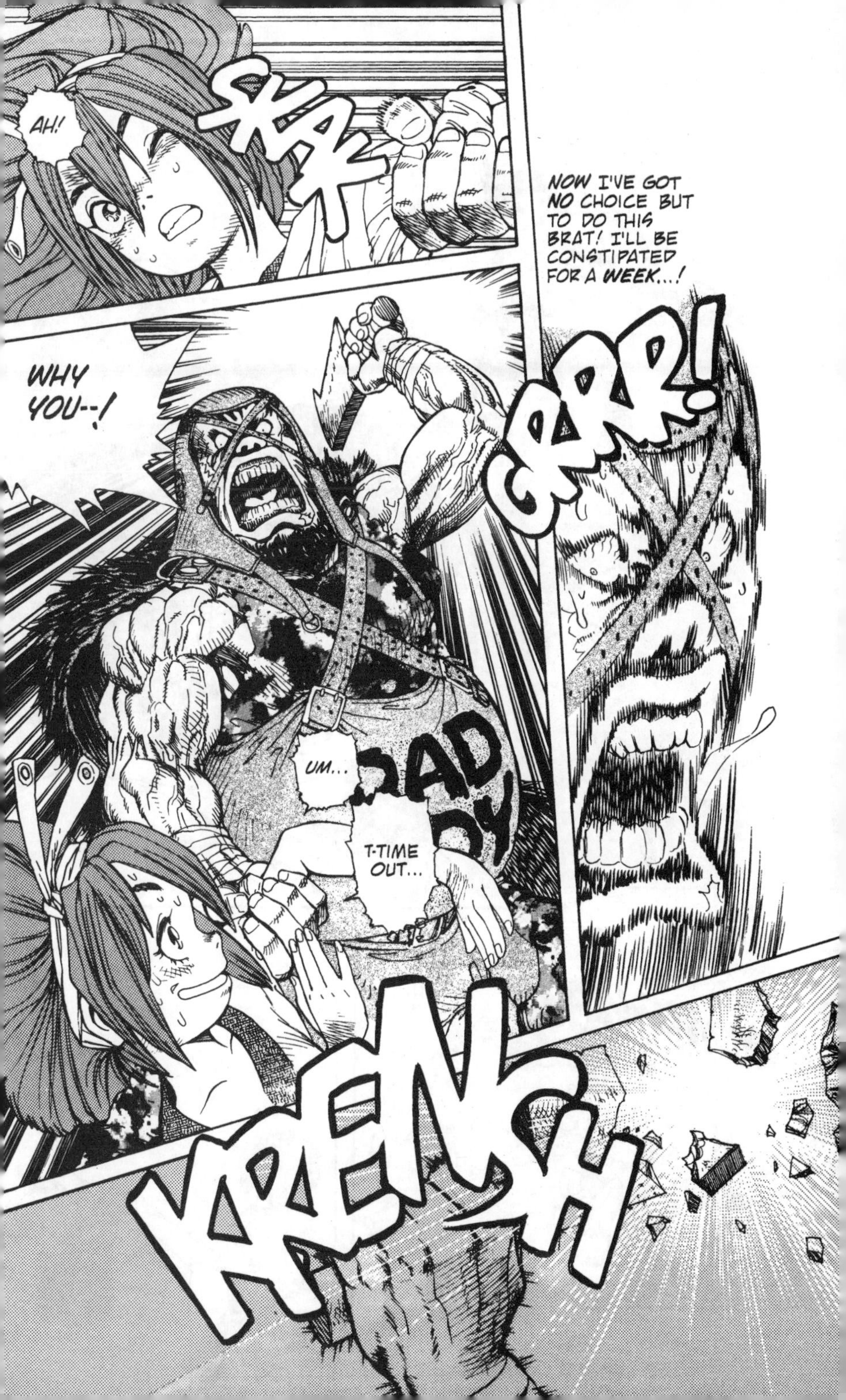
AH!
SKAK
NOW I'VE GOT NO CHOICE BUT TO DO THIS BRAT! I'LL BE CONSTIPATED FOR A WEEK...!
WHY YOU--!
UM...
T-TIME OUT...
GRRR!
KRENCH

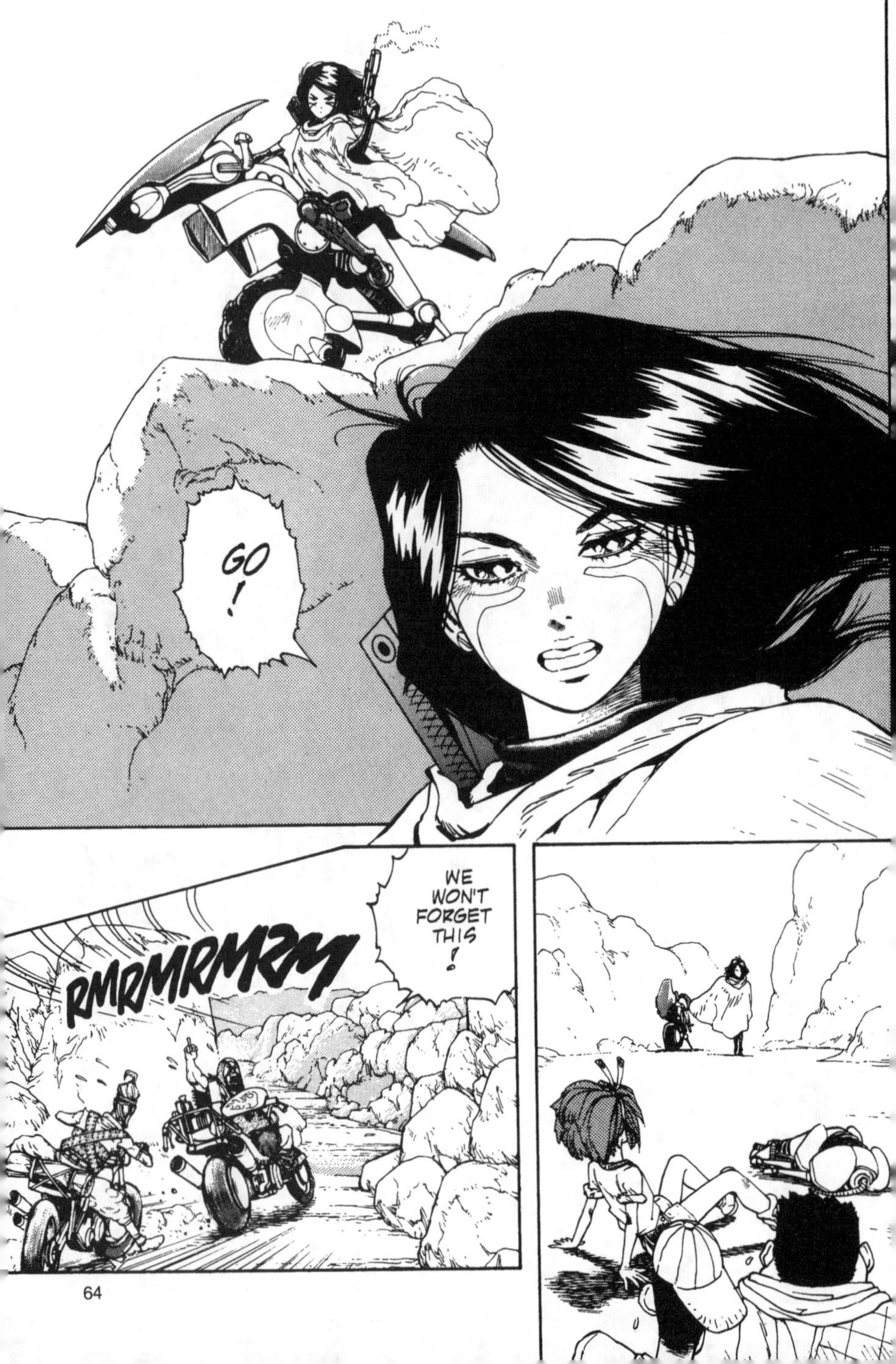
GO!
RMRMRMRM
WE WON'T FORGET THIS!

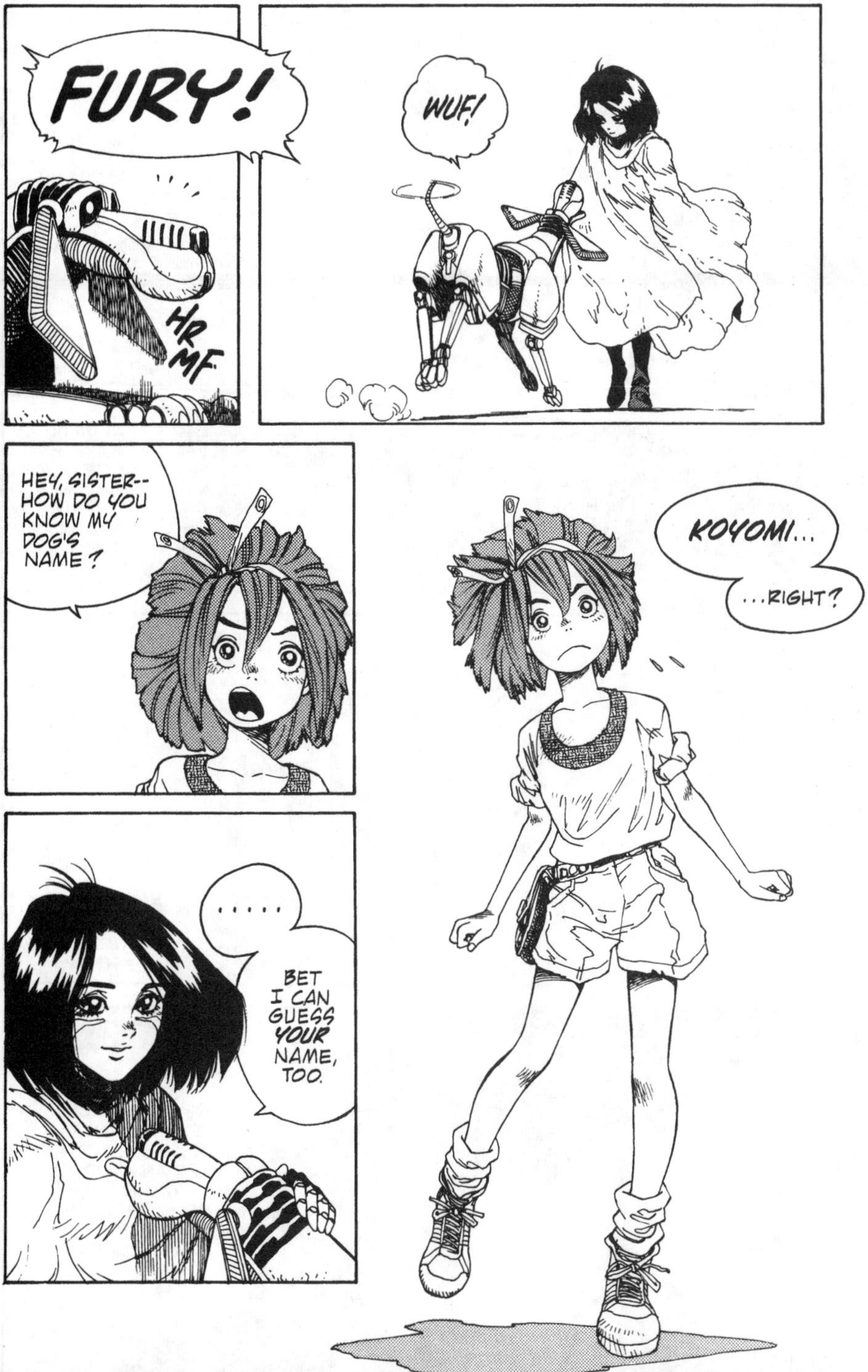
FURY!
HR MF
WUF!
HEY, SISTER-- HOW DO YOU KNOW MY DOG'S NAME?
KOYOMI...
...RIGHT?
.....
BET I CAN GUESS *YOUR* NAME, TOO.

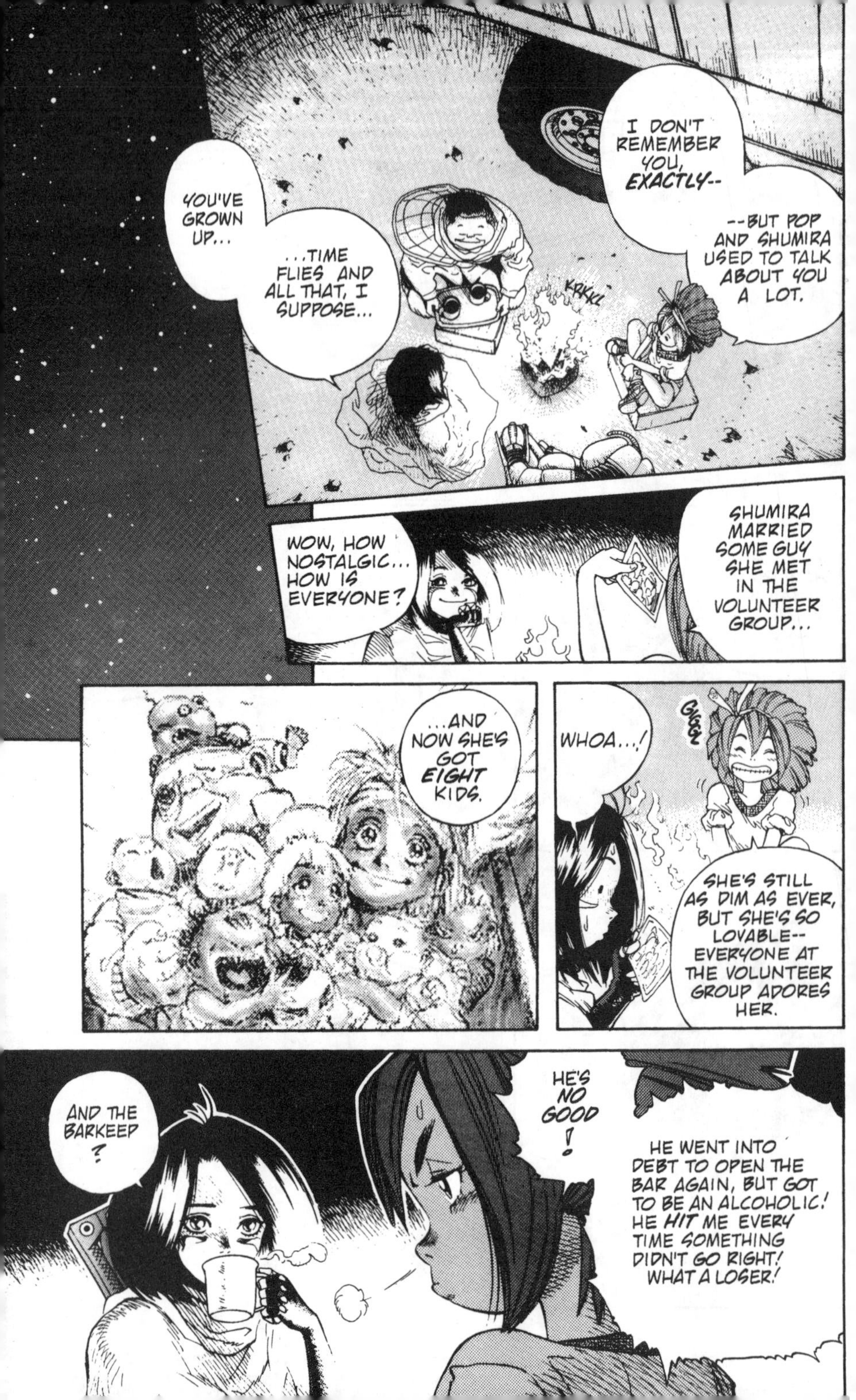
YOU'VE GROWN UP...
...TIME FLIES AND ALL THAT, I SUPPOSE...
KRKKL
I DON'T REMEMBER YOU, EXACTLY--
--BUT POP AND SHUMIRA USED TO TALK ABOUT YOU A LOT.
WOW, HOW NOSTALGIC... HOW IS EVERYONE?
SHUMIRA MARRIED SOME GUY SHE MET IN THE VOLUNTEER GROUP...
...AND NOW SHE'S GOT EIGHT KIDS.
WHOA...!
GIGGL
SHE'S STILL AS DIM AS EVER, BUT SHE'S SO LOVABLE-- EVERYONE AT THE VOLUNTEER GROUP ADORES HER.
AND THE BARKEEP?
HE'S NO GOOD!
HE WENT INTO DEBT TO OPEN THE BAR AGAIN, BUT GOT TO BE AN ALCOHOLIC! HE HIT ME EVERY TIME SOMETHING DIDN'T GO RIGHT! WHAT A LOSER!

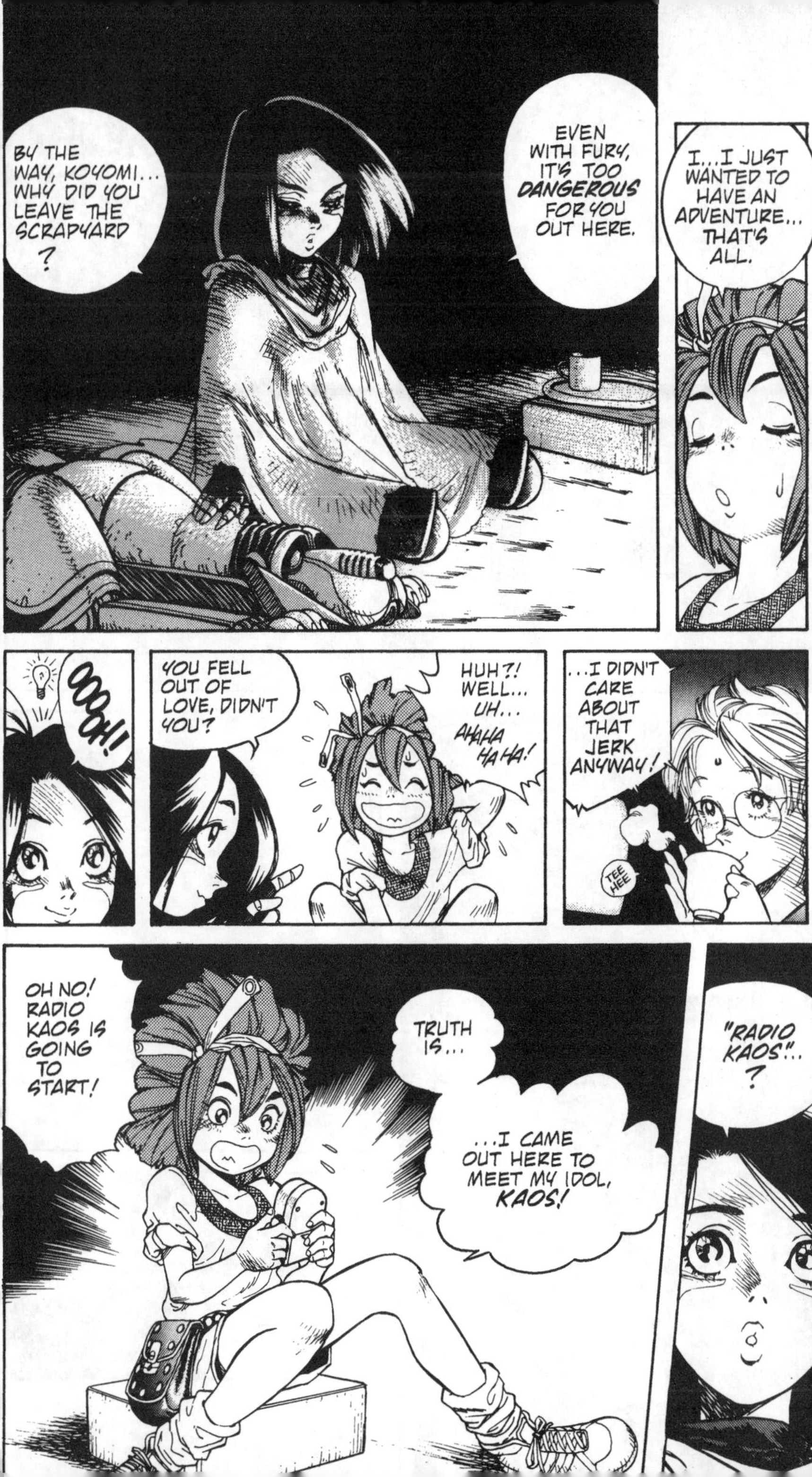
BY THE WAY, KOYOMI... WHY DID YOU LEAVE THE SCRAPYARD ?
EVEN WITH FURY, IT'S TOO DANGEROUS FOR YOU OUT HERE.
I...I JUST WANTED TO HAVE AN ADVENTURE... THAT'S ALL.
OOOOH!!
YOU FELL OUT OF LOVE, DIDN'T YOU?
HUH?! WELL... UH...
AHAHA HA HA!
...I DIDN'T CARE ABOUT THAT JERK ANYWAY!
TEE HEE
OH NO! RADIO KAOS IS GOING TO START!
TRUTH IS...
...I CAME OUT HERE TO MEET MY IDOL, KAOS!
"RADIO KAOS"... ?

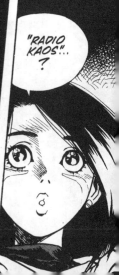

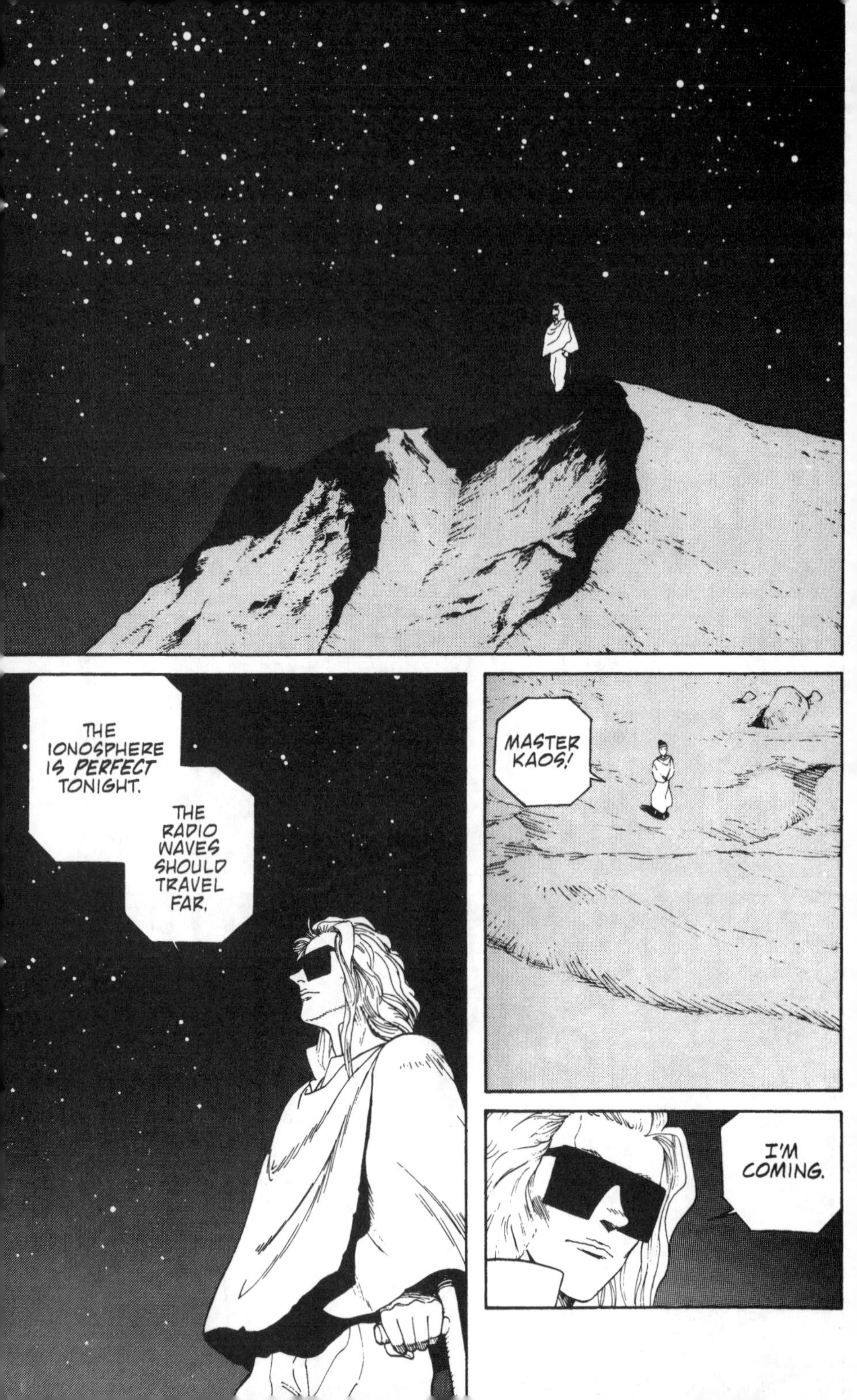
THE IONOSPHERE IS PERFECT TONIGHT.
THE RADIO WAVES SHOULD TRAVEL FAR.
MASTER KAOS!
I'M COMING.

TSSSH!

A MESSENGER FROM BARJACK IS HERE.

YOU PEOPLE AGAIN?

I APPRECIATE ALL THE SUPPORT DEN GIVES ME...

...BUT I WON'T RUN ANY PROPAGANDA FOR YOU.

MY MUSIC-- IT MUST RISE ABOVE THE DIFFERENCES BETWEEN PEOPLE... REACH THEIR HEARTS.

WON'T YOU RECONSIDER?

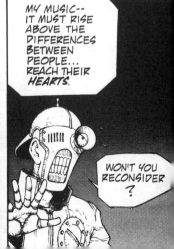

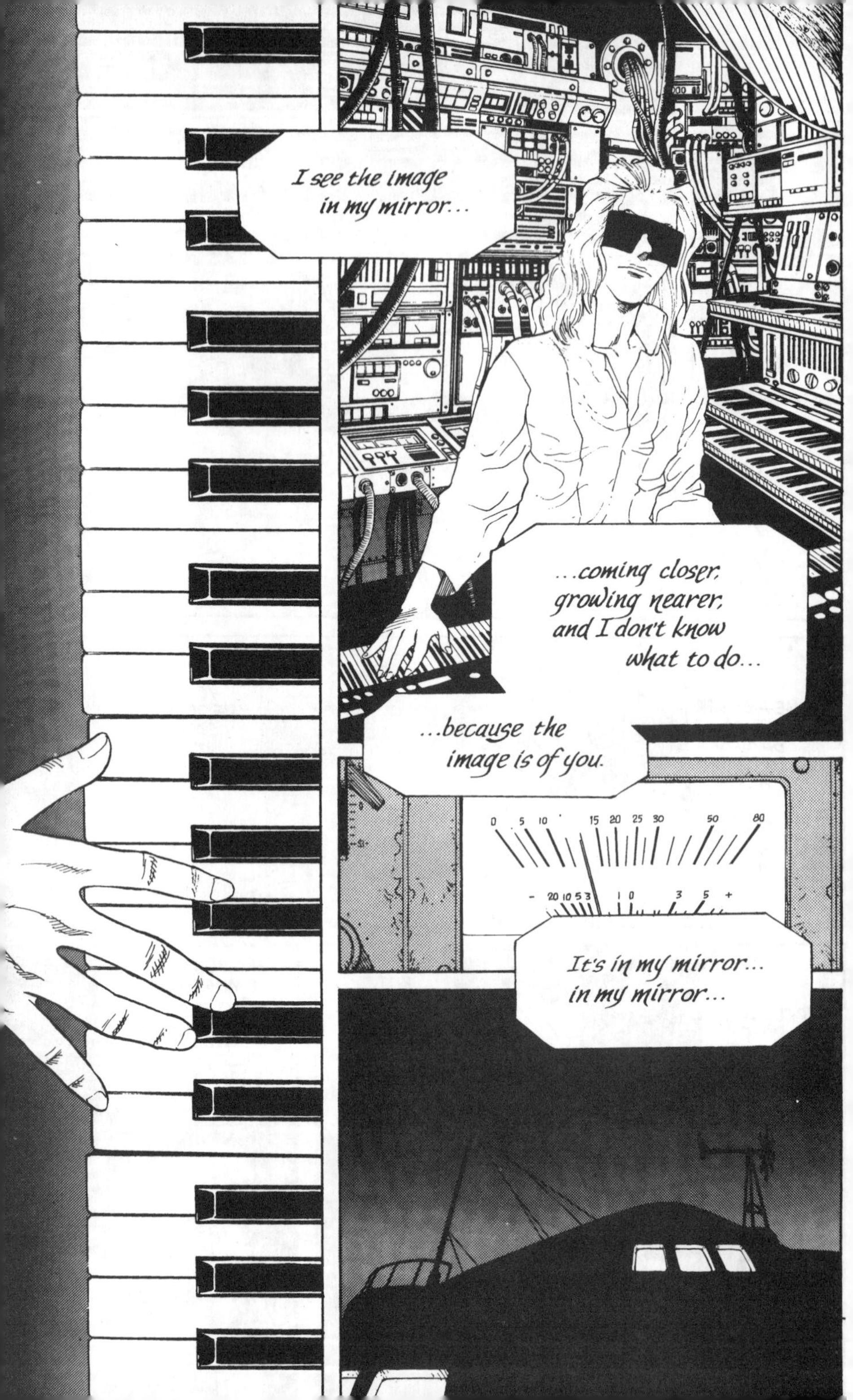
I see the image in my mirror...
...coming closer, growing nearer, and I don't know what to do...
...because the image is of you.
0 5 10 15 20 25 30 50 80
- 20 10 5 3 1 0 3 5 +
It's in my mirror... in my mirror...

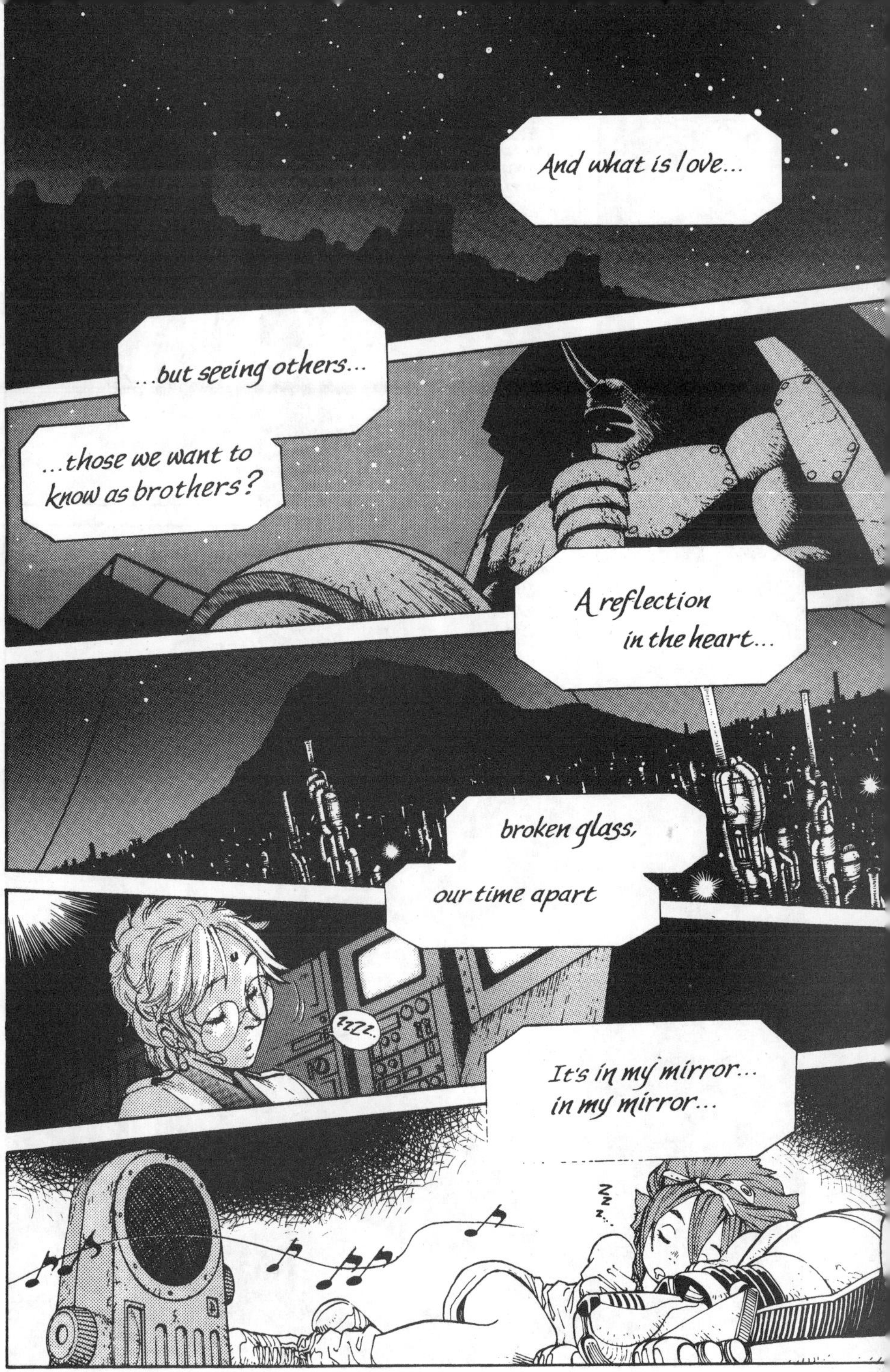
And what is love...
...but seeing others...
...those we want to know as brothers?
A reflection in the heart...
broken glass,
our time apart
ZZZZ..
It's in my mirror... in my mirror...
ZZZ...

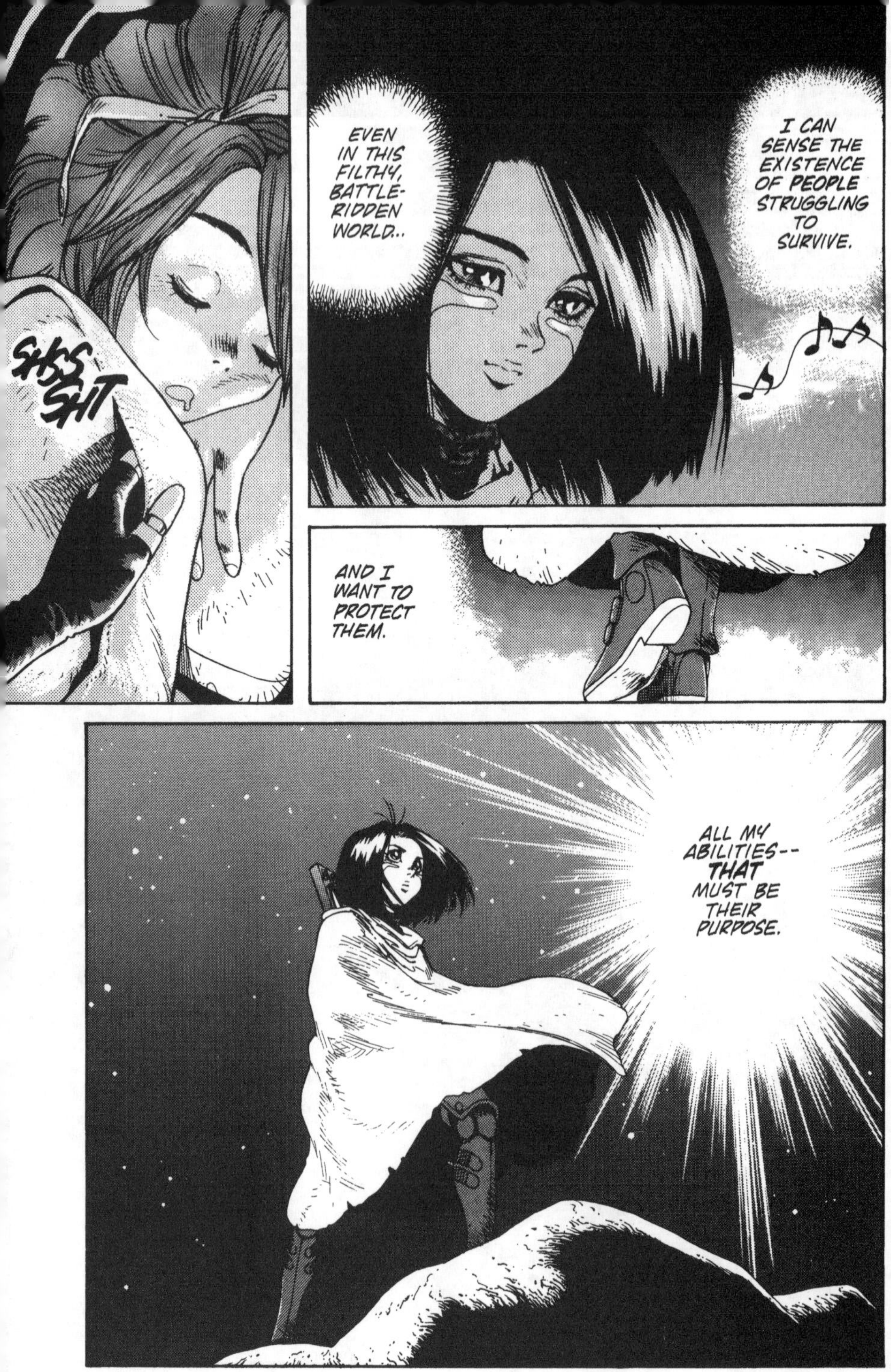
SHSS SHIT
EVEN IN THIS FILTHY, BATTLE-RIDDEN WORLD...
I CAN SENSE THE EXISTENCE OF PEOPLE STRUGGLING TO SURVIVE.
AND I WANT TO PROTECT THEM.
ALL MY ABILITIES-- **THAT** MUST BE THEIR PURPOSE.

PANZER BRIDE
Mission 3: Obsession

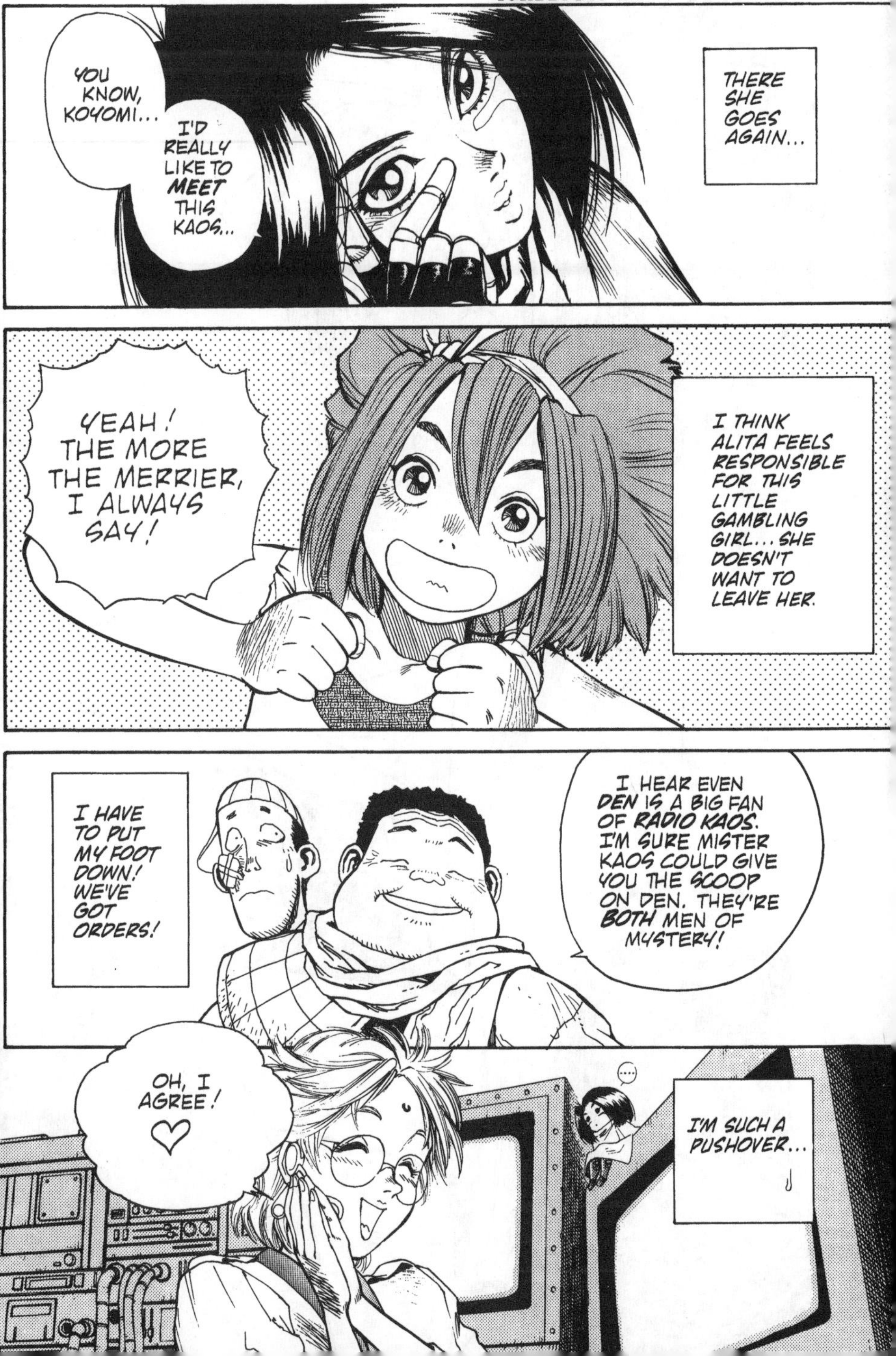

YOU KNOW, KOYOMI...
I'D REALLY LIKE TO MEET THIS KAOS...
THERE SHE GOES AGAIN...
YEAH! THE MORE THE MERRIER, I ALWAYS SAY!
I THINK ALITA FEELS RESPONSIBLE FOR THIS LITTLE GAMBLING GIRL... SHE DOESN'T WANT TO LEAVE HER.
I HAVE TO PUT MY FOOT DOWN! WE'VE GOT ORDERS!
I HEAR EVEN DEN IS A BIG FAN OF RADIO KAOS. I'M SURE MISTER KAOS COULD GIVE YOU THE SCOOP ON DEN. THEY'RE BOTH MEN OF MYSTERY!
OH, I AGREE! ♥
....
I'M SUCH A PUSHOVER...

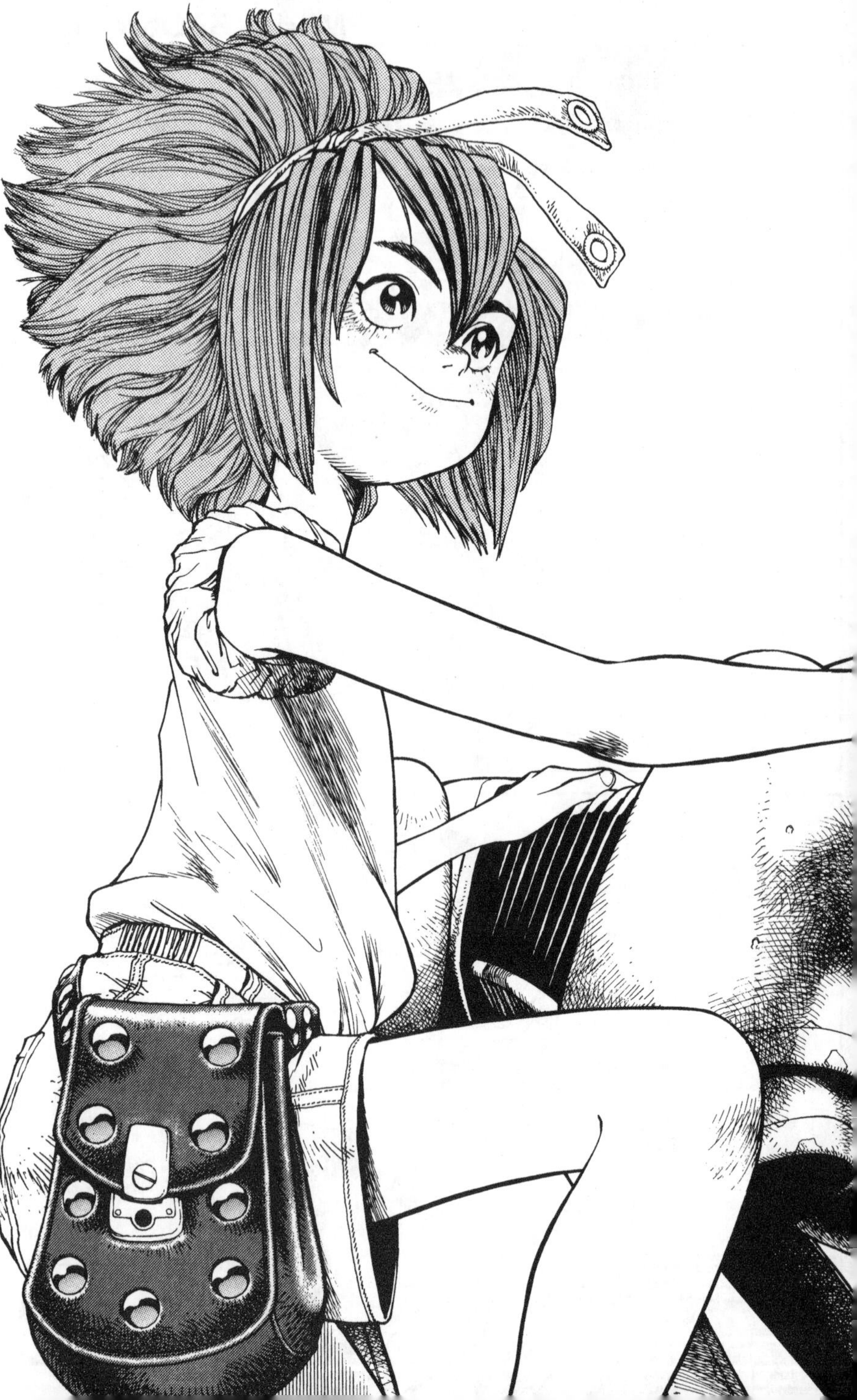

PANZER BRIDE

Mission 3: Obsession

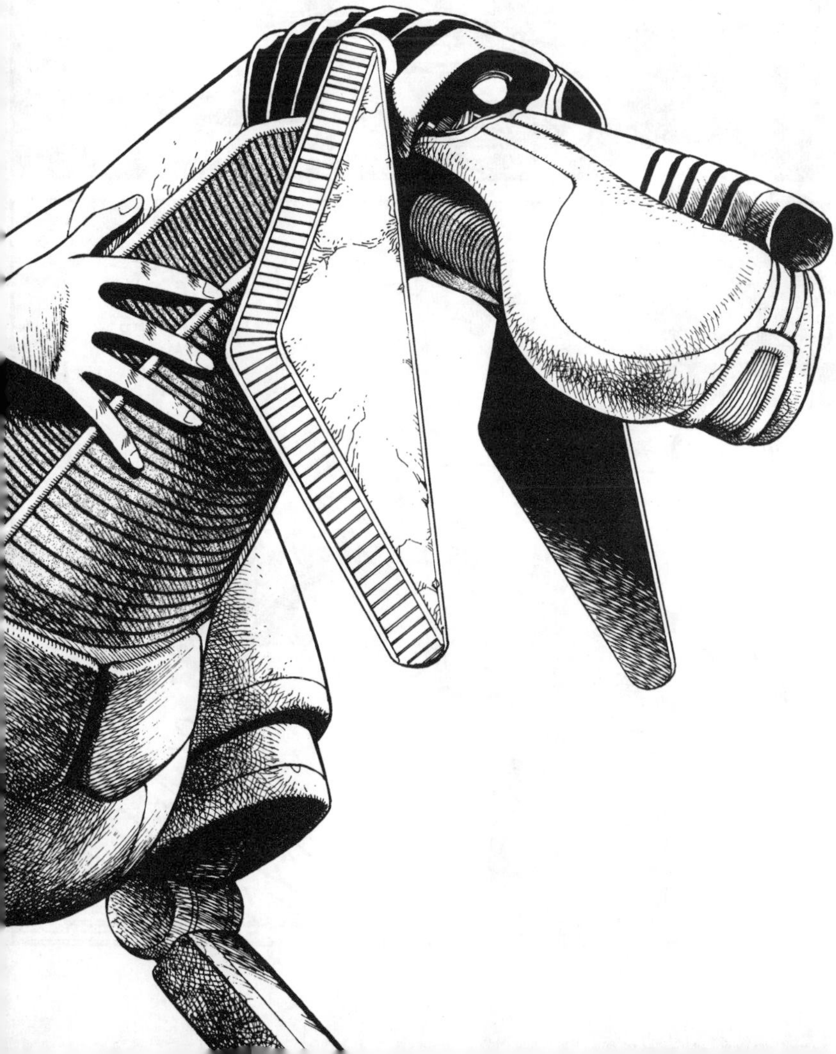

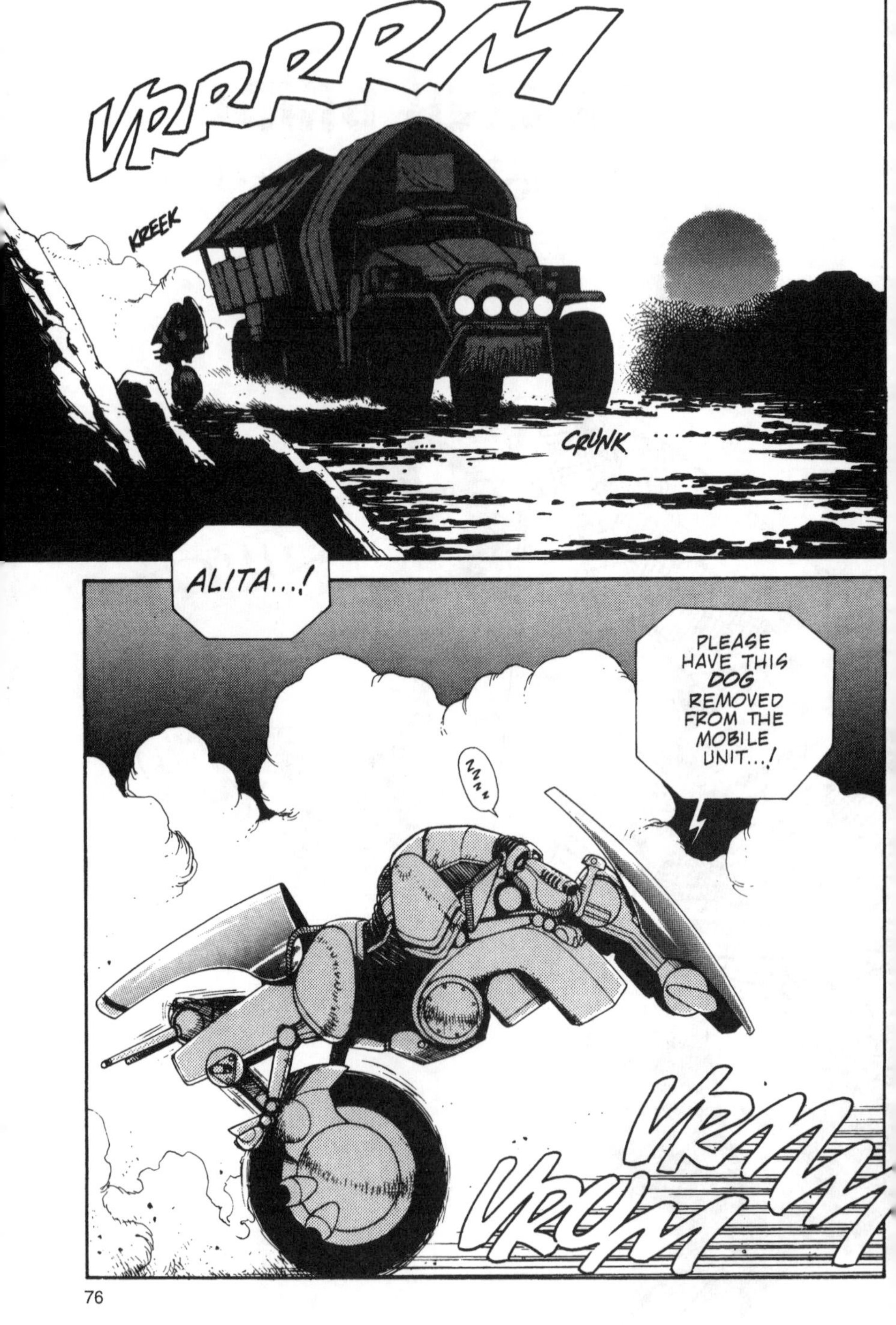

VRRRRM
KREEK
CRUNK
ALITA...!
PLEASE HAVE THIS DOG REMOVED FROM THE MOBILE UNIT...!
VRM
VRUM

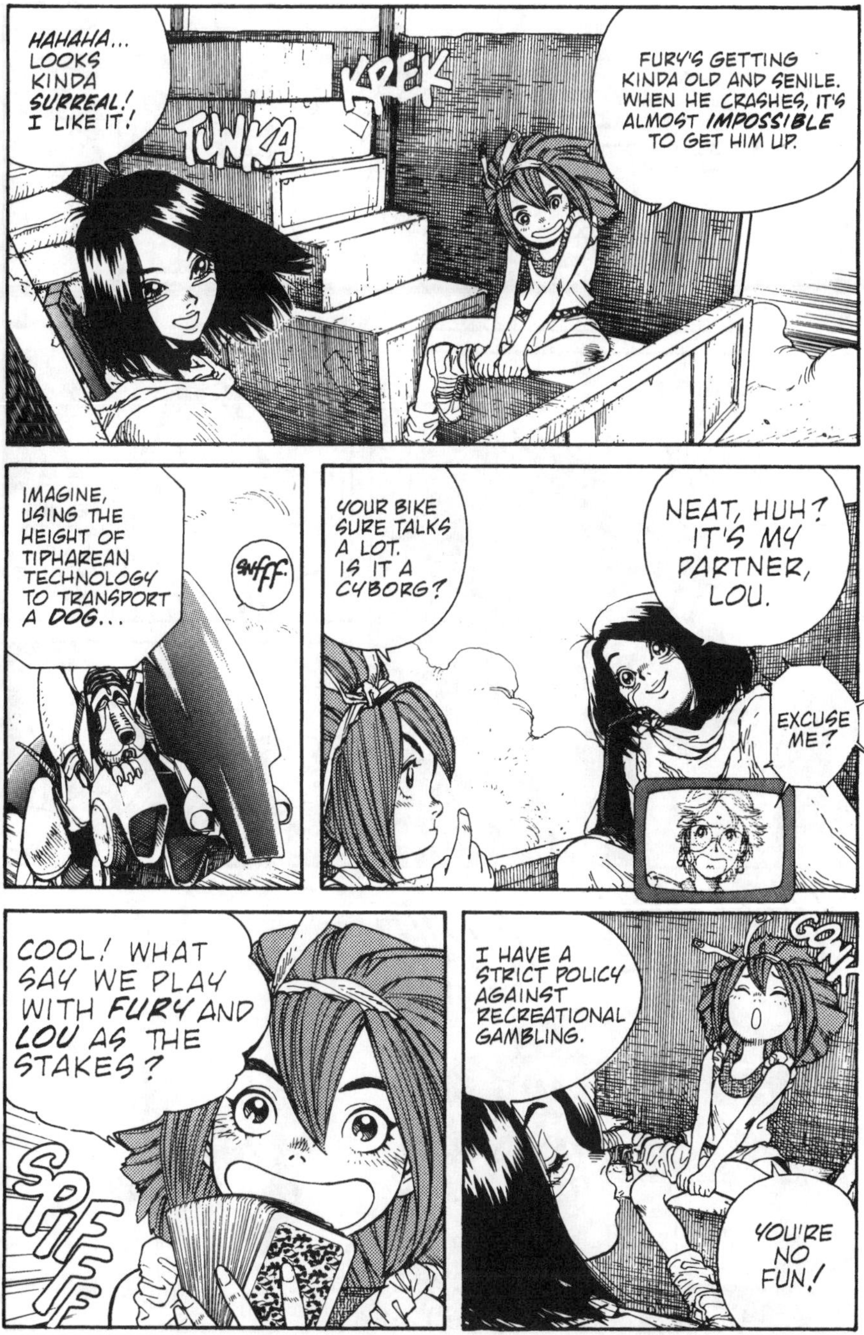
HAHAHA... LOOKS KINDA SURREAL! I LIKE IT!
KREK
TUNKA
FURY'S GETTING KINDA OLD AND SENILE. WHEN HE CRASHES, IT'S ALMOST IMPOSSIBLE TO GET HIM UP.
IMAGINE, USING THE HEIGHT OF TIPHAREAN TECHNOLOGY TO TRANSPORT A DOG...
SNIFF
YOUR BIKE SURE TALKS A LOT. IS IT A CYBORG?
NEAT, HUH? IT'S MY PARTNER, LOU.
EXCUSE ME?
COOL! WHAT SAY WE PLAY WITH FURY AND LOU AS THE STAKES?
SPIFFF
I HAVE A STRICT POLICY AGAINST RECREATIONAL GAMBLING.
GONK
YOU'RE NO FUN!

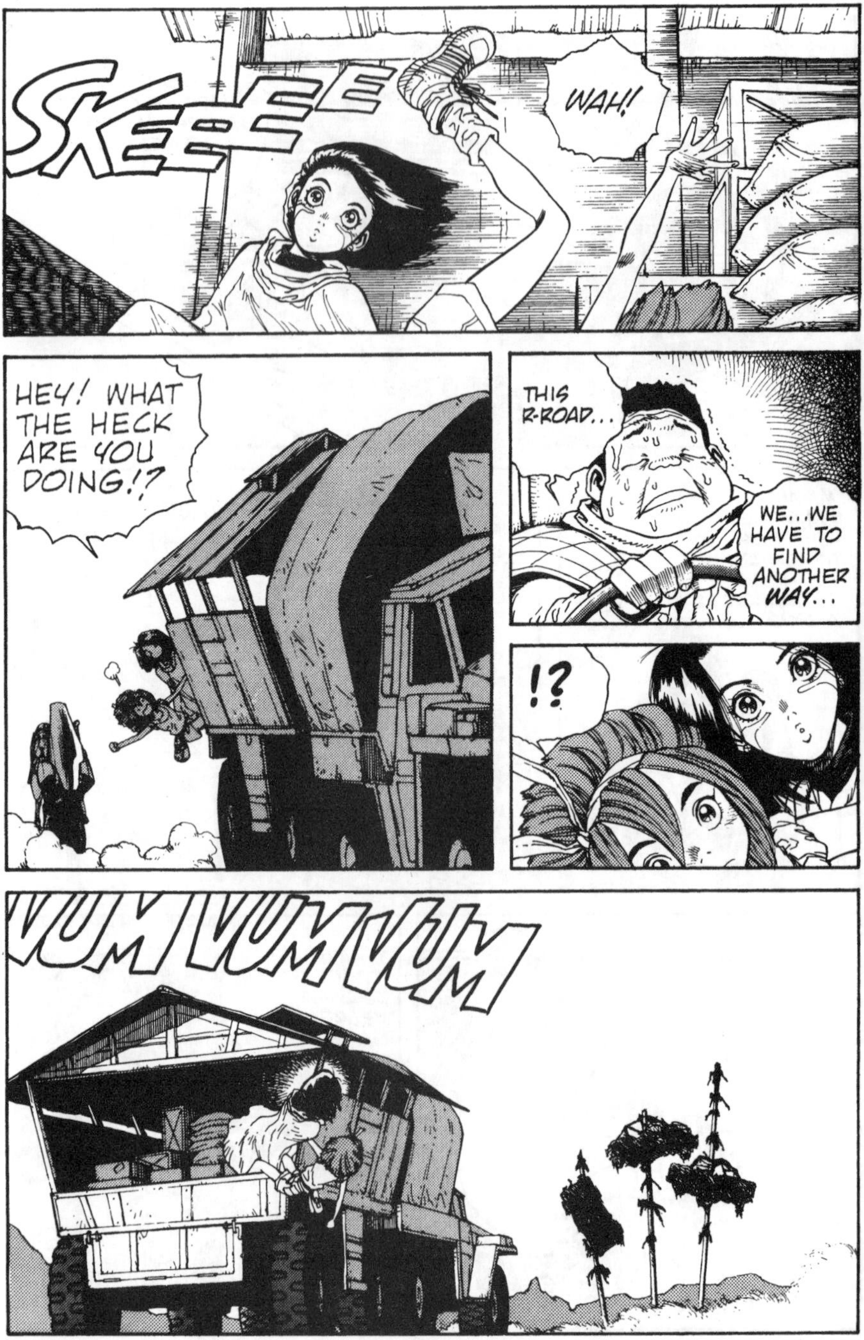
SKEEE
WAH!
HEY! WHAT THE HECK ARE YOU DOING!?
THIS R-ROAD...
WE...WE HAVE TO FIND ANOTHER WAY...
!?
VUM VUM VUM VUM

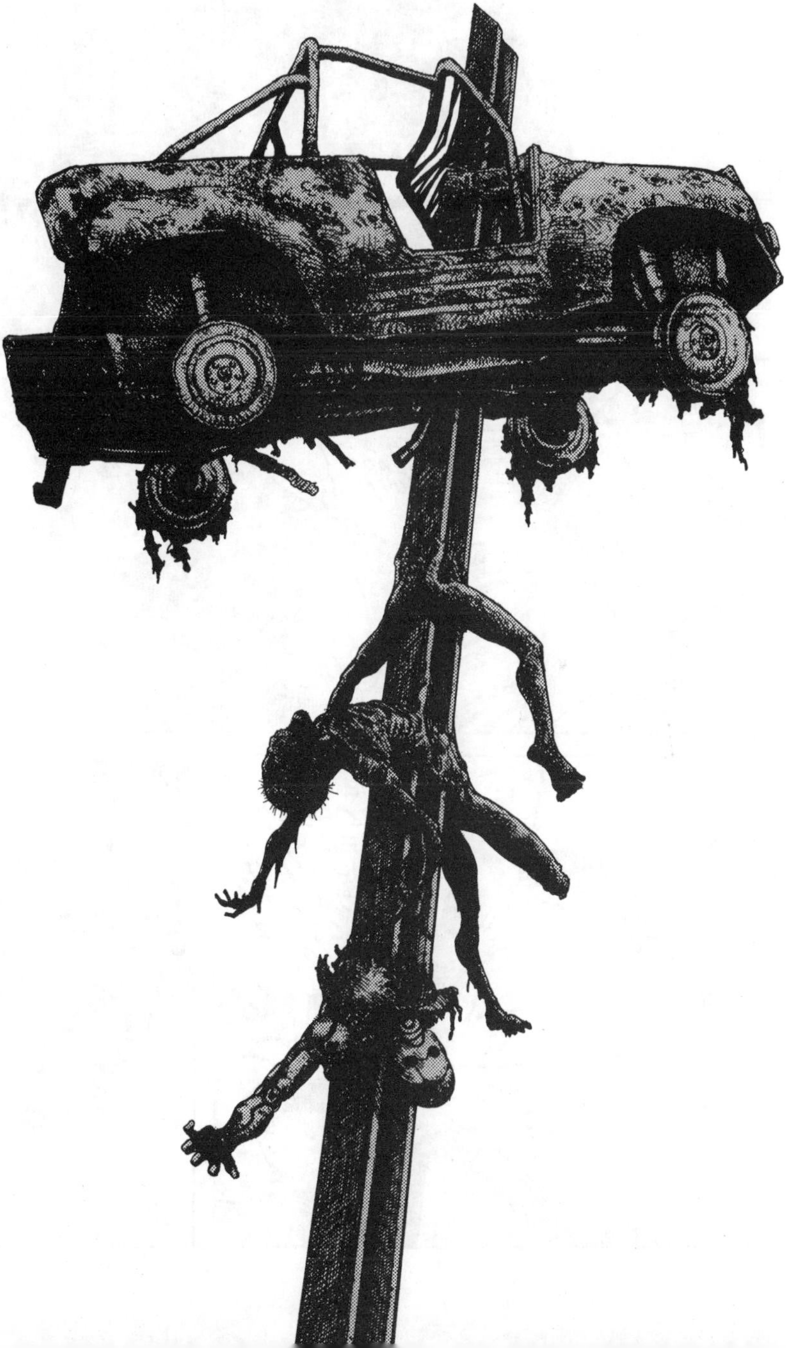

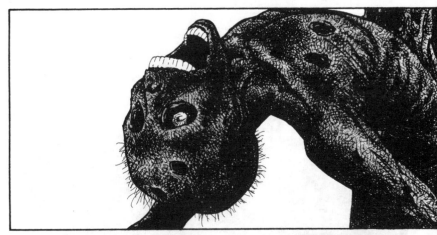

!

GROSS! IT'S A DEAD GUY!

...
....

IT'S A BOUNDARY MARKER-- FOR BARJACK TERRITORY!

WE'RE REALLY CLOSE TO MISTER KAOS, BUT WE *HAVE* TO FIND ANOTHER WAY!

BRMMMM

SKRK

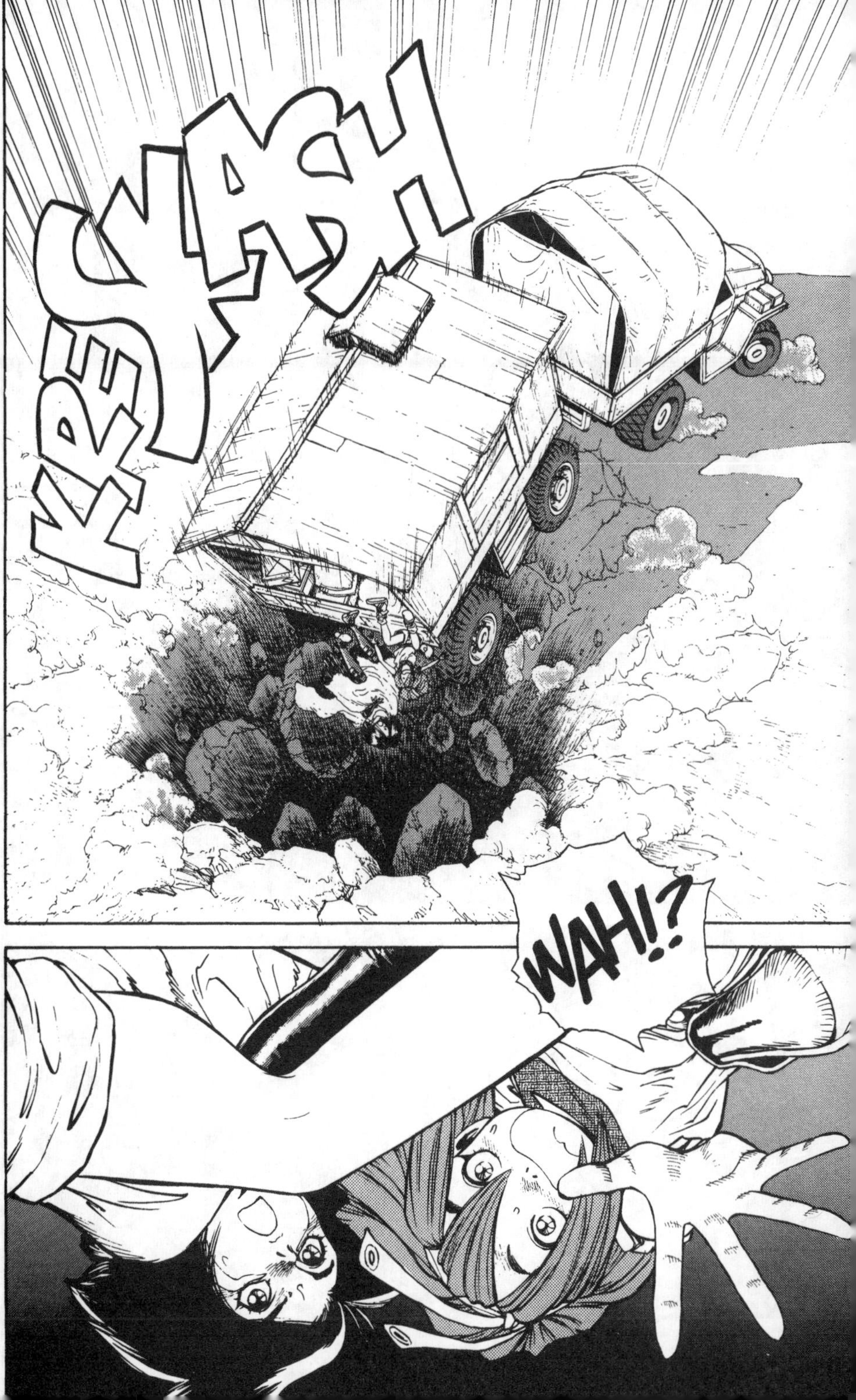
KRESKASH
WAH!?

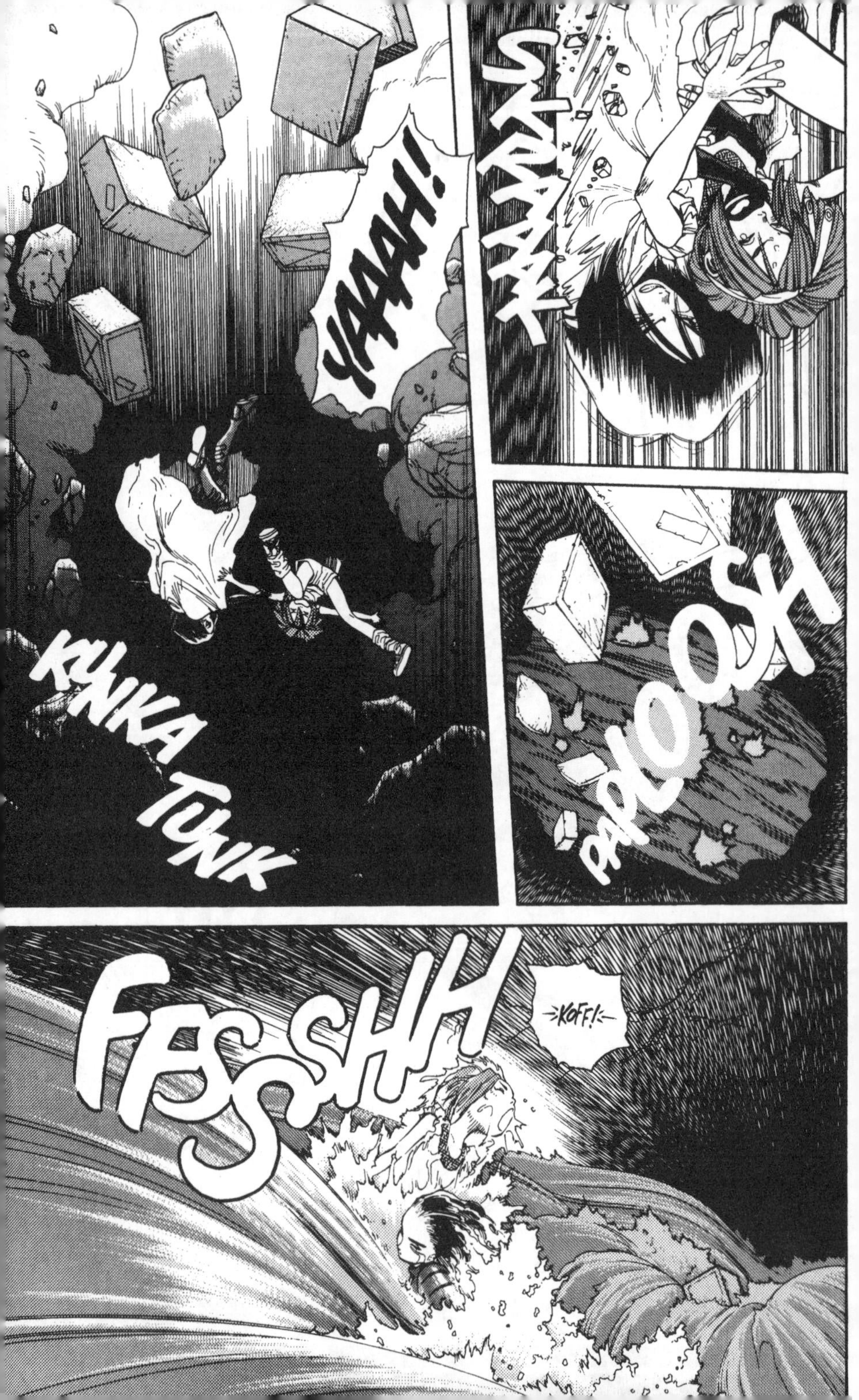
YAAAH!
KLINKA TUNK
SKRAAAK
PAPLOOSH
FSSSHH
KOFF!

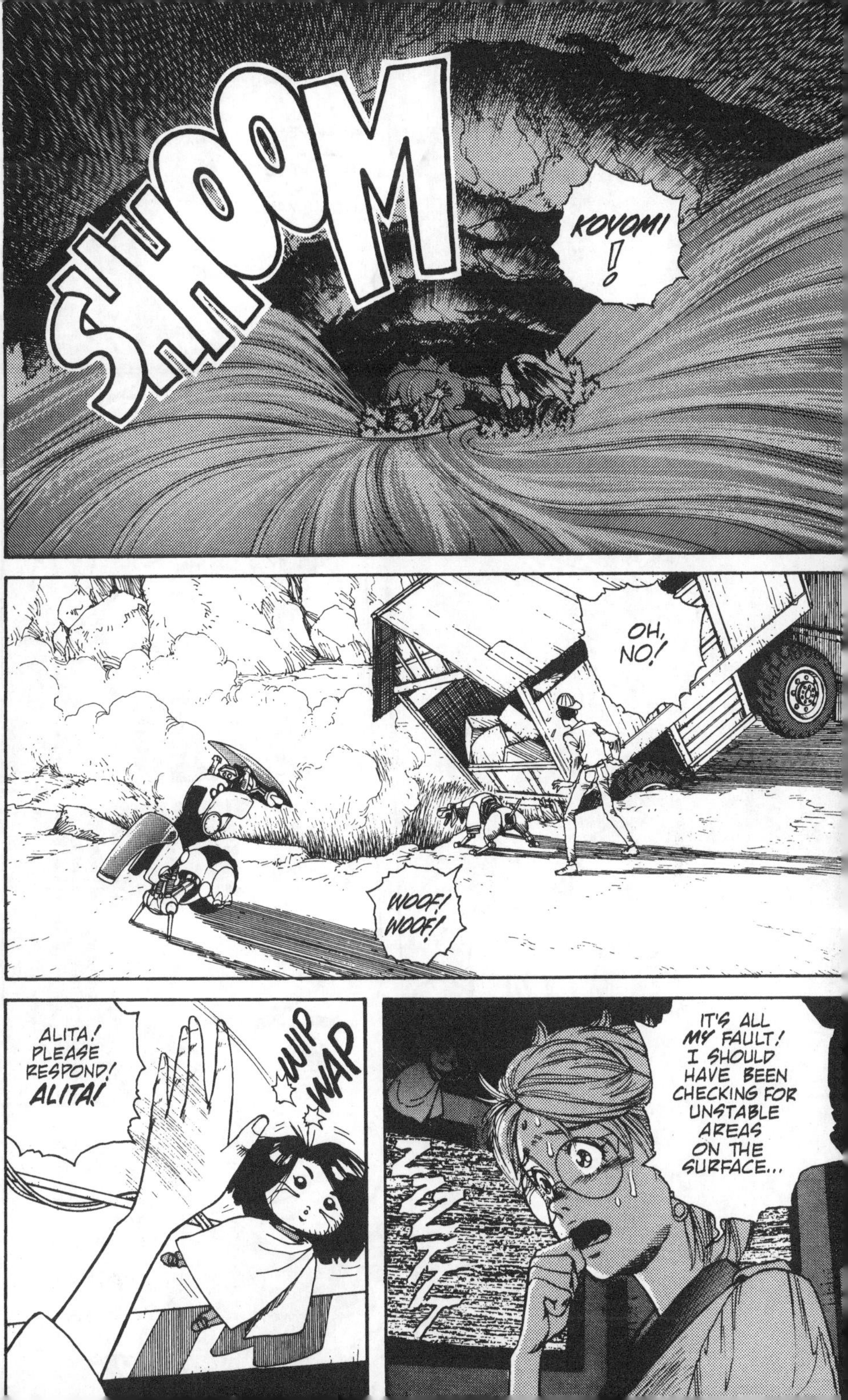
SHOOOM
KOYOMI!
OH, NO!
WOOF! WOOF!
ALITA! PLEASE RESPOND! ALITA!
WIP WAP
IT'S ALL MY FAULT! I SHOULD HAVE BEEN CHECKING FOR UNSTABLE AREAS ON THE SURFACE...
ZZZTTT

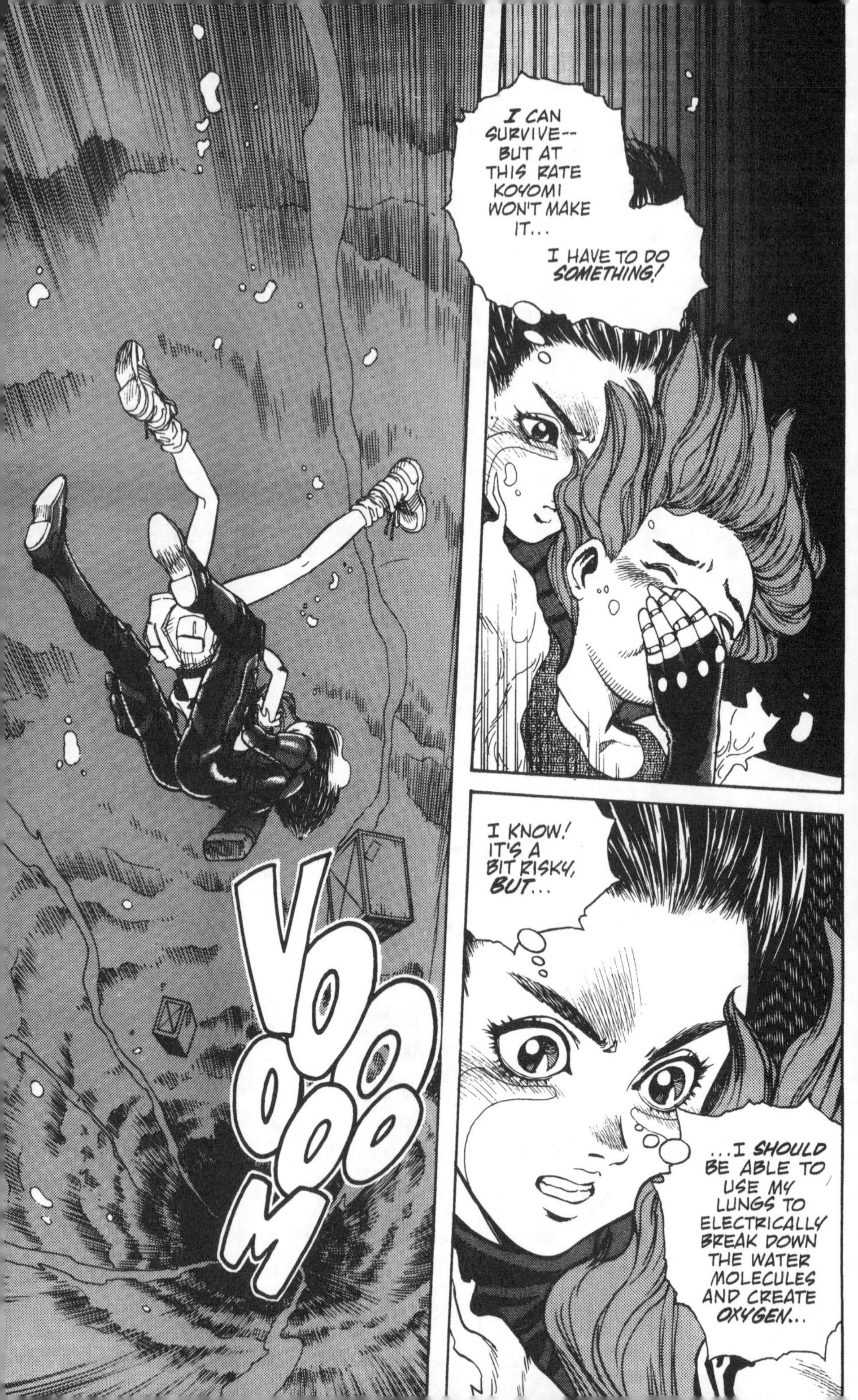
VOOOOOM
I CAN SURVIVE-- BUT AT THIS RATE KOYOMI WON'T MAKE IT...
I HAVE TO DO SOMETHING!
I KNOW! IT'S A BIT RISKY, BUT...
...I SHOULD BE ABLE TO USE MY LUNGS TO ELECTRICALLY BREAK DOWN THE WATER MOLECULES AND CREATE OXYGEN...

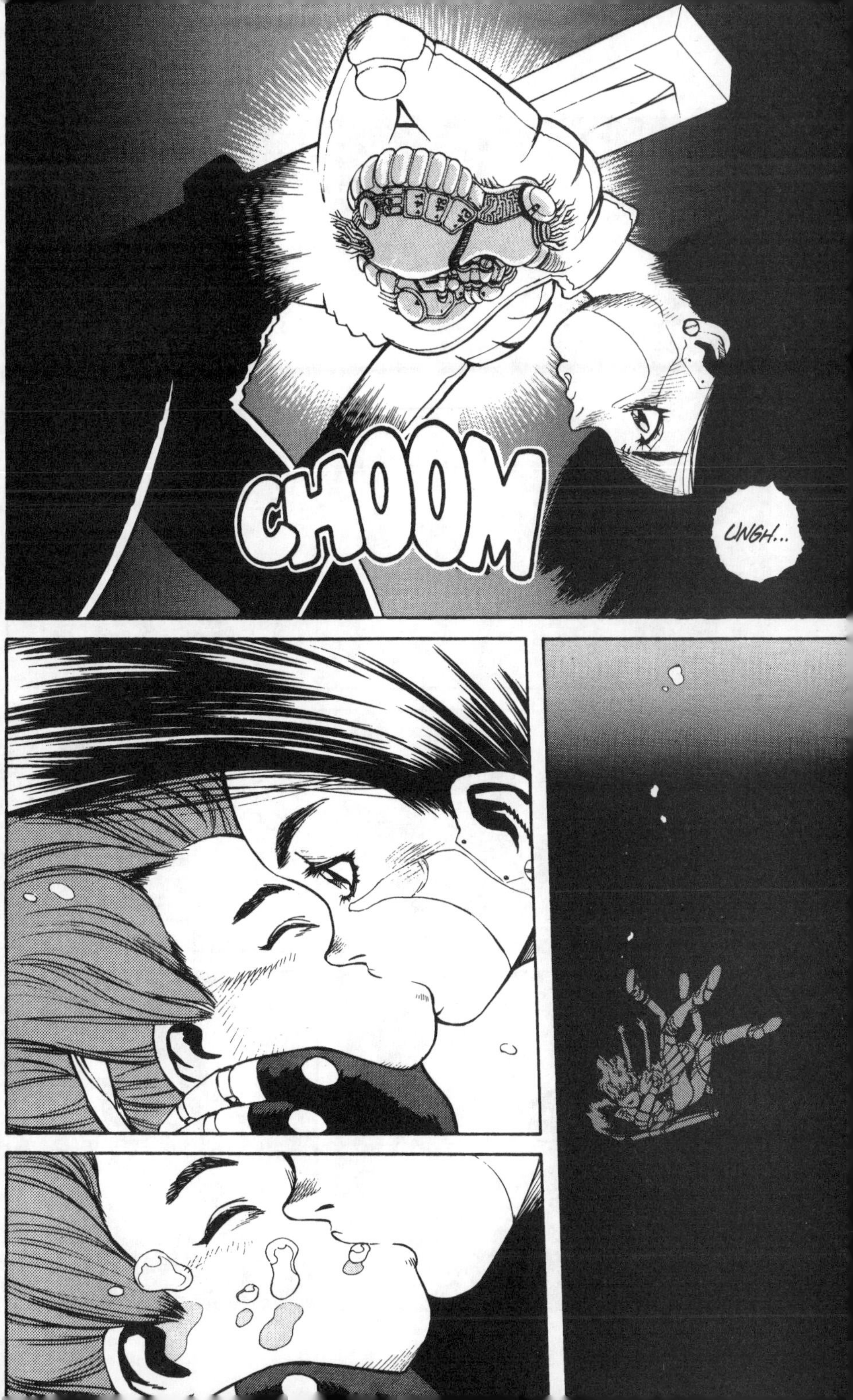
CHOOM
UNGH...

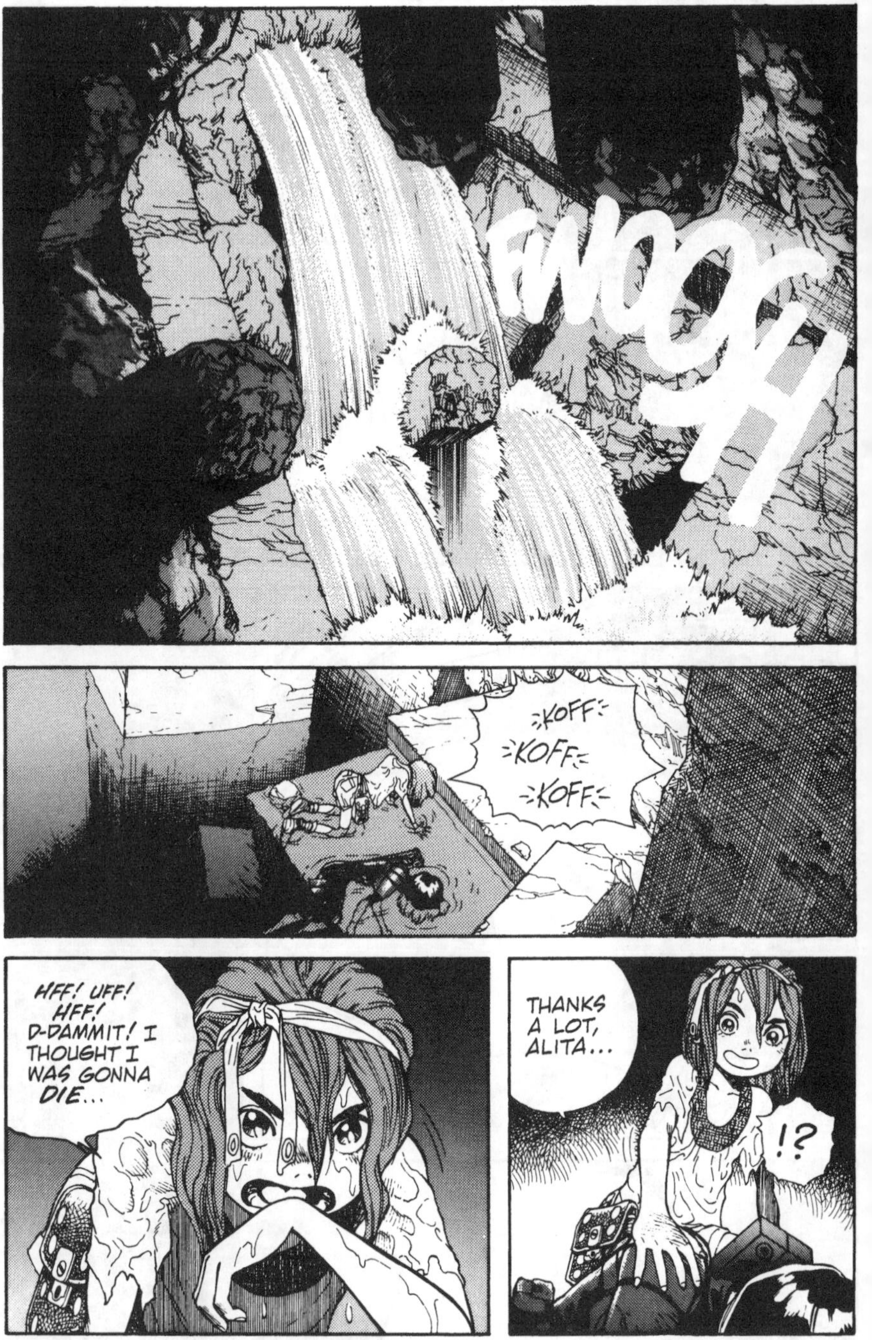
FWOOSH
KOFF
KOFF
KOFF
HFF! UFF! HFF! D-DAMMIT! I THOUGHT I WAS GONNA DIE...
THANKS A LOT, ALITA...
!?

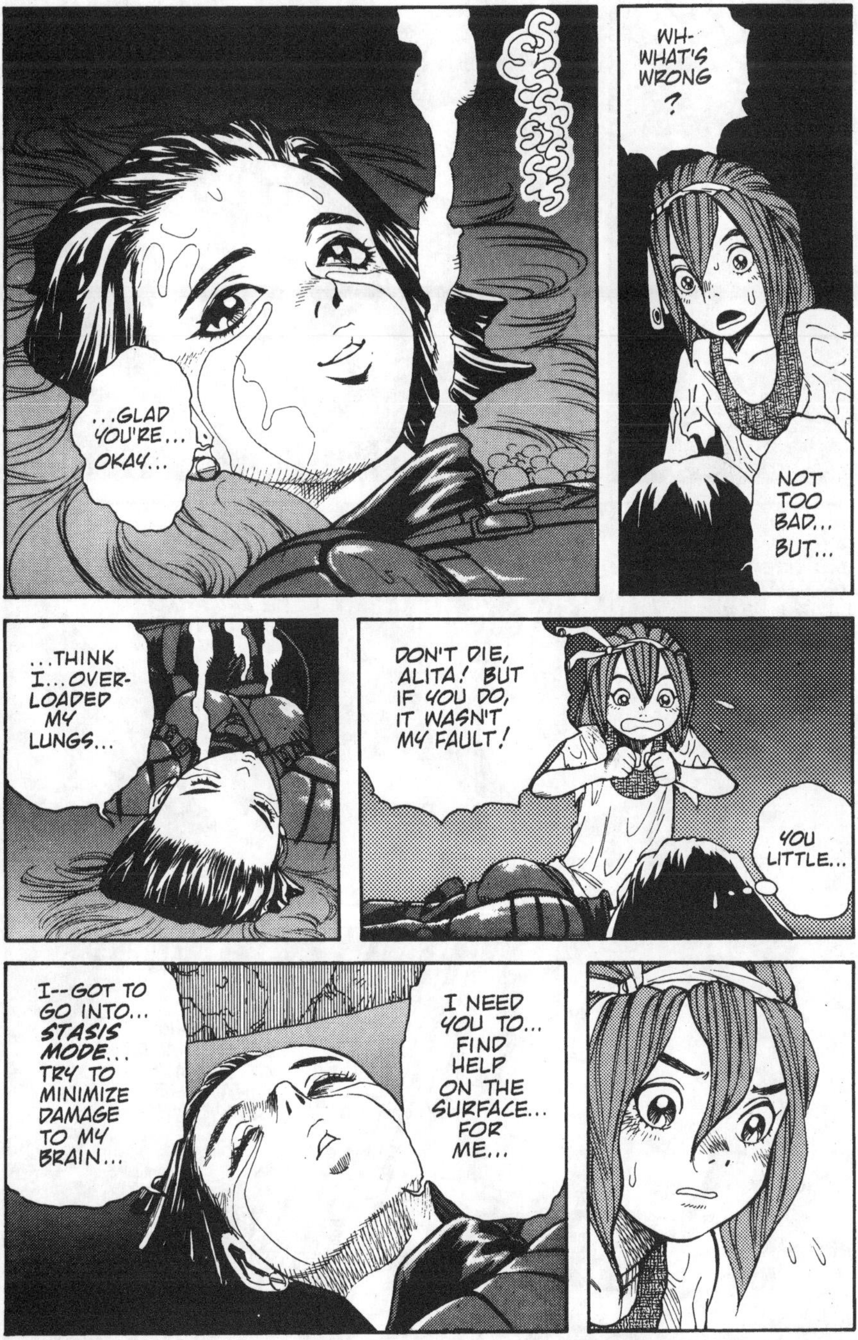
SSSSSSSS
...GLAD YOU'RE... OKAY...
WH-WHAT'S WRONG?
NOT TOO BAD... BUT...
...THINK I...OVER-LOADED MY LUNGS...
DON'T DIE, ALITA! BUT IF YOU DO, IT WASN'T MY FAULT!
YOU LITTLE...
I--GOT TO GO INTO... STASIS MODE... TRY TO MINIMIZE DAMAGE TO MY BRAIN...
I NEED YOU TO... FIND HELP ON THE SURFACE... FOR ME...

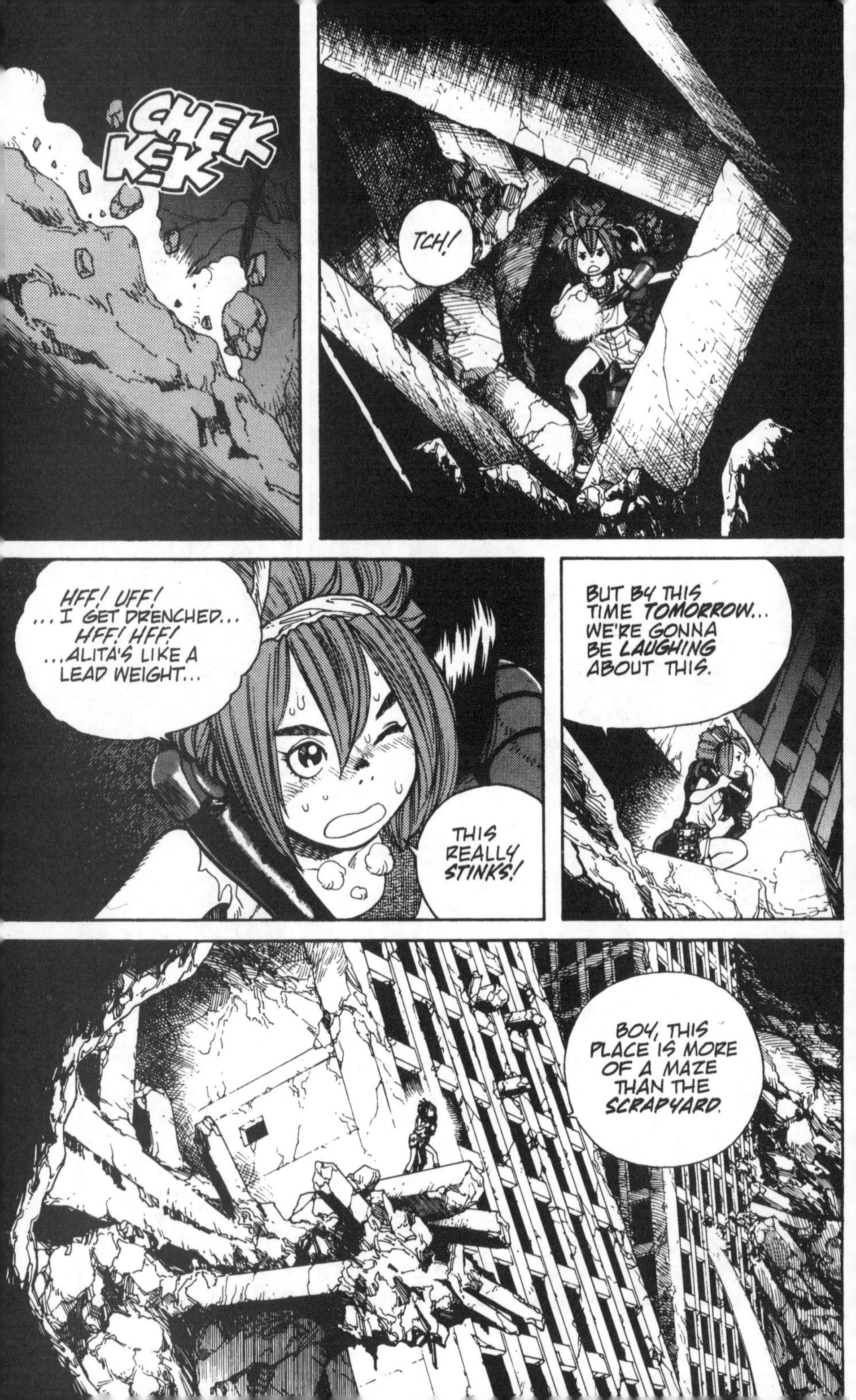
CHEK KEK
TCH!
HFF! UFF! ...I GET DRENCHED... HFF! HFF! ...ALITA'S LIKE A LEAD WEIGHT...
THIS REALLY STINKS!
BUT BY THIS TIME TOMORROW... WE'RE GONNA BE LAUGHING ABOUT THIS.
BOY, THIS PLACE IS MORE OF A MAZE THAN THE SCRAPYARD.

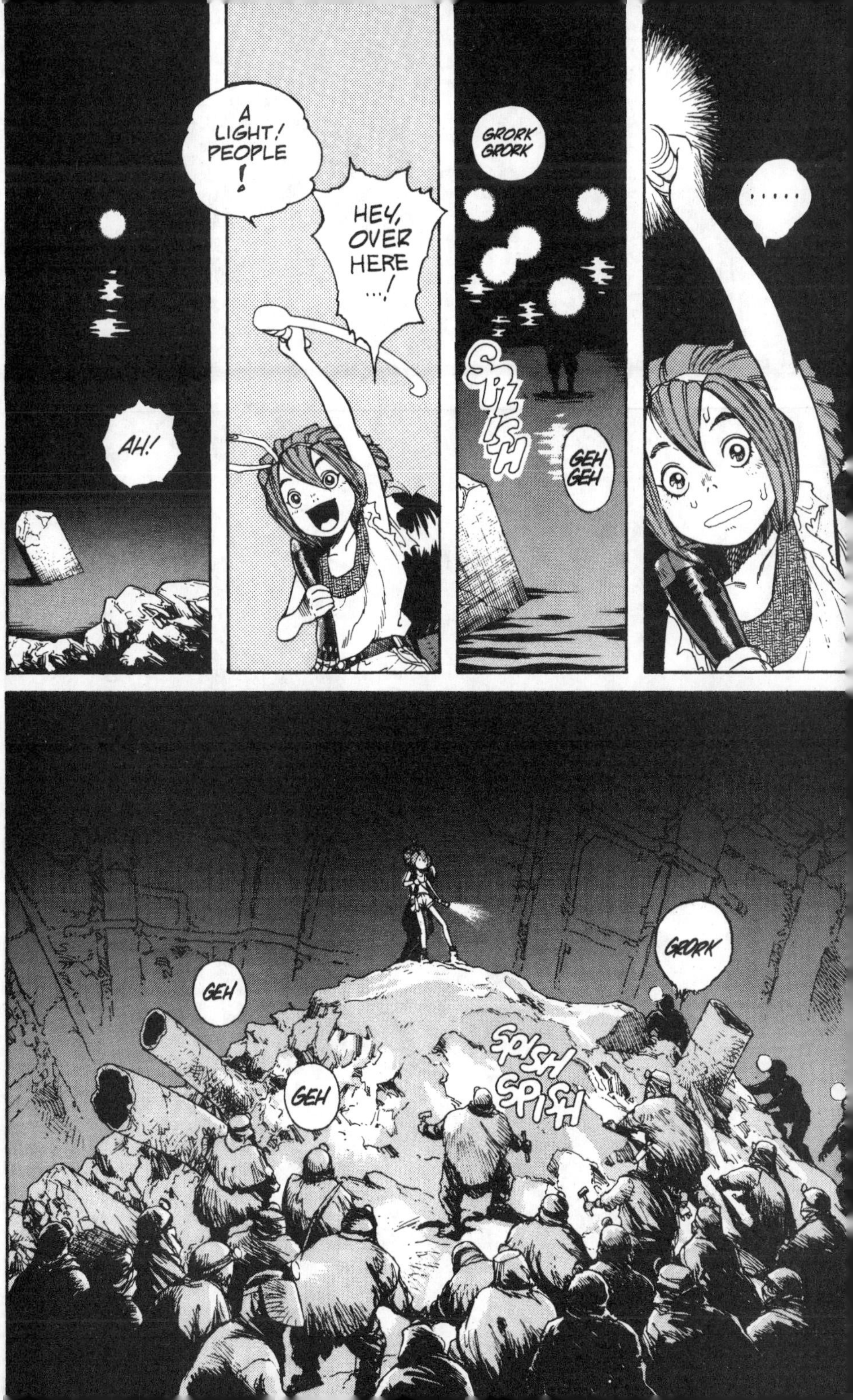
AH!
A LIGHT! PEOPLE!
HEY, OVER HERE ...!
GRORK GRORK
SPLISH
GEH GEH
......
GEH
GEH
GRORK
SPLISH SPLISH

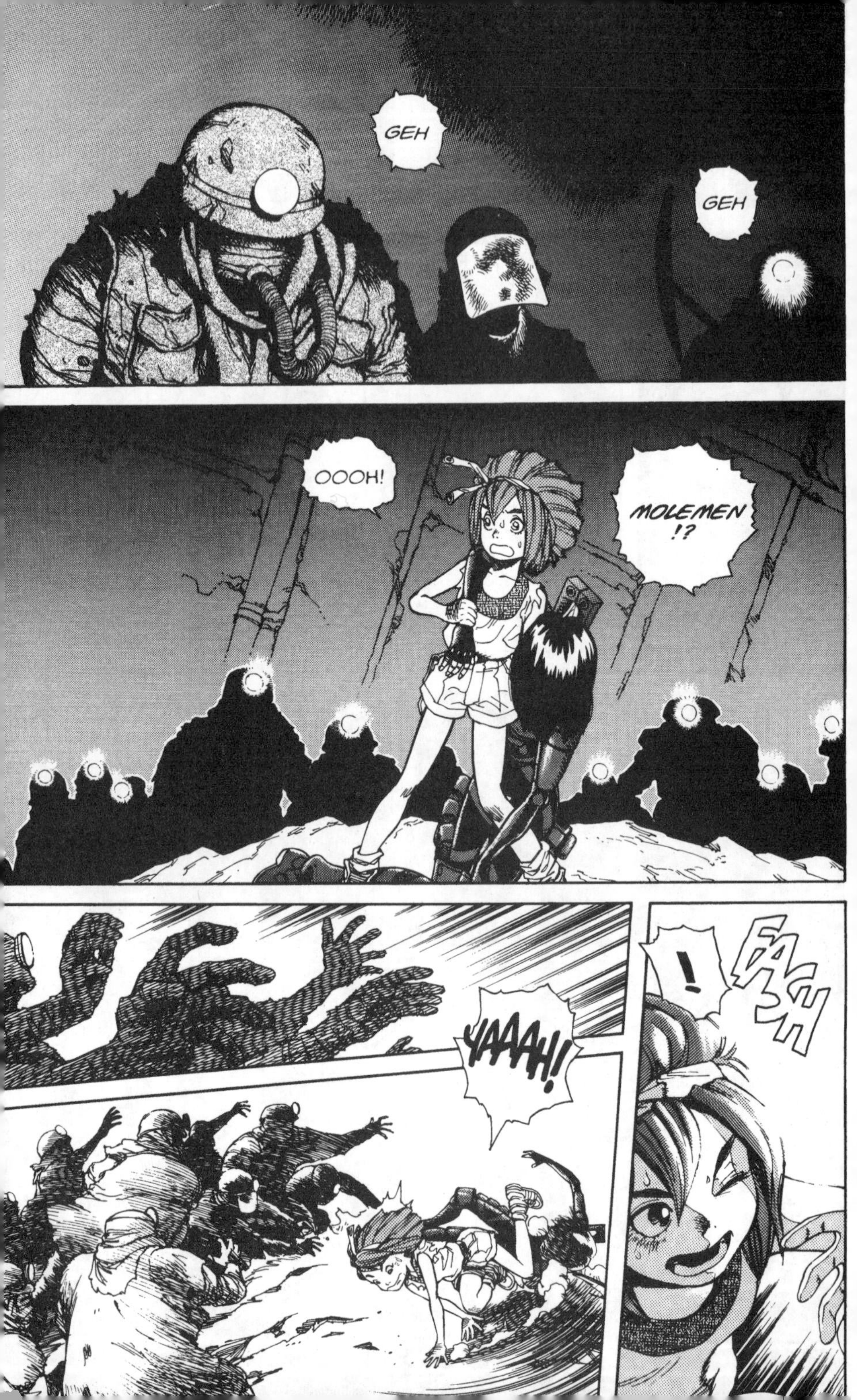
GEH
GEH
OOOH!
MOLEMEN !?
YAAAAH!
!
FACH

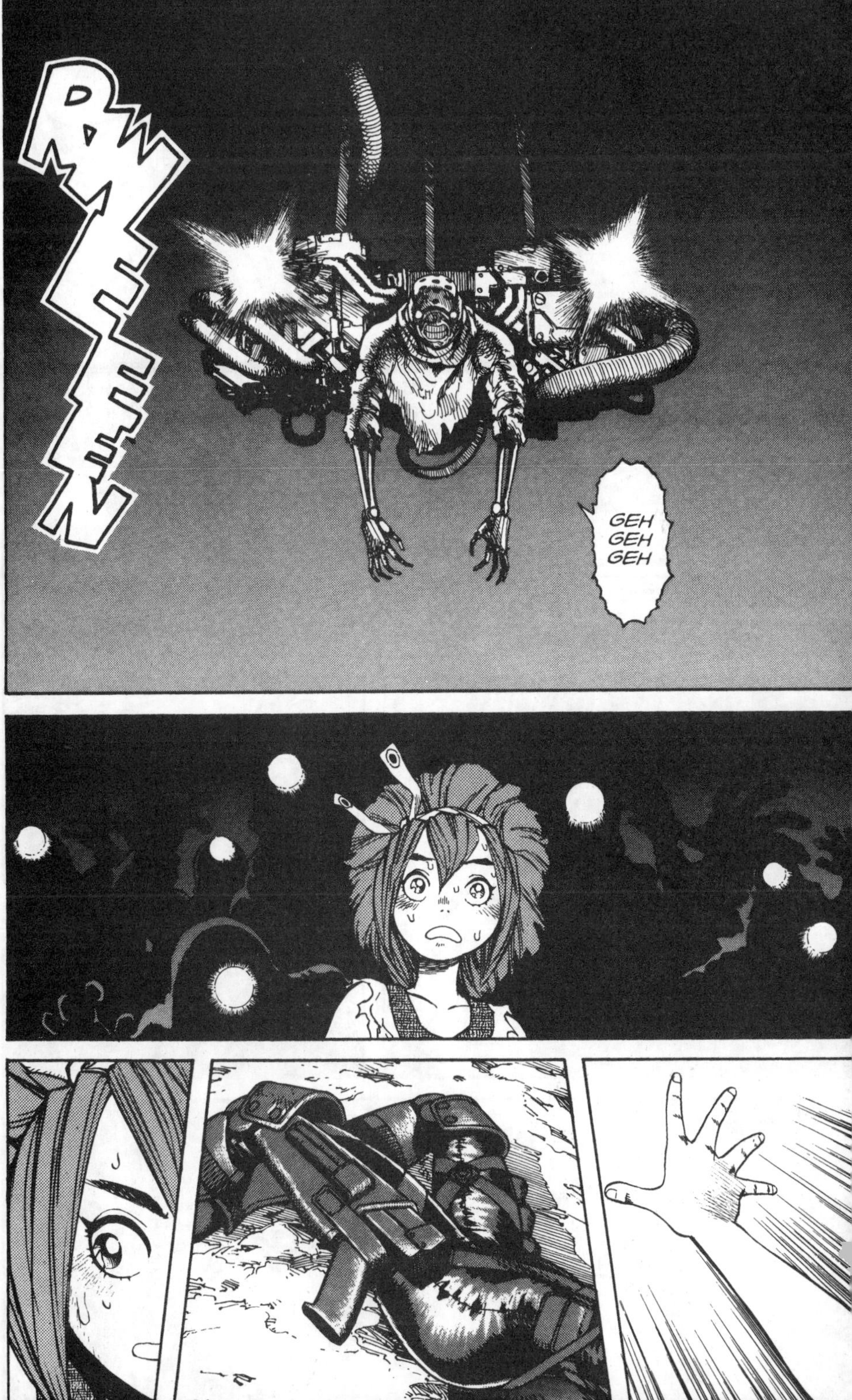
RAWEEEEN
GEH GEH GEH

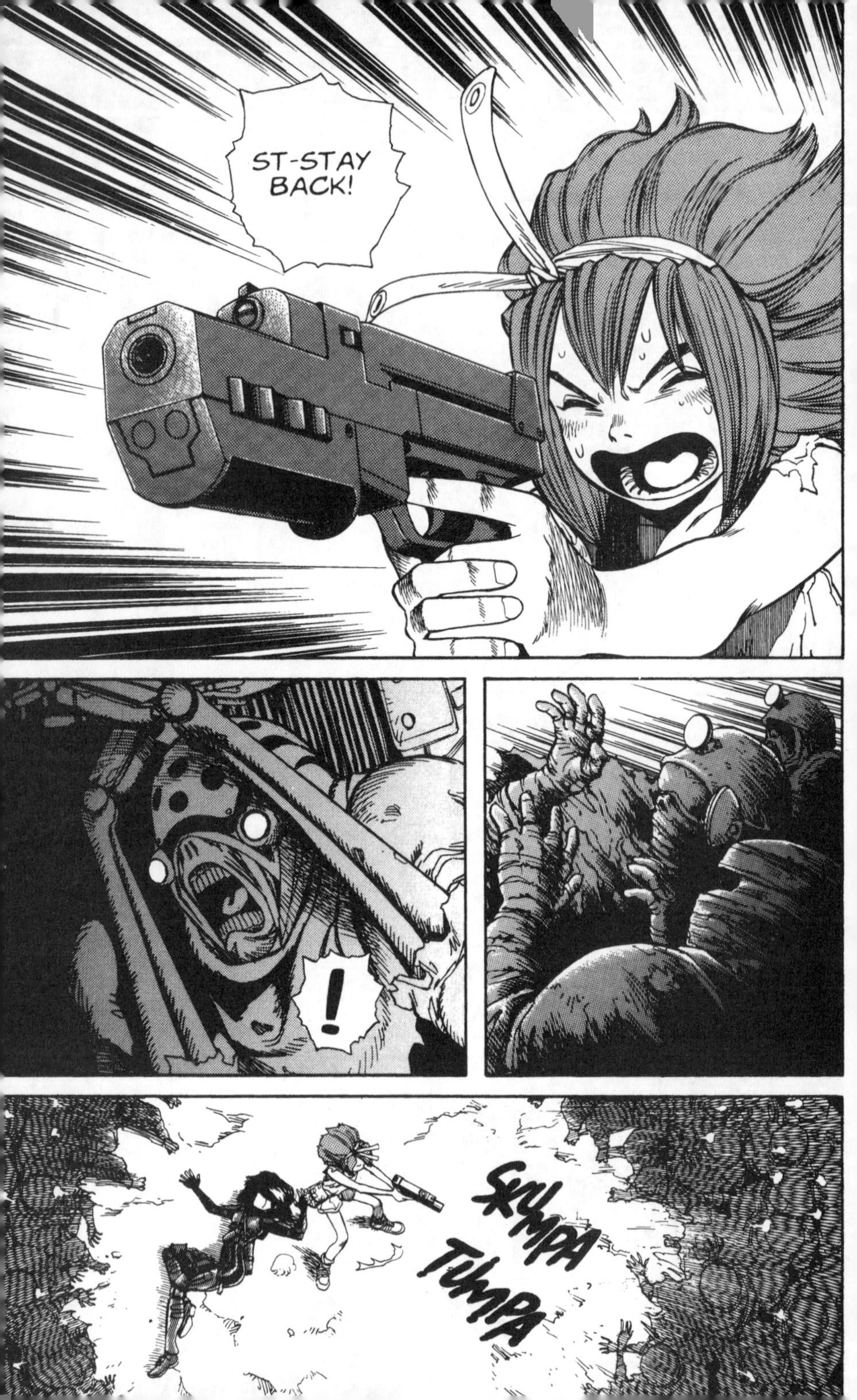
ST-STAY BACK!
!
SKUMPA
TUMPA

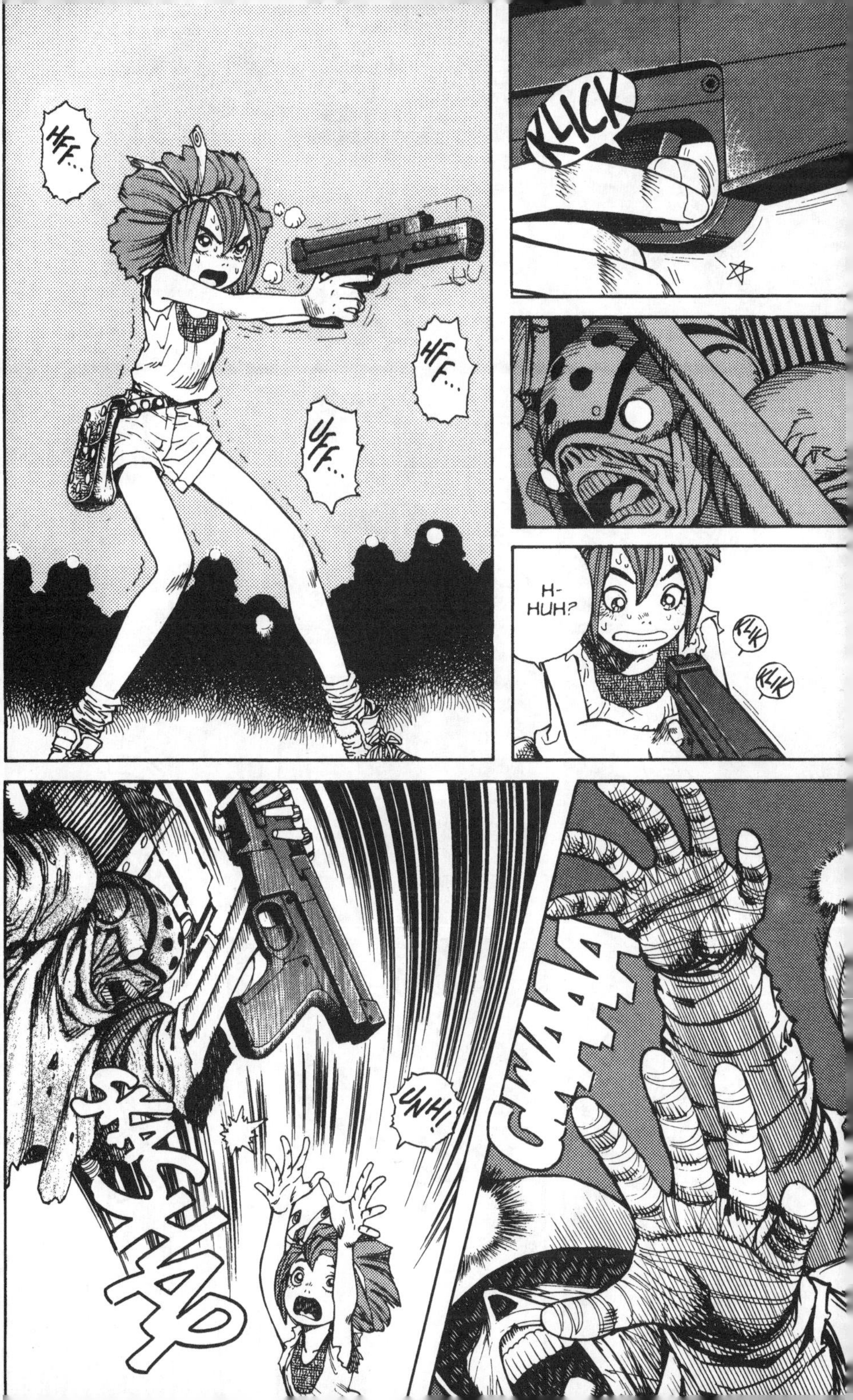
HFF...
HFF...
UFF...
KLICK
H-HUH?
KLIK
KLIK
SNAP
UNH!
GWAAA

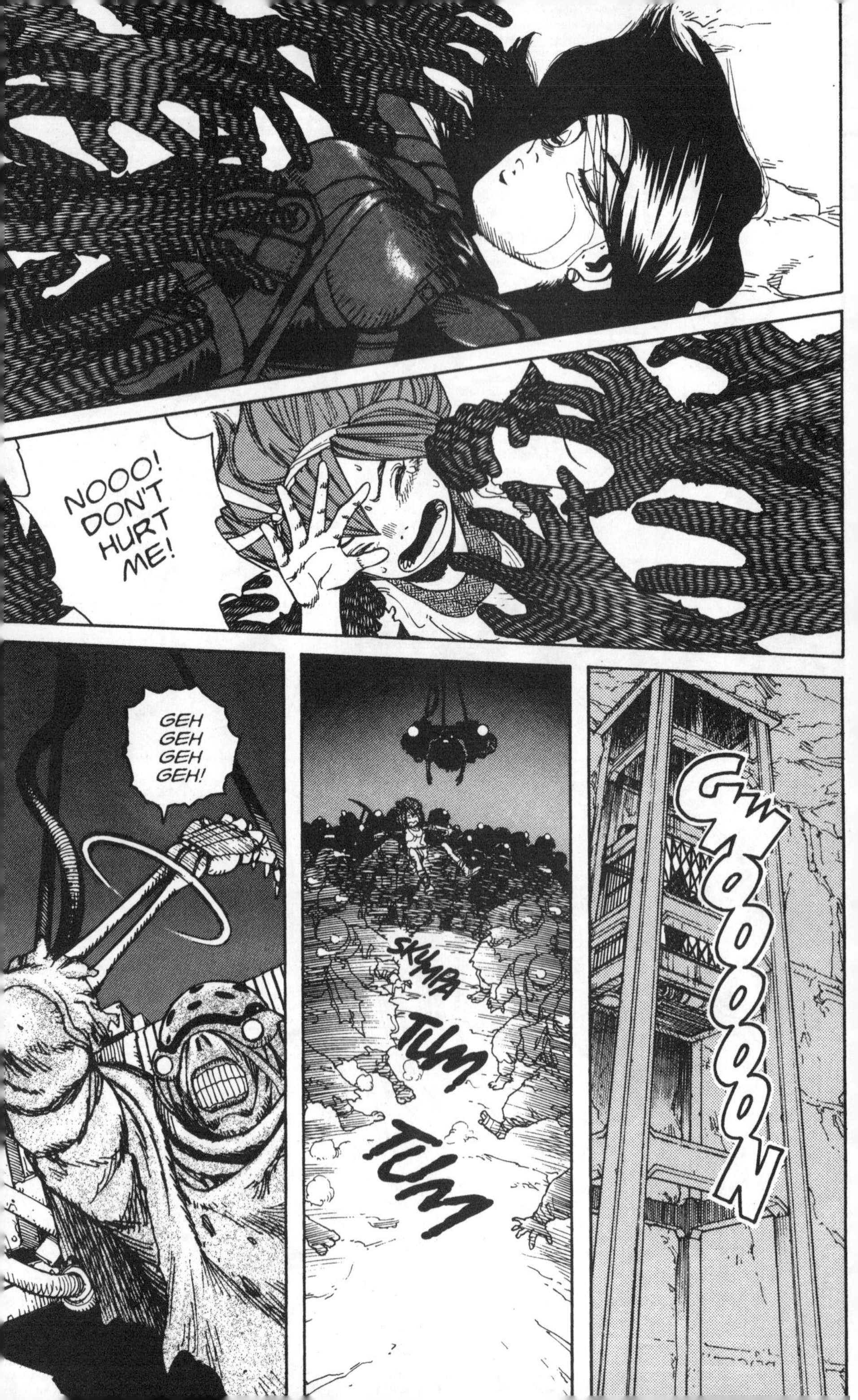
NOOO! DON'T HURT ME!
GEH GEH GEH GEH!
SKYMPA
TUM
TUM
GWOOOOOON

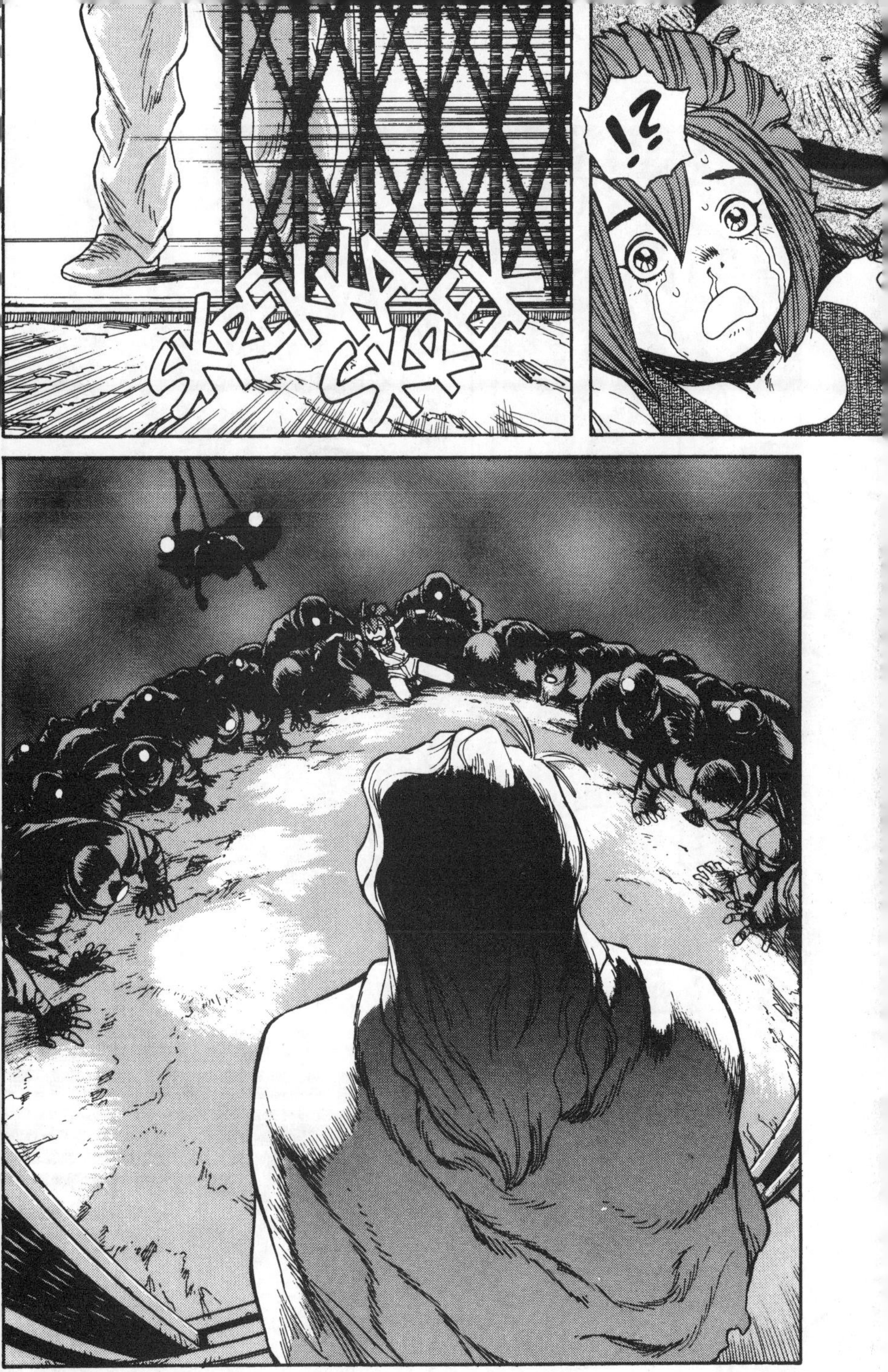
SKREEKA
SKREEK
!?

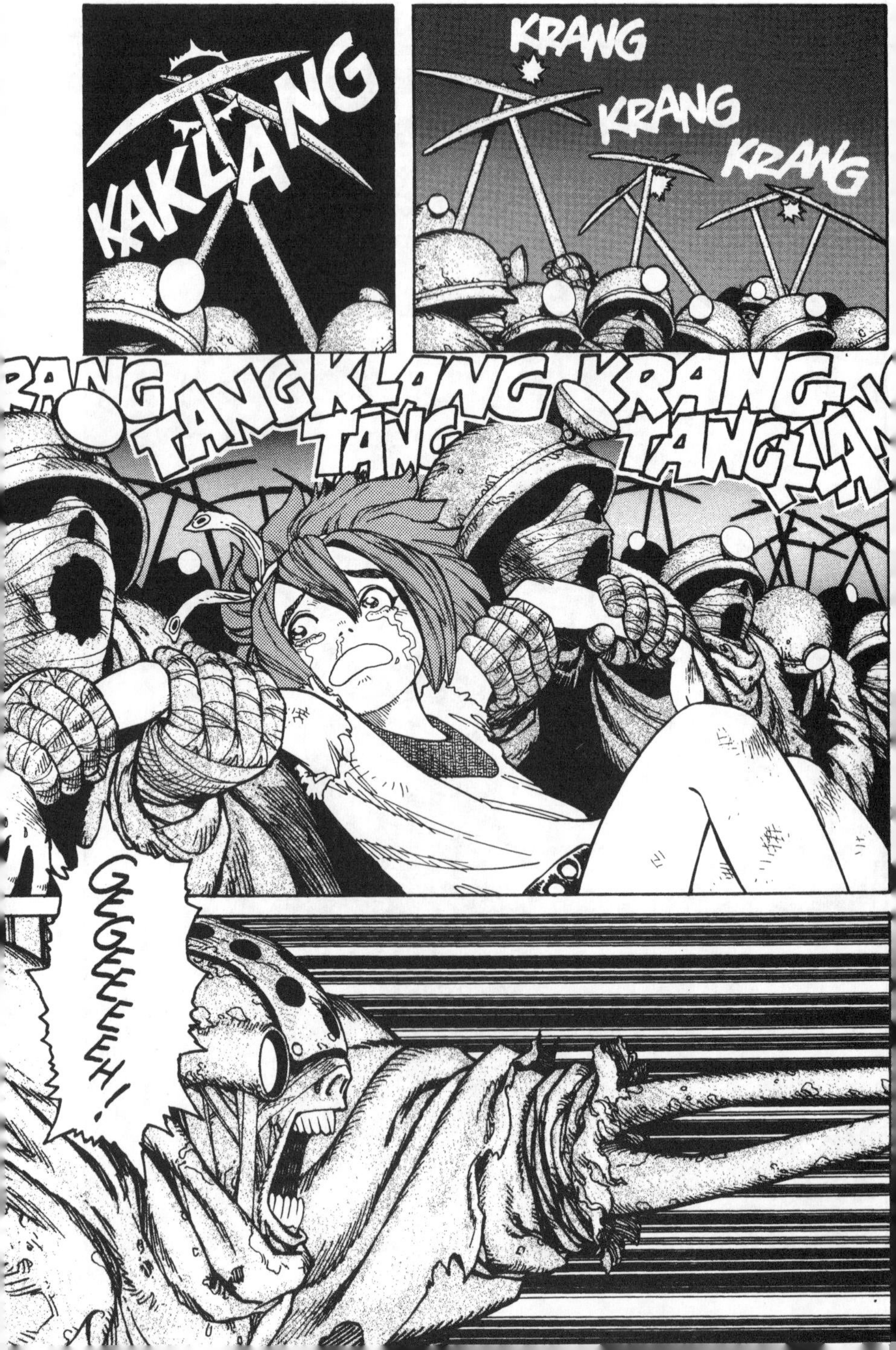

KAKLANG
KRANG
KRANG
KRANG
RANG
TANG
KLANG
TANG
KRANG
TANG
GEGEEEEEH!

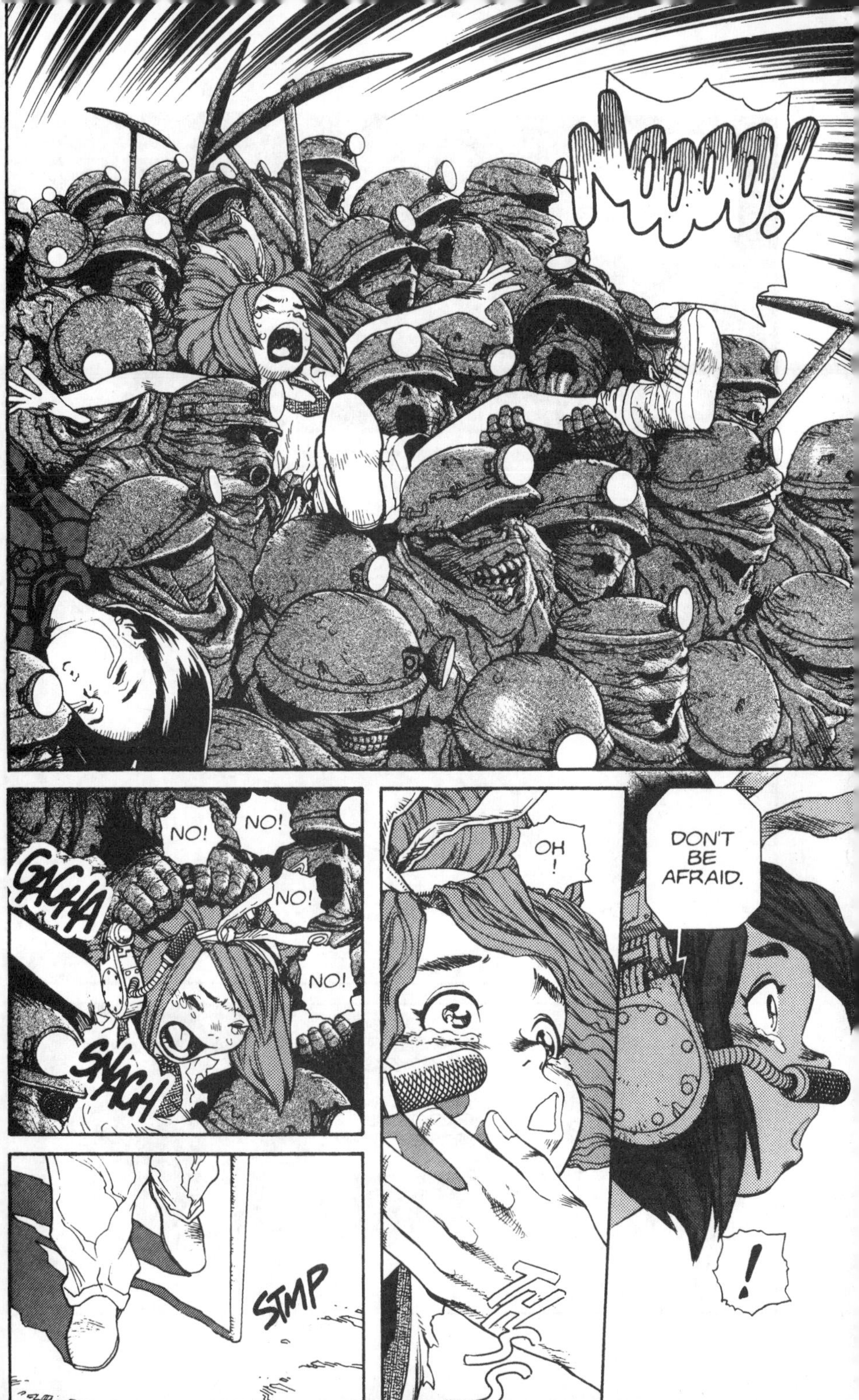
NOOOO!!
GACHA
NO!
NO!
NO!
NO!
SNACH
OH!
DON'T BE AFRAID.
STMP
!

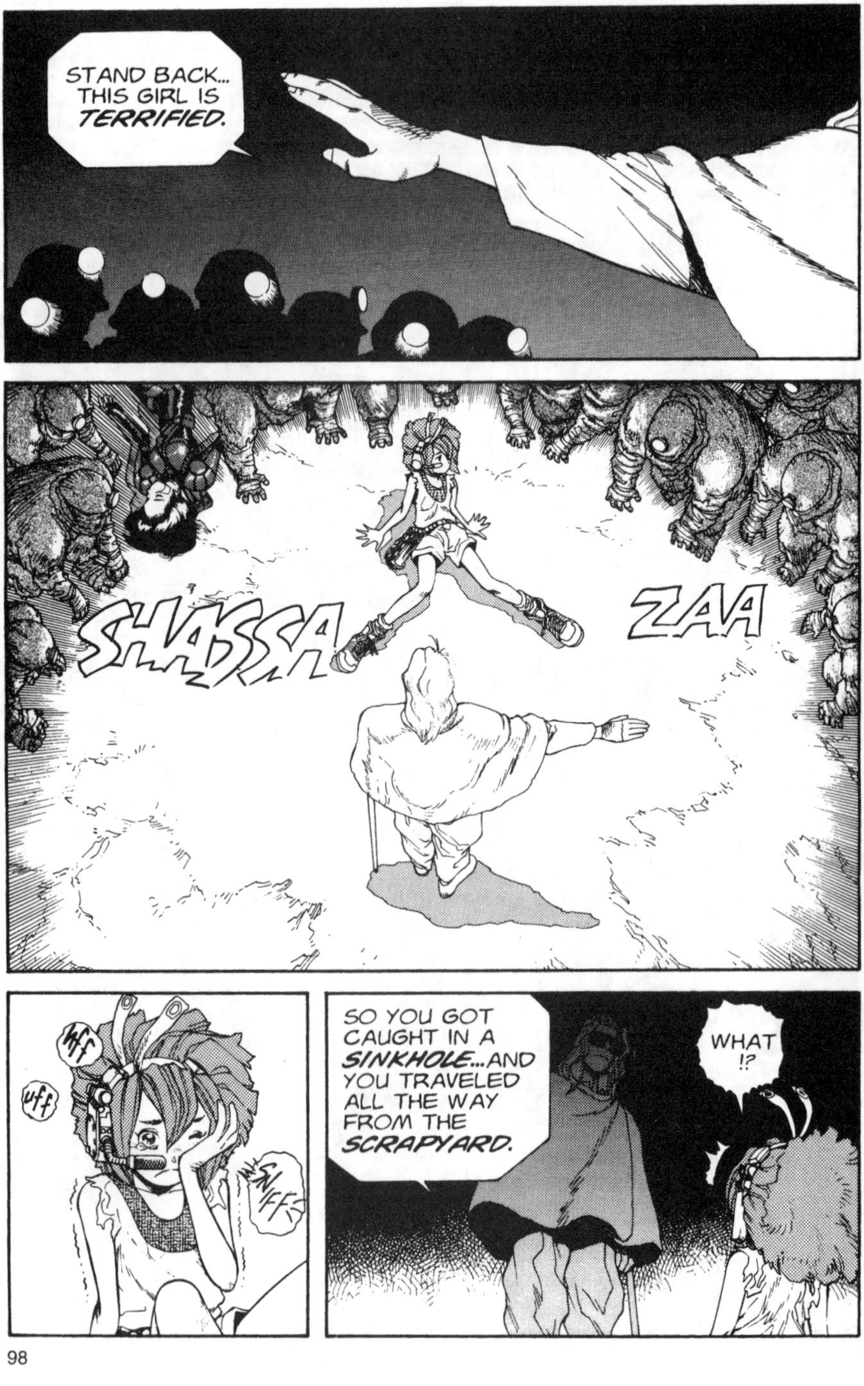
STAND BACK... THIS GIRL IS *TERRIFIED.*
SHASSCA
ZAA
uff
SNIFF
SO YOU GOT CAUGHT IN A *SINKHOLE*...AND YOU TRAVELED ALL THE WAY FROM THE *SCRAPYARD.*
WHAT !?

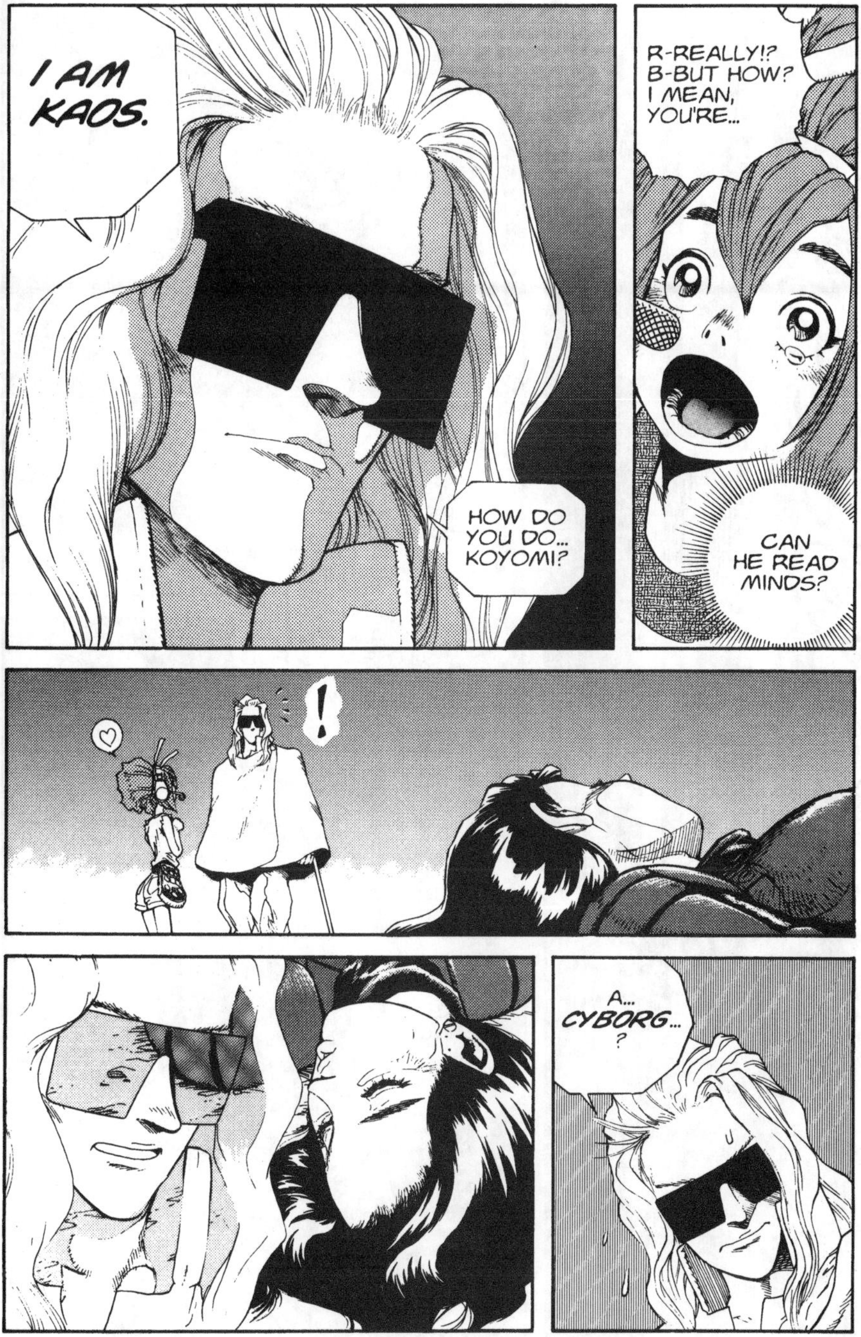
I AM KAOS.
HOW DO YOU DO... KOYOMI?
R-REALLY!? B-BUT HOW? I MEAN, YOU'RE...
CAN HE READ MINDS?
!
A... CYBORG... ?

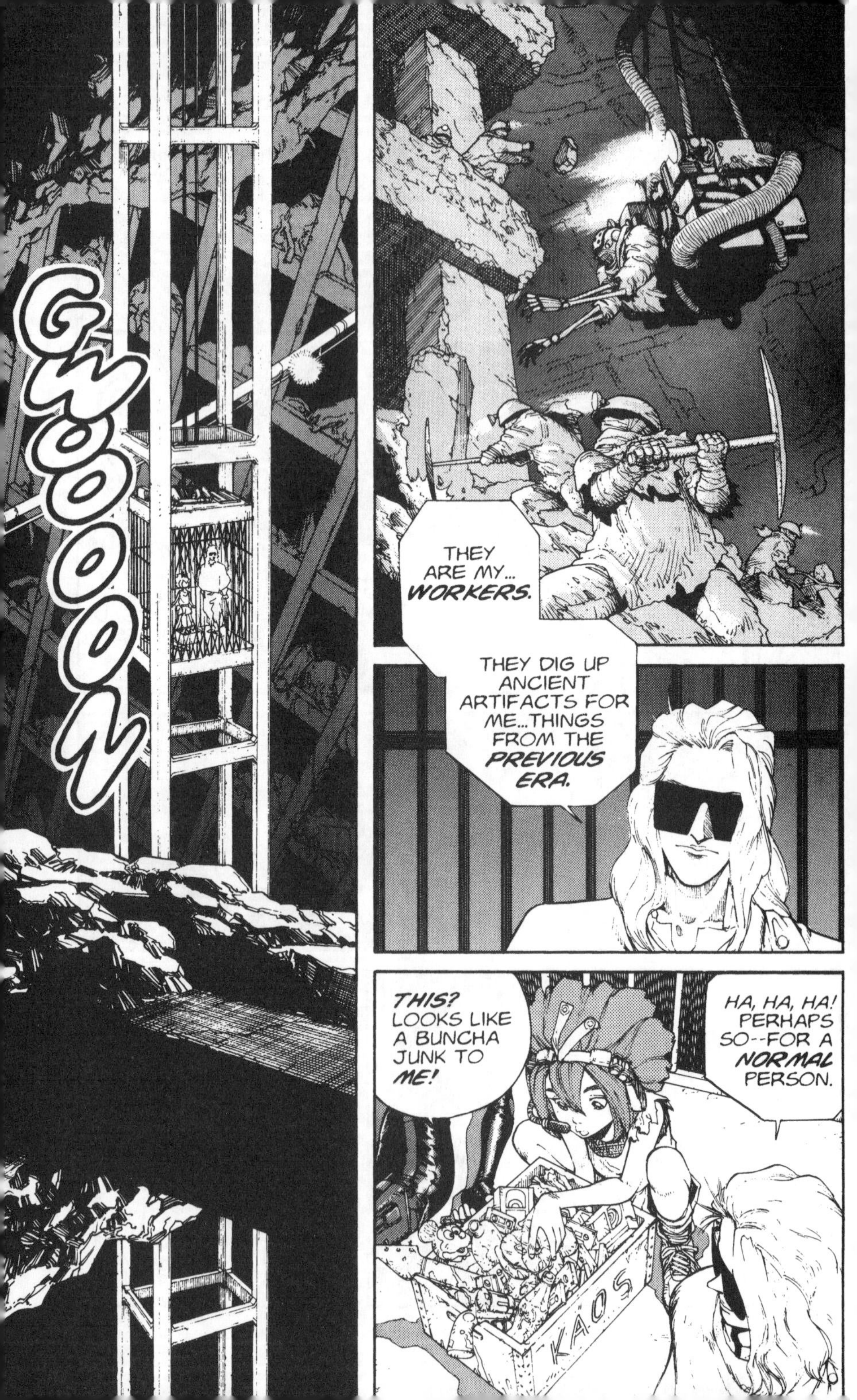
GWOOOOON
THEY ARE MY... WORKERS.
THEY DIG UP ANCIENT ARTIFACTS FOR ME...THINGS FROM THE PREVIOUS ERA.
THIS? LOOKS LIKE A BUNCHA JUNK TO ME!
HA, HA, HA! PERHAPS SO--FOR A NORMAL PERSON.
KAOS

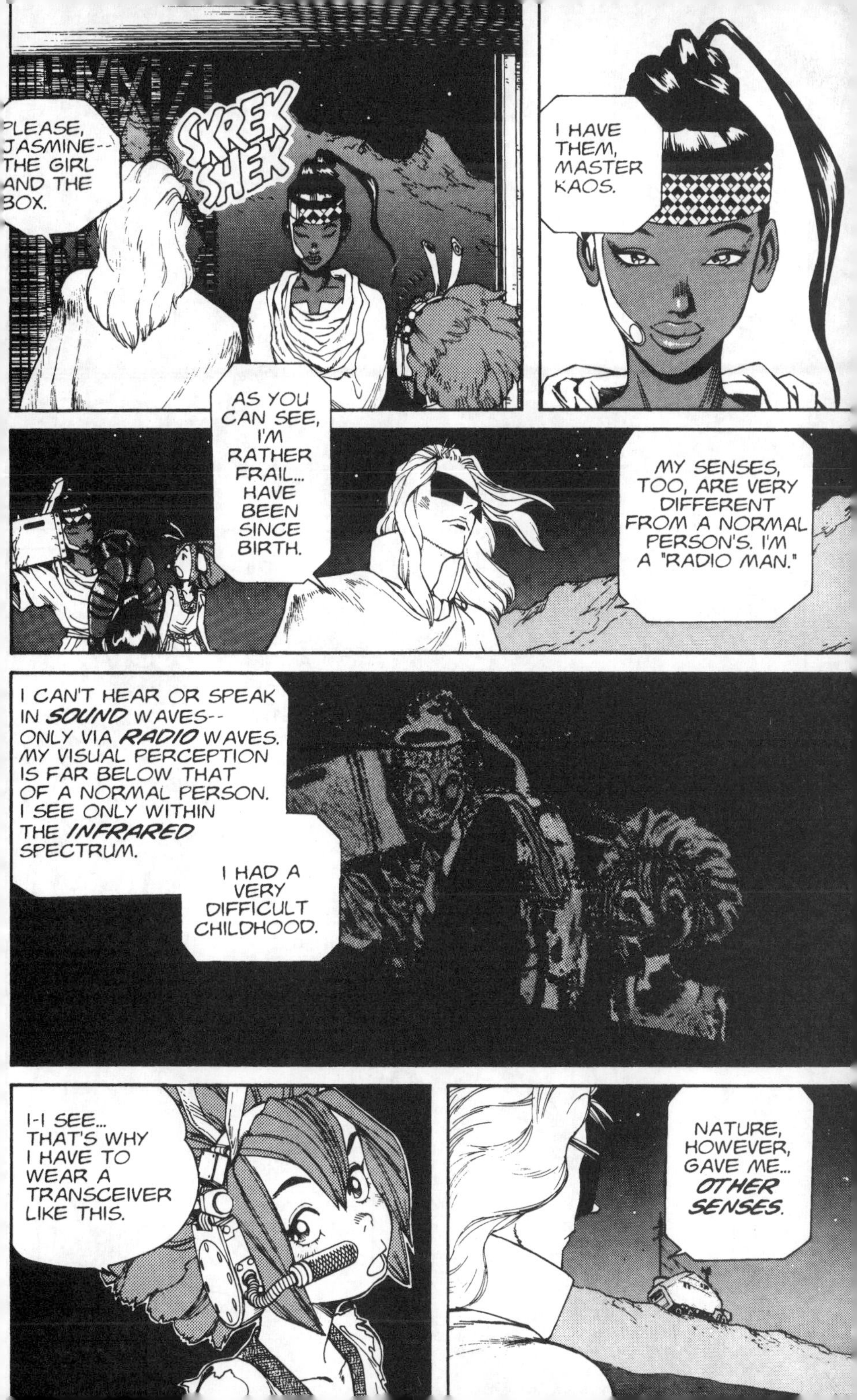
PLEASE, JASMINE-- THE GIRL AND THE BOX.
SKREK SHEK
I HAVE THEM, MASTER KAOS.
AS YOU CAN SEE, I'M RATHER FRAIL... HAVE BEEN SINCE BIRTH.
MY SENSES, TOO, ARE VERY DIFFERENT FROM A NORMAL PERSON'S. I'M A "RADIO MAN."
I CAN'T HEAR OR SPEAK IN SOUND WAVES-- ONLY VIA RADIO WAVES. MY VISUAL PERCEPTION IS FAR BELOW THAT OF A NORMAL PERSON. I SEE ONLY WITHIN THE INFRARED SPECTRUM.
I HAD A VERY DIFFICULT CHILDHOOD.
I-I SEE... THAT'S WHY I HAVE TO WEAR A TRANSCEIVER LIKE THIS.
NATURE, HOWEVER, GAVE ME... OTHER SENSES.

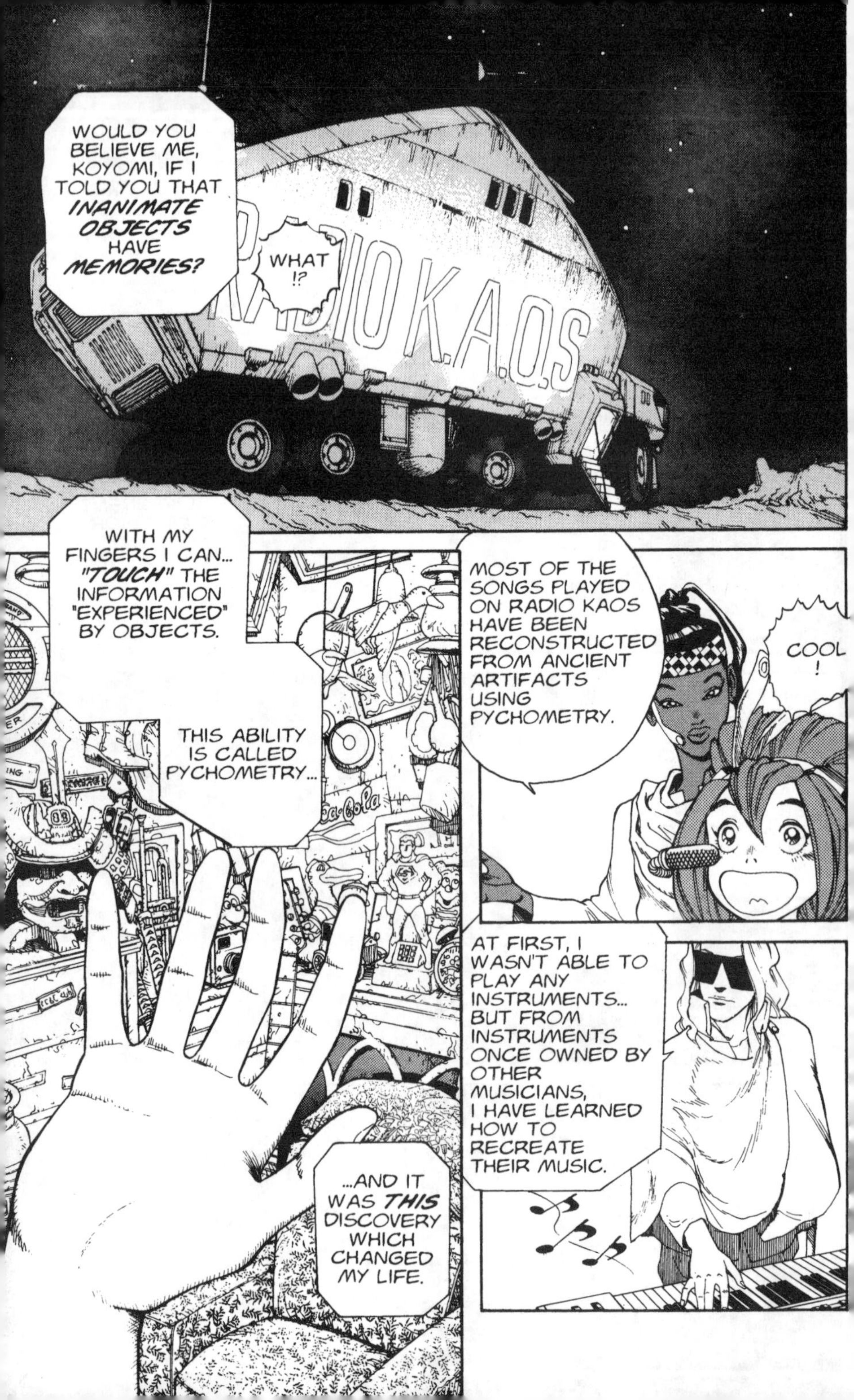
WOULD YOU BELIEVE ME, KOYOMI, IF I TOLD YOU THAT *INANIMATE OBJECTS* HAVE *MEMORIES?*
WHAT !?
RADIO K.A.O.S
WITH MY FINGERS I CAN... "*TOUCH*" THE INFORMATION "EXPERIENCED" BY OBJECTS.
THIS ABILITY IS CALLED PYCHOMETRY...
...AND IT WAS *THIS* DISCOVERY WHICH CHANGED MY LIFE.
MOST OF THE SONGS PLAYED ON RADIO KAOS HAVE BEEN RECONSTRUCTED FROM ANCIENT ARTIFACTS USING PYCHOMETRY.
COOL !
AT FIRST, I WASN'T ABLE TO PLAY ANY INSTRUMENTS... BUT FROM INSTRUMENTS ONCE OWNED BY OTHER MUSICIANS, I HAVE LEARNED HOW TO RECREATE THEIR MUSIC.

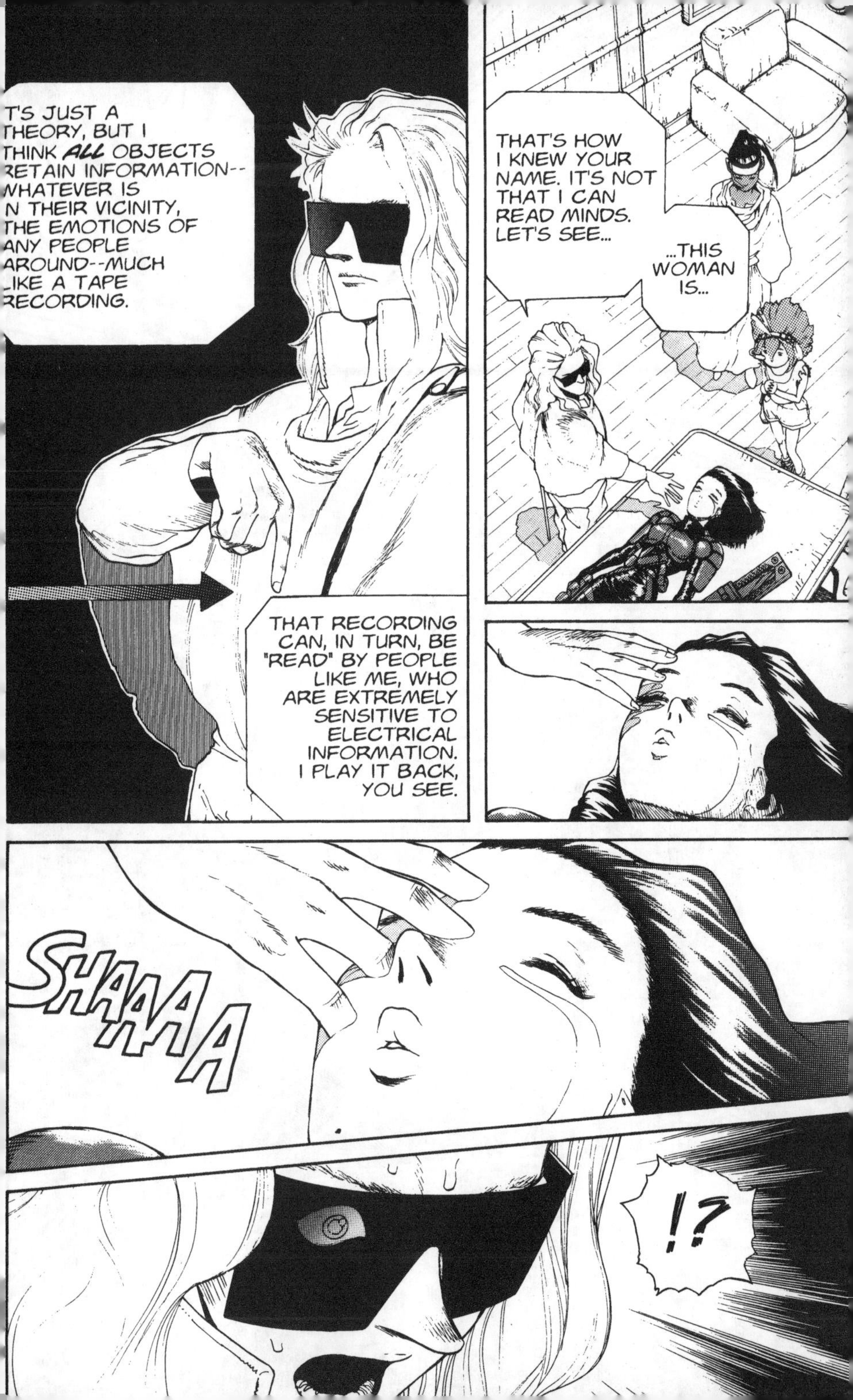
T'S JUST A THEORY, BUT I THINK ALL OBJECTS RETAIN INFORMATION-- WHATEVER IS N THEIR VICINITY, THE EMOTIONS OF ANY PEOPLE AROUND--MUCH LIKE A TAPE RECORDING.
THAT RECORDING CAN, IN TURN, BE "READ" BY PEOPLE LIKE ME, WHO ARE EXTREMELY SENSITIVE TO ELECTRICAL INFORMATION. I PLAY IT BACK, YOU SEE.
THAT'S HOW I KNEW YOUR NAME. IT'S NOT THAT I CAN READ MINDS. LET'S SEE...
...THIS WOMAN IS...
SHAAAA
!?

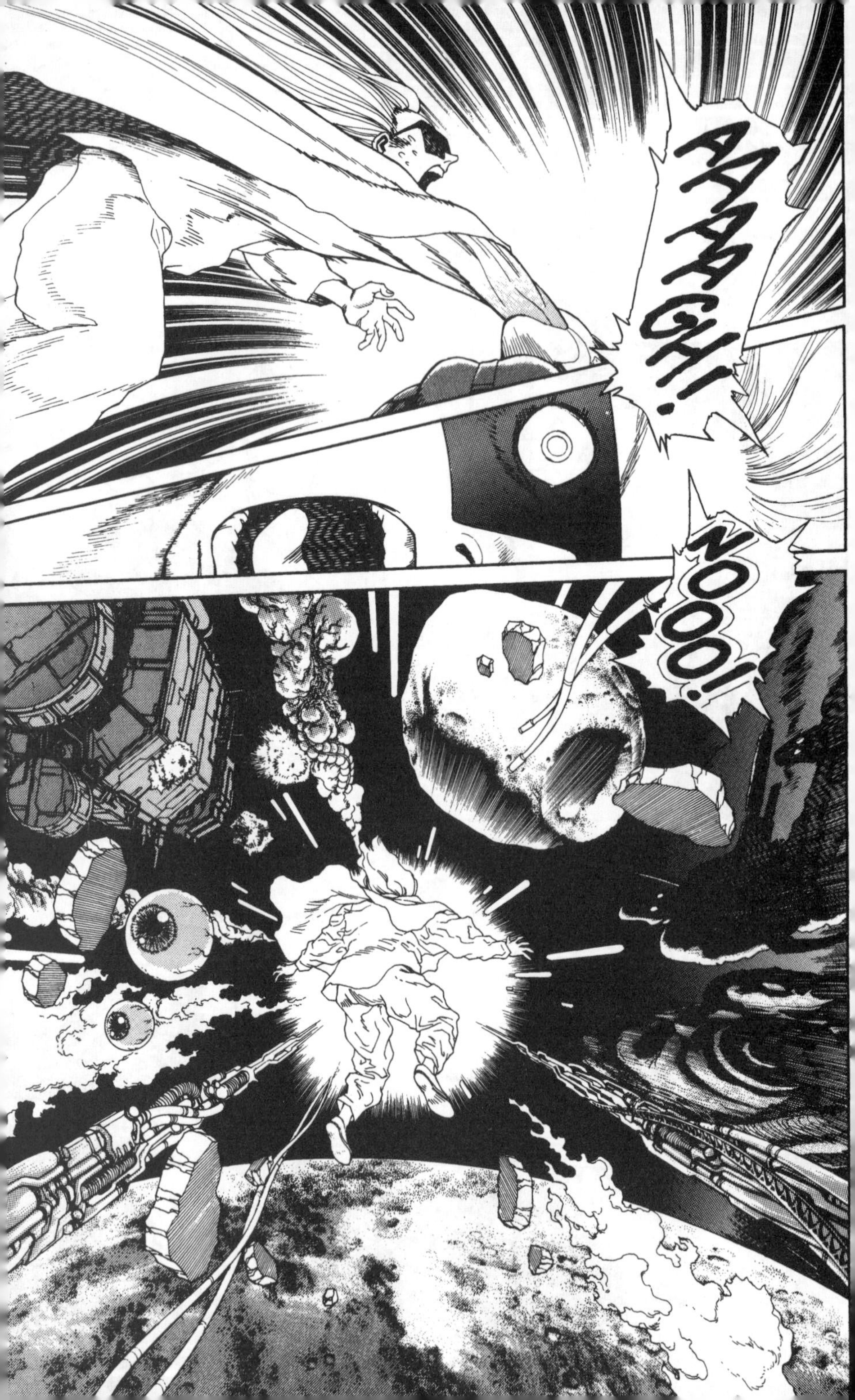
AAAAGH!!
NOOOO!!

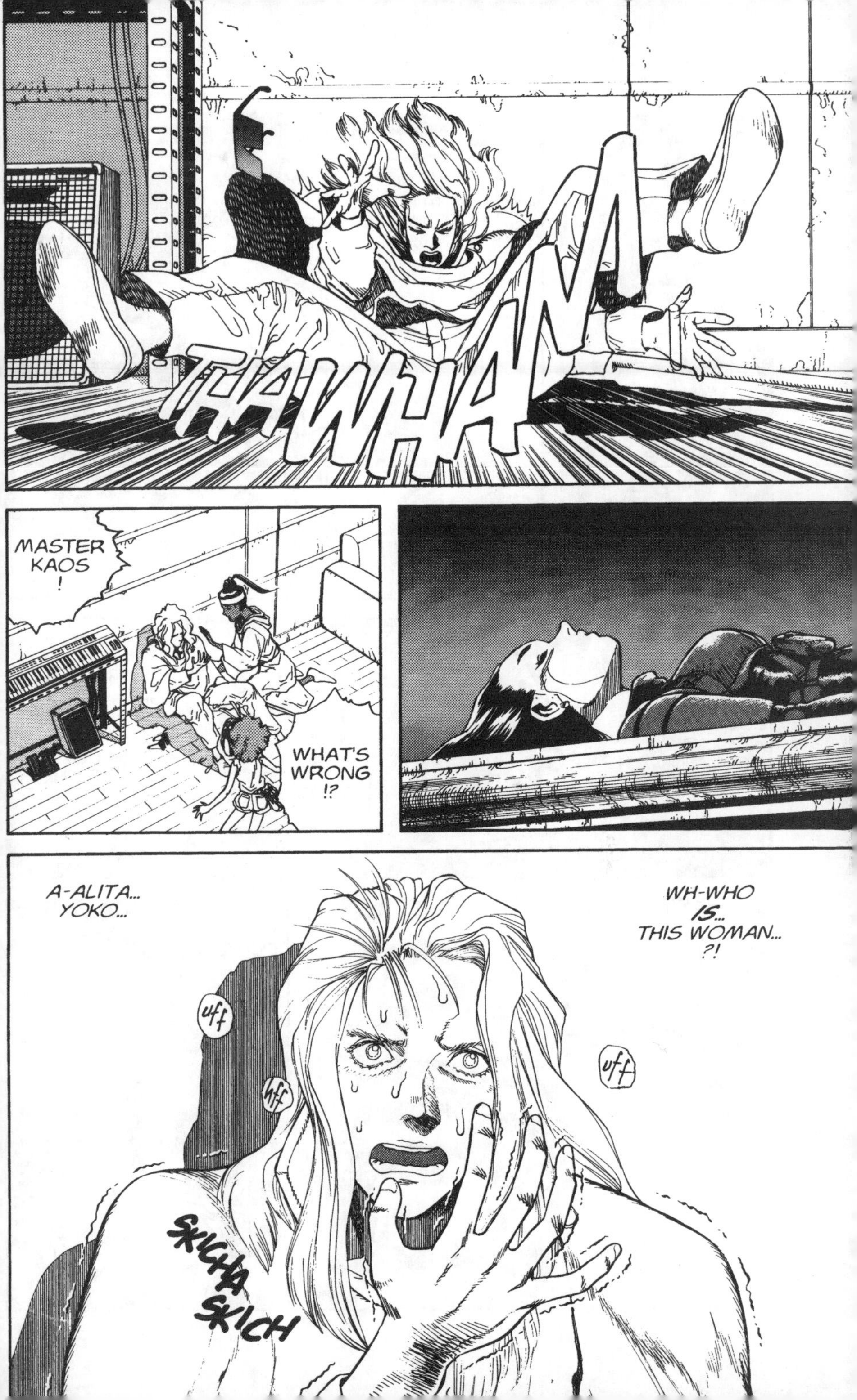
THAWHAM
MASTER KAOS !
WHAT'S WRONG !?
A-ALITA... YOKO...
WH-WHO IS... THIS WOMAN... ?!
uff
uff
uff
SKICHA SKICH

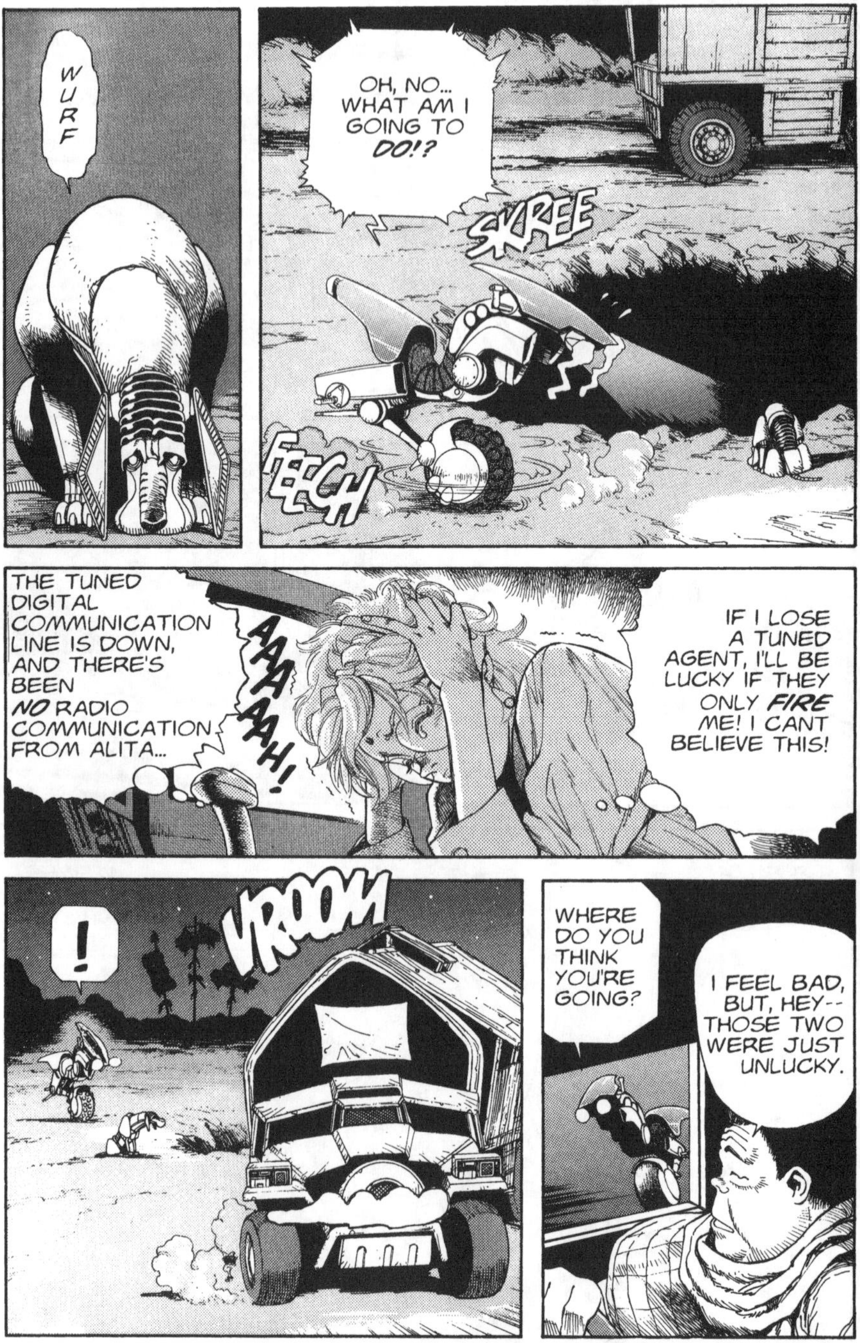
WURF
OH, NO... WHAT AM I GOING TO DO!?
SKREE
FEECH
THE TUNED DIGITAL COMMUNICATION LINE IS DOWN, AND THERE'S BEEN NO RADIO COMMUNICATION FROM ALITA...
AAAAAAH!
IF I LOSE A TUNED AGENT, I'LL BE LUCKY IF THEY ONLY FIRE ME! I CANT BELIEVE THIS!
!
VROOM
WHERE DO YOU THINK YOU'RE GOING?
I FEEL BAD, BUT, HEY-- THOSE TWO WERE JUST UNLUCKY.

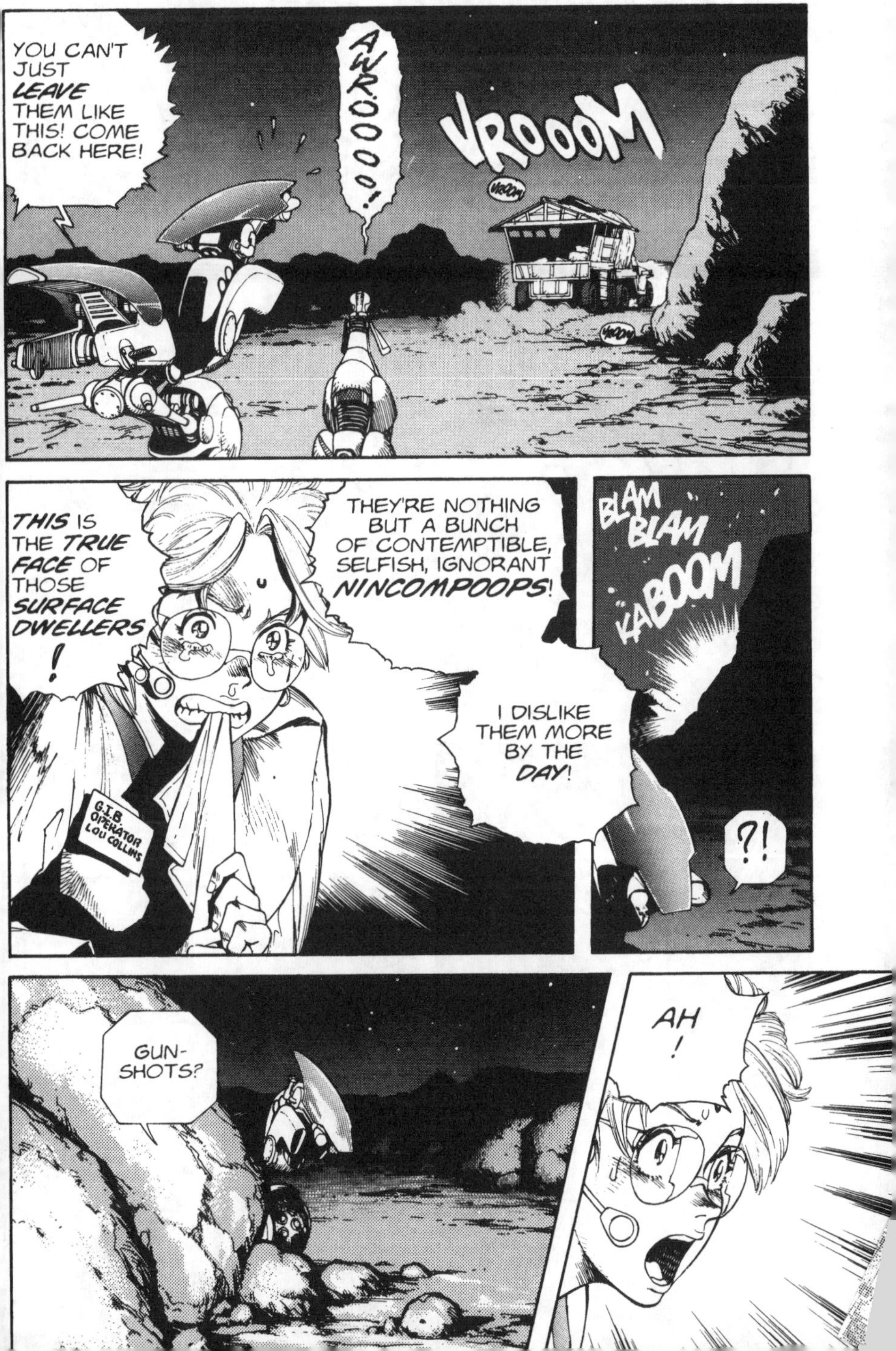
YOU CAN'T JUST *LEAVE* THEM LIKE THIS! COME BACK HERE!
AWROOOOO!
VROOOM
VROOM
VROOM
THIS IS THE *TRUE FACE* OF THOSE *SURFACE DWELLERS*!
THEY'RE NOTHING BUT A BUNCH OF CONTEMPTIBLE, SELFISH, IGNORANT *NINCOMPOOPS*!
G.I.B. OPERATOR LOU COLLINS
I DISLIKE THEM MORE BY THE *DAY*!
BLAM BLAM
KABOOM
?!
GUN-SHOTS?
AH!

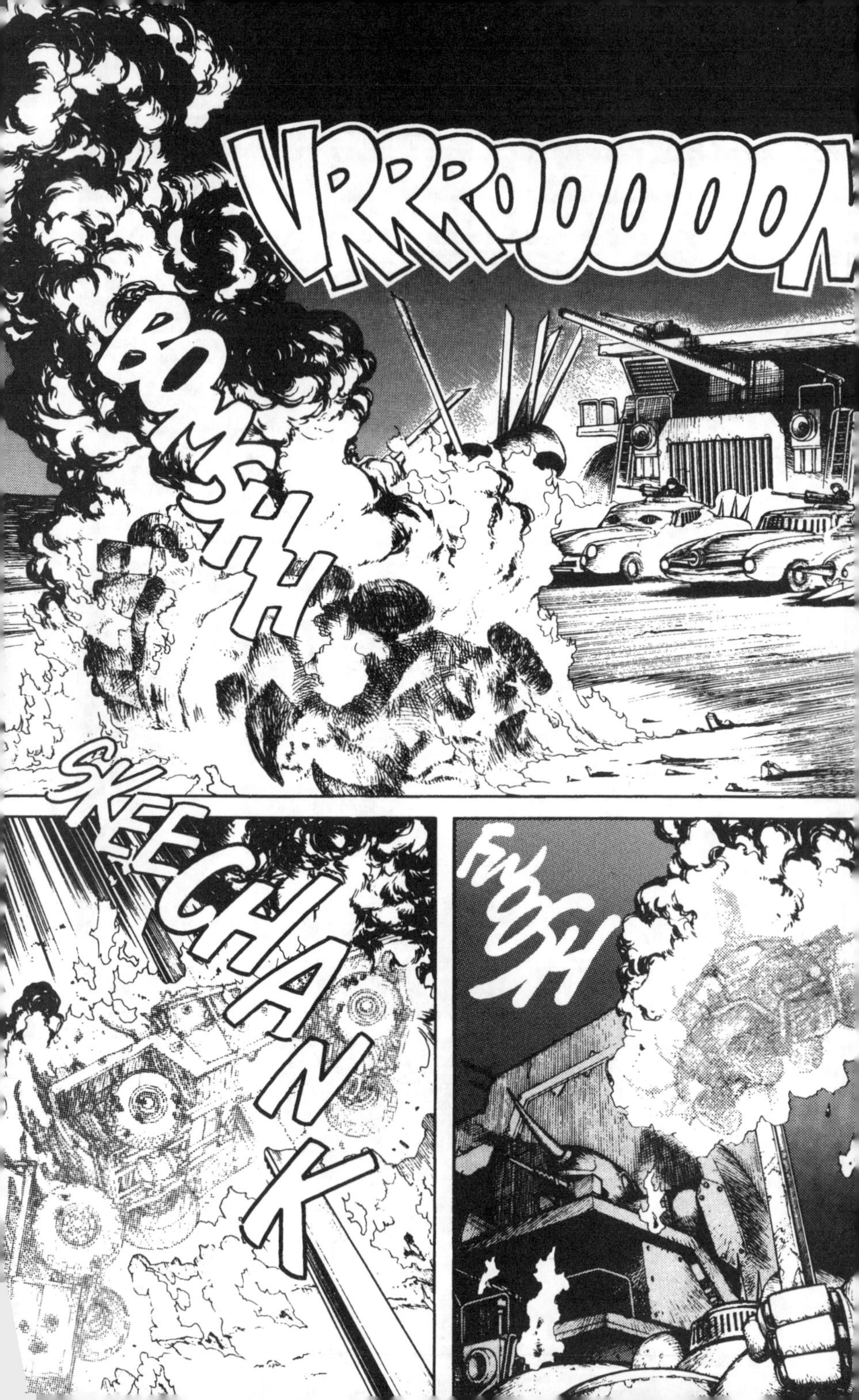
VRRROOOOOM
BOMCHH
SKEECHANK
FWSH

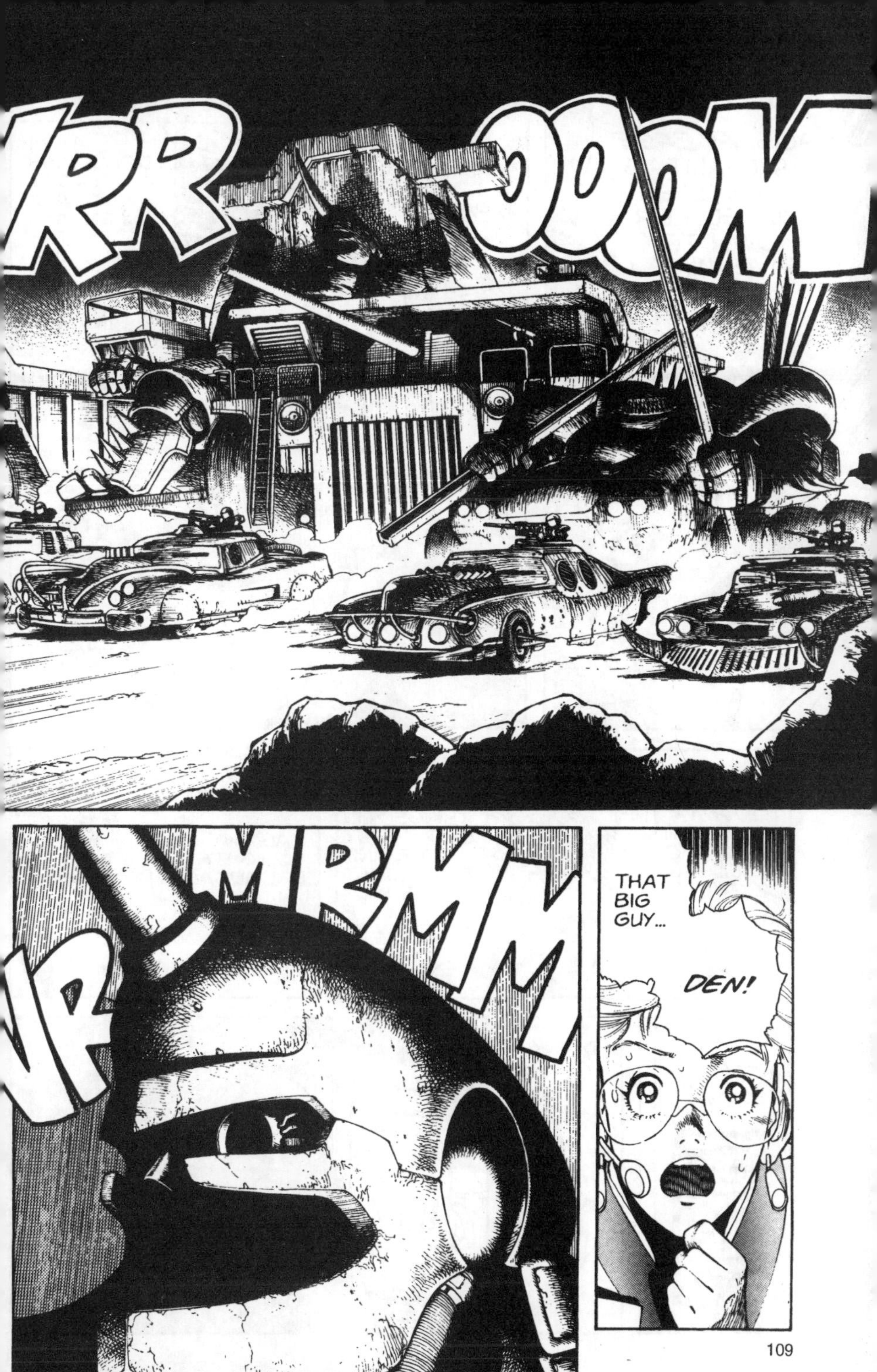
RR OOOM
VRMRMM
THAT BIG GUY...
DEN!

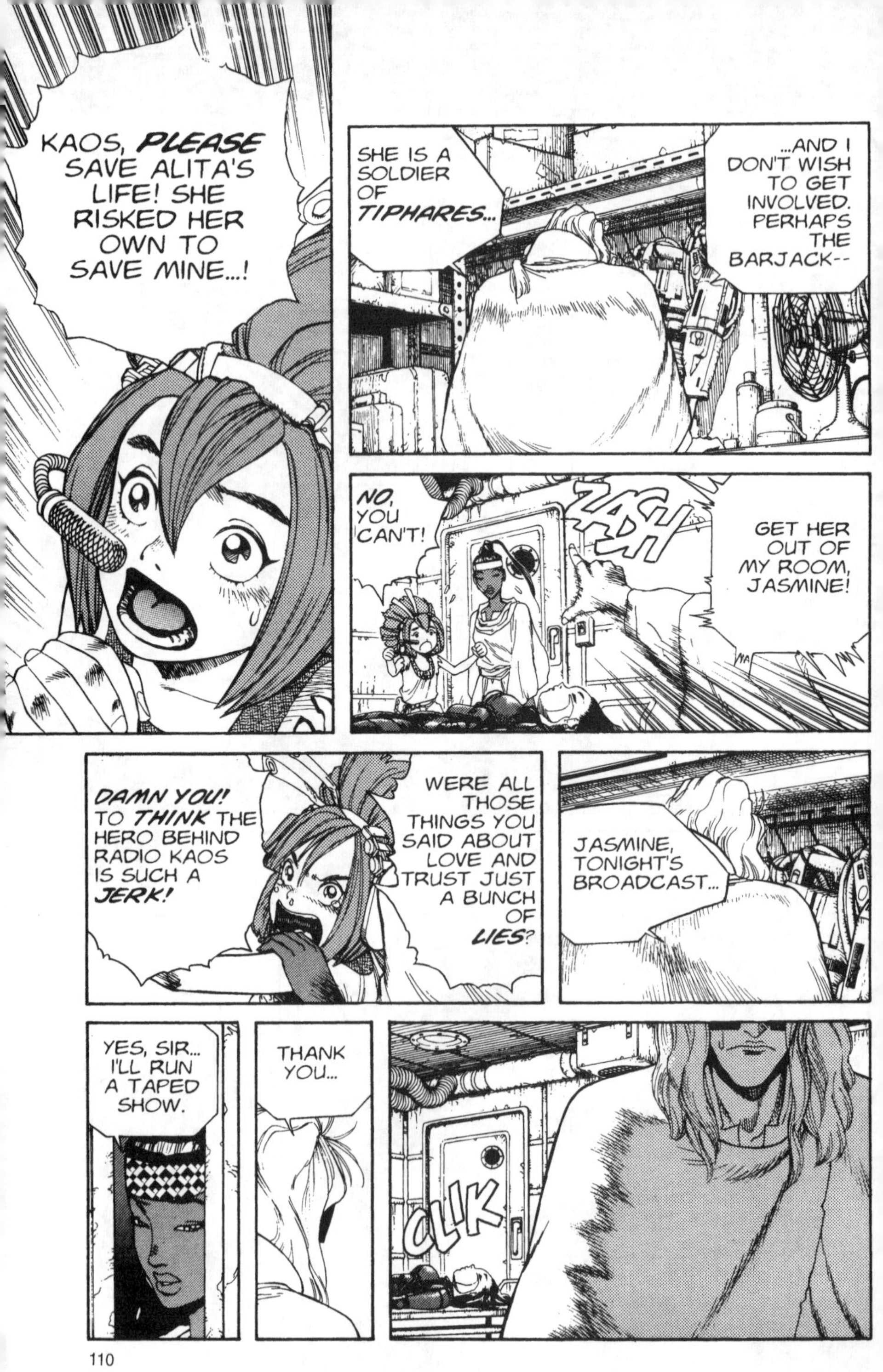
KAOS, PLEASE SAVE ALITA'S LIFE! SHE RISKED HER OWN TO SAVE MINE...!
SHE IS A SOLDIER OF TIPHARES...
...AND I DON'T WISH TO GET INVOLVED. PERHAPS THE BARJACK--
NO, YOU CAN'T!
ZASH
GET HER OUT OF MY ROOM, JASMINE!
DAMN YOU! TO THINK THE HERO BEHIND RADIO KAOS IS SUCH A JERK!
WERE ALL THOSE THINGS YOU SAID ABOUT LOVE AND TRUST JUST A BUNCH OF LIES?
JASMINE, TONIGHT'S BROADCAST...
YES, SIR... I'LL RUN A TAPED SHOW.
THANK YOU...
CLIK

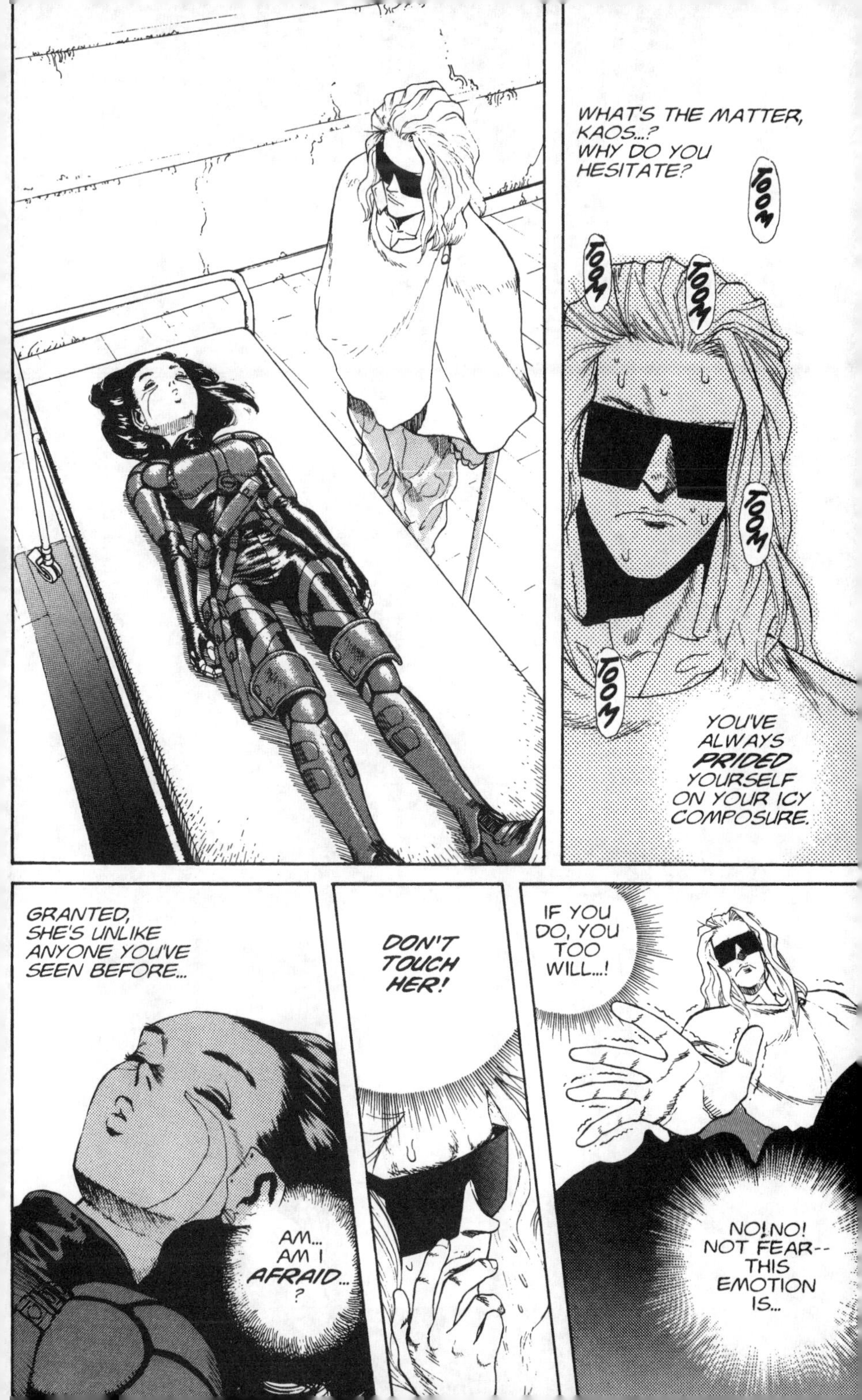
WHAT'S THE MATTER, KAOS...? WHY DO YOU HESITATE?
TOOM
TOOM
TOOM
TOOM
TOOM
YOU'VE ALWAYS PRIDED YOURSELF ON YOUR ICY COMPOSURE.
GRANTED, SHE'S UNLIKE ANYONE YOU'VE SEEN BEFORE...
AM... AM I AFRAID...?
DON'T TOUCH HER!
IF YOU DO, YOU TOO WILL...!
NO! NO! NOT FEAR-- THIS EMOTION IS...

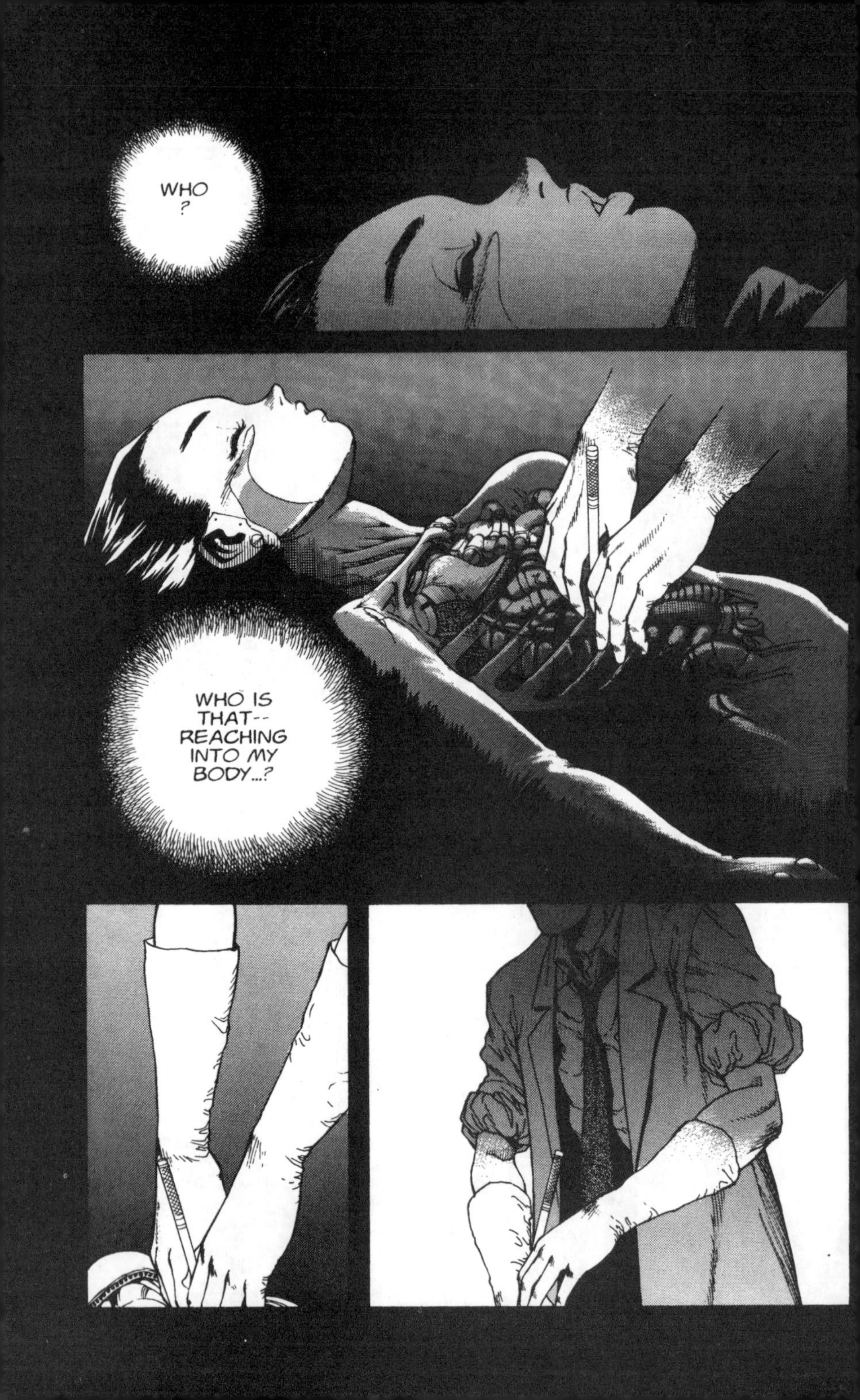
WHO ?
WHO IS THAT-- REACHING INTO MY BODY...?

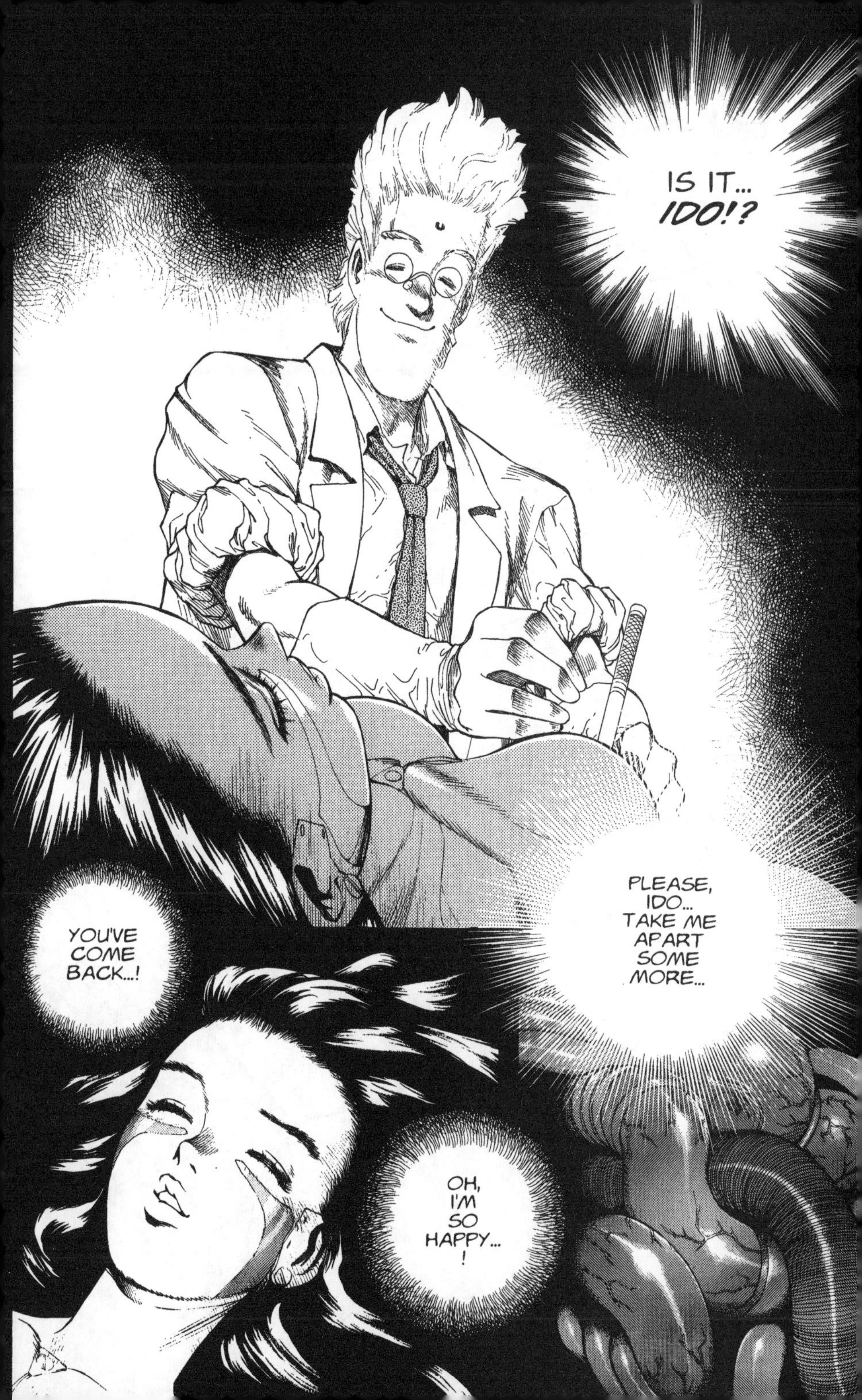
IS IT... IDO!?
YOU'VE COME BACK...!
PLEASE, IDO... TAKE ME APART SOME MORE...
OH, I'M SO HAPPY...!

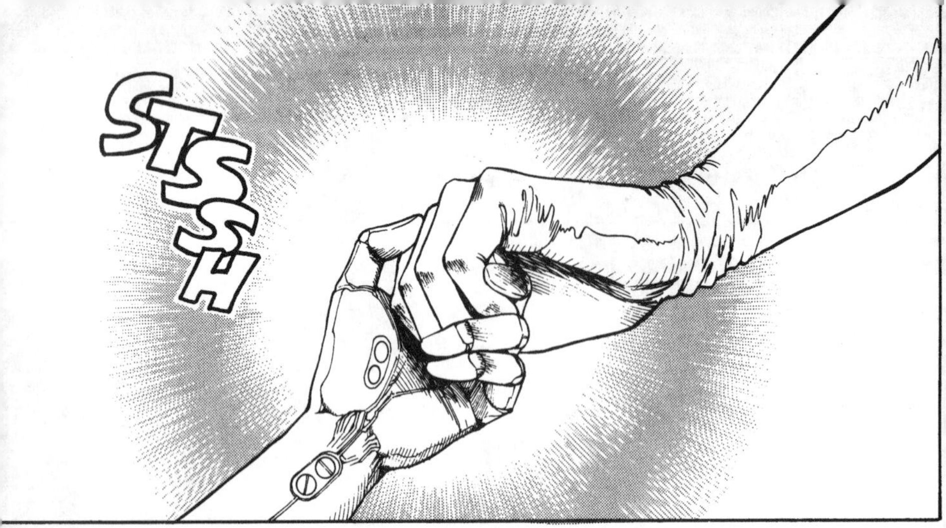
STSSH
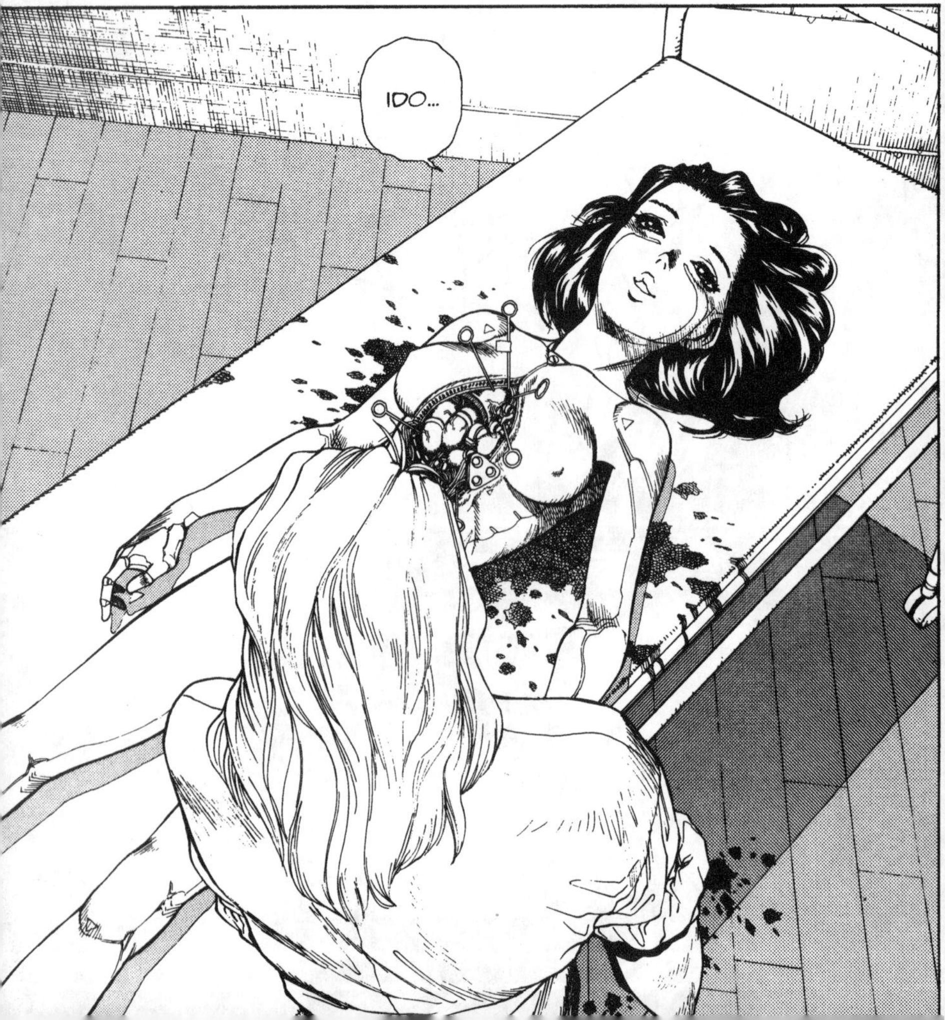
IDO...

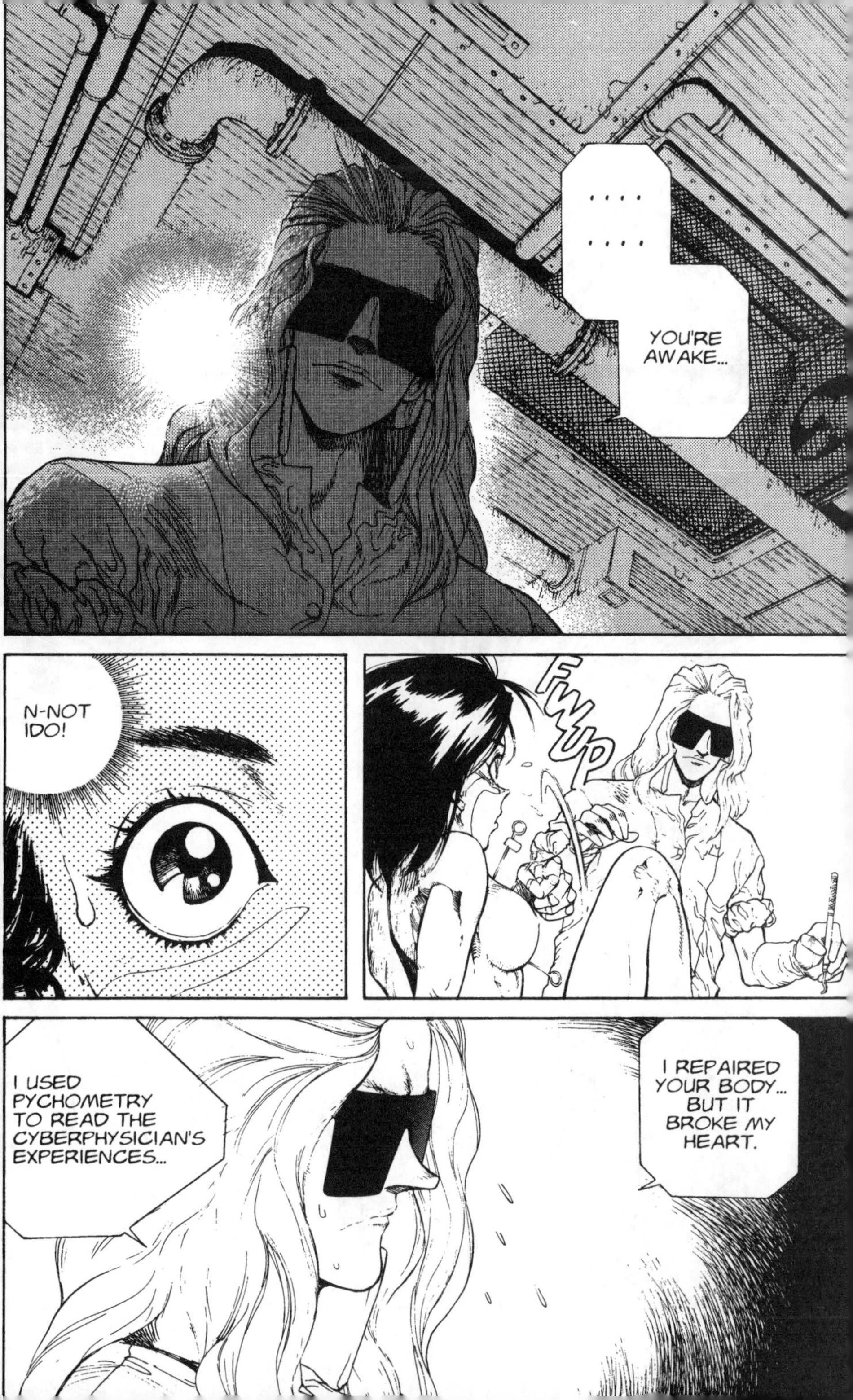
....
....
YOU'RE AWAKE...
N-NOT IDO!
FWUP
I USED PYCHOMETRY TO READ THE CYBERPHYSICIAN'S EXPERIENCES...
I REPAIRED YOUR BODY... BUT IT BROKE MY HEART.

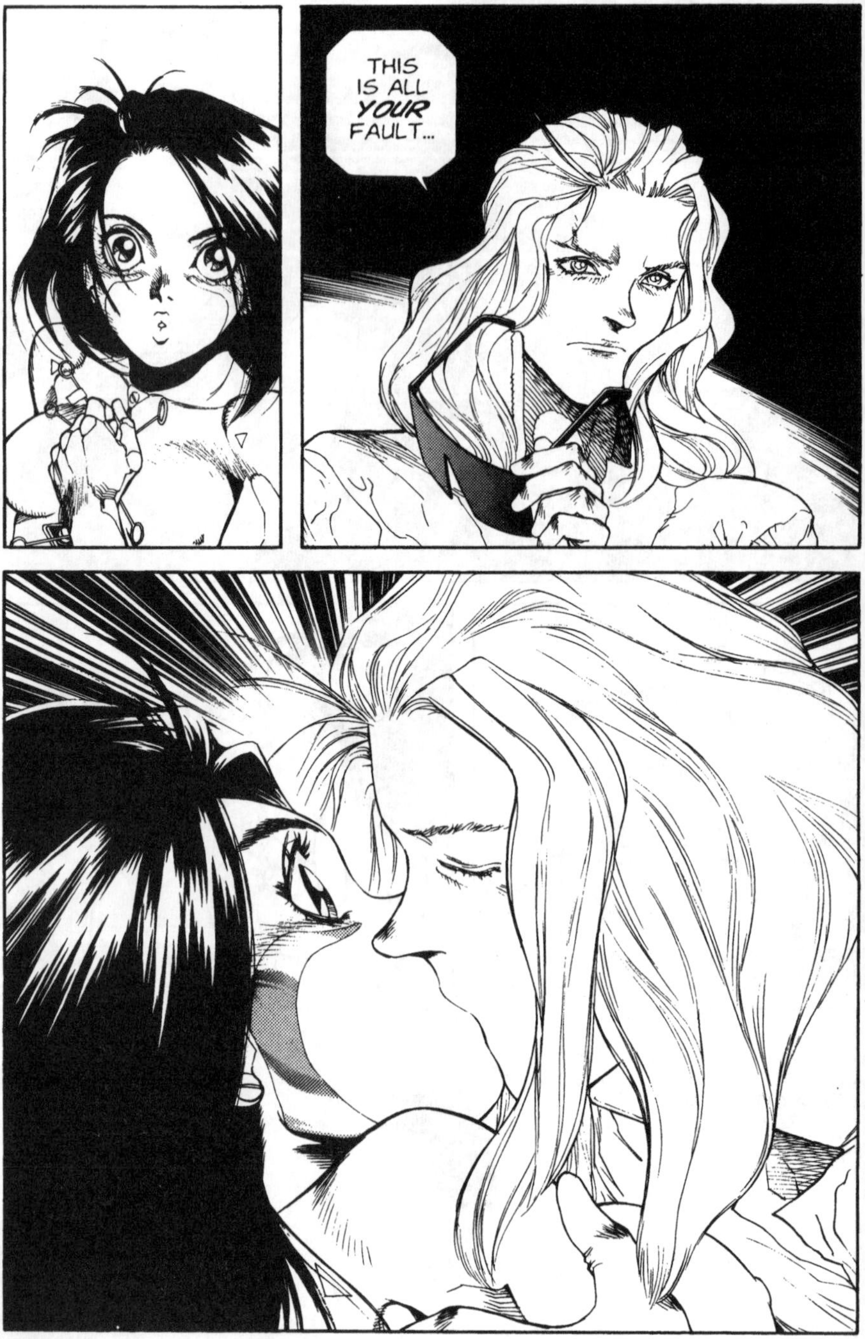
THIS IS ALL YOUR FAULT...

DEN OF BARJACK

Mission 4: Loyalties

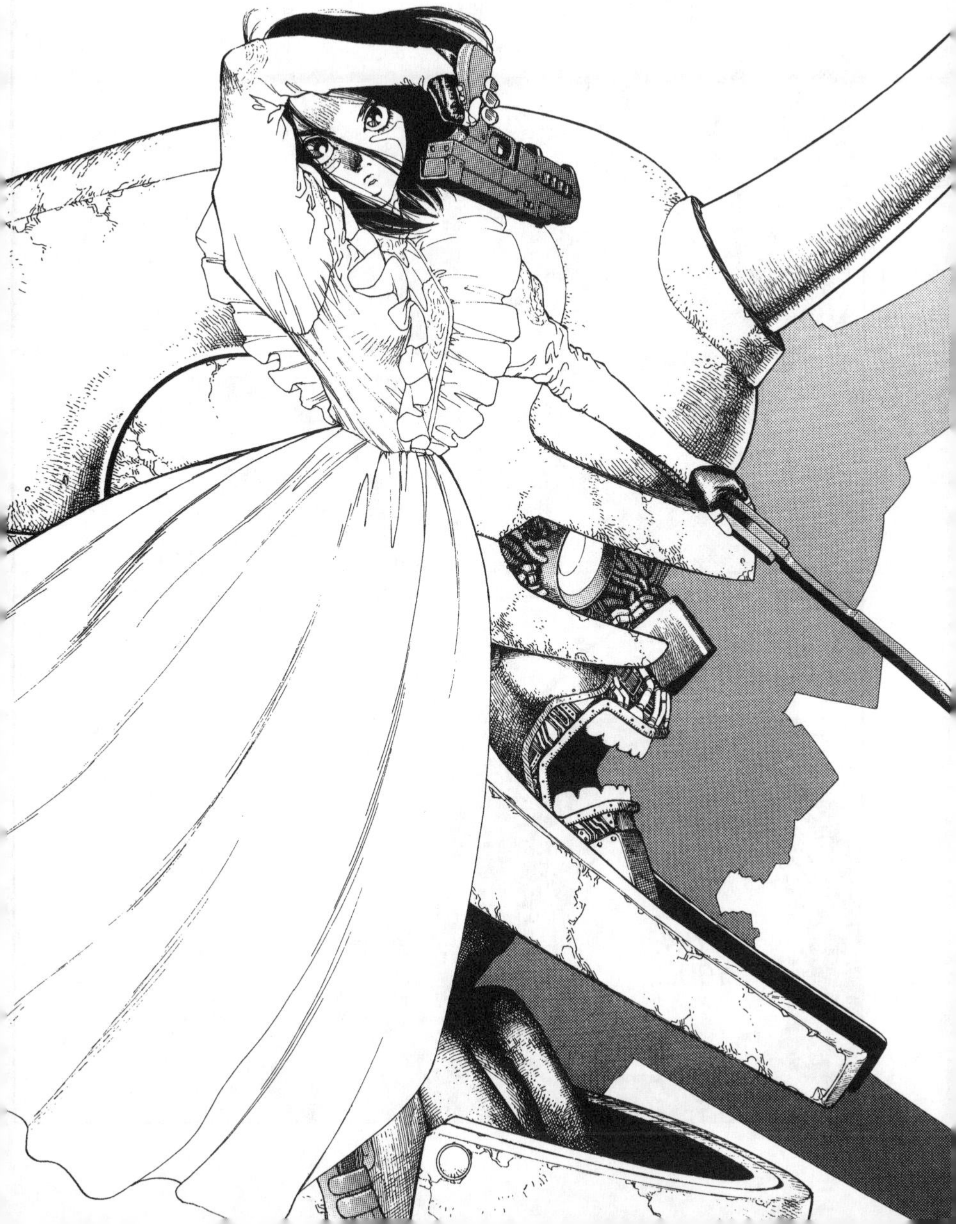

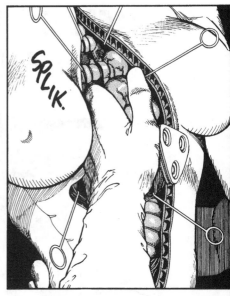

SPLIK.

NNN NH...

I--I *LOVE* YOU....

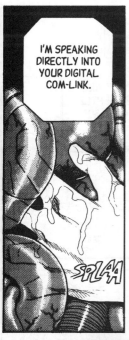

I'M SPEAKING DIRECTLY INTO YOUR DIGITAL COM-LINK.

CAN'T YOU FEEL MY *LOVE*... BEING TRANSMITTED *INTO* YOU ?

SPLAA

YOKO....

!

KLANG
TINK

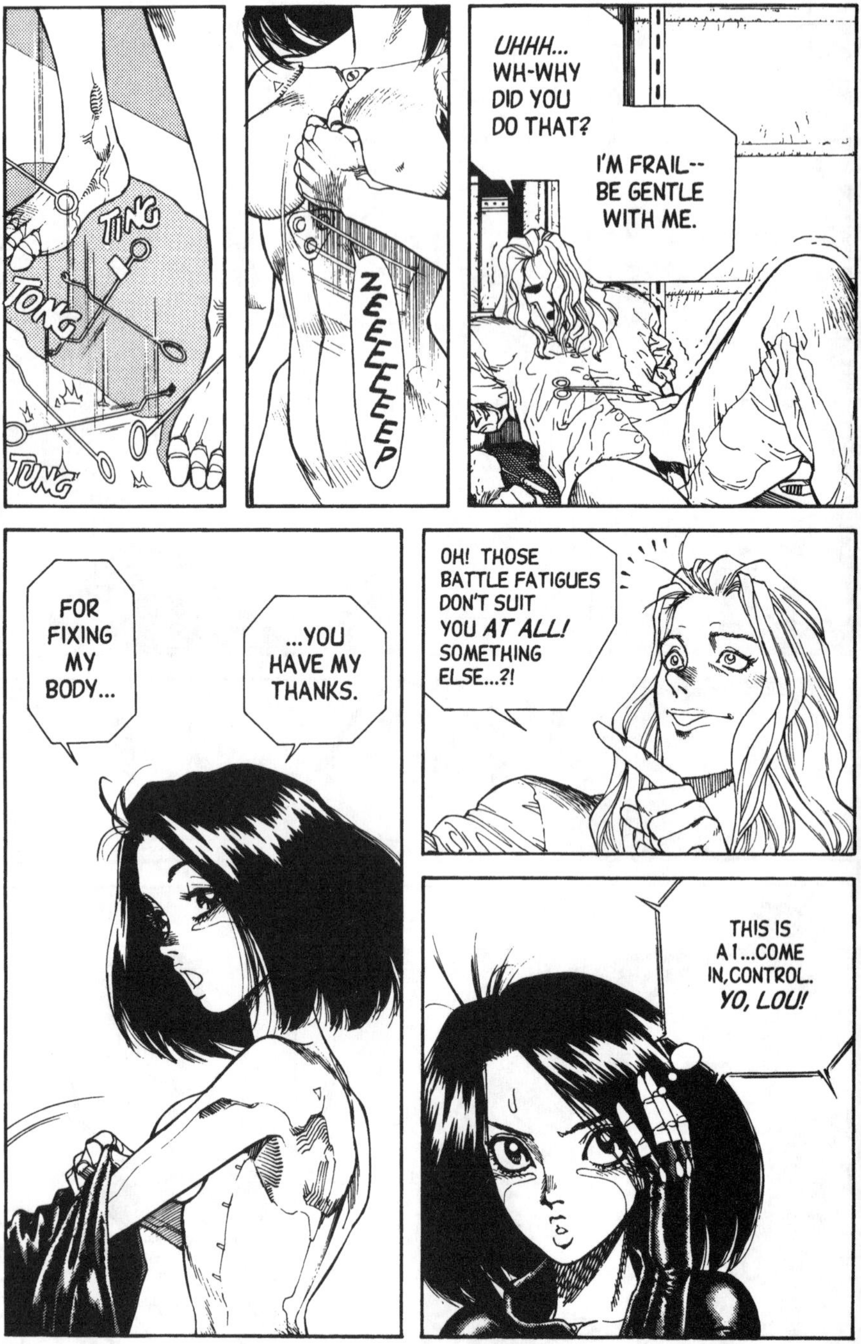
TING
TONG
TUNG
ZEEEEEEEP
UHHH... WH-WHY DID YOU DO THAT?
I'M FRAIL-- BE GENTLE WITH ME.
FOR FIXING MY BODY...
...YOU HAVE MY THANKS.
OH! THOSE BATTLE FATIGUES DON'T SUIT YOU AT ALL! SOMETHING ELSE...?!
THIS IS A1...COME IN,CONTROL. YO, LOU!

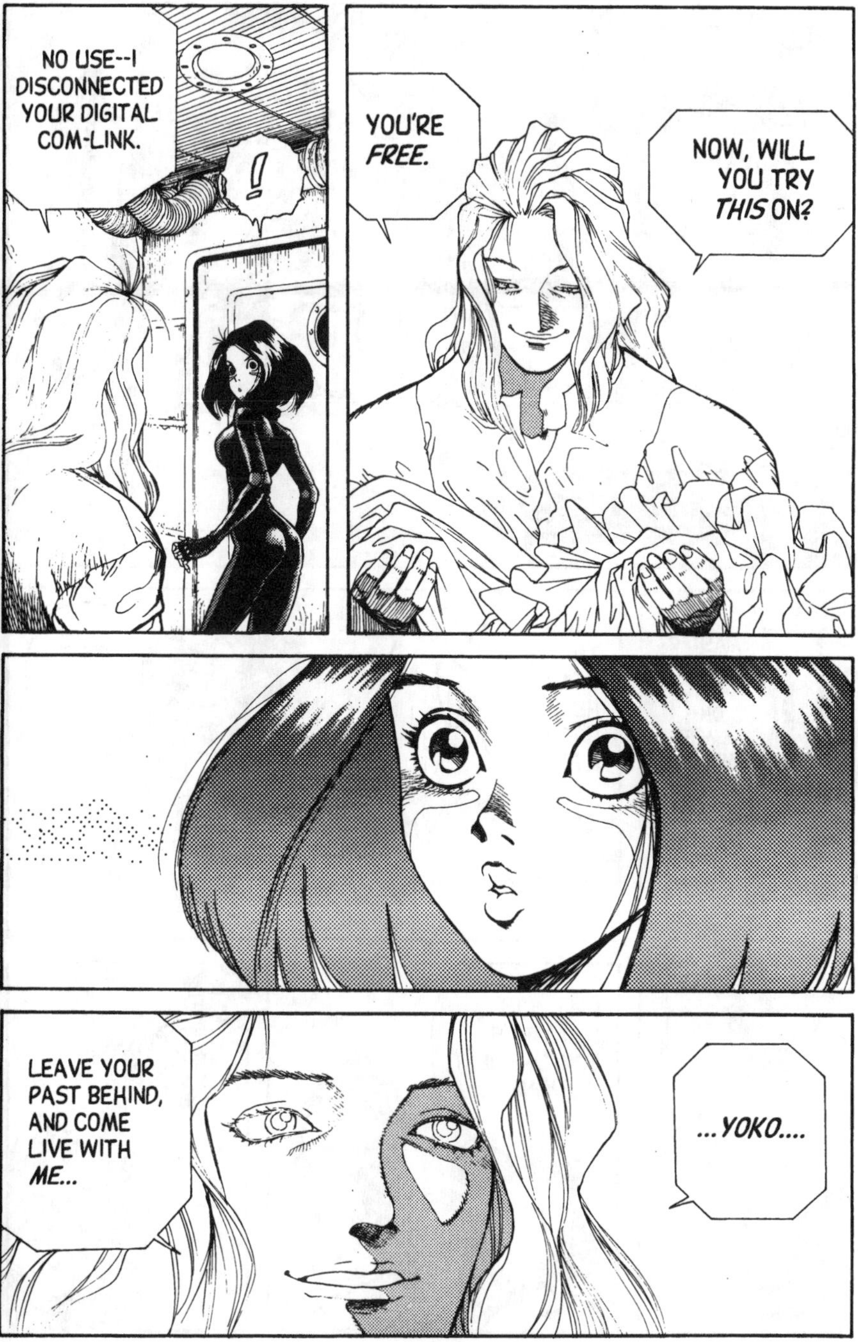
NO USE--I DISCONNECTED YOUR DIGITAL COM-LINK.
!
YOU'RE *FREE.*
NOW, WILL YOU TRY *THIS* ON?
LEAVE YOUR PAST BEHIND, AND COME LIVE WITH *ME...*
...YOKO....

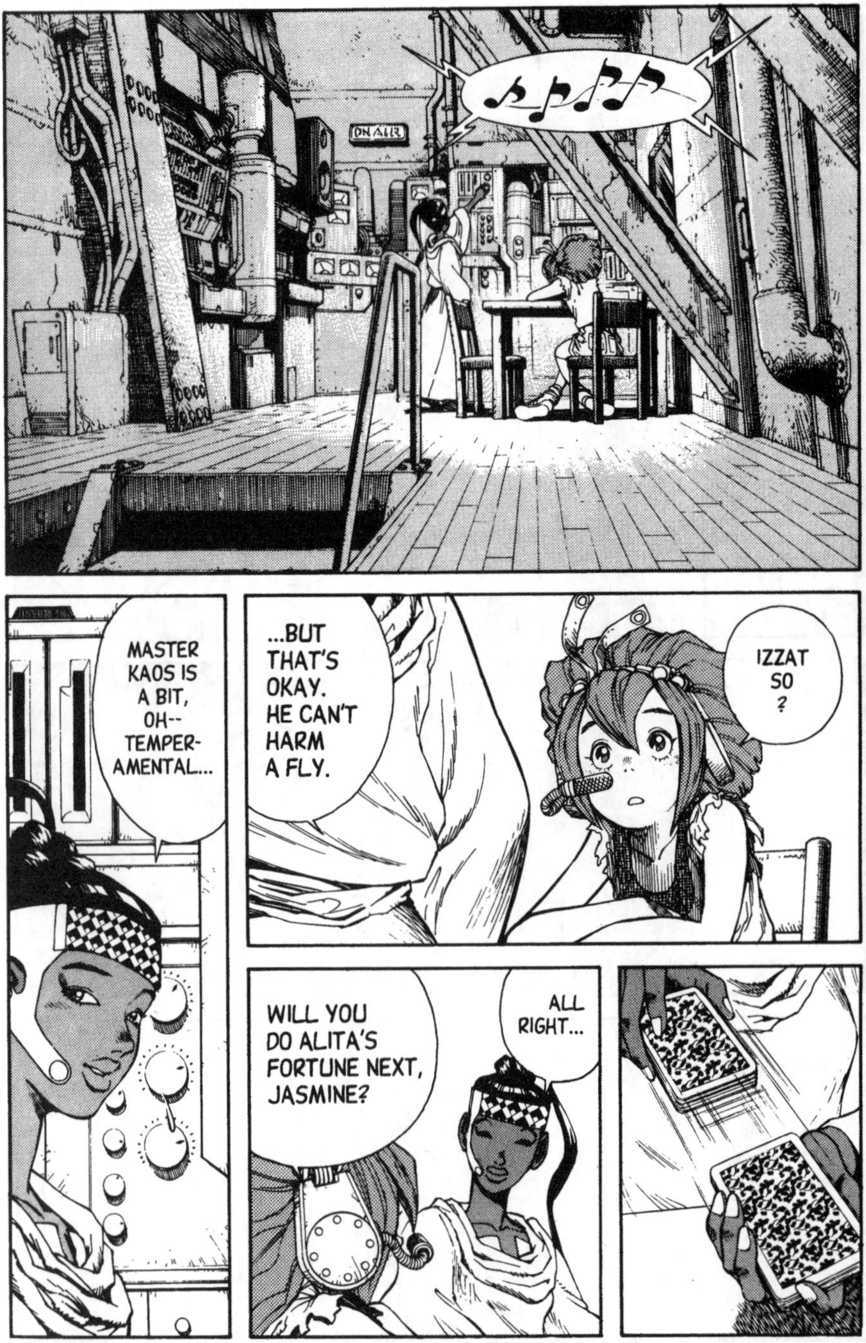
MASTER KAOS IS A BIT, OH-- TEMPER-AMENTAL...
...BUT THAT'S OKAY. HE CAN'T HARM A FLY.
IZZAT SO ?
WILL YOU DO ALITA'S FORTUNE NEXT, JASMINE?
ALL RIGHT...

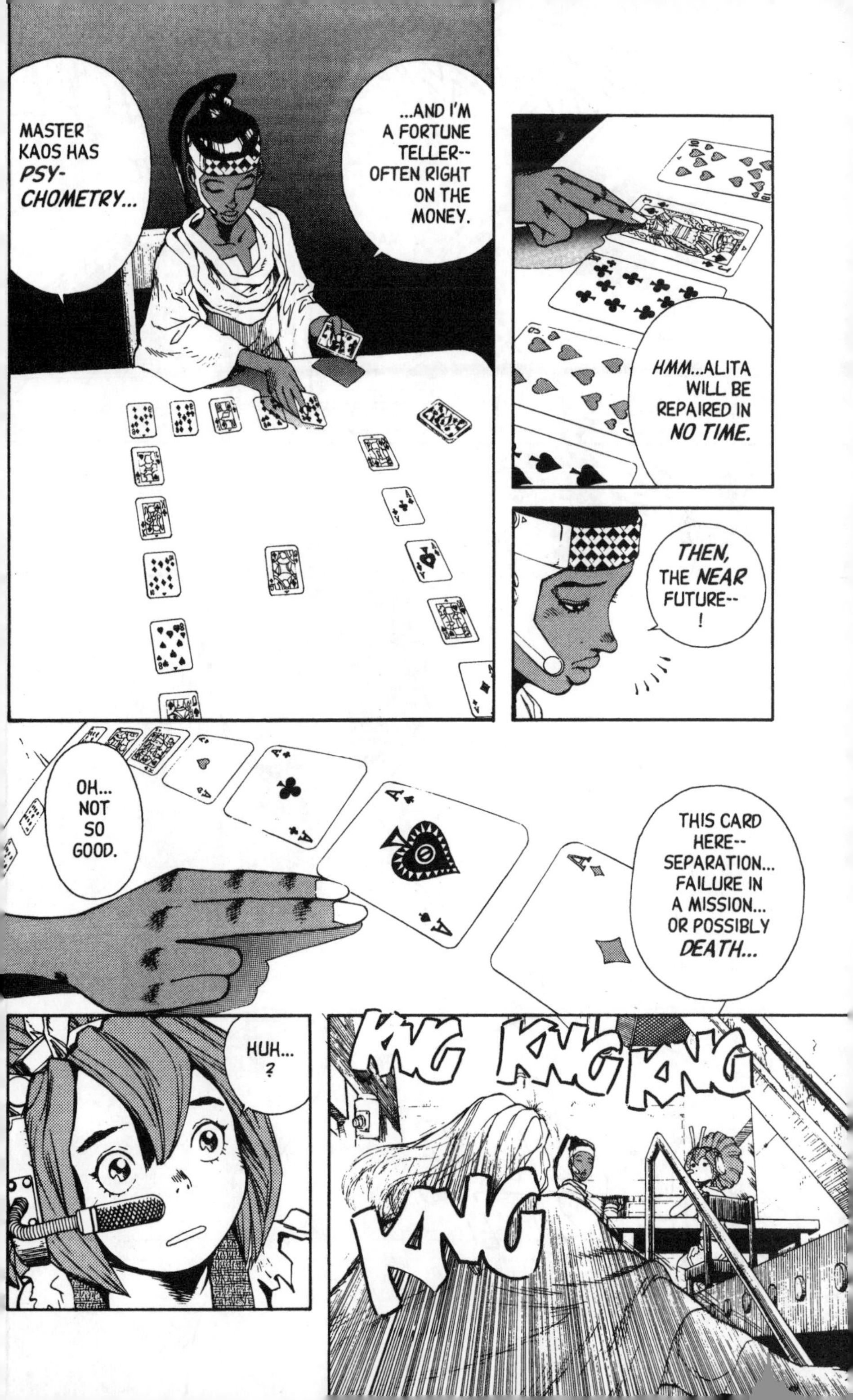
MASTER KAOS HAS PSY-CHOMETRY...
...AND I'M A FORTUNE TELLER-- OFTEN RIGHT ON THE MONEY.
HMM...ALITA WILL BE REPAIRED IN NO TIME.
THEN, THE NEAR FUTURE-- !
OH... NOT SO GOOD.
THIS CARD HERE-- SEPARATION... FAILURE IN A MISSION... OR POSSIBLY DEATH...
HUH... ?
KNG KNG KNG KNG
KNG

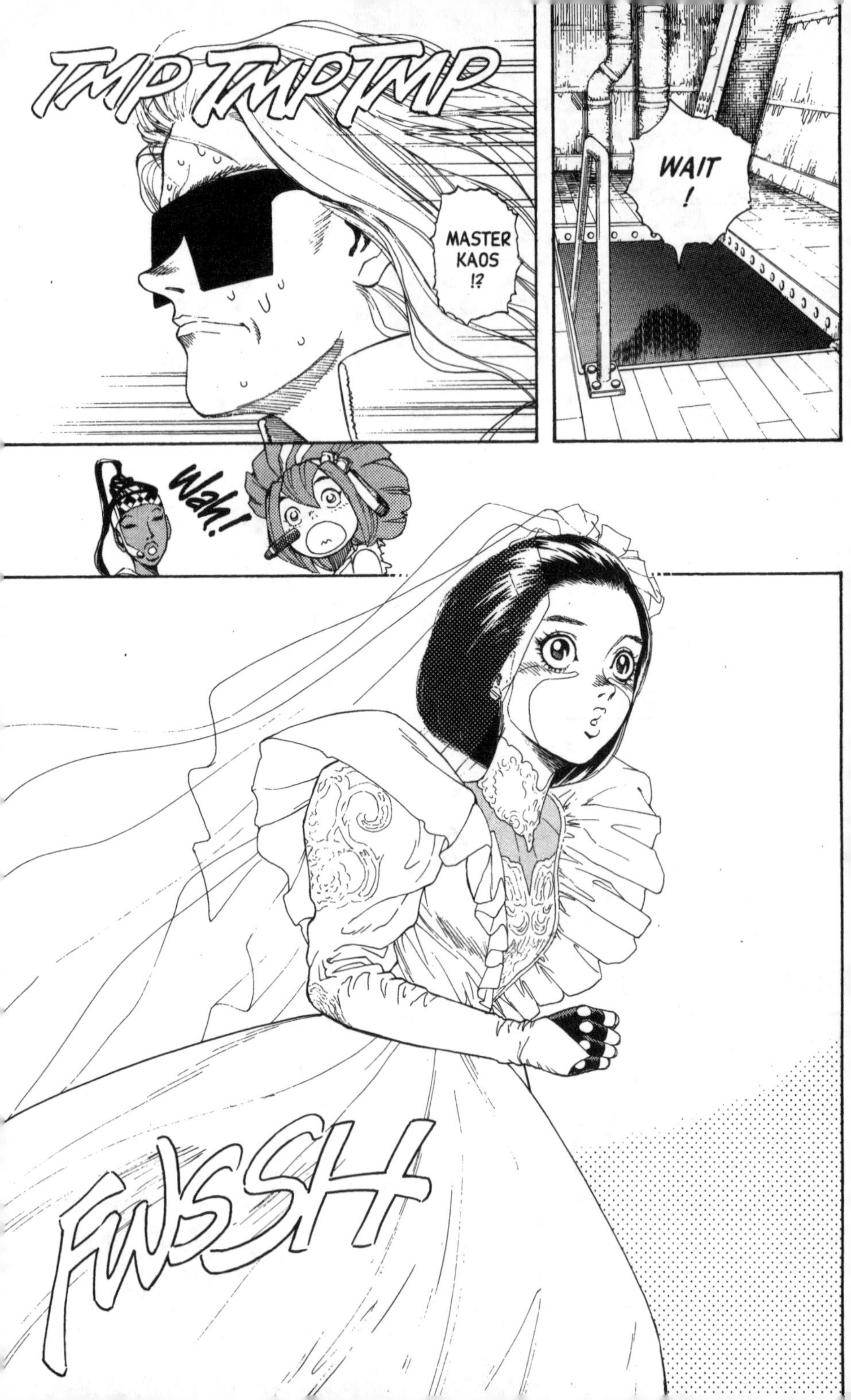
TMP TMP TMP
MASTER KAOS !?
WAIT !
Wah!
FWSSH

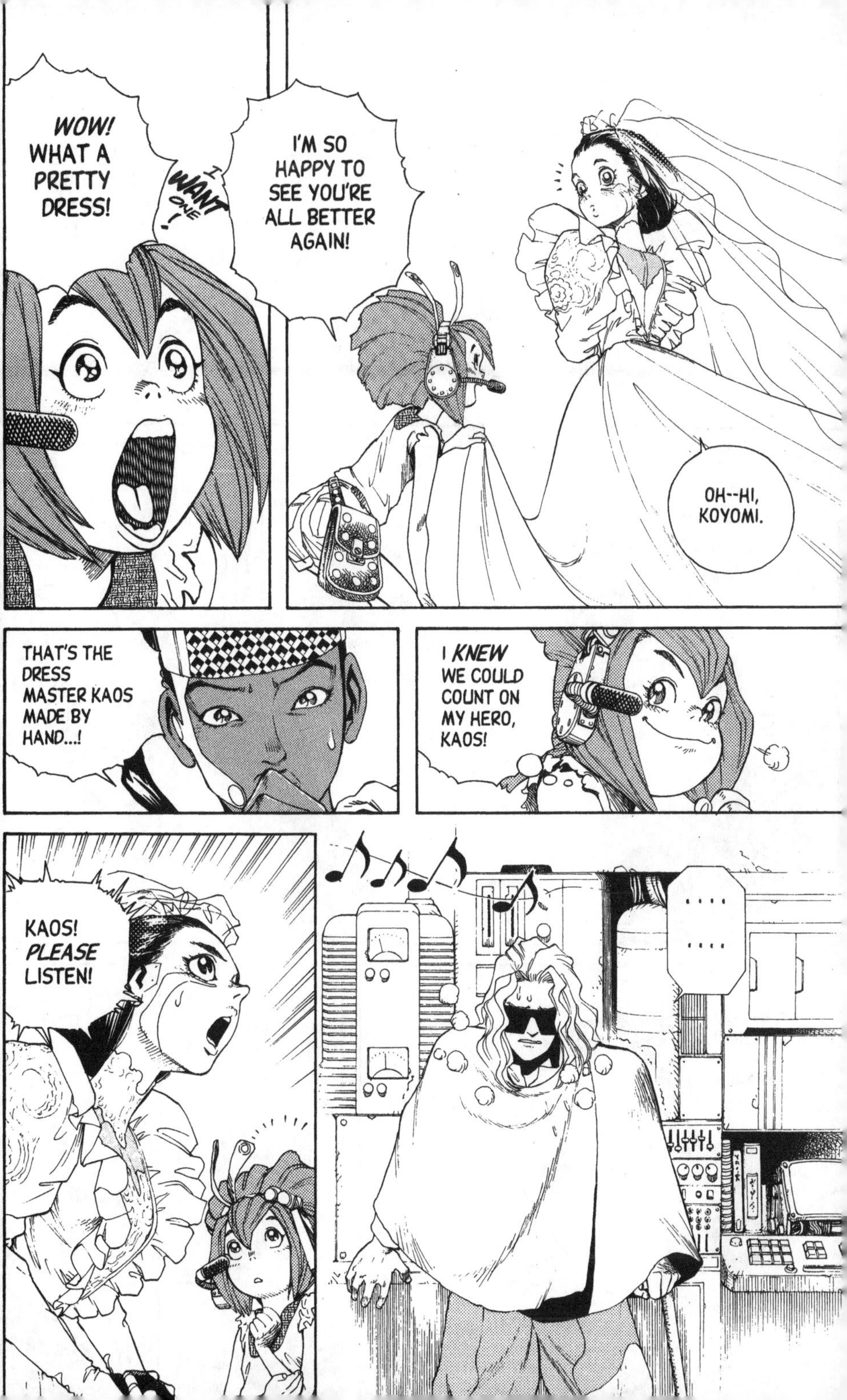

WOW! WHAT A PRETTY DRESS!
I *WANT* ONE!
I'M SO HAPPY TO SEE YOU'RE ALL BETTER AGAIN!
OH--HI, KOYOMI.
THAT'S THE DRESS MASTER KAOS MADE BY HAND...!
I *KNEW* WE COULD COUNT ON MY HERO, KAOS!
KAOS! *PLEASE* LISTEN!
....
....

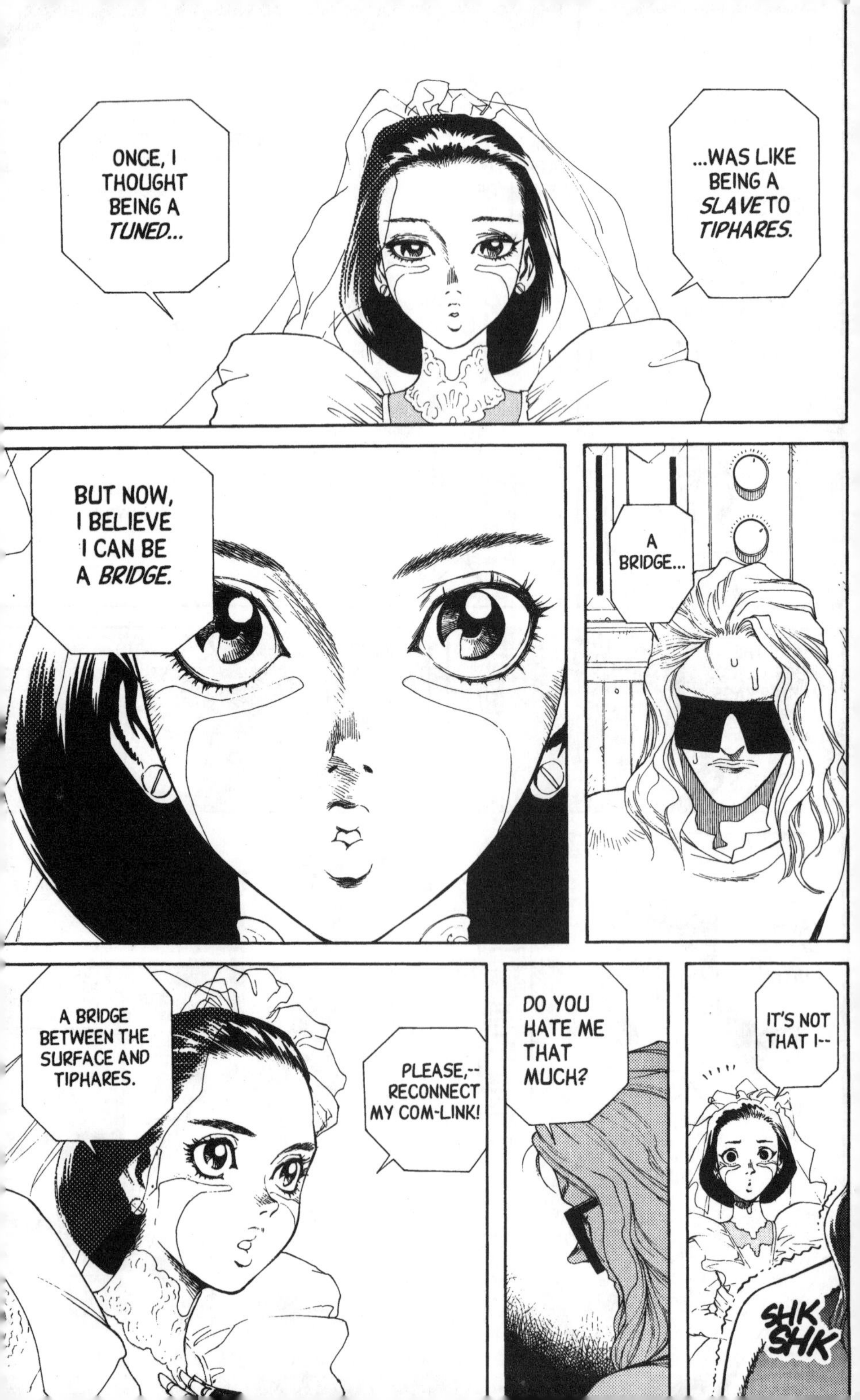

ONCE, I THOUGHT BEING A *TUNED*...
...WAS LIKE BEING A *SLAVE* TO *TIPHARES*.
BUT NOW, I BELIEVE I CAN BE A *BRIDGE*.
A BRIDGE...
A BRIDGE BETWEEN THE SURFACE AND TIPHARES.
PLEASE,-- RECONNECT MY COM-LINK!
DO YOU HATE ME THAT MUCH?
IT'S NOT THAT I--
SHK SHK

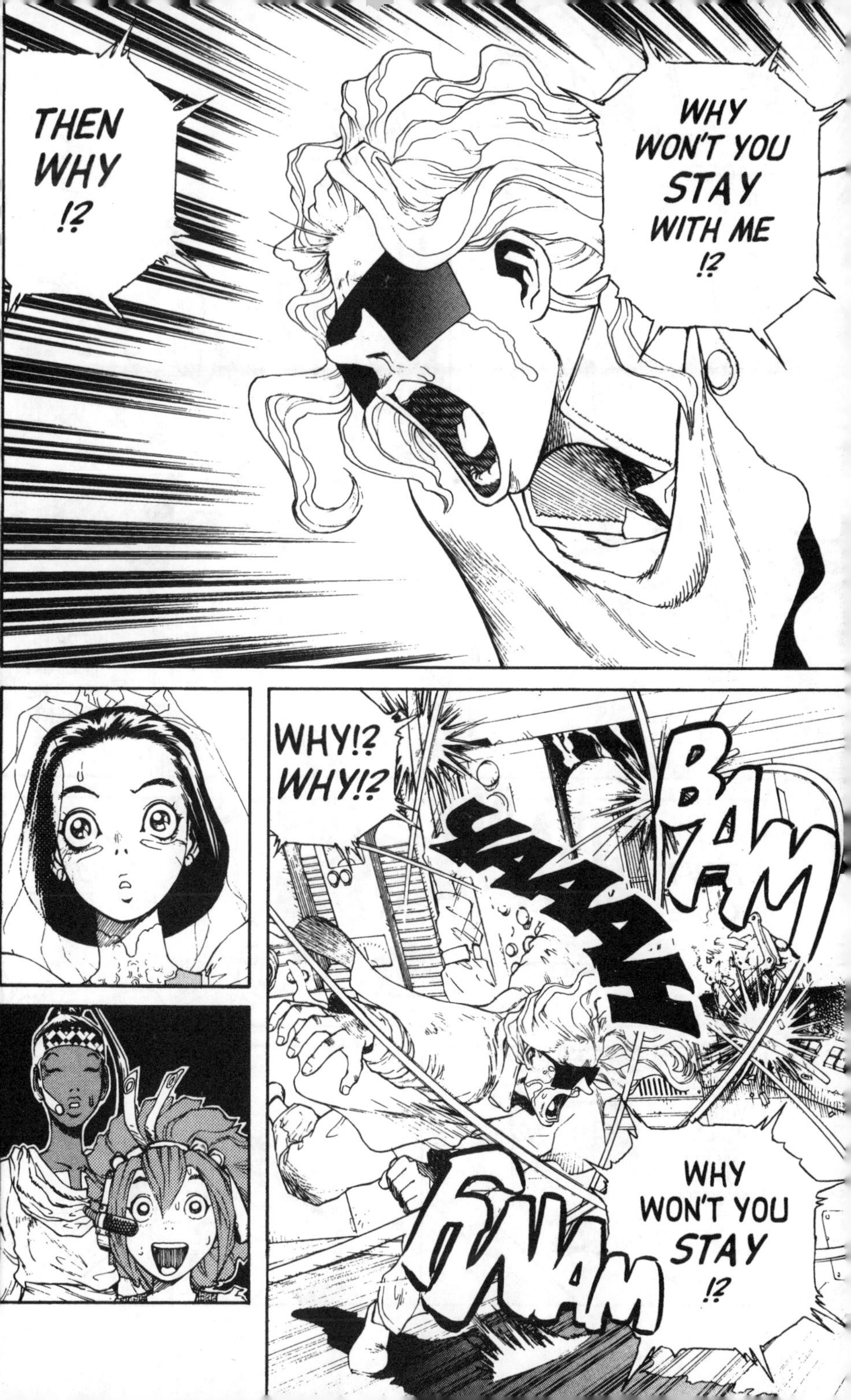
THEN WHY !?
WHY WON'T YOU STAY WITH ME !?
WHY!? WHY!?
BAM
SLAAAAM
WHY WON'T YOU STAY !?
FWAM

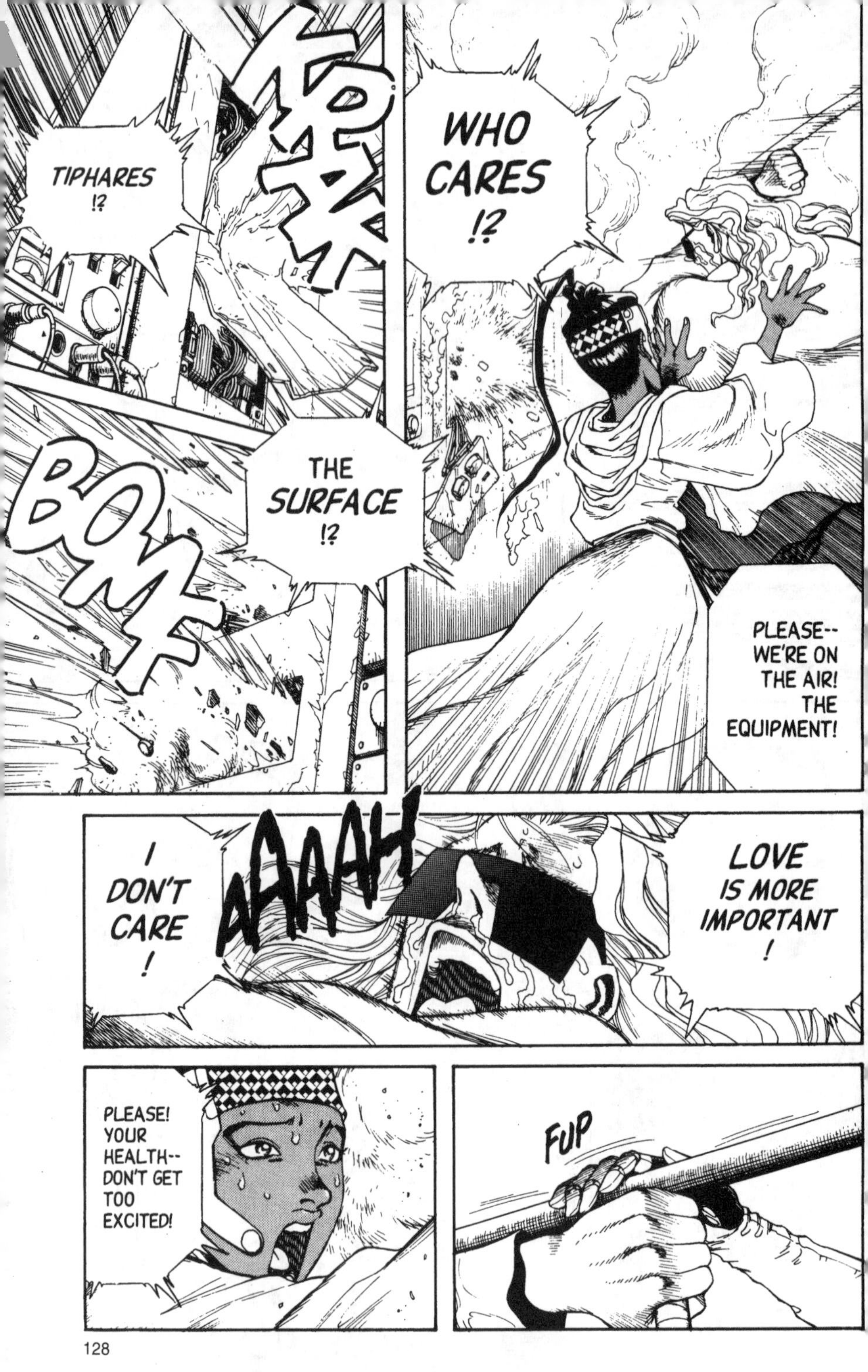
TIPHARES !?
THE SURFACE !?
WHO CARES !?
PLEASE-- WE'RE ON THE AIR! THE EQUIPMENT!
I DON'T CARE !
AAAAH
LOVE IS MORE IMPORTANT !
PLEASE! YOUR HEALTH-- DON'T GET TOO EXCITED!
FUP

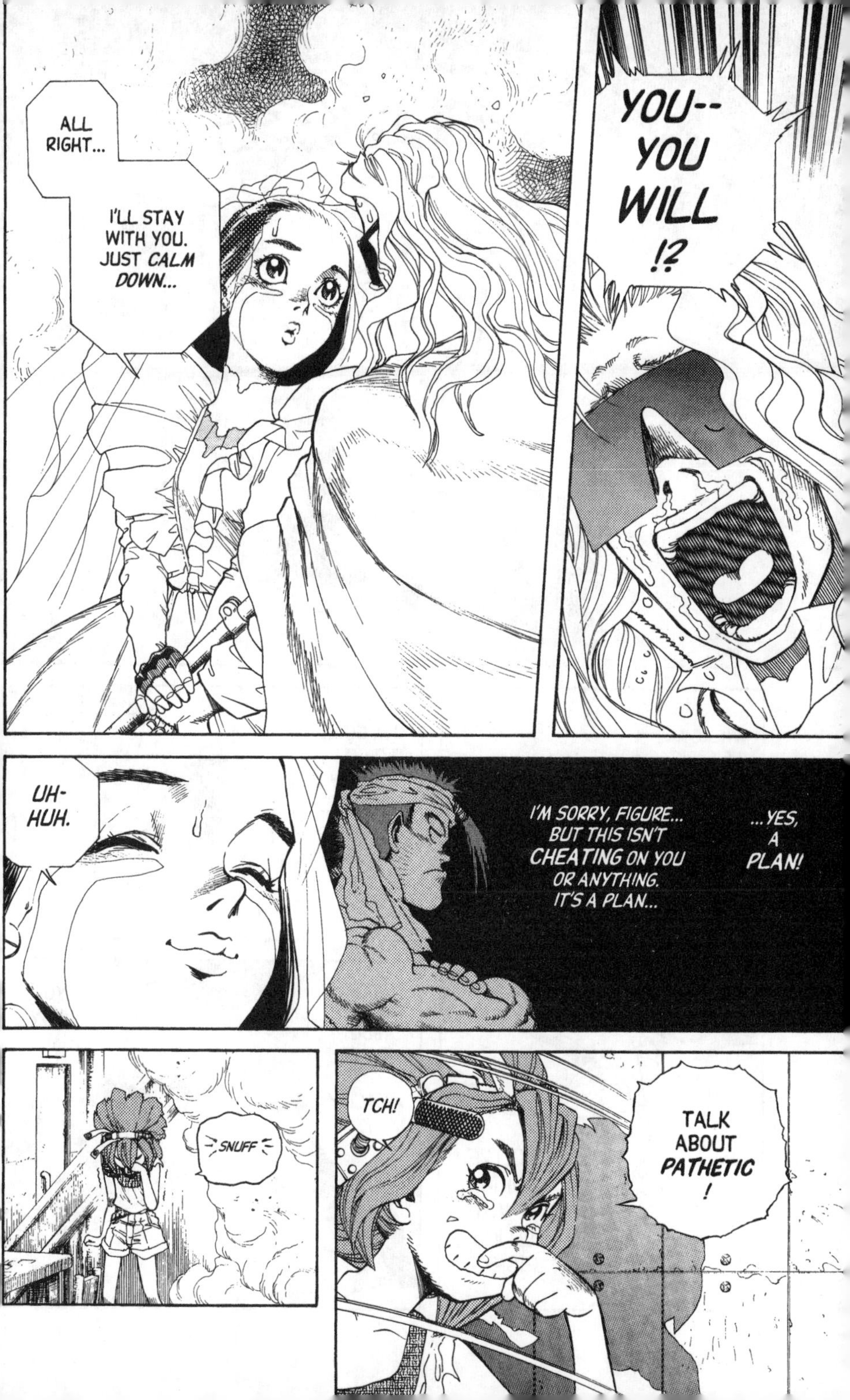
ALL RIGHT...
I'LL STAY WITH YOU. JUST CALM DOWN...
YOU-- YOU WILL !?
UH-HUH.
I'M SORRY, FIGURE... BUT THIS ISN'T CHEATING ON YOU OR ANYTHING. IT'S A PLAN...
...YES, A PLAN!
SNUFF
TCH!
TALK ABOUT PATHETIC !

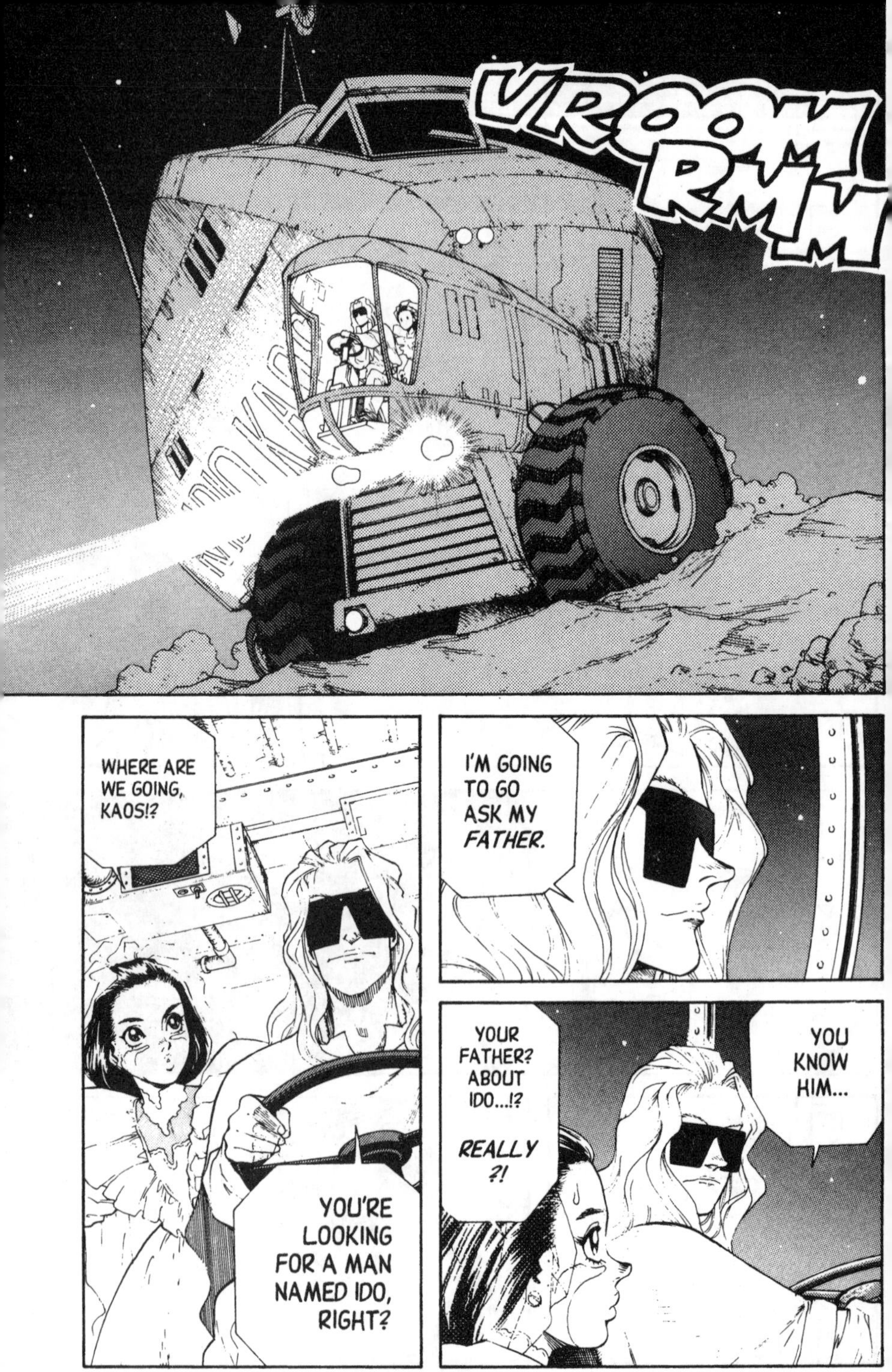
VROOM RMM
WHERE ARE WE GOING, KAOS!?
YOU'RE LOOKING FOR A MAN NAMED IDO, RIGHT?
I'M GOING TO GO ASK MY *FATHER.*
YOUR FATHER? ABOUT IDO...!?
REALLY ?!
YOU KNOW HIM...

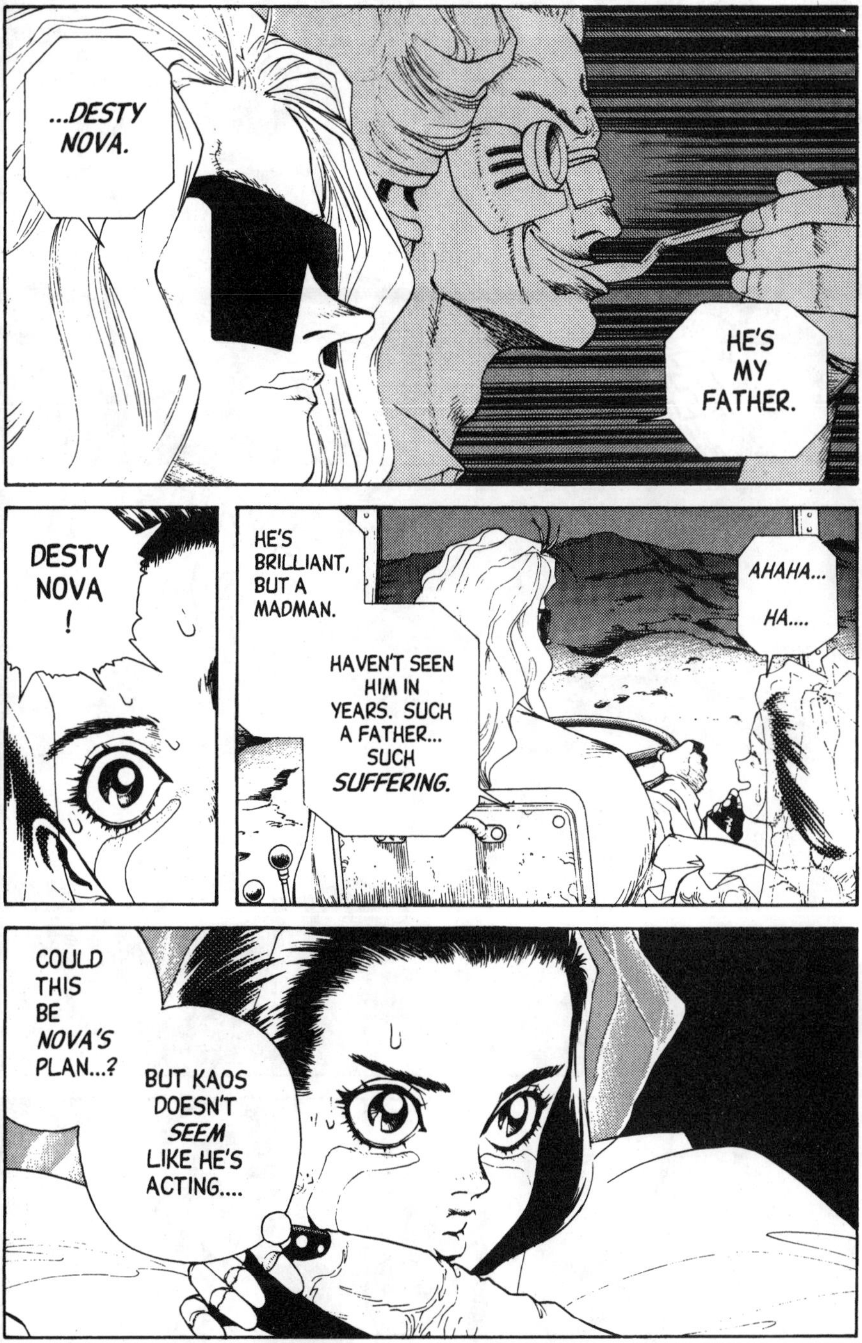
...DESTY NOVA.
HE'S MY FATHER.
DESTY NOVA !
HE'S BRILLIANT, BUT A MADMAN.
HAVEN'T SEEN HIM IN YEARS. SUCH A FATHER... SUCH SUFFERING.
AHAHA... HA....
COULD THIS BE NOVA'S PLAN...?
BUT KAOS DOESN'T SEEM LIKE HE'S ACTING....

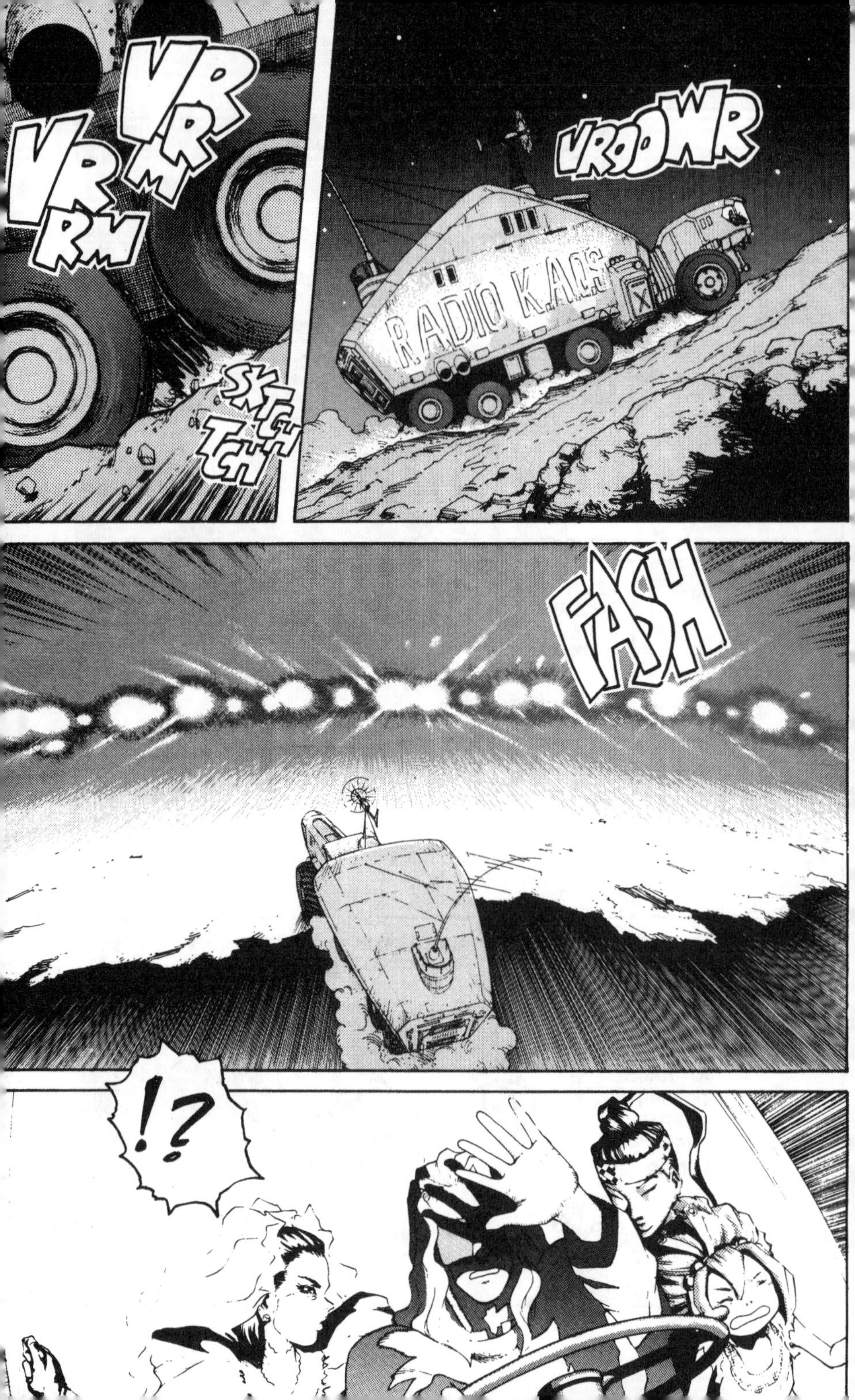

VRRM
VRRM
SKTCH TCH
VROOWR
RADIO KAOS
FASH
!?

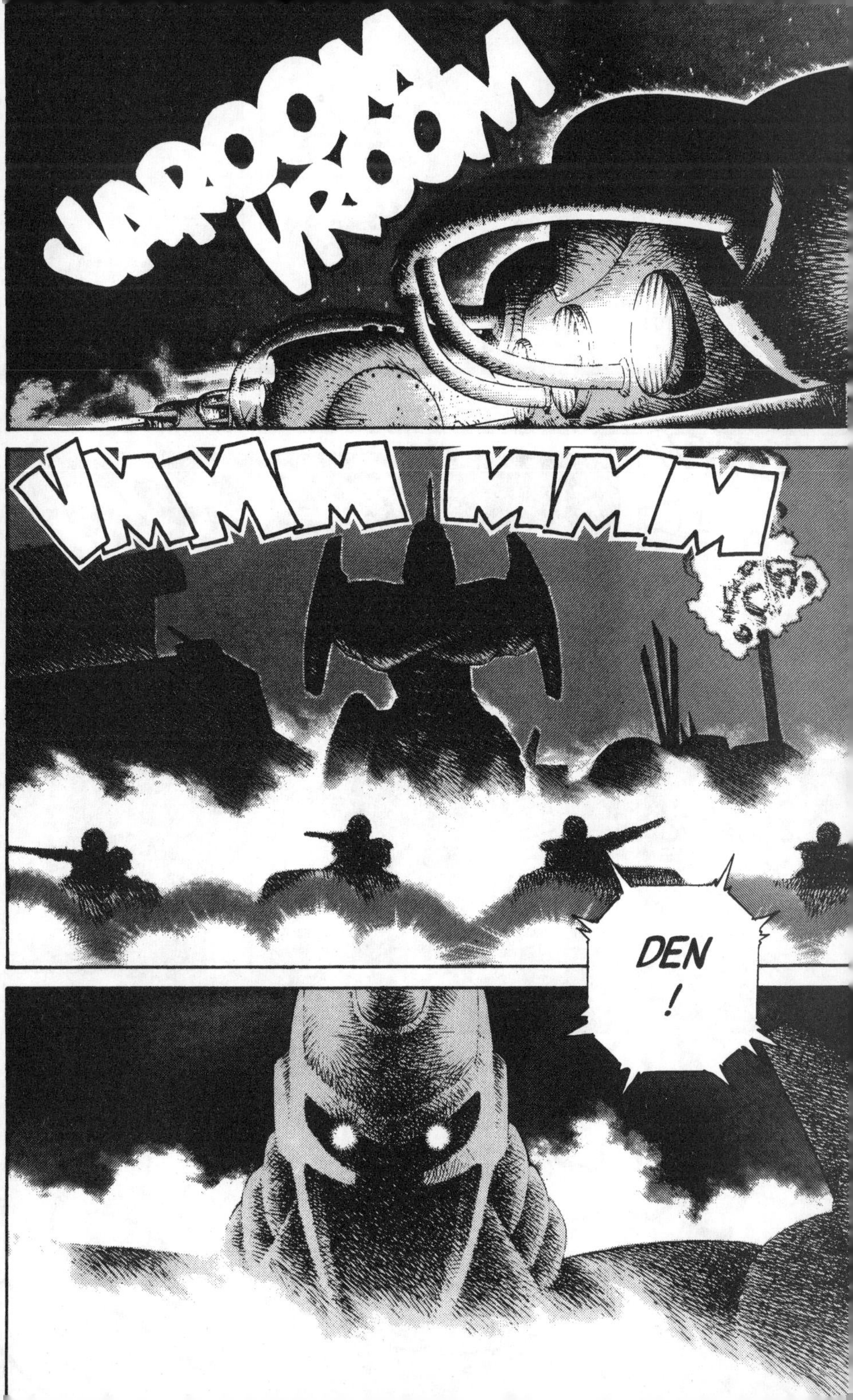
VAROOOM
VROOOM
VMMM MMMM
DEN
!

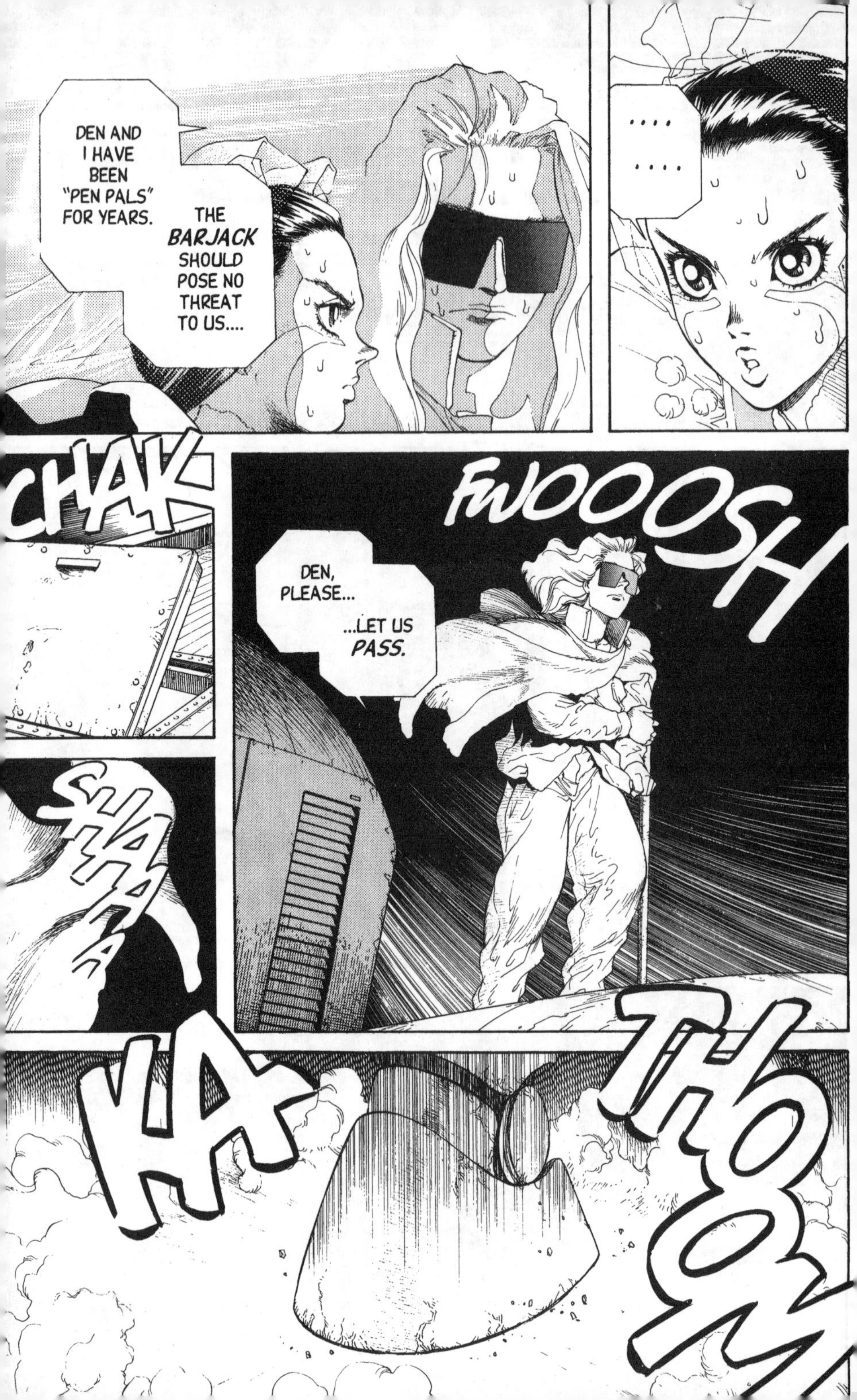
DEN AND I HAVE BEEN "PEN PALS" FOR YEARS.
THE *BARJACK* SHOULD POSE NO THREAT TO US....
....
....
CHAK
FWOOOSH
DEN, PLEASE...
...LET US *PASS.*
SHAAAA
KA-THOOM

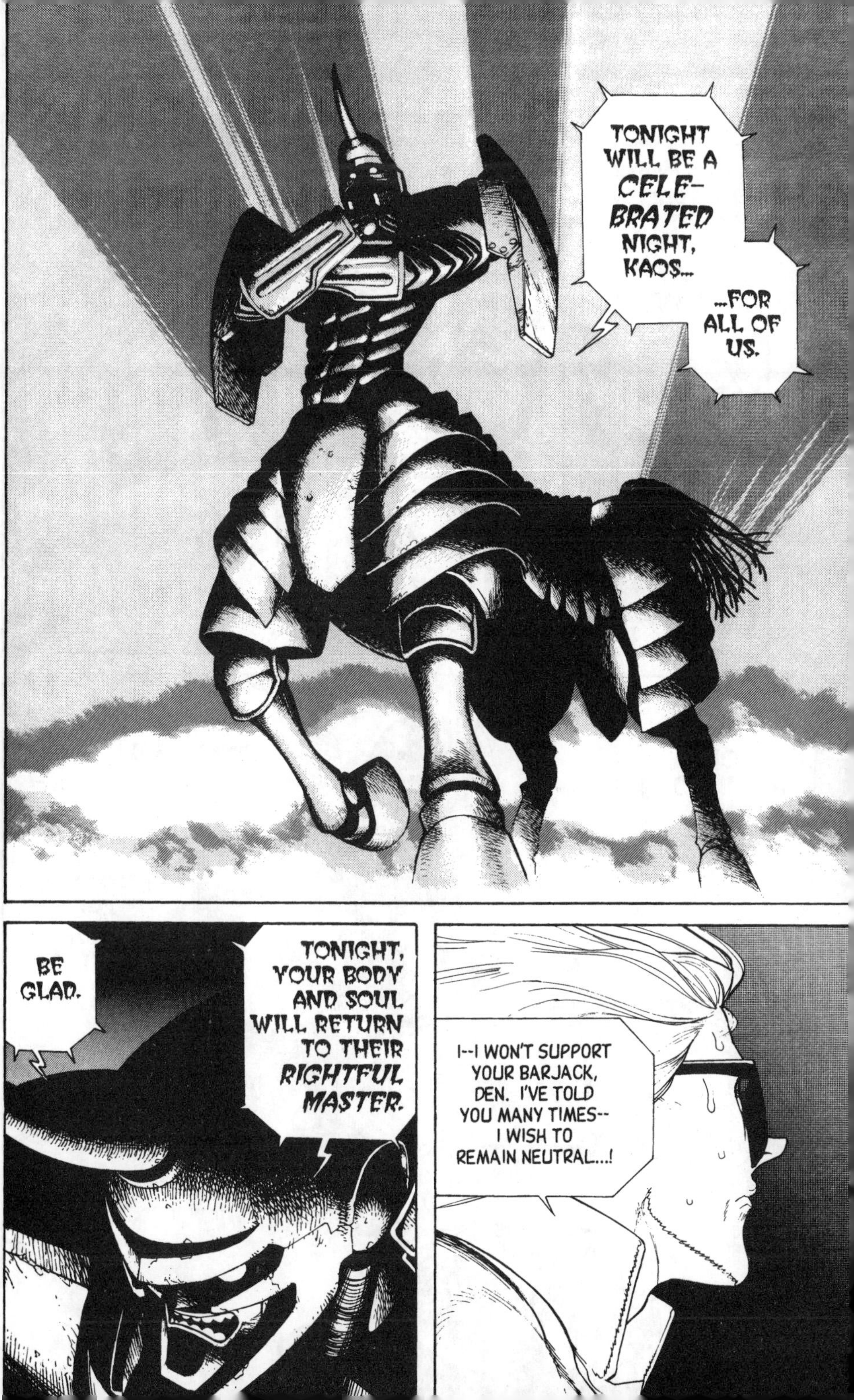
TONIGHT WILL BE A CELE-BRATED NIGHT, KAOS...
...FOR ALL OF US.
BE GLAD.
TONIGHT, YOUR BODY AND SOUL WILL RETURN TO THEIR RIGHTFUL MASTER.
I--I WON'T SUPPORT YOUR BARJACK, DEN. I'VE TOLD YOU MANY TIMES-- I WISH TO REMAIN NEUTRAL...!

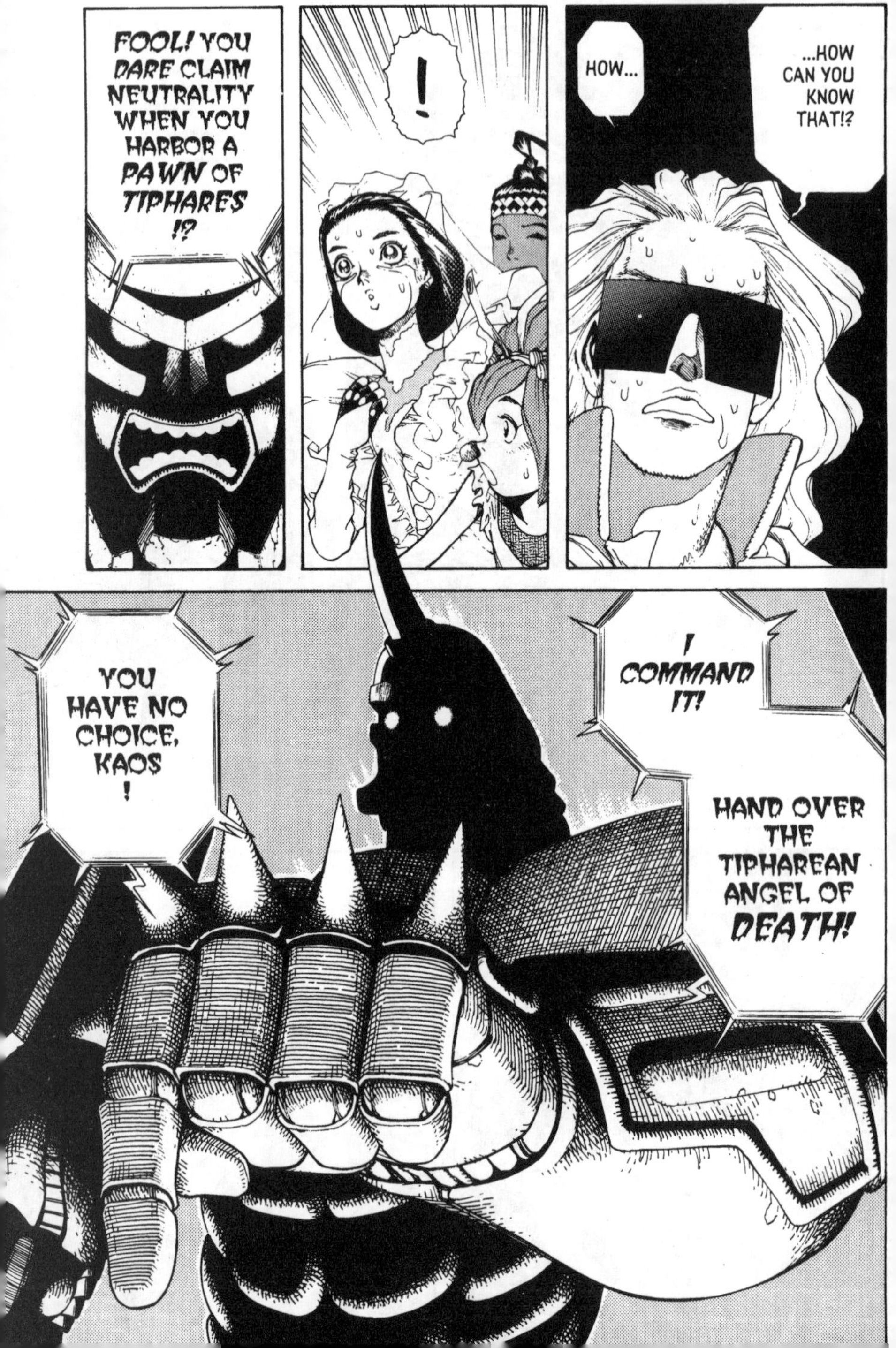

FOOL! YOU DARE CLAIM NEUTRALITY WHEN YOU HARBOR A PAWN OF TIPHARES !?
!
HOW...
...HOW CAN YOU KNOW THAT!?
YOU HAVE NO CHOICE, KAOS !
I COMMAND IT!
HAND OVER THE TIPHAREAN ANGEL OF DEATH!

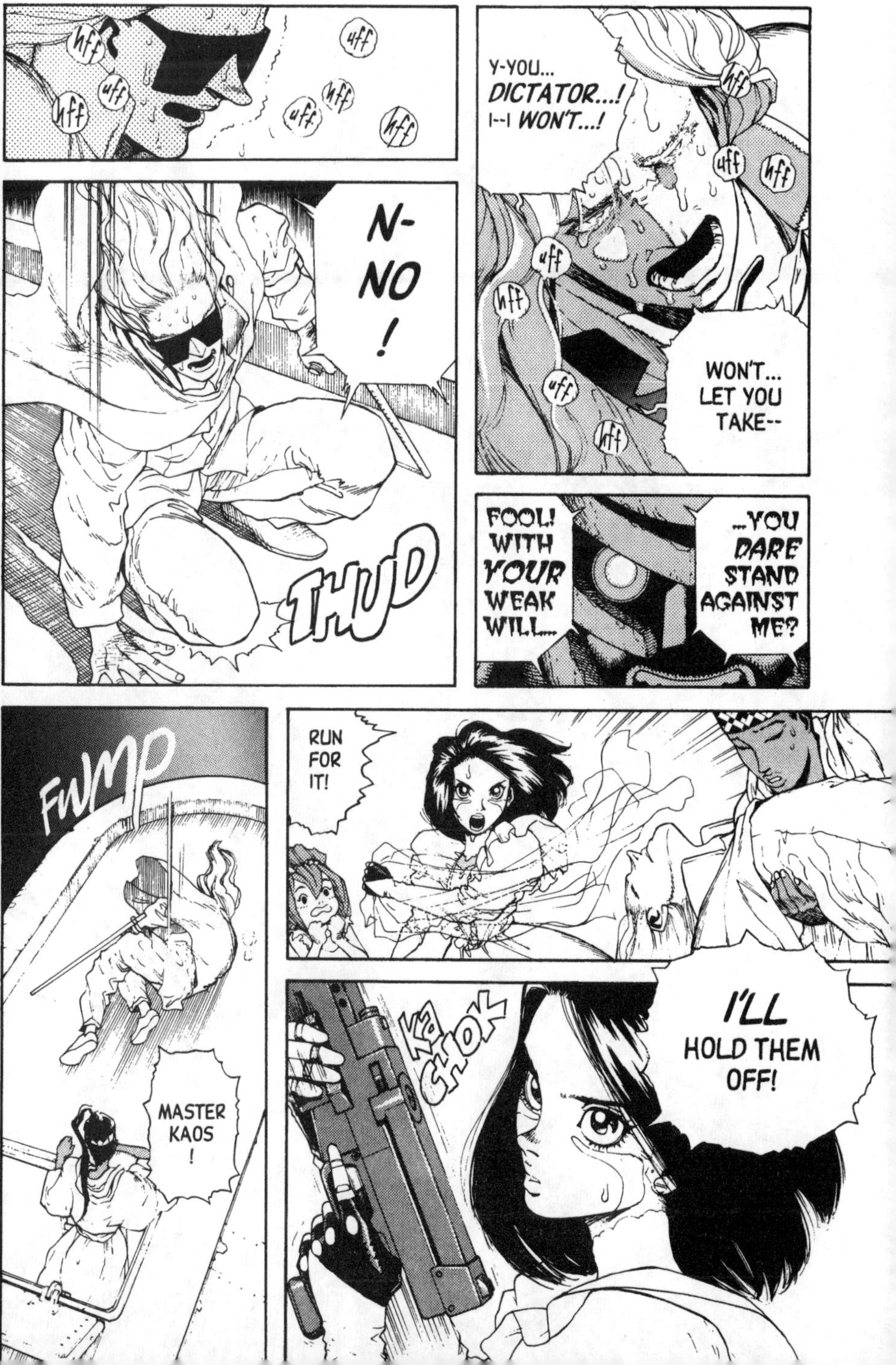
hff
uff
hff
uff
hff
uff
hff
Y-YOU... DICTATOR...! I--I WON'T...!
hff
hff
uff
uff
hff
uff
hff
WON'T... LET YOU TAKE--
N-NO!
THUD
FOOL! WITH YOUR WEAK WILL...
...YOU DARE STAND AGAINST ME?
FWMP
MASTER KAOS!
RUN FOR IT!
KA CHOK
I'LL HOLD THEM OFF!

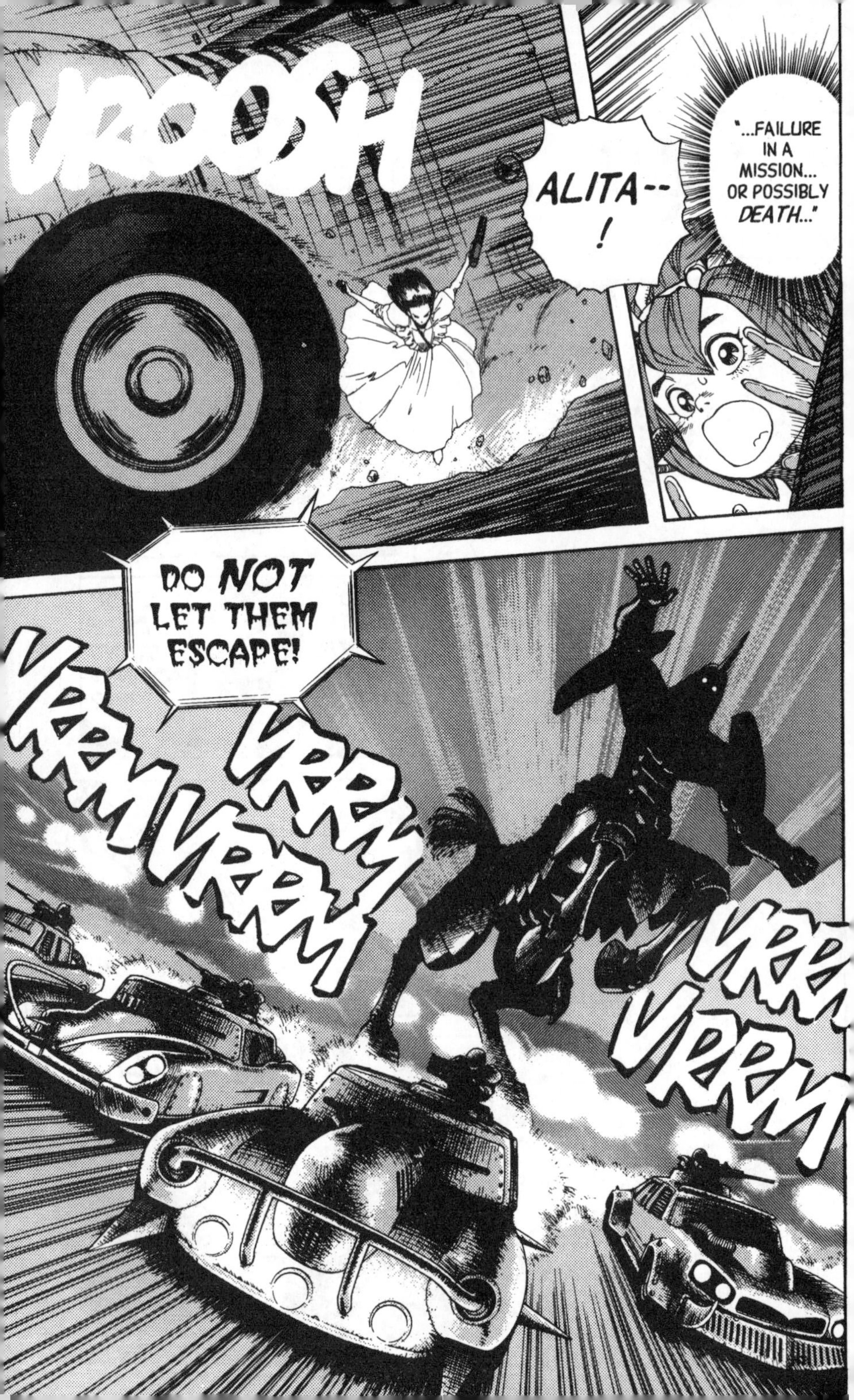
VROOSH
ALITA-- !
"...FAILURE IN A MISSION... OR POSSIBLY DEATH..."
DO NOT LET THEM ESCAPE!
VRRM VRRM VRRM
VRRM VRRM

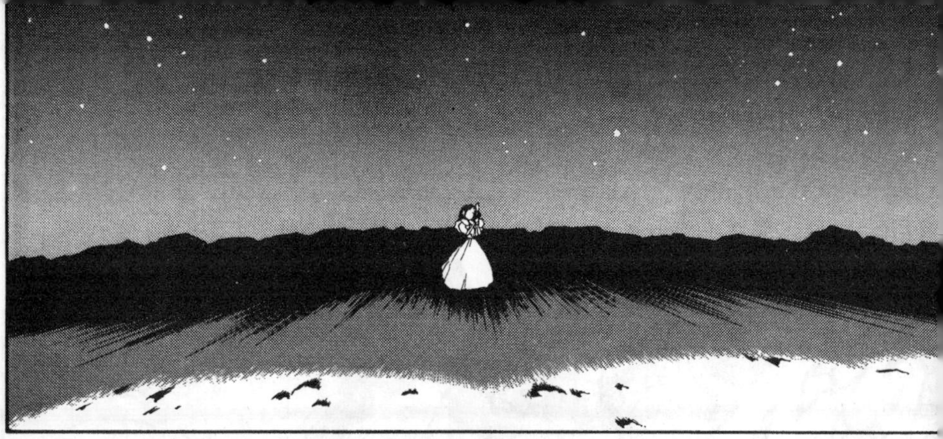

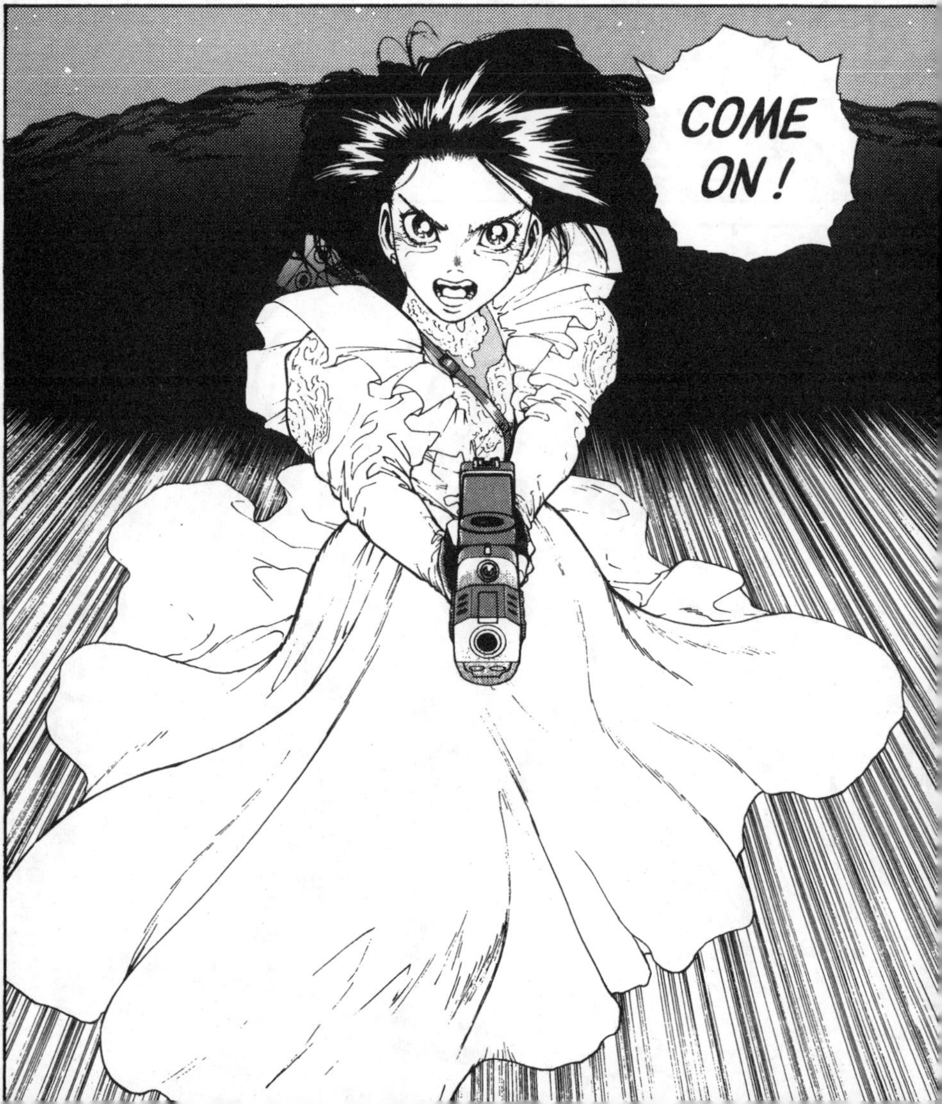
COME ON!

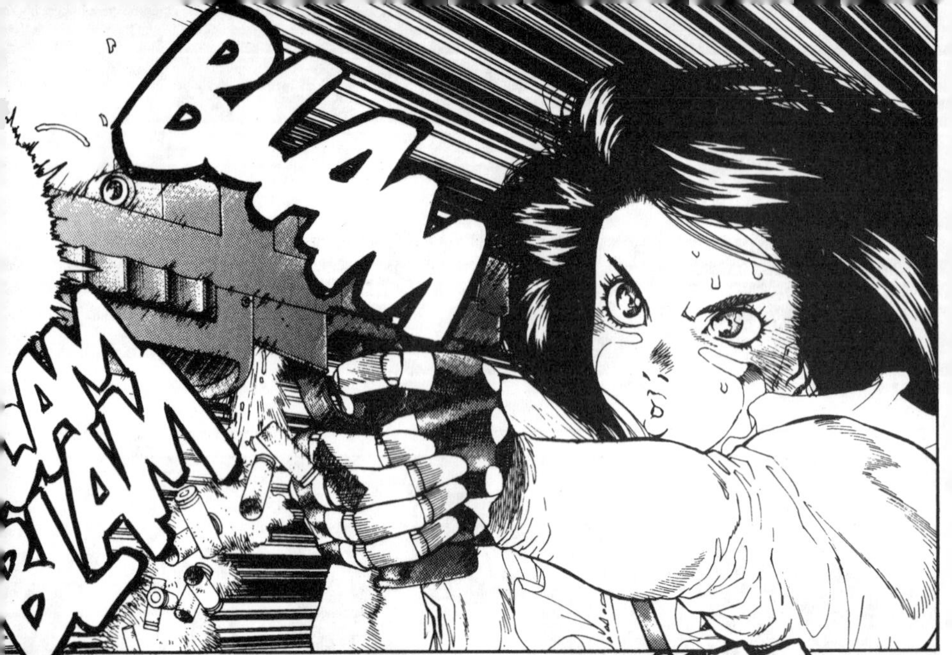
BLAM
BLAM
BLAM
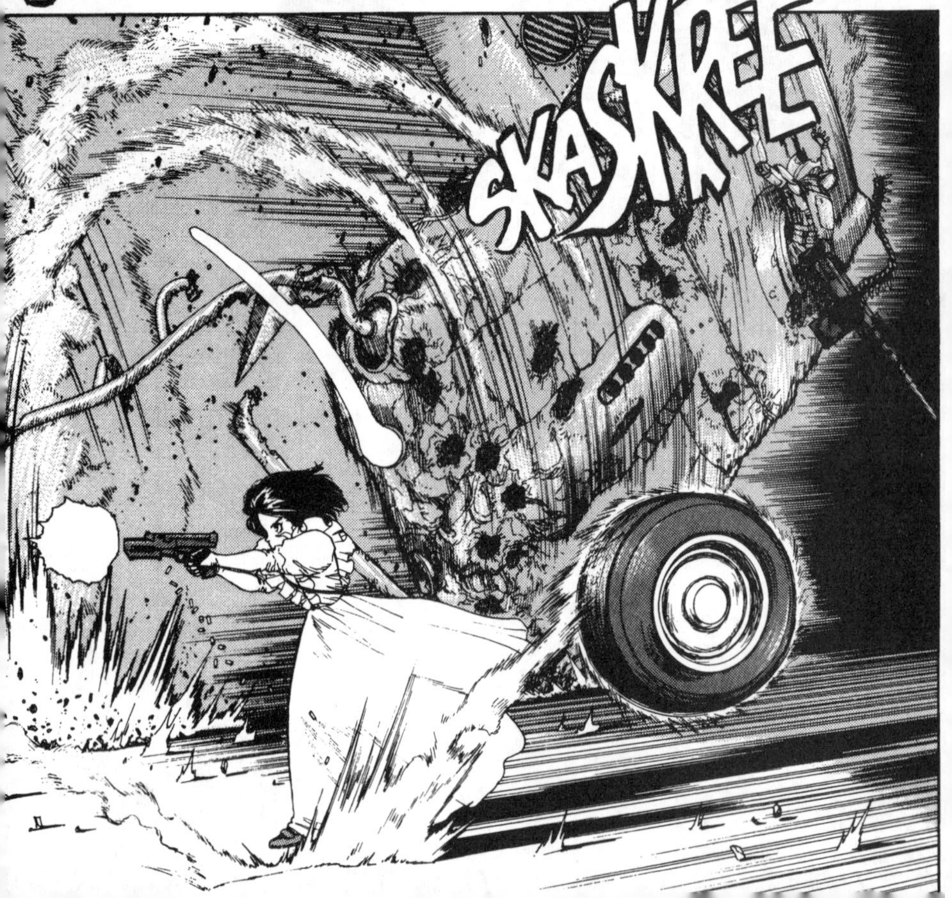
SKASKREE

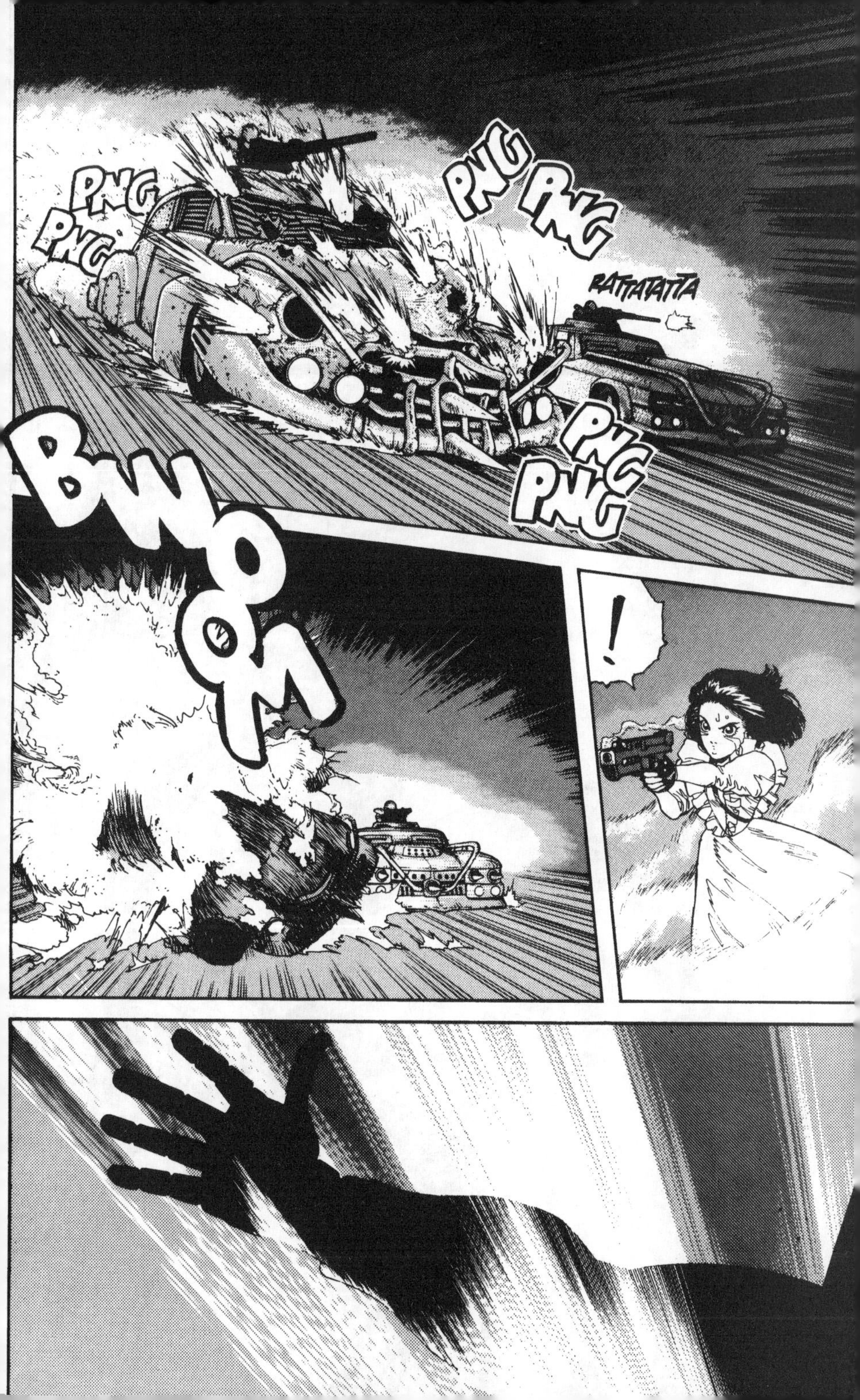
PNG PNG
PNG PNG
RATTATATTA
PNG PNG
BWOOM
!

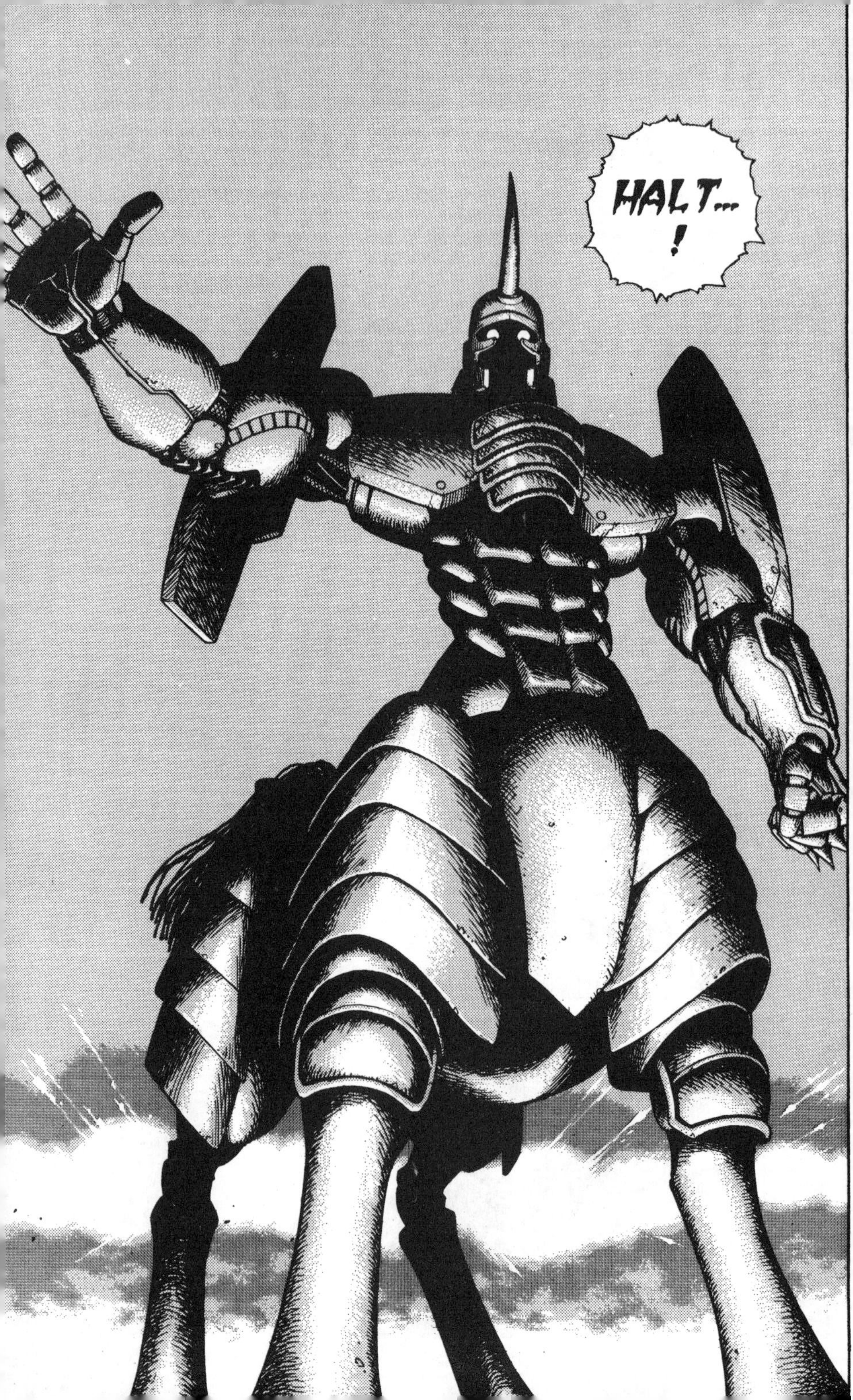
HALT... !

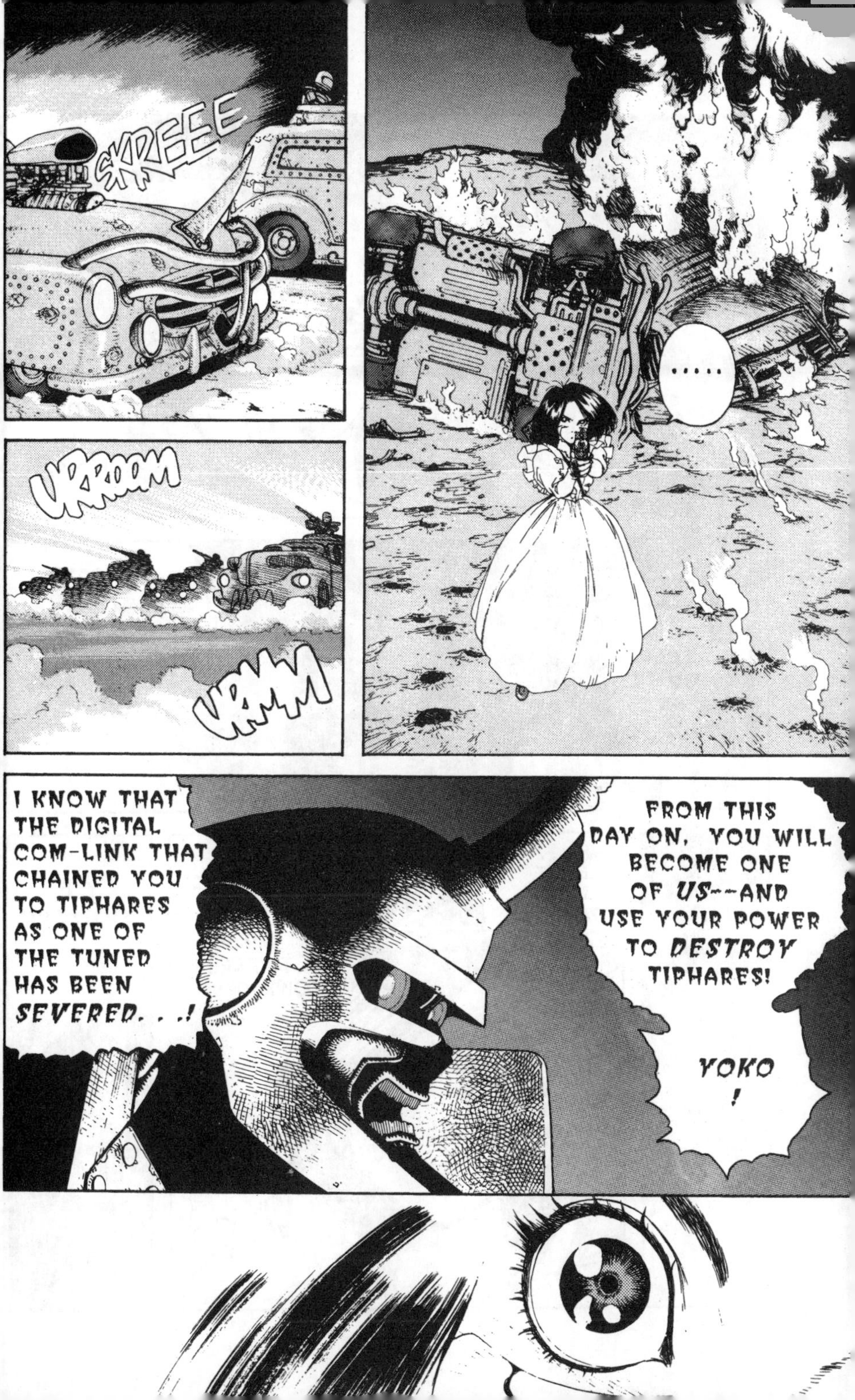
SKREEE
.....
VRAROOM
VRAM
I KNOW THAT THE DIGITAL COM-LINK THAT CHAINED YOU TO TIPHARES AS ONE OF THE TUNED HAS BEEN SEVERED. . .!
FROM THIS DAY ON, YOU WILL BECOME ONE OF US--AND USE YOUR POWER TO DESTROY TIPHARES!
YOKO !

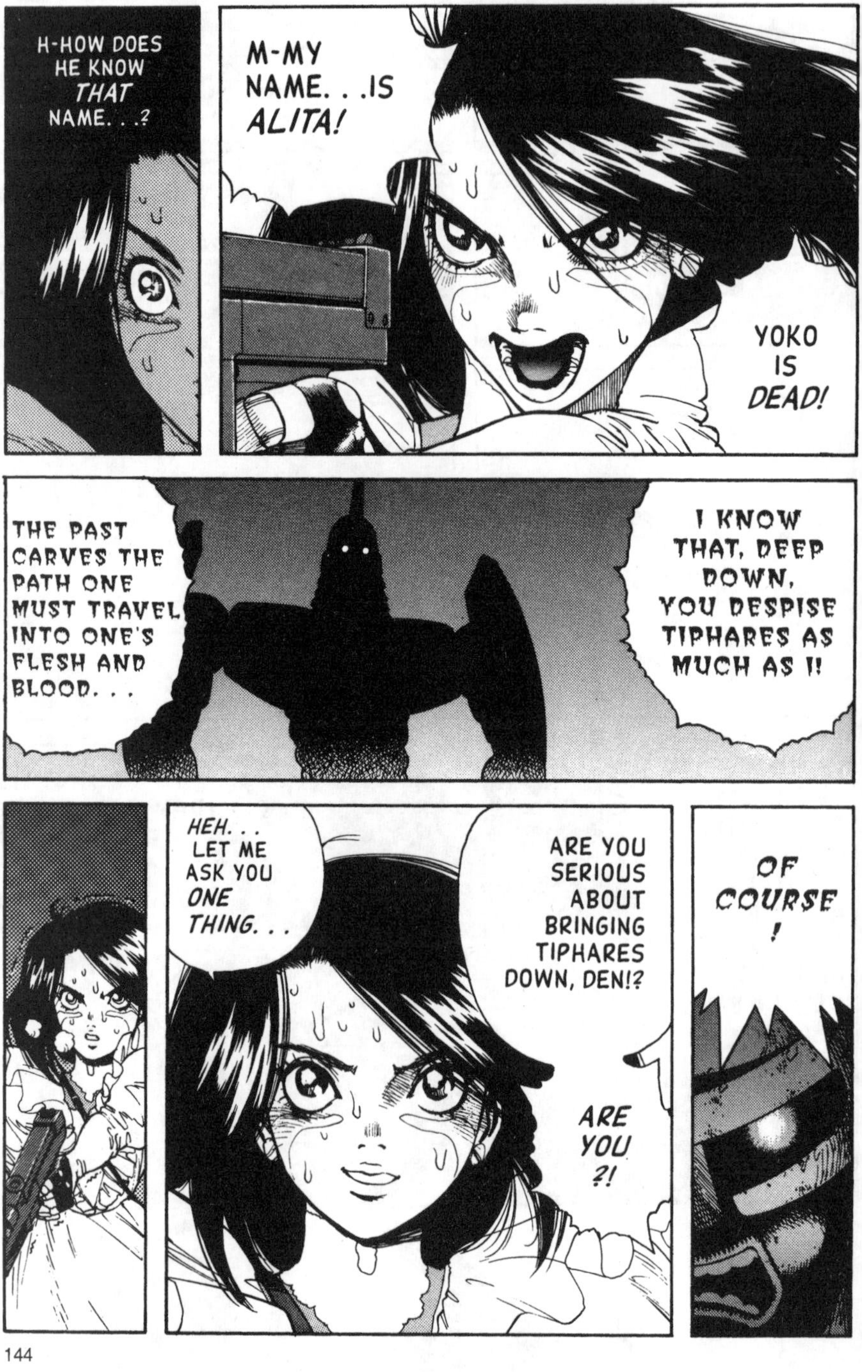
H-HOW DOES HE KNOW *THAT* NAME. . .?
M-MY NAME. . .IS *ALITA!*
YOKO IS *DEAD!*
THE PAST CARVES THE PATH ONE MUST TRAVEL INTO ONE'S FLESH AND BLOOD. . .
I KNOW THAT, DEEP DOWN, YOU DESPISE TIPHARES AS MUCH AS I!
HEH. . . LET ME ASK YOU *ONE THING. . .*
ARE YOU SERIOUS ABOUT BRINGING TIPHARES DOWN, DEN!?
ARE YOU ?!
OF COURSE !

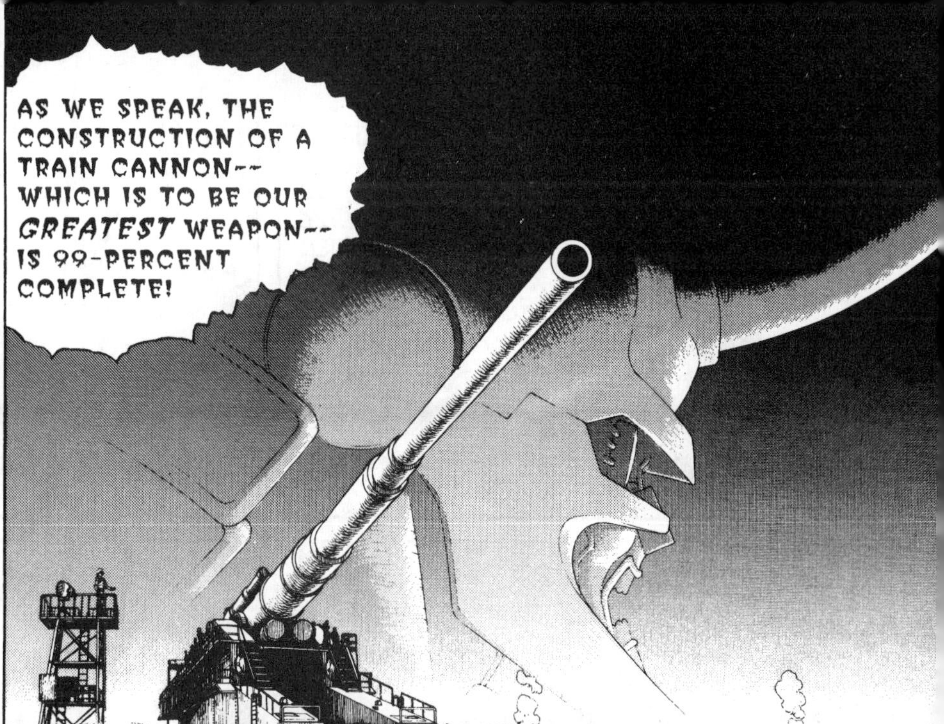
AS WE SPEAK, THE CONSTRUCTION OF A TRAIN CANNON-- WHICH IS TO BE OUR *GREATEST* WEAPON-- IS 99-PERCENT COMPLETE!
WITH IT, WE WILL SHOOT DOWN THE 4000-METER-HIGH SHAFT SUPPORTING TIPHARES.
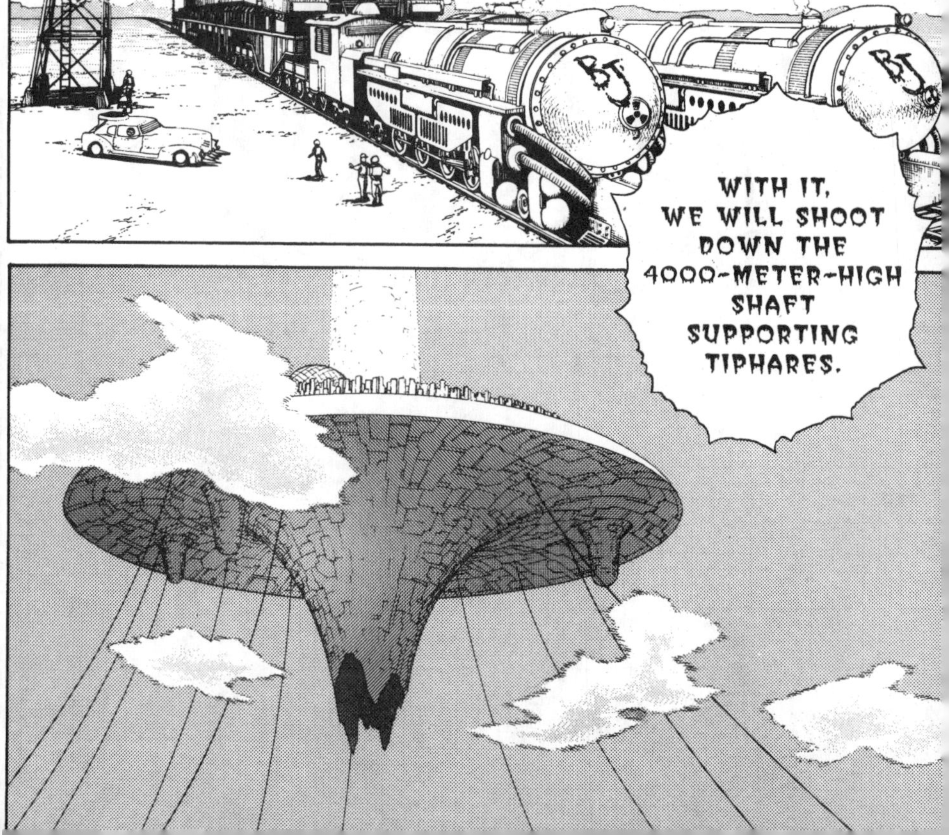

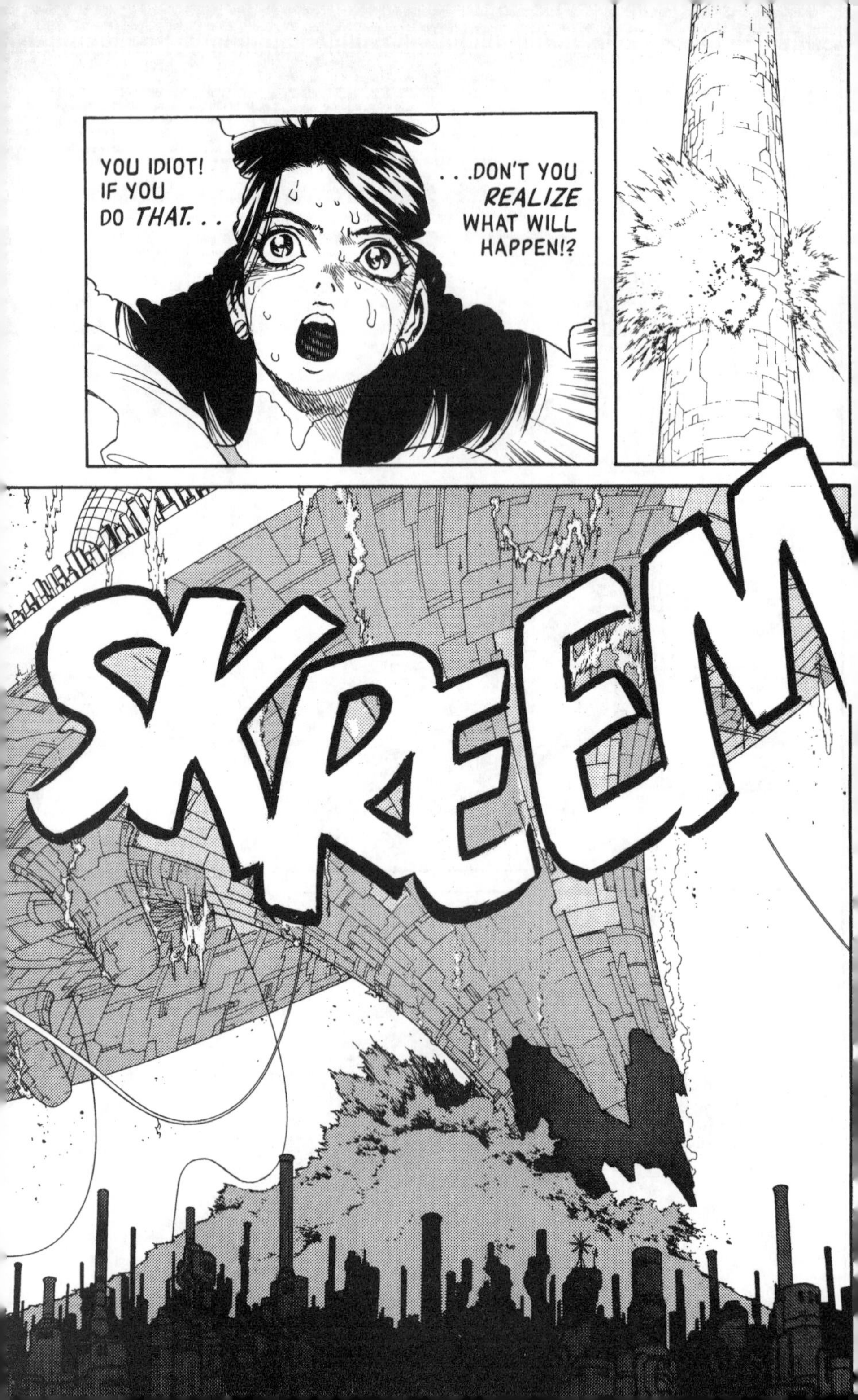
YOU IDIOT! IF YOU DO *THAT*. . .
. . .DON'T YOU *REALIZE* WHAT WILL HAPPEN!?
SKREEM

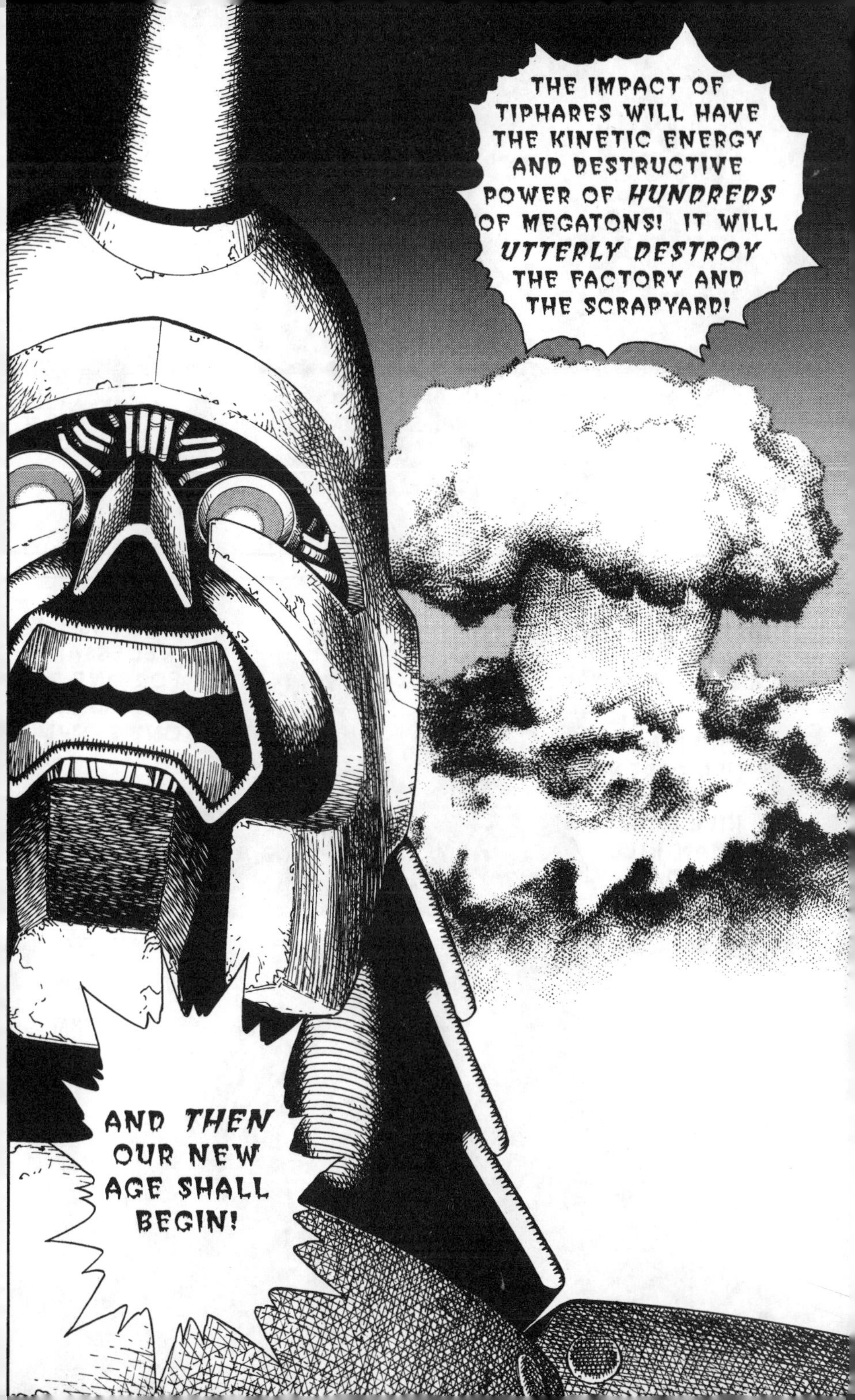
THE IMPACT OF TIPHARES WILL HAVE THE KINETIC ENERGY AND DESTRUCTIVE POWER OF HUNDREDS OF MEGATONS! IT WILL UTTERLY DESTROY THE FACTORY AND THE SCRAPYARD!
AND THEN OUR NEW AGE SHALL BEGIN!

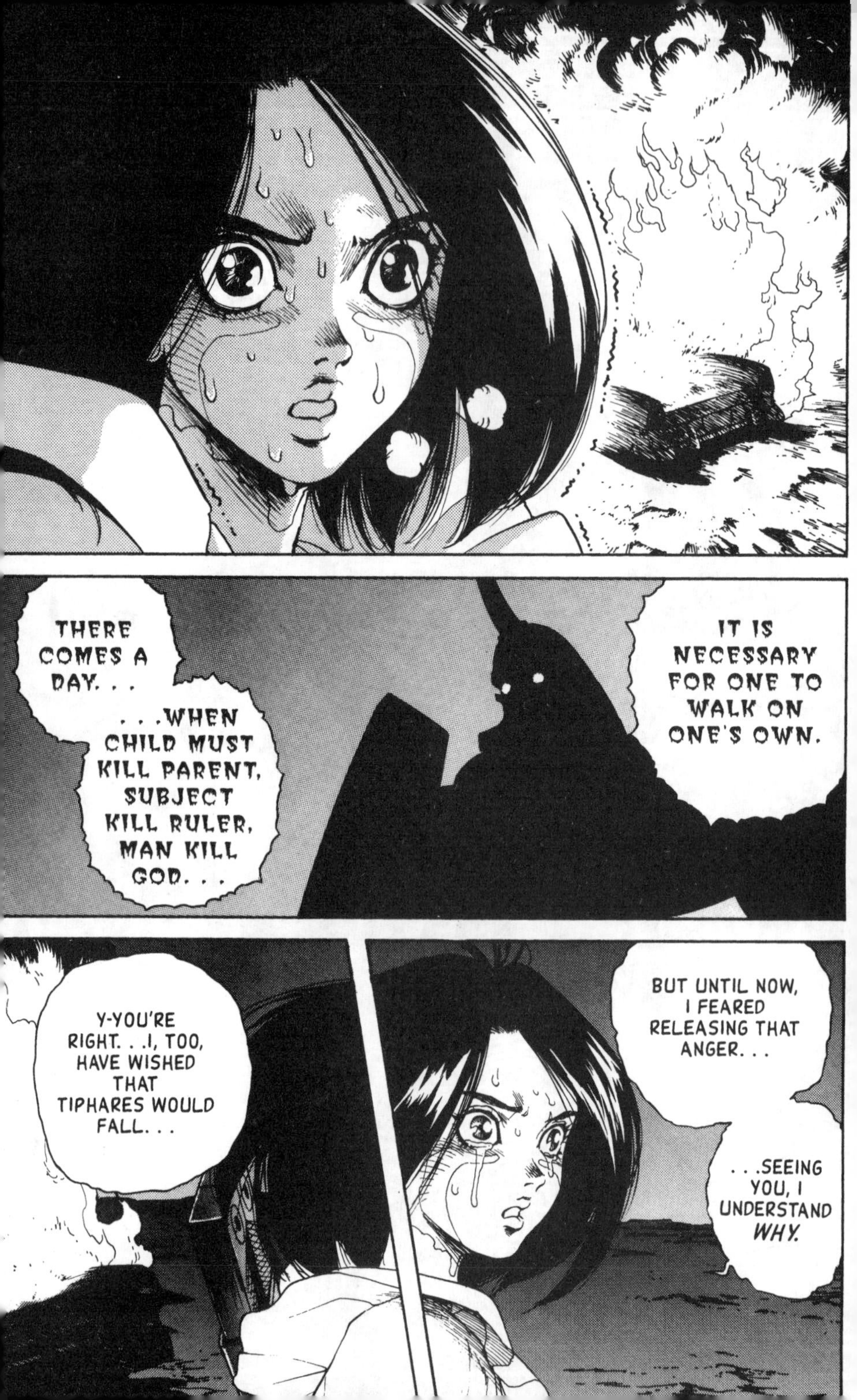
THERE COMES A DAY. . .
. . .WHEN CHILD MUST KILL PARENT, SUBJECT KILL RULER, MAN KILL GOD. . .
IT IS NECESSARY FOR ONE TO WALK ON ONE'S OWN.
Y-YOU'RE RIGHT. . .I, TOO, HAVE WISHED THAT TIPHARES WOULD FALL. . .
BUT UNTIL NOW, I FEARED RELEASING THAT ANGER. . .
. . .SEEING YOU, I UNDERSTAND WHY.

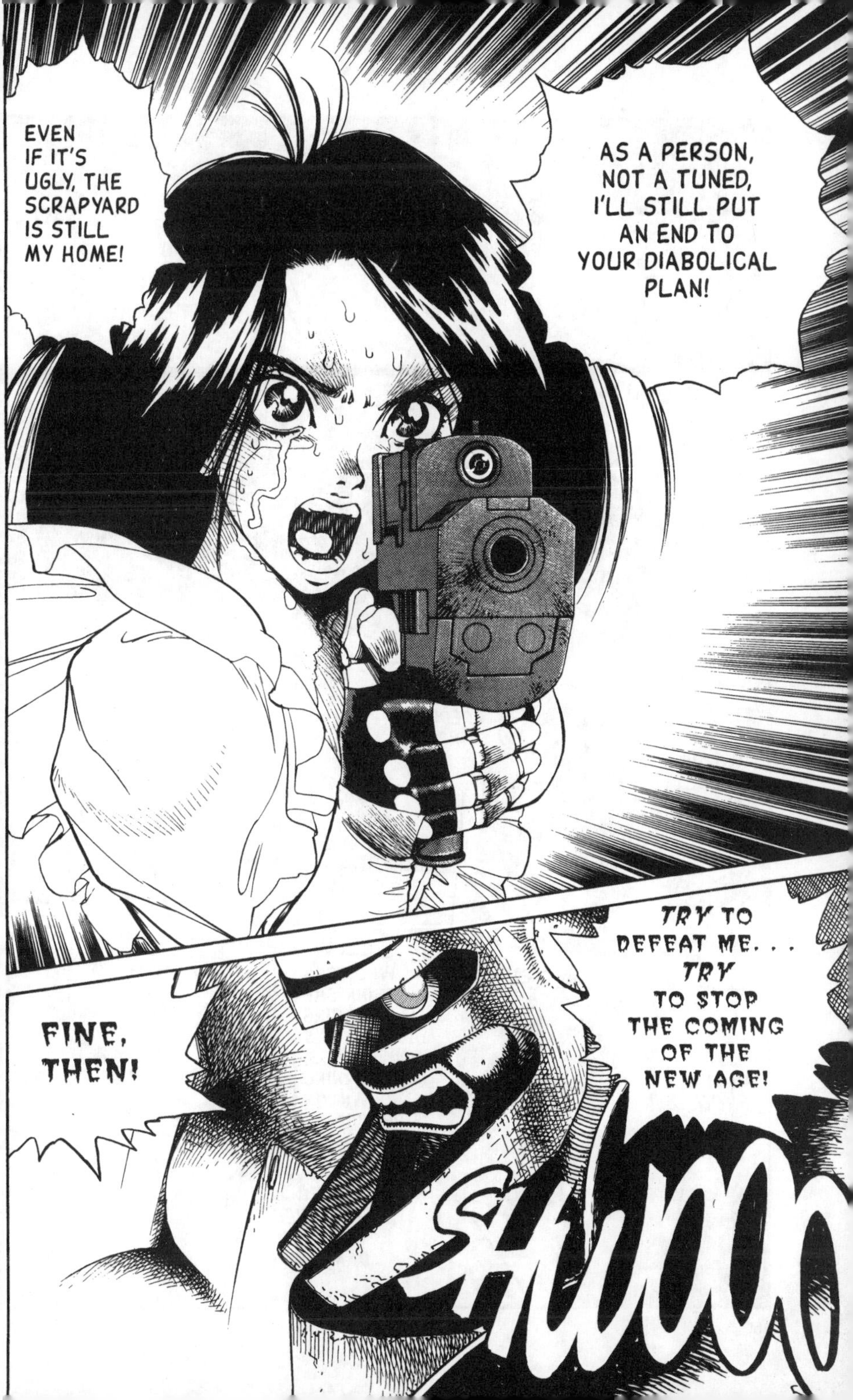
EVEN IF IT'S UGLY, THE SCRAPYARD IS STILL MY HOME!
AS A PERSON, NOT A TUNED, I'LL STILL PUT AN END TO YOUR DIABOLICAL PLAN!
FINE, THEN!
TRY TO DEFEAT ME. . . TRY TO STOP THE COMING OF THE NEW AGE!

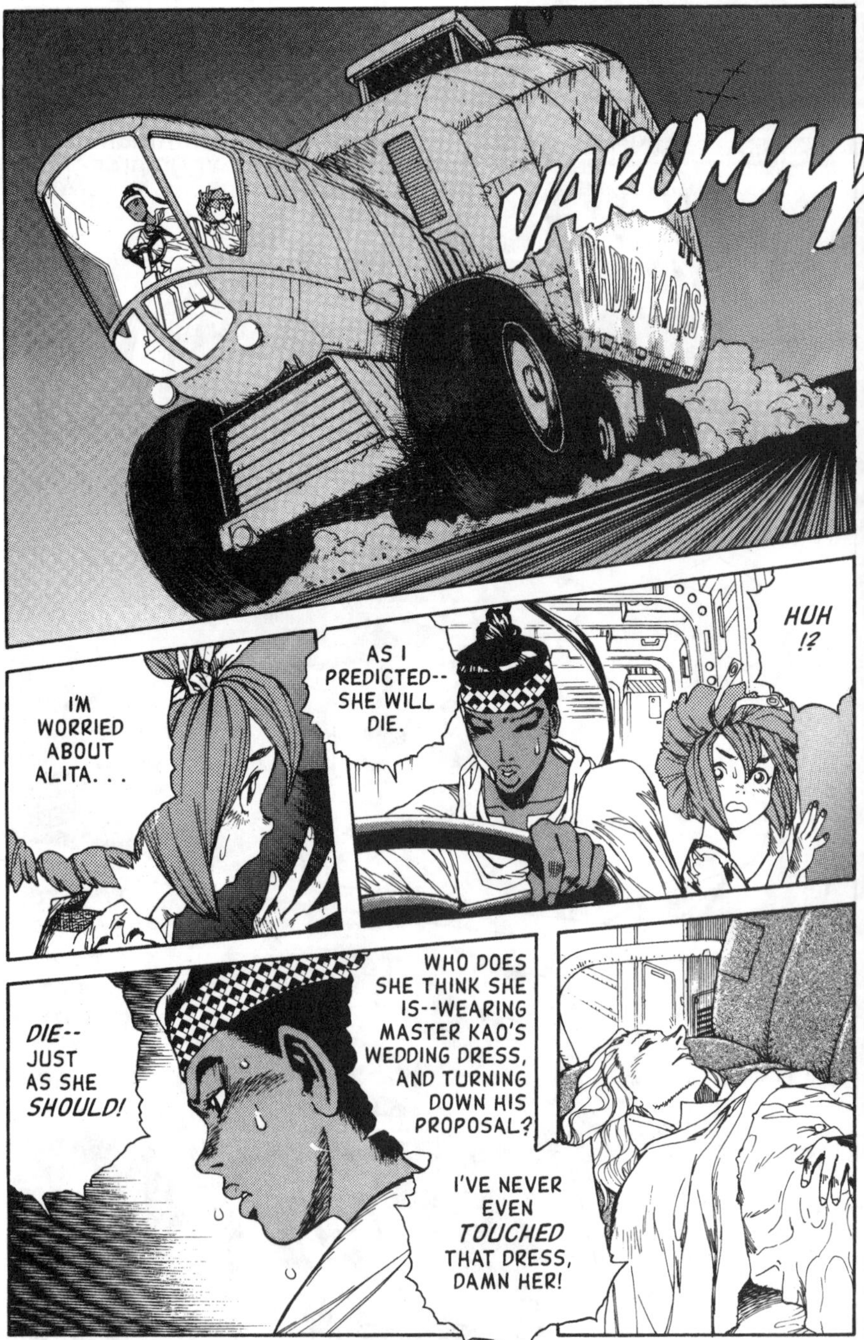
VARUMM
RADIO KAOS
I'M WORRIED ABOUT ALITA. . .
AS I PREDICTED-- SHE WILL DIE.
HUH !?
DIE-- JUST AS SHE *SHOULD!*
WHO DOES SHE THINK SHE IS--WEARING MASTER KAO'S WEDDING DRESS, AND TURNING DOWN HIS PROPOSAL?
I'VE NEVER EVEN *TOUCHED* THAT DRESS, DAMN HER!

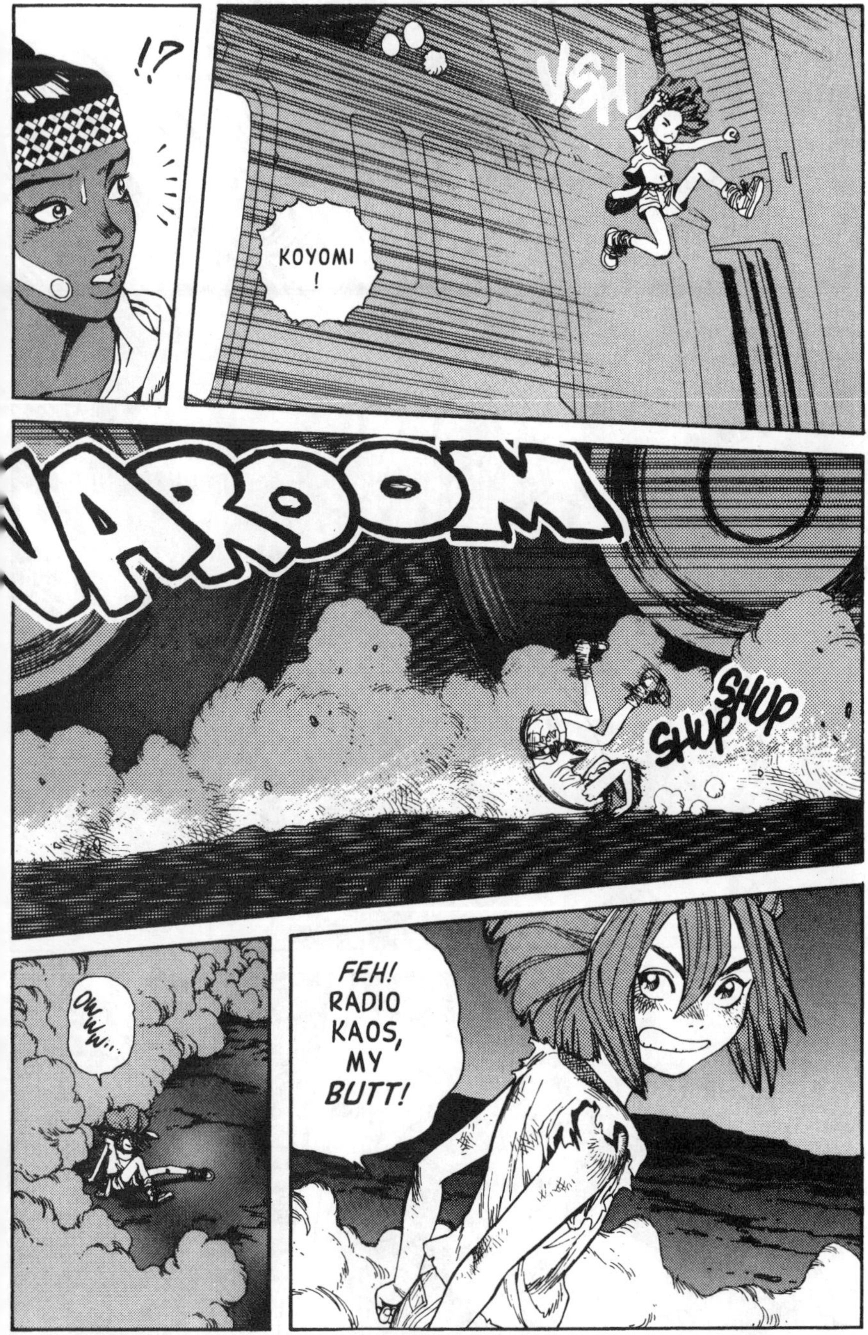
!?
VSH
KOYOMI!
VAROOM
SHUP SHUP
OWWW...
FEH! RADIO KAOS, MY BUTT!

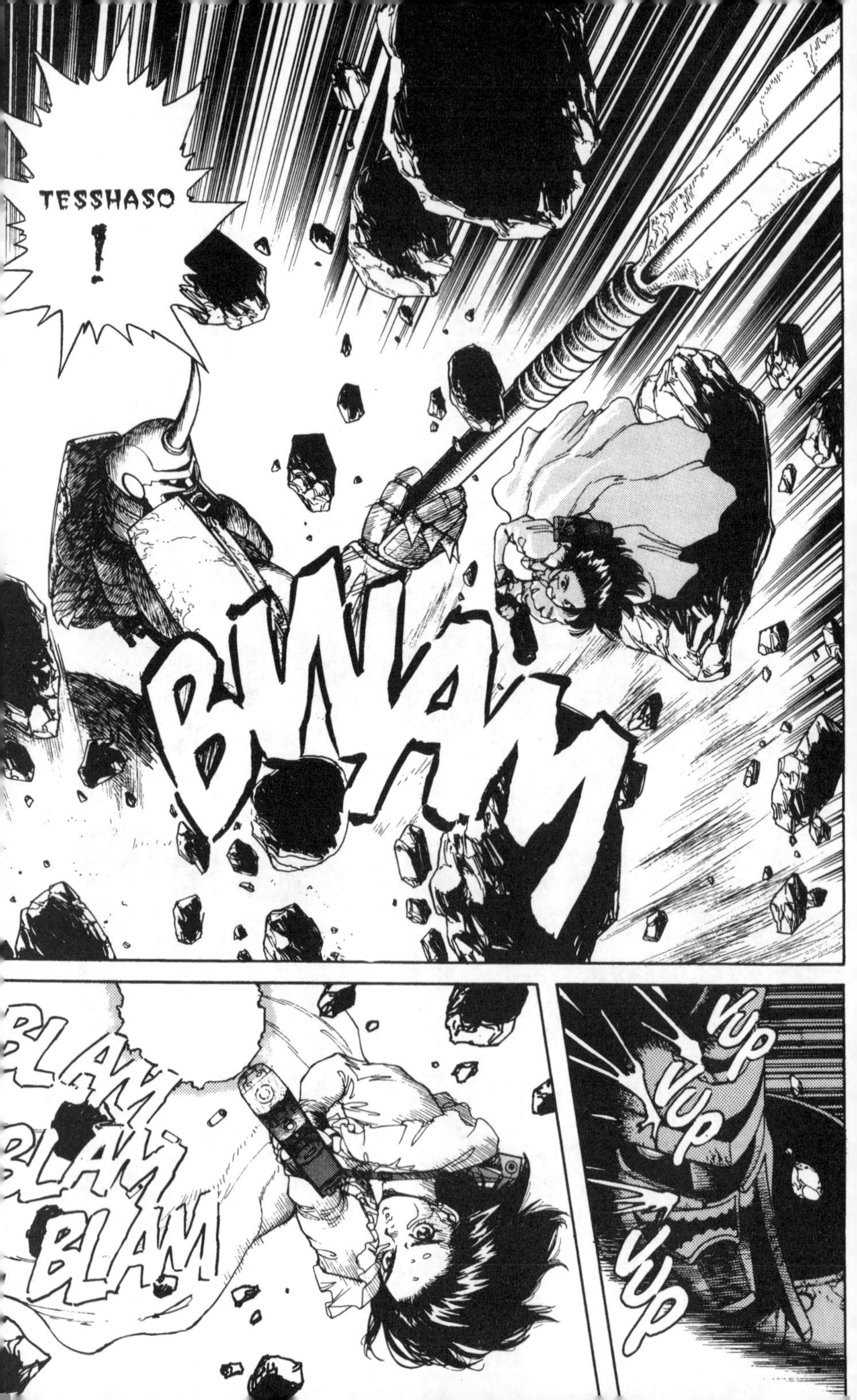
TESSHASO !
BWAM
BLAM
BLAM
BLAM
VUP
VUP
VUP

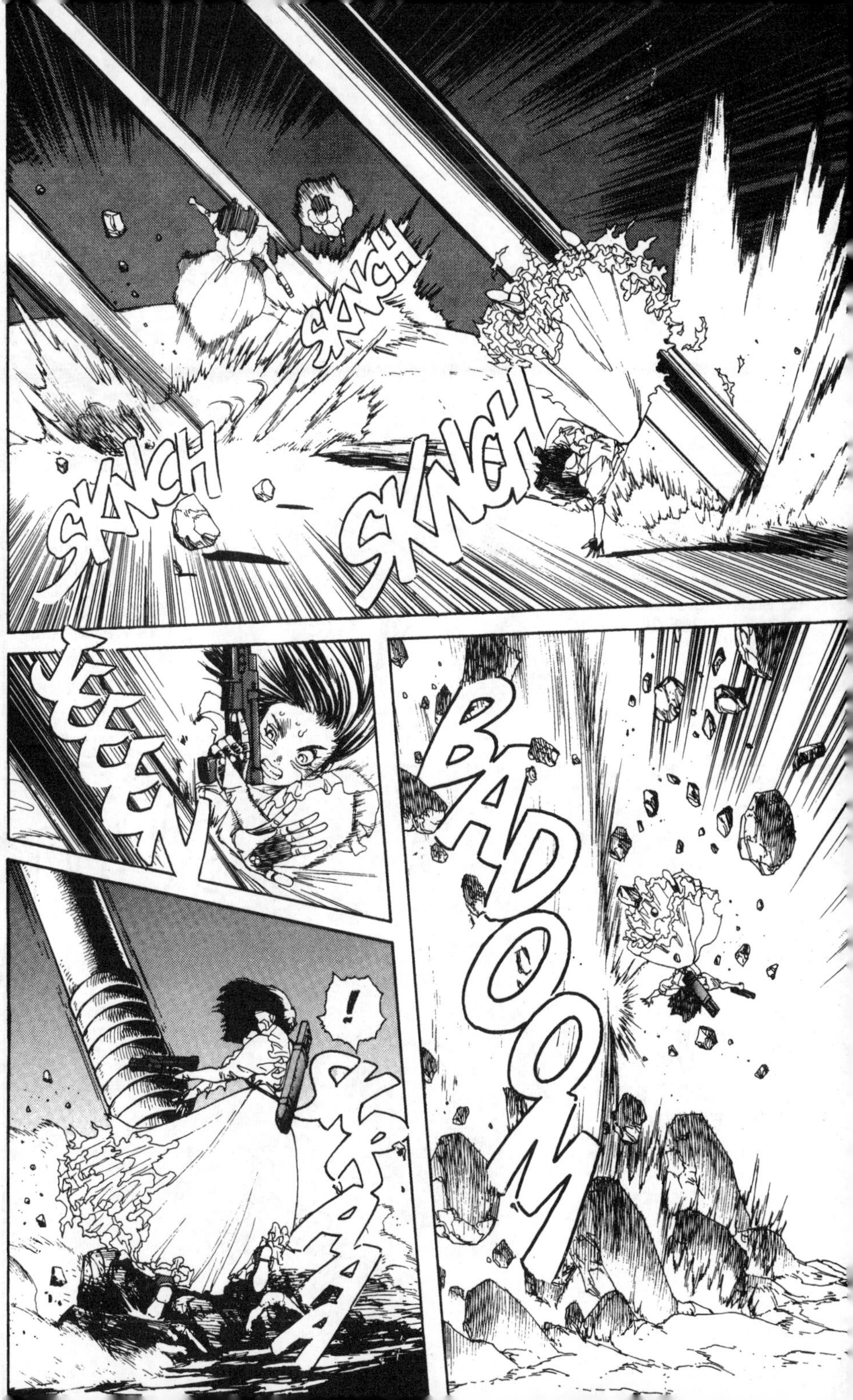
SKNCH
SKNCH
SKNCH
SKNCH
JEEEEN
!
SKRAAA
BADOOOM

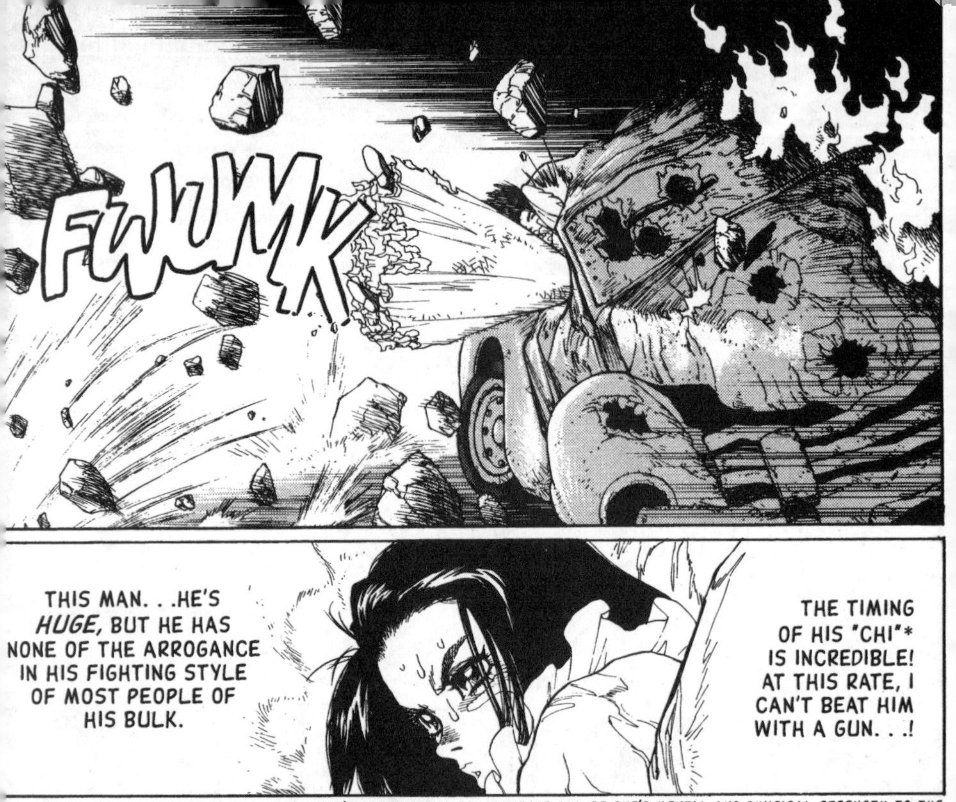
FWUMK
THIS MAN. . .HE'S *HUGE,* BUT HE HAS NONE OF THE ARROGANCE IN HIS FIGHTING STYLE OF MOST PEOPLE OF HIS BULK.
THE TIMING OF HIS "CHI"* IS INCREDIBLE! AT THIS RATE, I CAN'T BEAT HIM WITH A GUN. . .!

*CHI: THE ABILITY TO READ AN OPPONENT'S ACTIONS AND CONCENTRATE ALL OF ONE'S MENTAL AND PHYSICAL STRENGTH TO THE ONE POINT THAT WILL BE MOST EFFECTIVE. A WELL-FOCUSED CHI BRINGS FORTH INCREDIBLE POWER. FOR MORE ON CHI, SEE THE *BATTLE ANGEL ALITA* GRAPHIC NOVELS *KILLING ANGEL* AND *ANGEL OF VICTORY.*

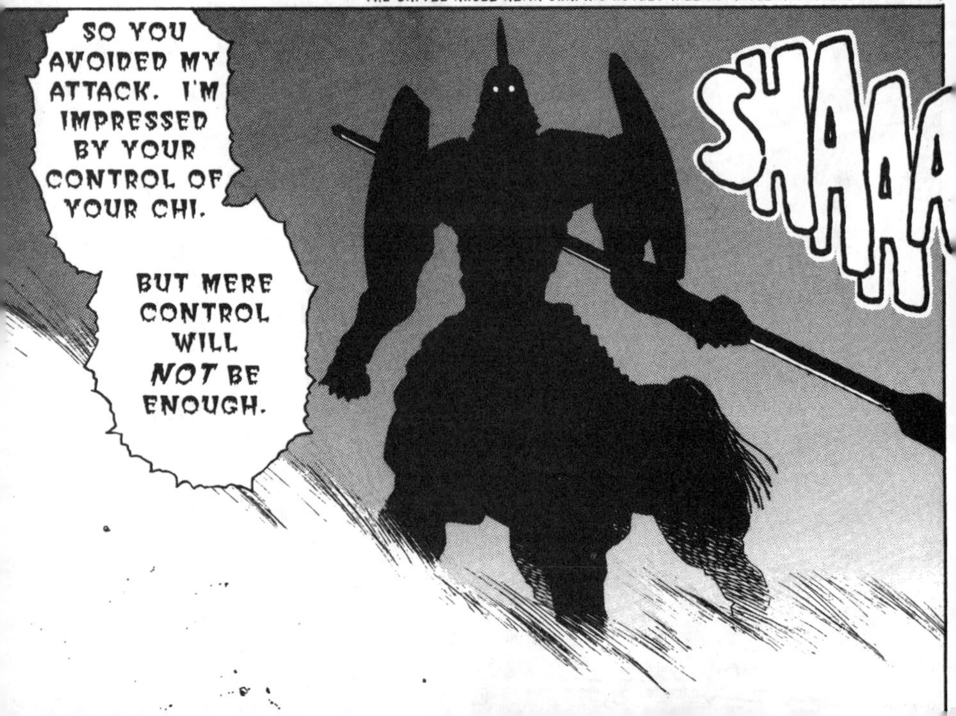
SO YOU AVOIDED MY ATTACK. I'M IMPRESSED BY YOUR CONTROL OF YOUR CHI.
BUT MERE CONTROL WILL *NOT* BE ENOUGH.
SHAAA

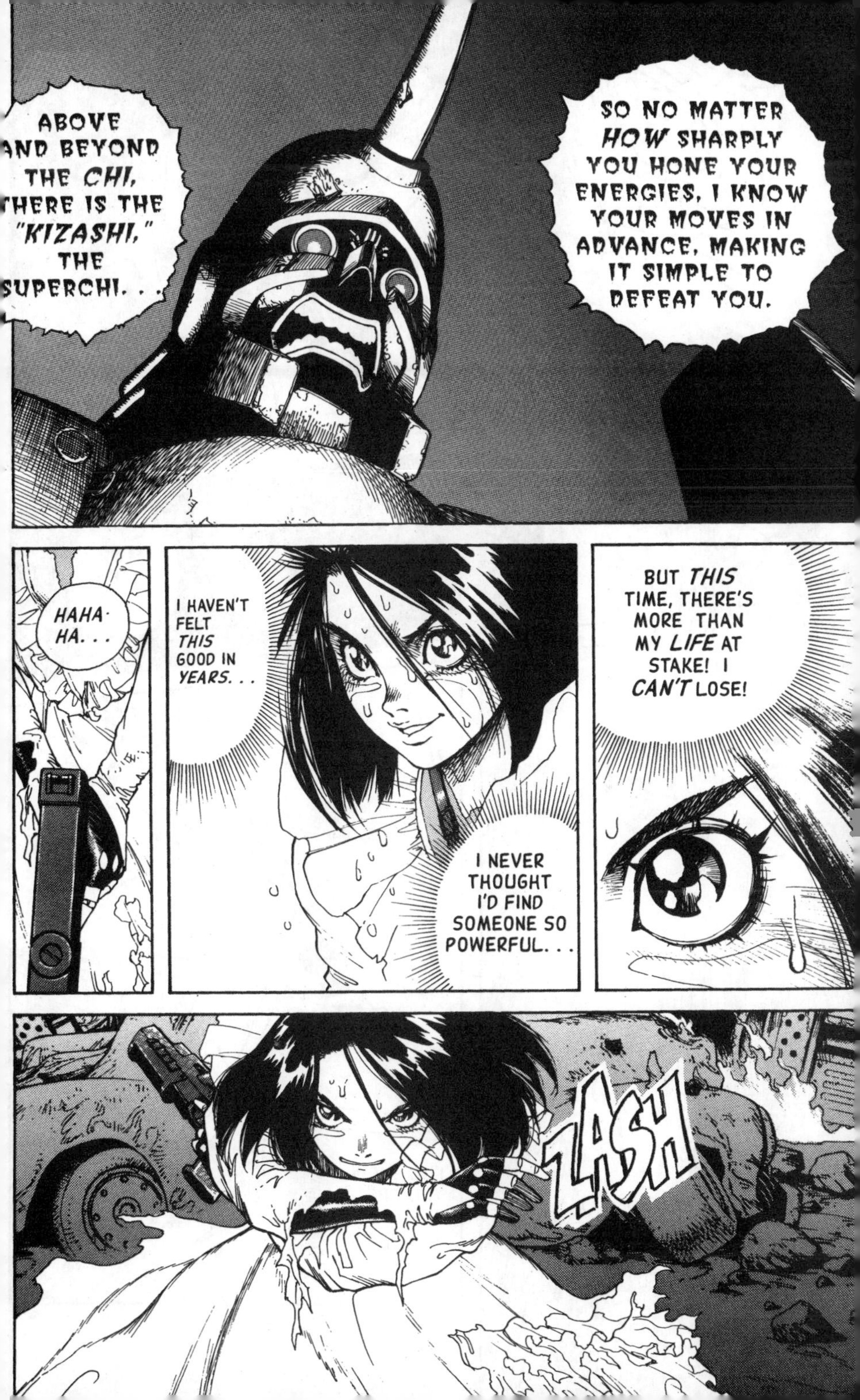
ABOVE AND BEYOND THE *CHI*, THERE IS THE "*KIZASHI*," THE SUPERCHI. . .
SO NO MATTER *HOW* SHARPLY YOU HONE YOUR ENERGIES, I KNOW YOUR MOVES IN ADVANCE, MAKING IT SIMPLE TO DEFEAT YOU.
HAHA-HA. . .
I HAVEN'T FELT *THIS* GOOD IN *YEARS*. . .
I NEVER THOUGHT I'D FIND SOMEONE SO POWERFUL. . .
BUT *THIS* TIME, THERE'S MORE THAN MY *LIFE* AT STAKE! I *CAN'T* LOSE!
ZASH

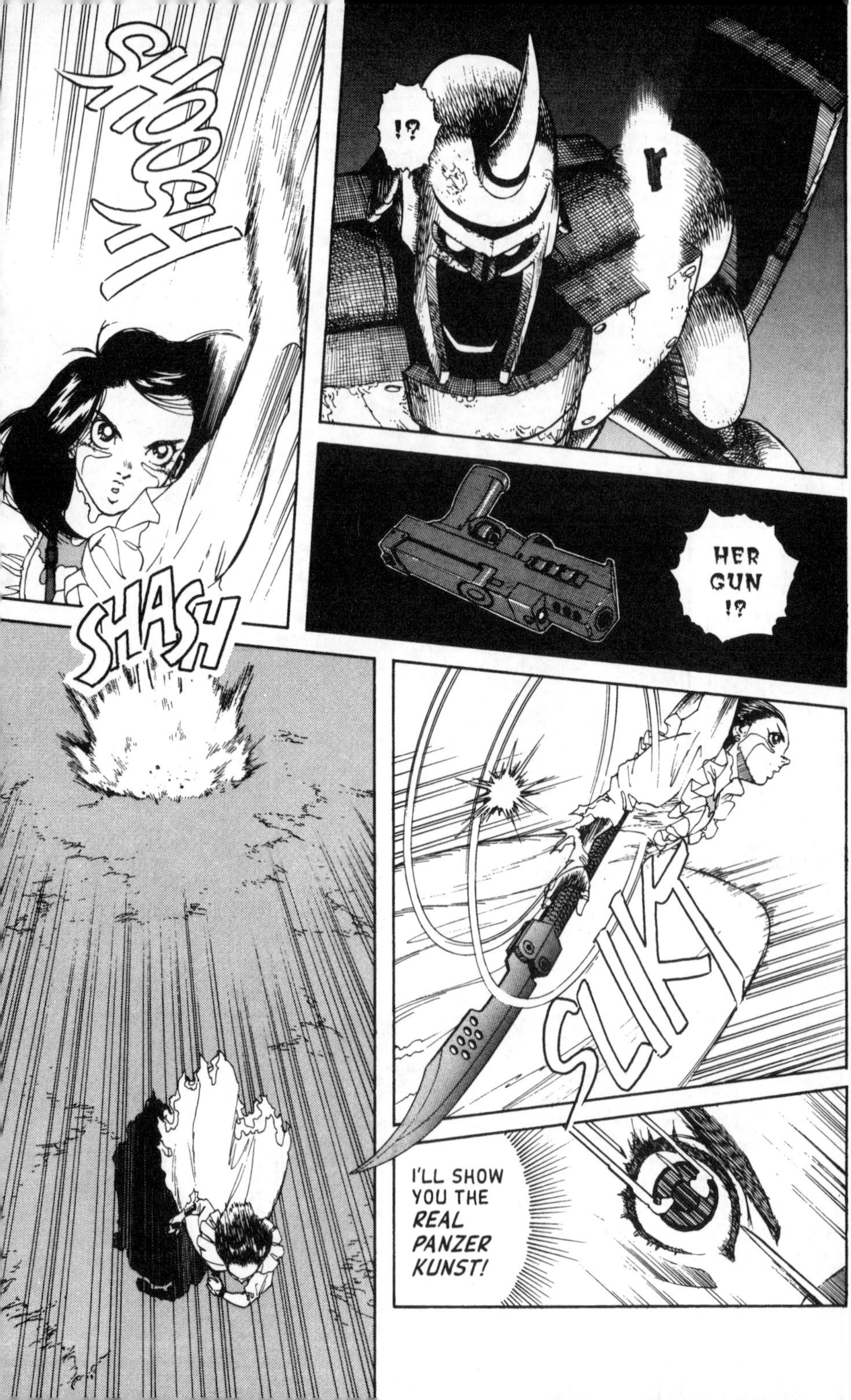
SHOOOSH
!?
r
HER GUN !?
SHASH
SLIK
I'LL SHOW YOU THE *REAL* PANZER KUNST!

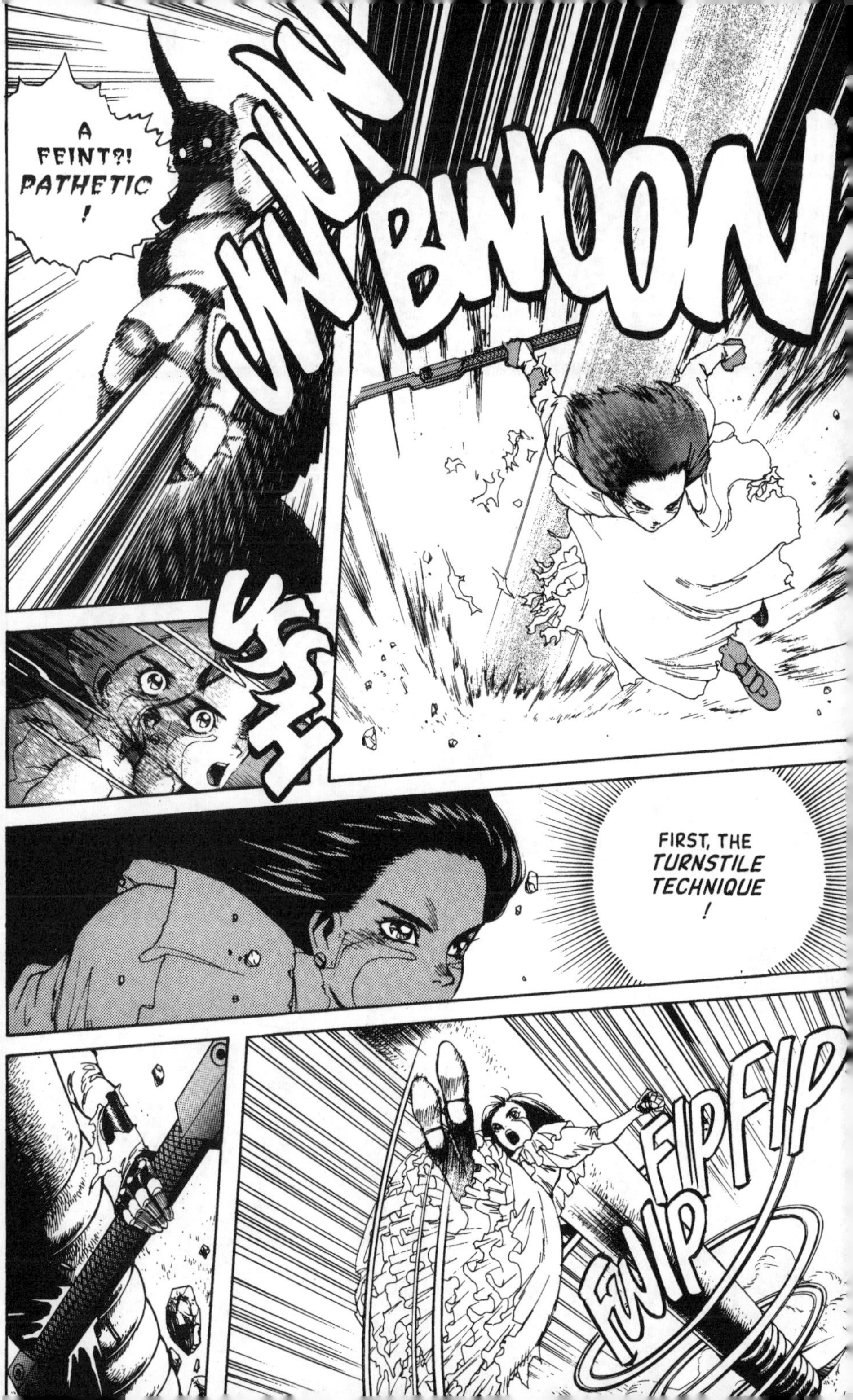
A FEINT?! PATHETIC !
WHUM
WHBMOOM
SWSH
FIRST, THE TURNSTILE TECHNIQUE !
FWIP
FIP FIP

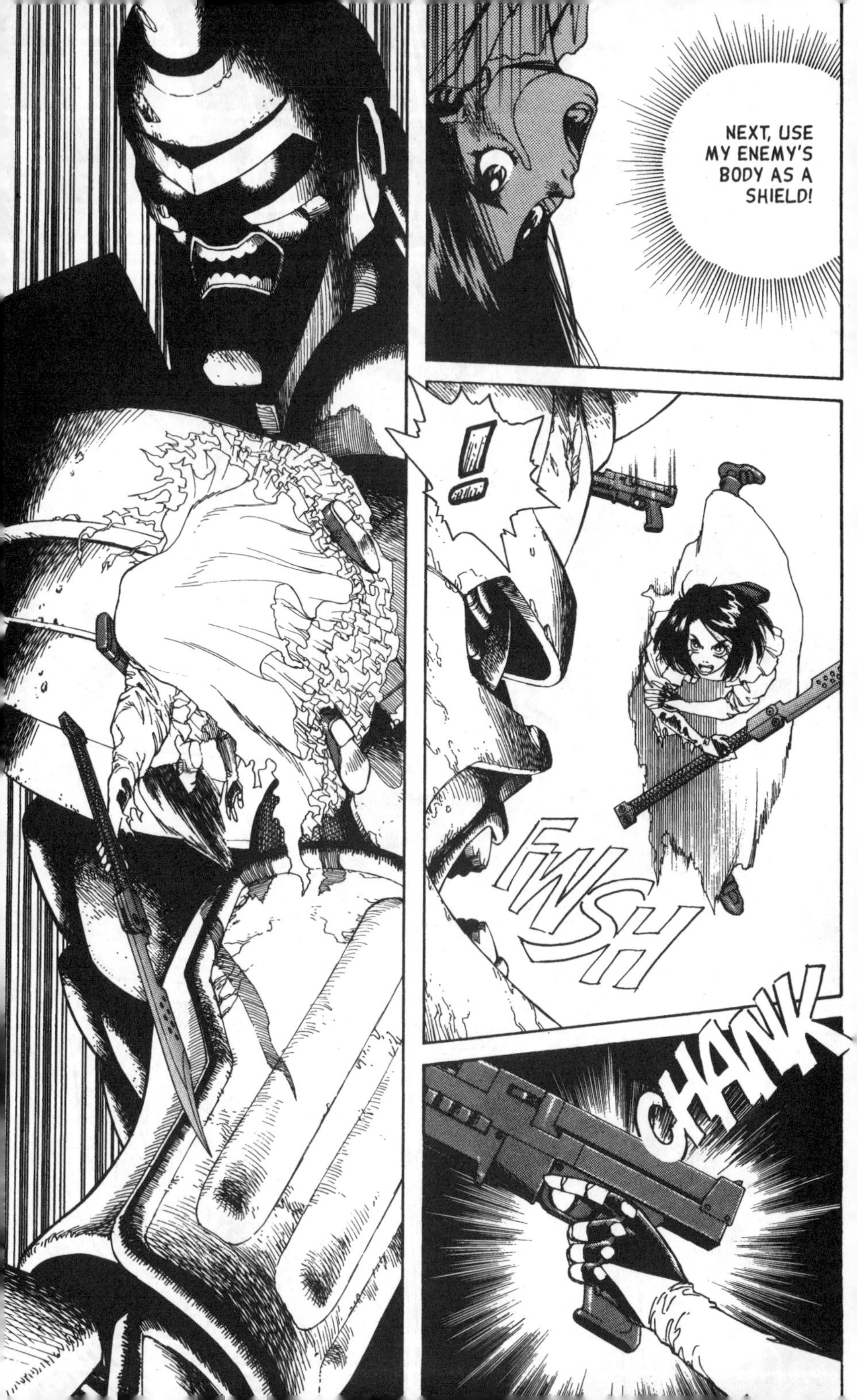

NEXT, USE MY ENEMY'S BODY AS A SHIELD!
!
FWISH
CHANK

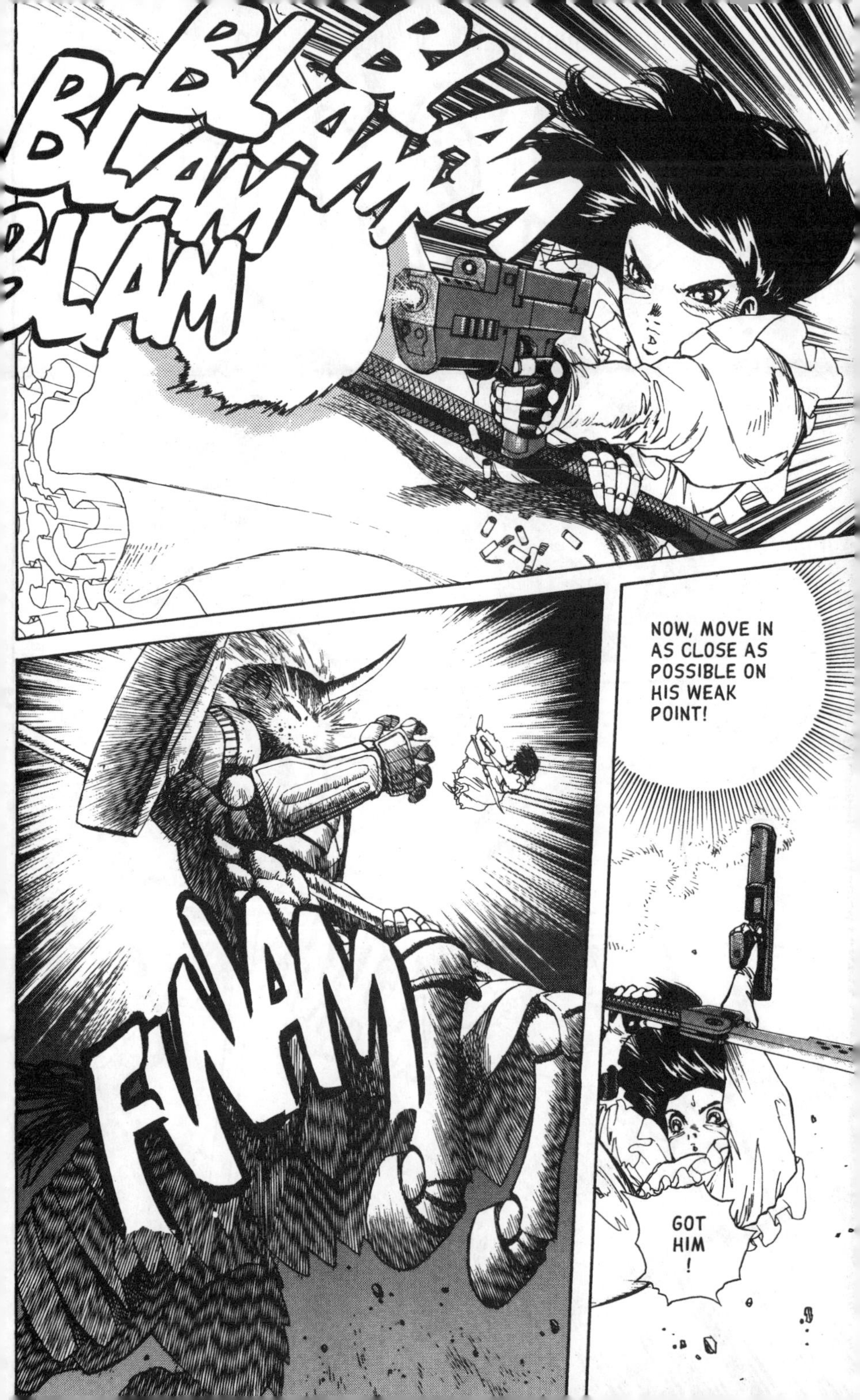
BLBLAMM
BLAM
BLAM
FWAM!
NOW, MOVE IN AS CLOSE AS POSSIBLE ON HIS WEAK POINT!
GOT HIM!

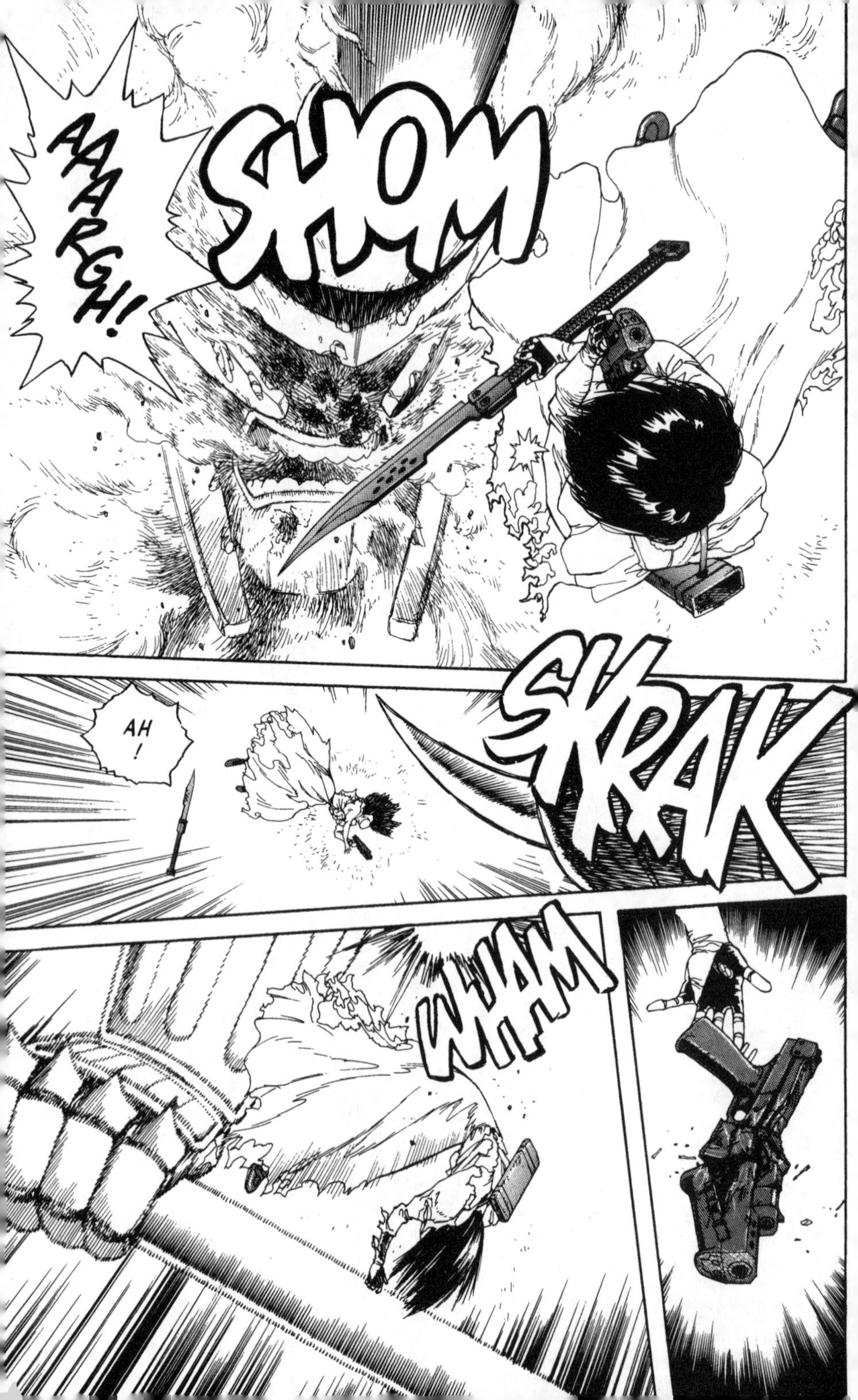
AAARGH!
SHOM
AH!
SKRAK
WHAM

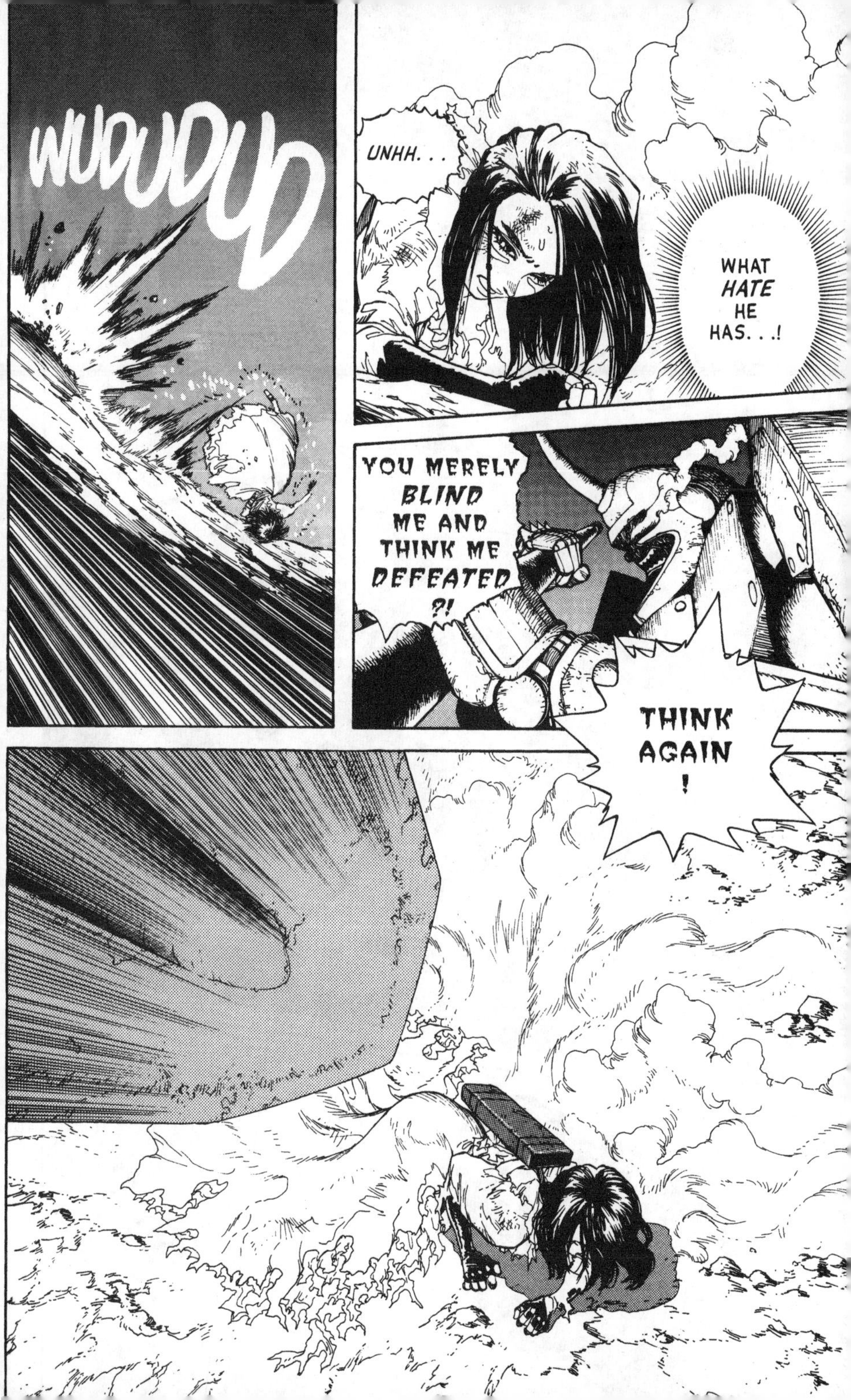
WUDUDUD
UNHH. . .
WHAT HATE HE HAS. . .!
YOU MERELY BLIND ME AND THINK ME DEFEATED ?!
THINK AGAIN !

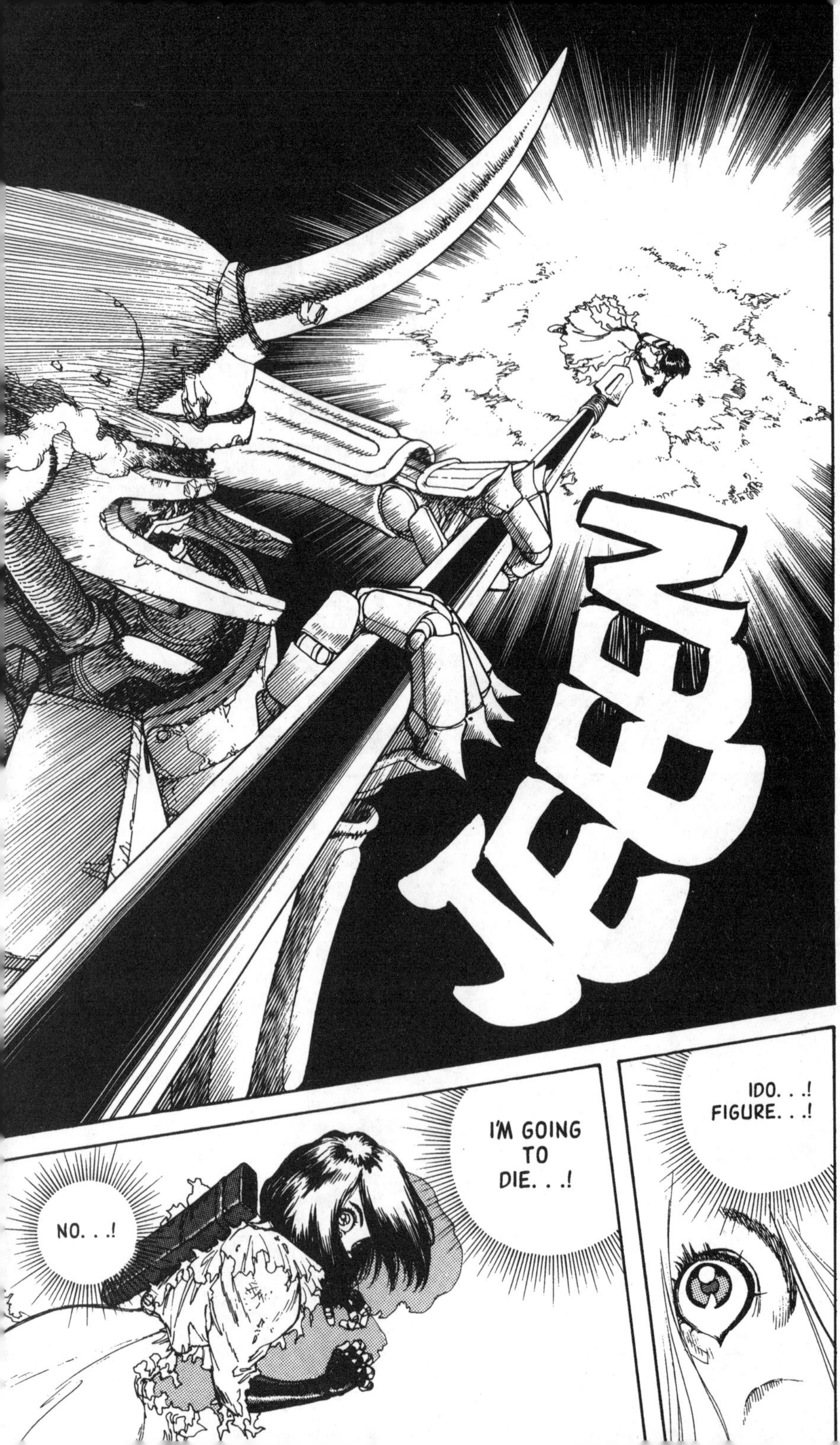
NO. . .!
I'M GOING TO DIE. . .!
IDO. . .! FIGURE. . .!

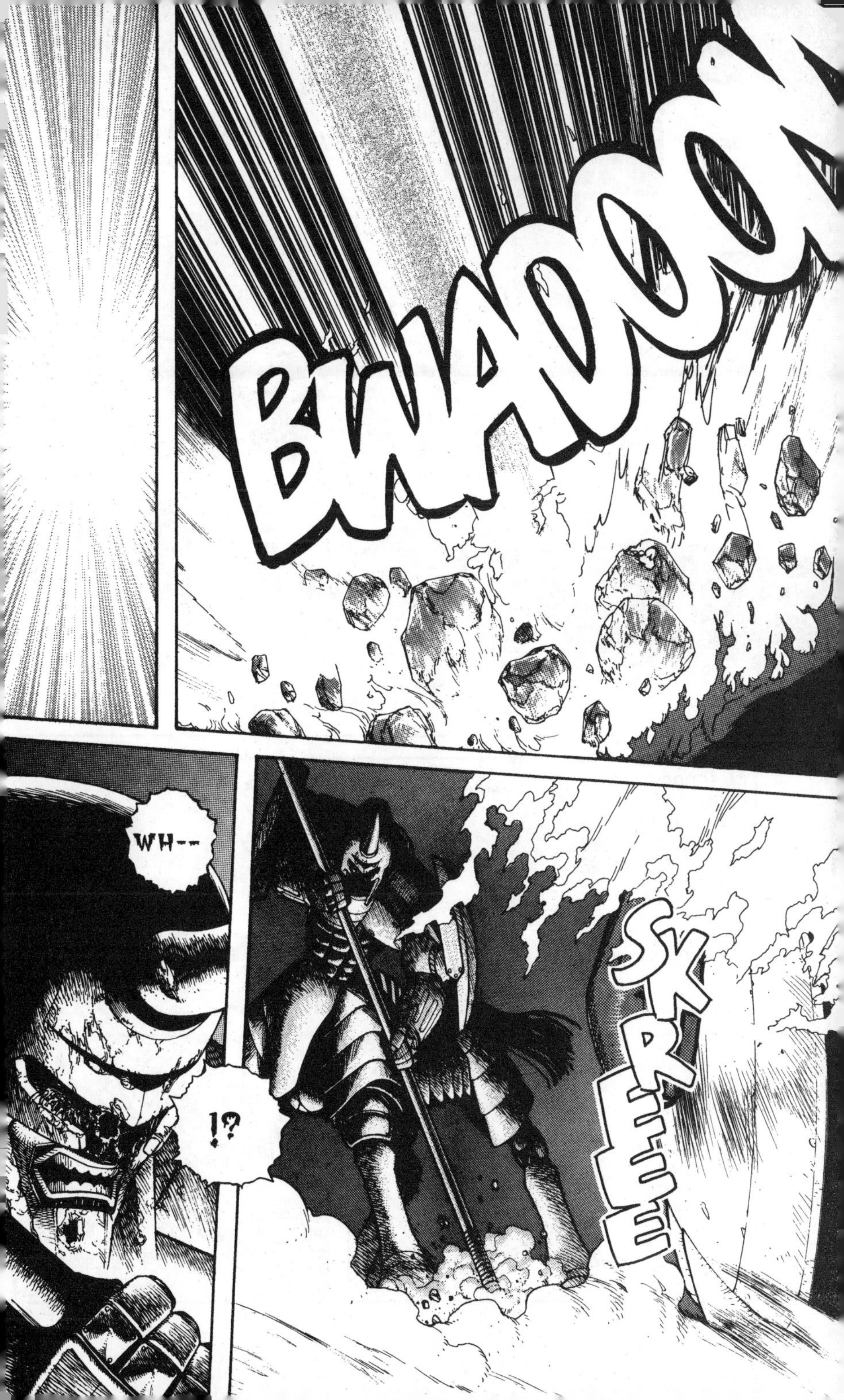
BWABOOM
WH--
!?
SKREEEE

VRUM VRUM

PHEW, THAT WAS CLOSE. . .

BUT SHE'S SAFE--!

I'M SOOOO GLAD I FOUND YOU, ALITA! WHEN I SAW THE WEDDING DRESS, I DIDN'T RECOGNIZE YOU AT FIRST.

AND BESIDES, YOUR COM-LINK WAS DOWN. . .

HFF UFF

LOU. . . THANKS. A LOT'S HAPPENED SINCE THEN.

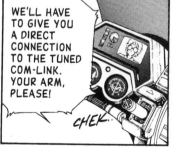

WE'LL HAVE TO GIVE YOU A DIRECT CONNECTION TO THE TUNED COM-LINK. YOUR ARM, PLEASE!

CHEK.

OKAY.

CHUK.

CHUK.

FEEP

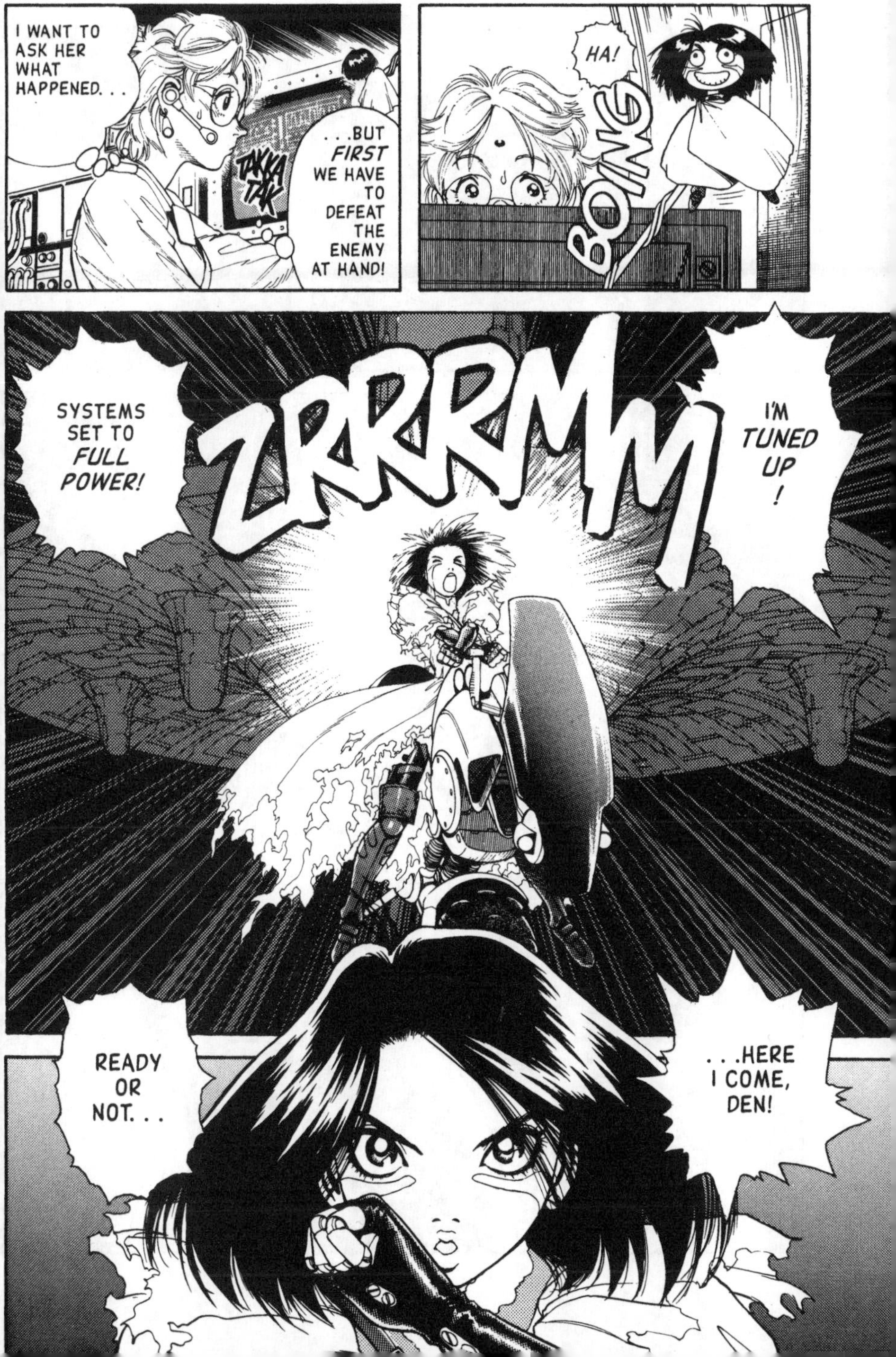
I WANT TO ASK HER WHAT HAPPENED. . .
TAKKA TAK
. . .BUT FIRST WE HAVE TO DEFEAT THE ENEMY AT HAND!
HA!
BOING
SYSTEMS SET TO FULL POWER!
ZRRRMM
I'M TUNED UP!
READY OR NOT. . .
. . .HERE I COME, DEN!

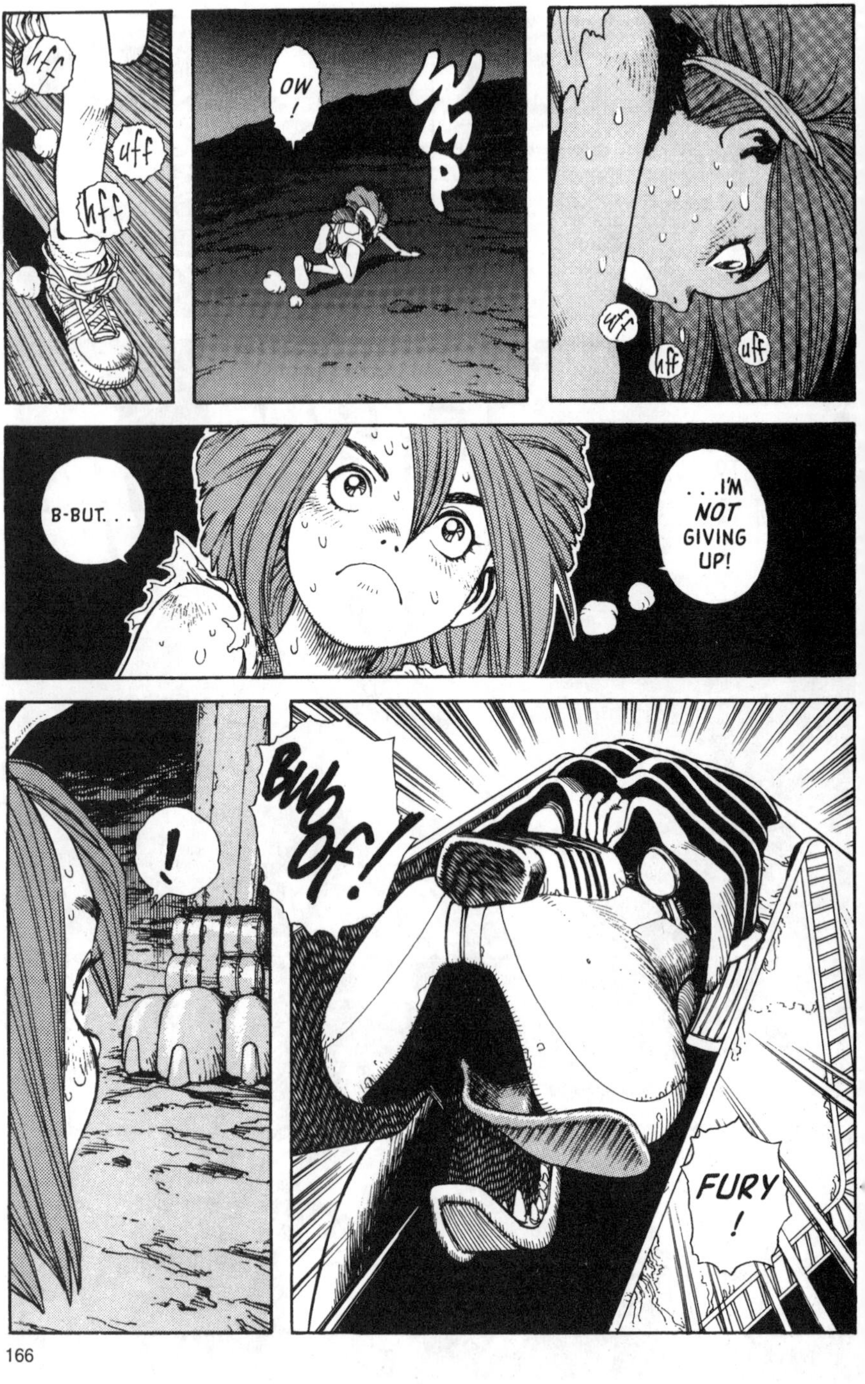
hff
uff
hff
OW!
WMP
uff
hff
uff
B-BUT. . .
. . .I'M *NOT* GIVING UP!
!
BUOOF!
FURY!

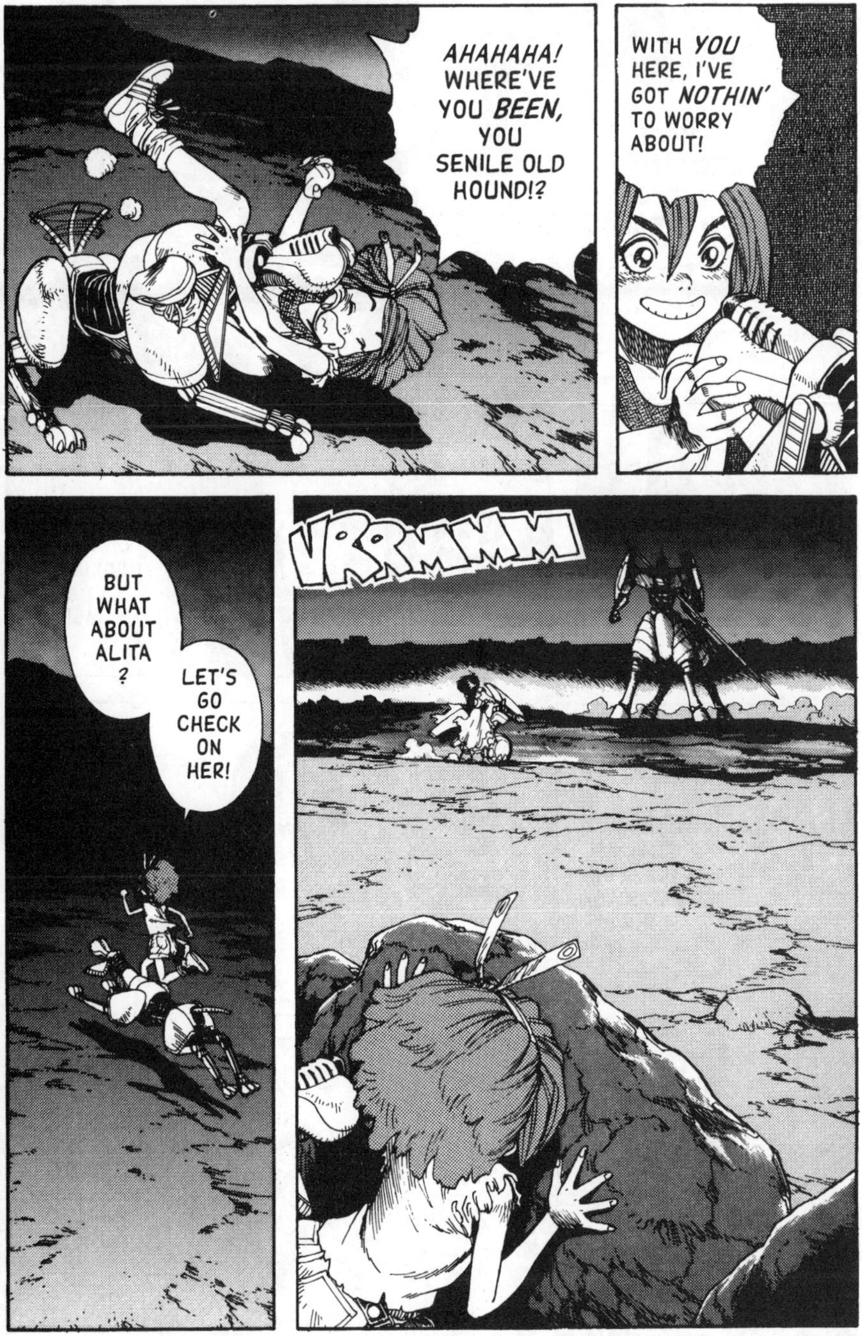
AHAHAHA! WHERE'VE YOU BEEN, YOU SENILE OLD HOUND!?
WITH YOU HERE, I'VE GOT NOTHIN' TO WORRY ABOUT!
BUT WHAT ABOUT ALITA?
LET'S GO CHECK ON HER!
VRRMMM

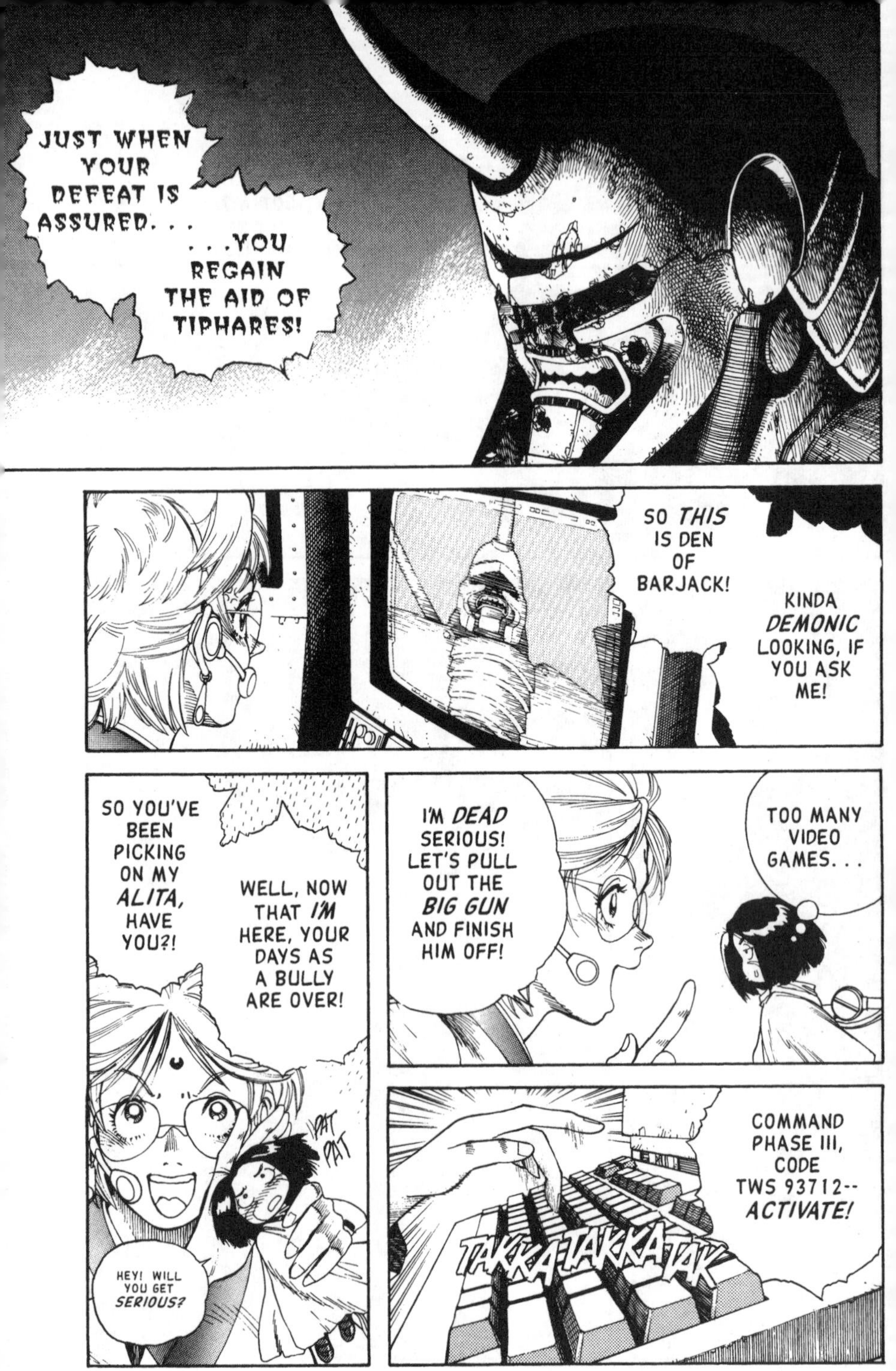
JUST WHEN YOUR DEFEAT IS ASSURED. . .
. . .YOU REGAIN THE AID OF TIPHARES!
SO THIS IS DEN OF BARJACK!
KINDA DEMONIC LOOKING, IF YOU ASK ME!
SO YOU'VE BEEN PICKING ON MY ALITA, HAVE YOU?!
WELL, NOW THAT I'M HERE, YOUR DAYS AS A BULLY ARE OVER!
PAT PAT
HEY! WILL YOU GET SERIOUS?
I'M DEAD SERIOUS! LET'S PULL OUT THE BIG GUN AND FINISH HIM OFF!
TOO MANY VIDEO GAMES. . .
COMMAND PHASE III, CODE TWS 93712-- ACTIVATE!
TAKKA TAKKA TAK

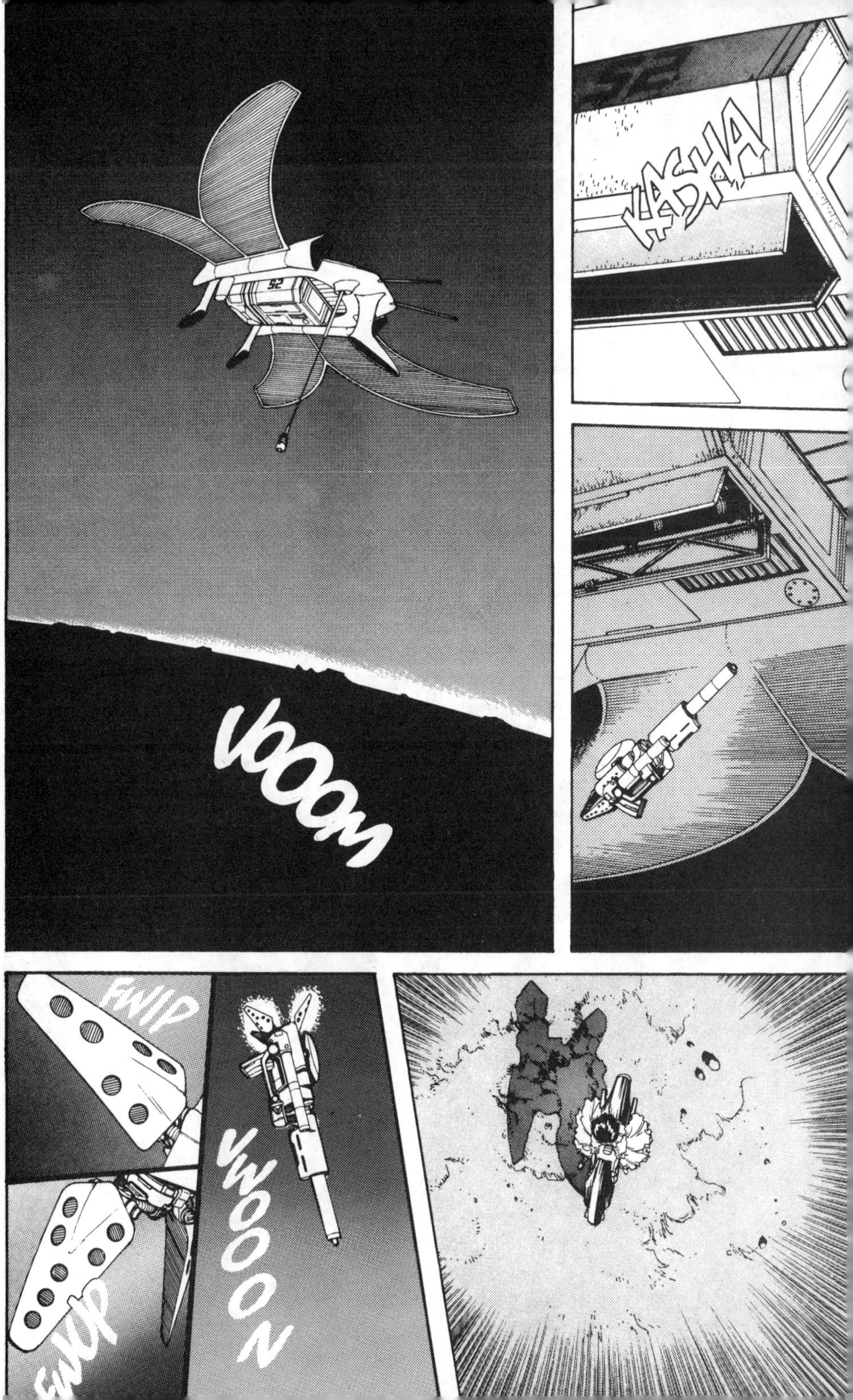
VOOOM
KASHA
FWIP
FWIP
VWOOON

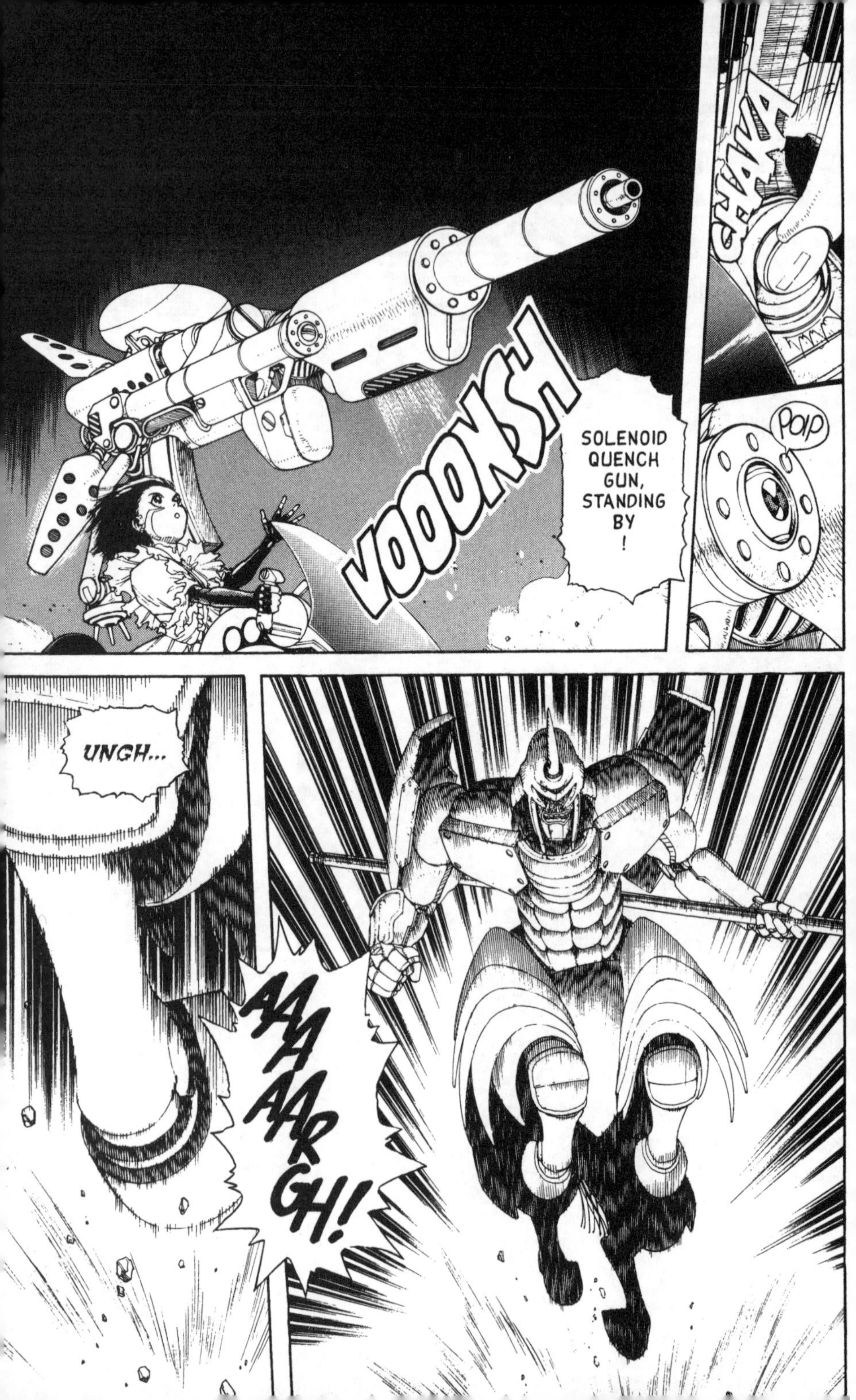
VOOONSH
SOLENOID QUENCH GUN, STANDING BY!
CHAKA
POIP
UNGH...
AAAAAARGH!

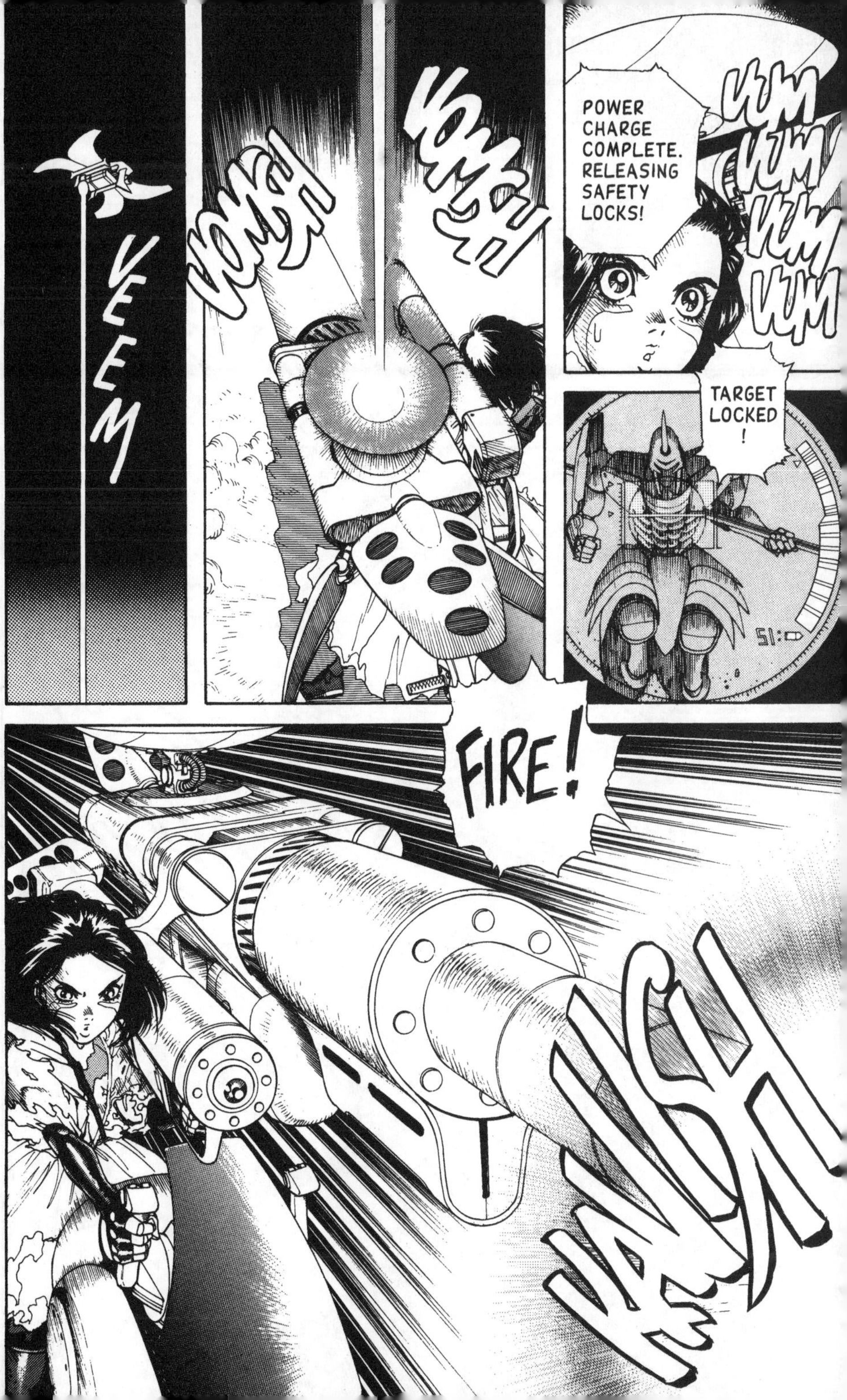
VEEM
VOMSH!
VOMSH!
POWER CHARGE COMPLETE. RELEASING SAFETY LOCKS!
VUM VUM VUM VUM
TARGET LOCKED !
FIRE!

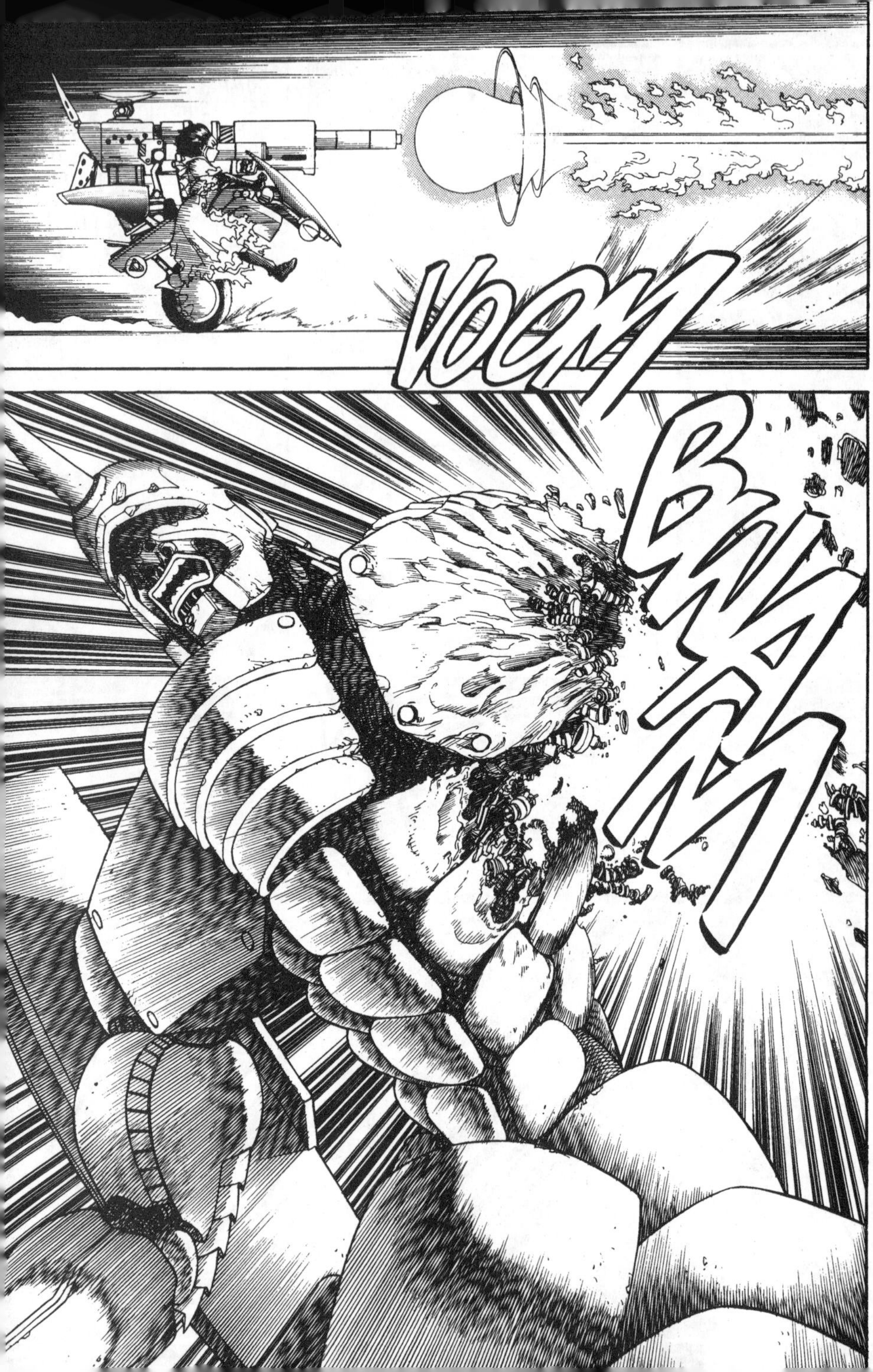
VOOM
BWAM

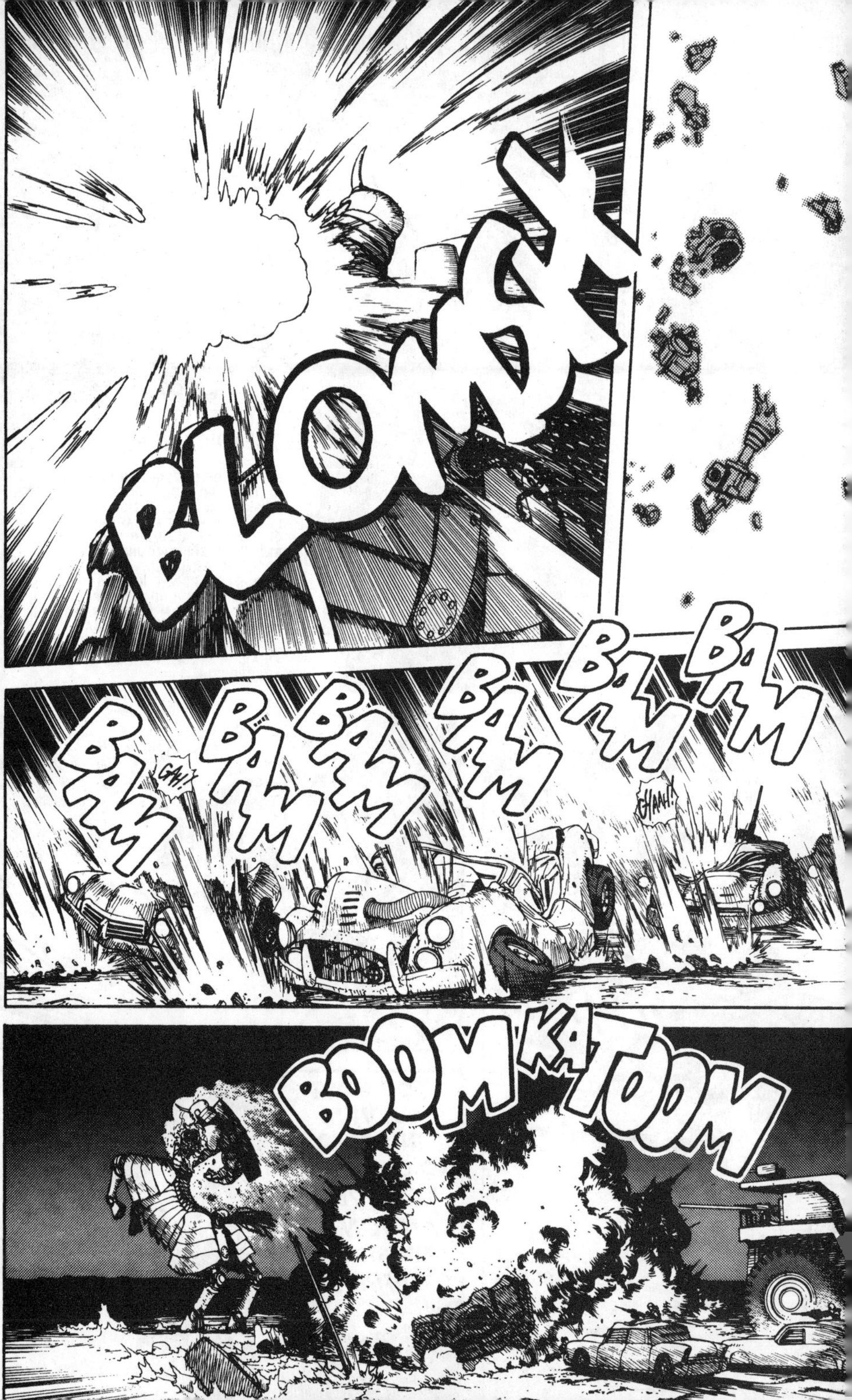
BLOWCK
BAM
GAH!
BAM
BAM
BAM
BAM
BAM
GHAAH!
BOOM KA-TOOM

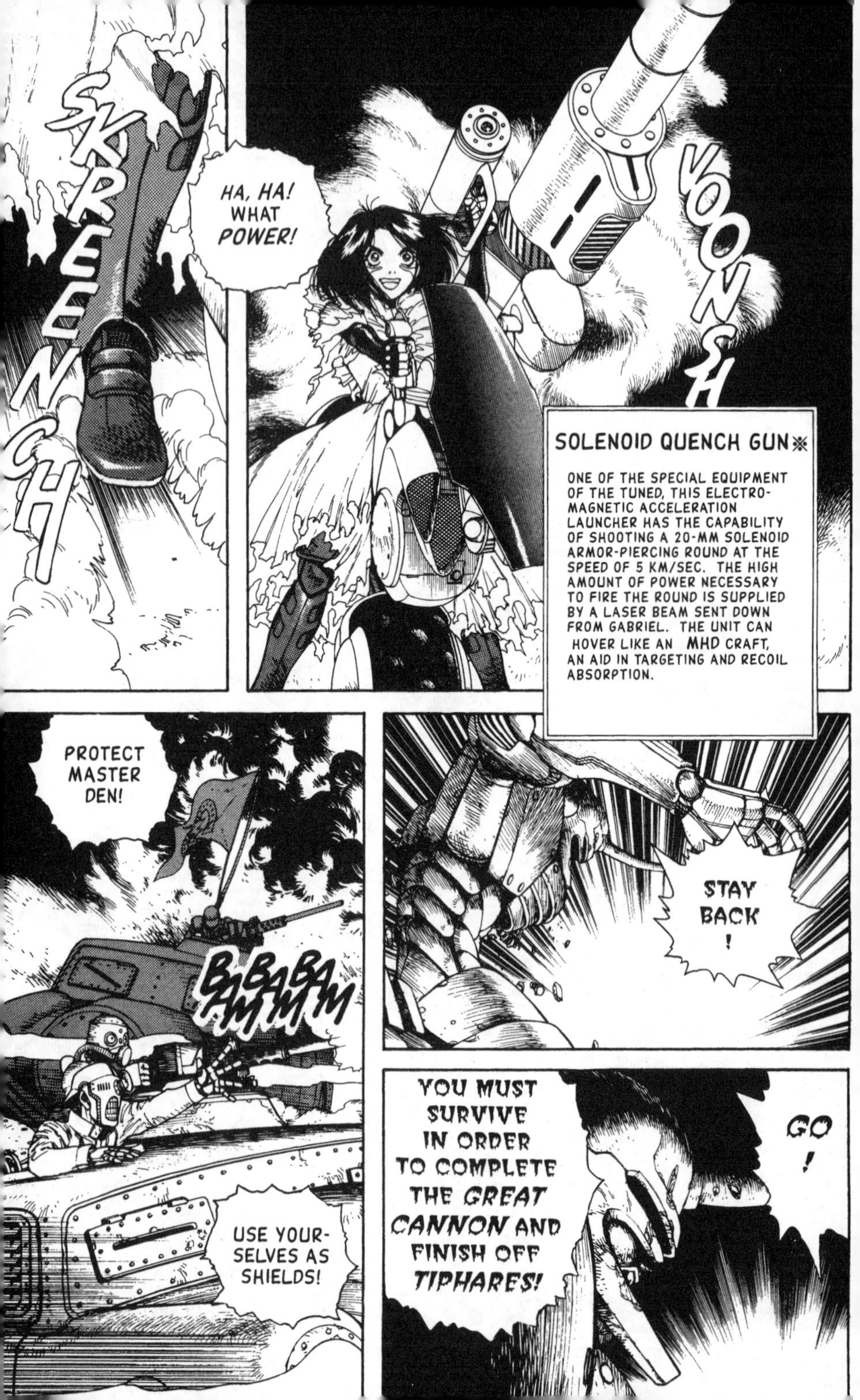
SKREEENCH
HA, HA! WHAT POWER!
VOONSH
SOLENOID QUENCH GUN※
ONE OF THE SPECIAL EQUIPMENT OF THE TUNED, THIS ELECTRO-MAGNETIC ACCELERATION LAUNCHER HAS THE CAPABILITY OF SHOOTING A 20-MM SOLENOID ARMOR-PIERCING ROUND AT THE SPEED OF 5 KM/SEC. THE HIGH AMOUNT OF POWER NECESSARY TO FIRE THE ROUND IS SUPPLIED BY A LASER BEAM SENT DOWN FROM GABRIEL. THE UNIT CAN HOVER LIKE AN MHD CRAFT, AN AID IN TARGETING AND RECOIL ABSORPTION.
PROTECT MASTER DEN!
BABABAM
USE YOURSELVES AS SHIELDS!
STAY BACK!
YOU MUST SURVIVE IN ORDER TO COMPLETE THE GREAT CANNON AND FINISH OFF TIPHARES!
GO!

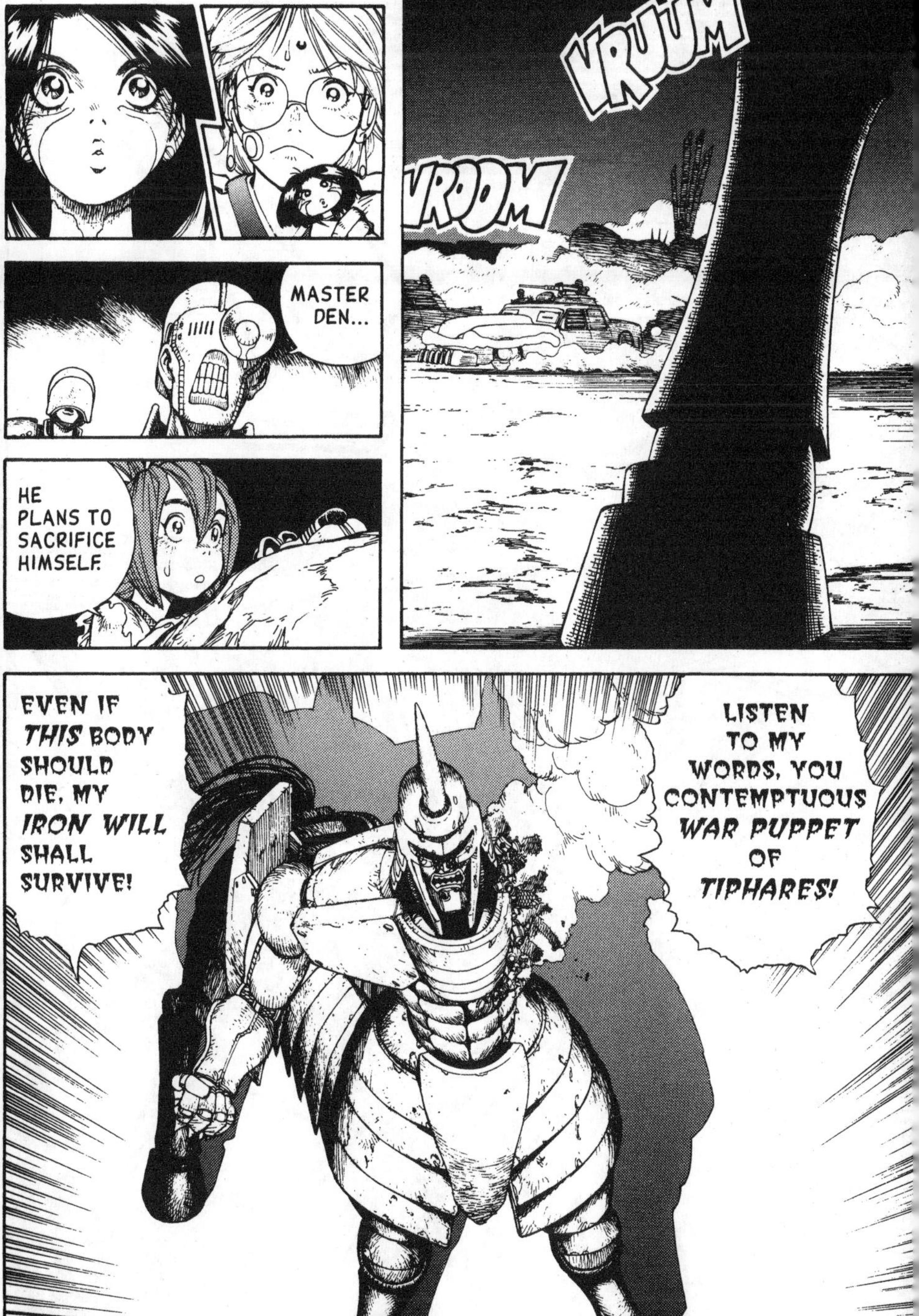
MASTER DEN...
HE PLANS TO SACRIFICE HIMSELF.
VRUUM
VROOM
EVEN IF *THIS* BODY SHOULD DIE, MY *IRON WILL* SHALL SURVIVE!
LISTEN TO MY WORDS, YOU CONTEMPTUOUS *WAR PUPPET* OF *TIPHARES!*

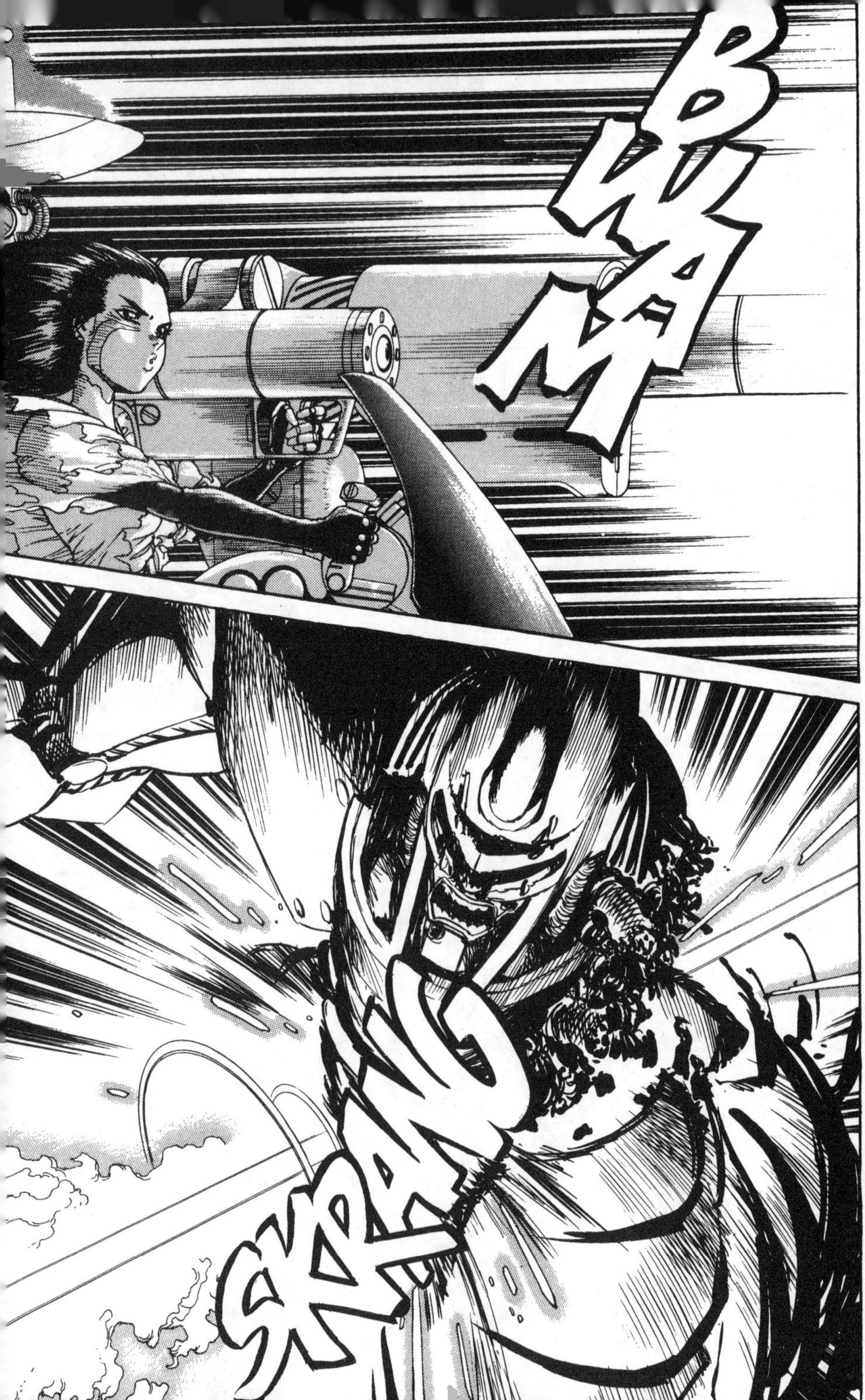
BUWAM
SKRANG

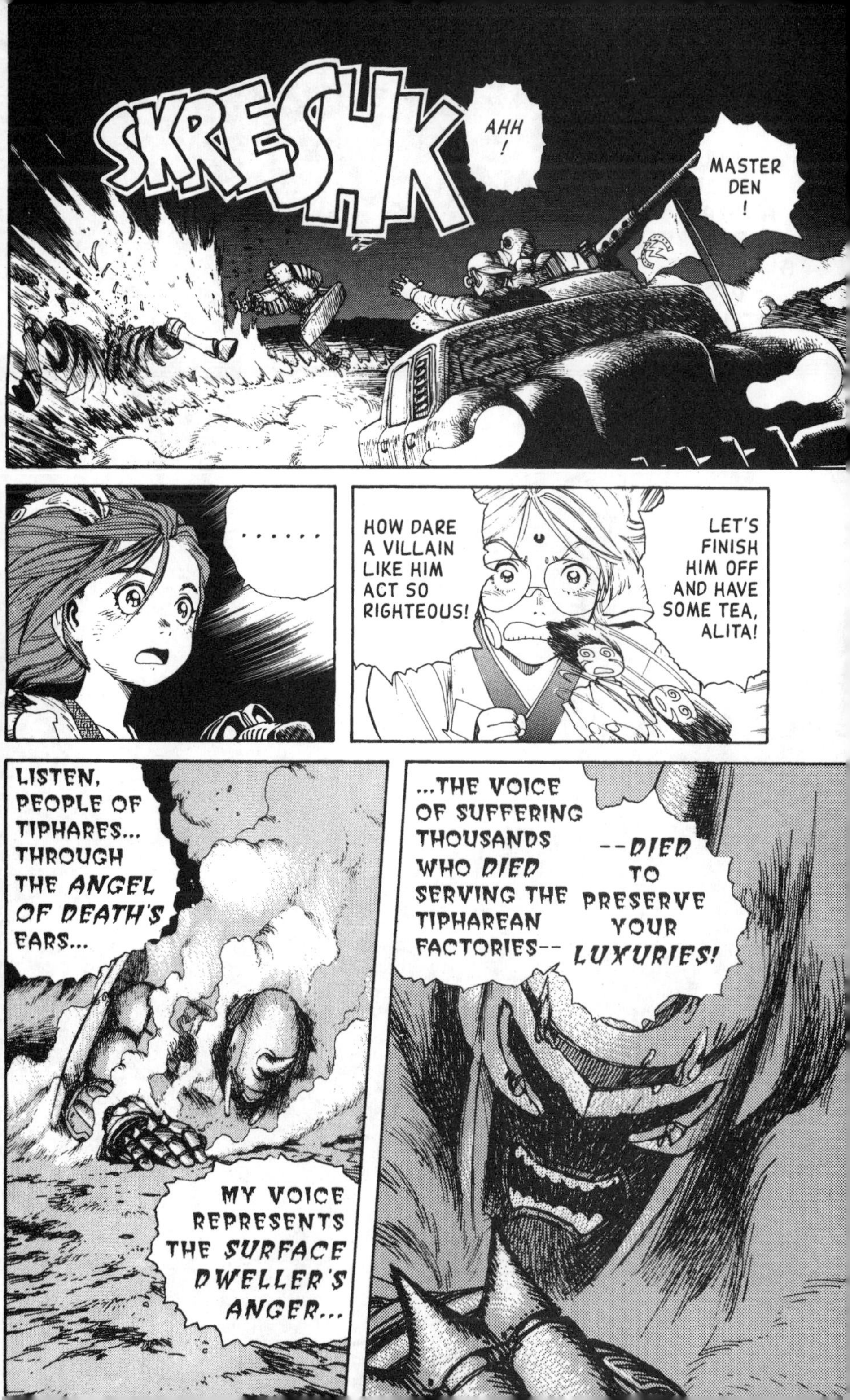
SKRESHK
AHH!
MASTER DEN!
......
HOW DARE A VILLAIN LIKE HIM ACT SO RIGHTEOUS!
LET'S FINISH HIM OFF AND HAVE SOME TEA, ALITA!
LISTEN, PEOPLE OF TIPHARES... THROUGH THE ANGEL OF DEATH'S EARS...
MY VOICE REPRESENTS THE SURFACE DWELLER'S ANGER...
...THE VOICE OF SUFFERING THOUSANDS WHO DIED SERVING THE TIPHAREAN FACTORIES--
--DIED TO PRESERVE YOUR LUXURIES!

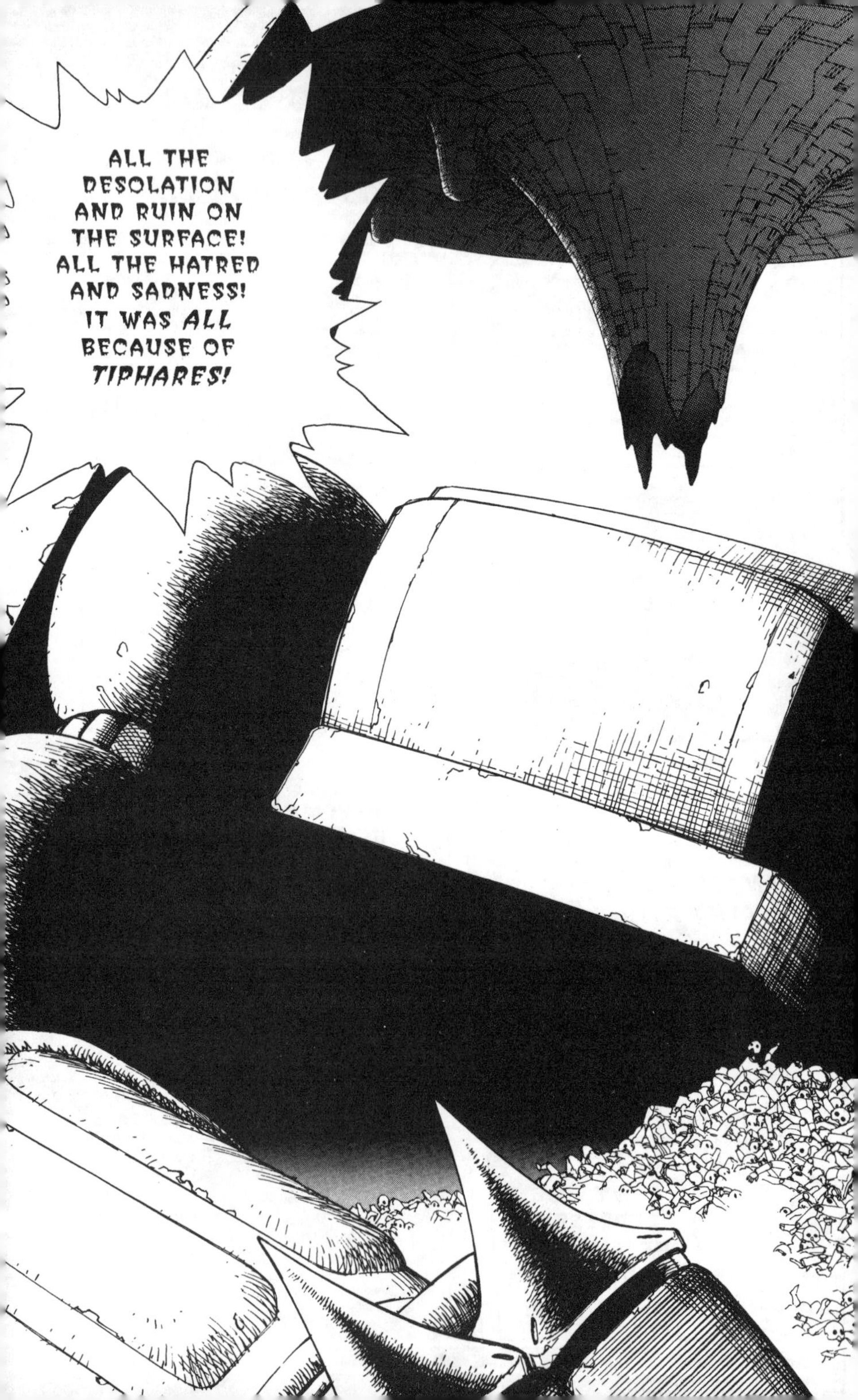
ALL THE DESOLATION AND RUIN ON THE SURFACE! ALL THE HATRED AND SADNESS! IT WAS *ALL* BECAUSE OF *TIPHARES!*

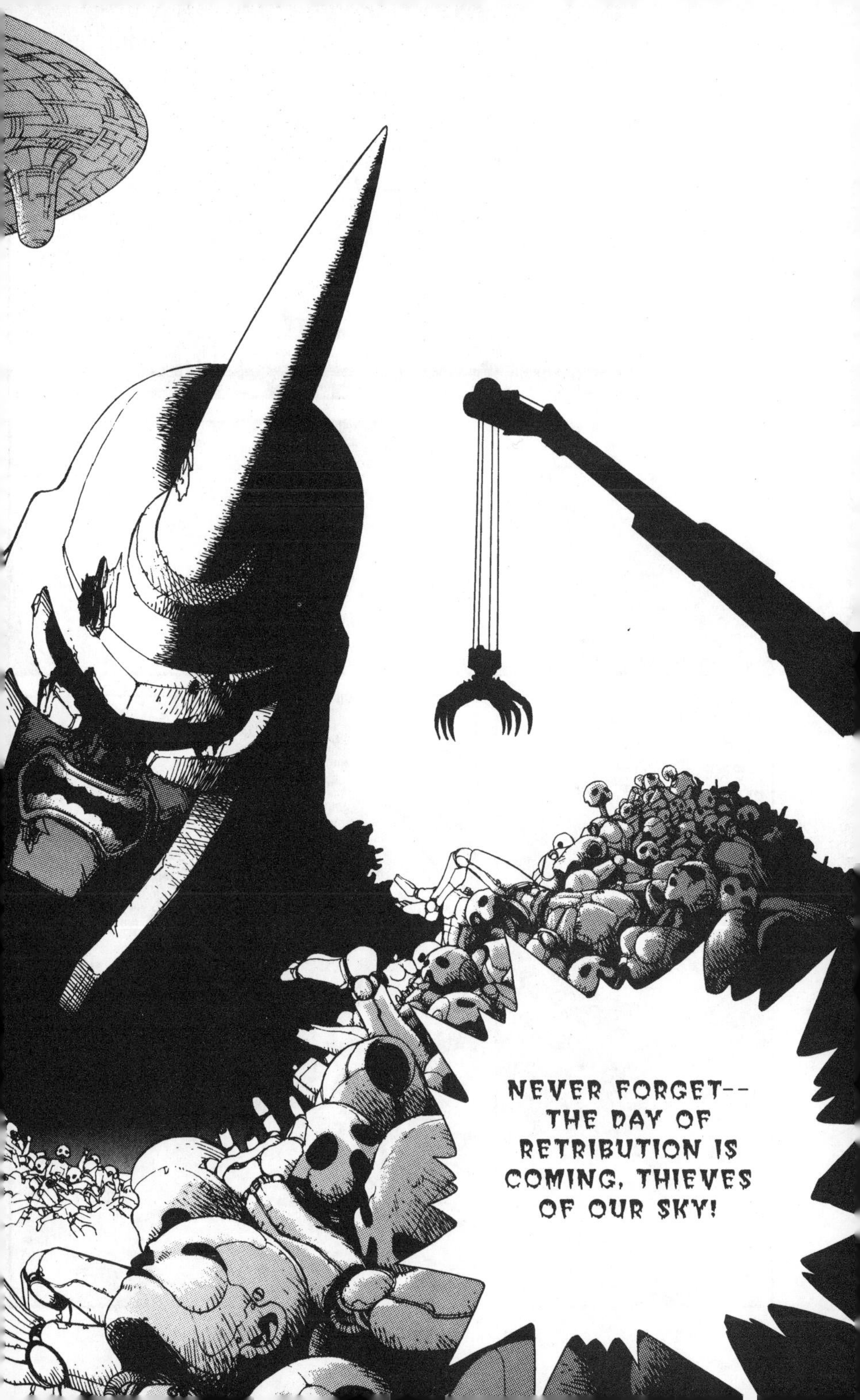
NEVER FORGET--
THE DAY OF
RETRIBUTION IS
COMING, THIEVES
OF OUR SKY!

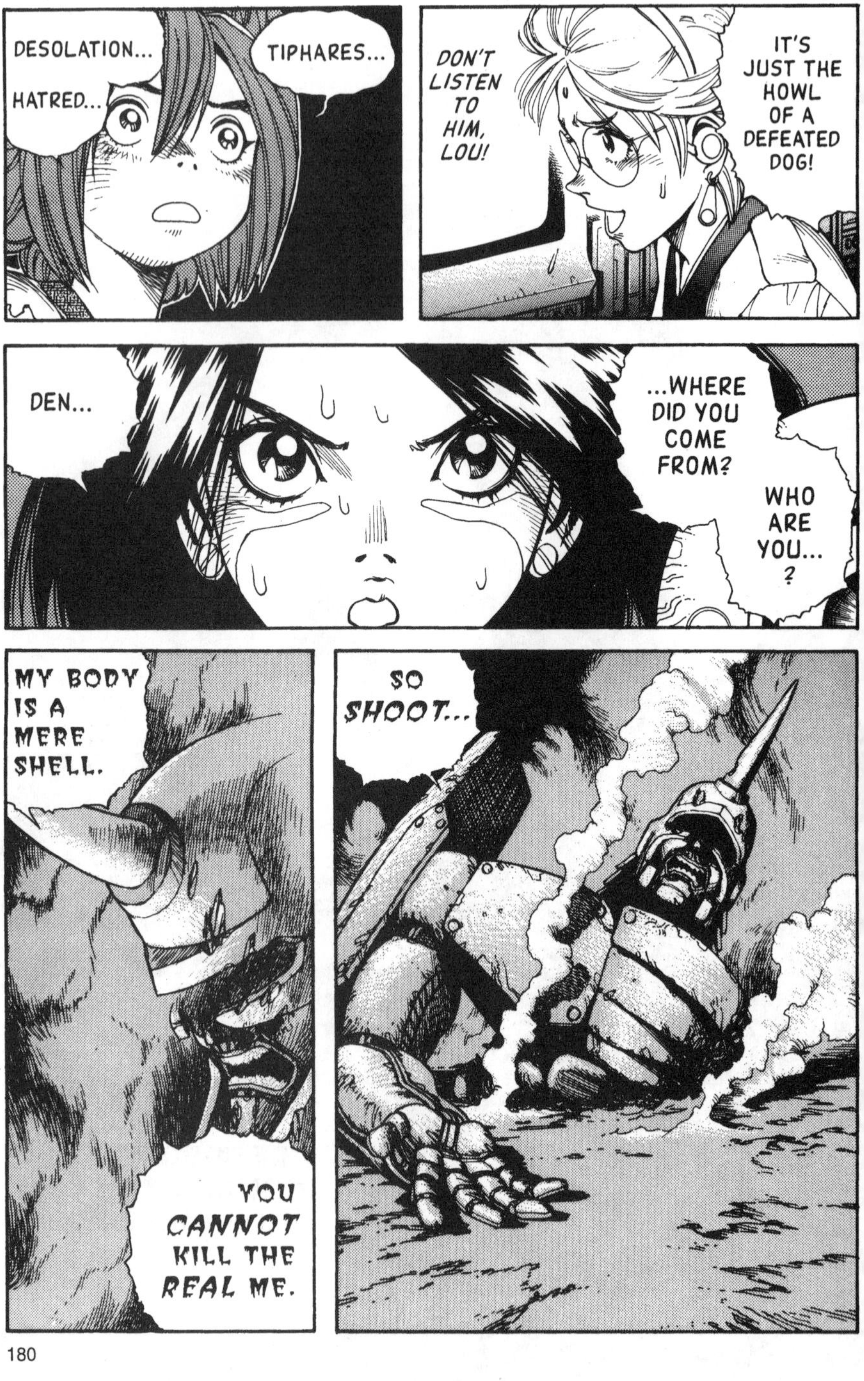
DESOLATION...
HATRED...
TIPHARES...
DON'T LISTEN TO HIM, LOU!
IT'S JUST THE HOWL OF A DEFEATED DOG!
DEN...
...WHERE DID YOU COME FROM?
WHO ARE YOU...?
MY BODY IS A MERE SHELL.
YOU CANNOT KILL THE REAL ME.
SO SHOOT...

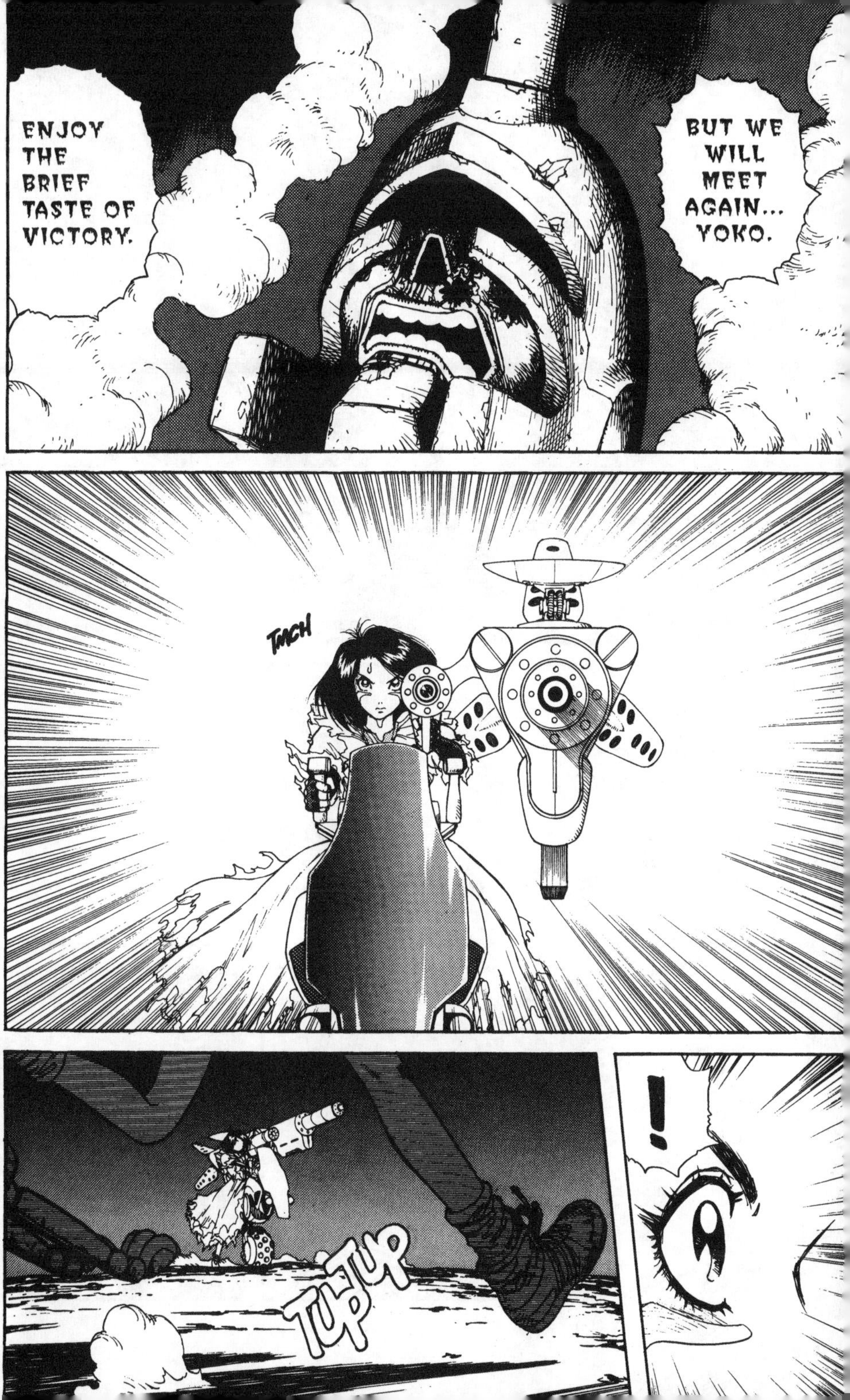
ENJOY THE BRIEF TASTE OF VICTORY.
BUT WE WILL MEET AGAIN... YOKO.
TMCH
TUPTUP
!

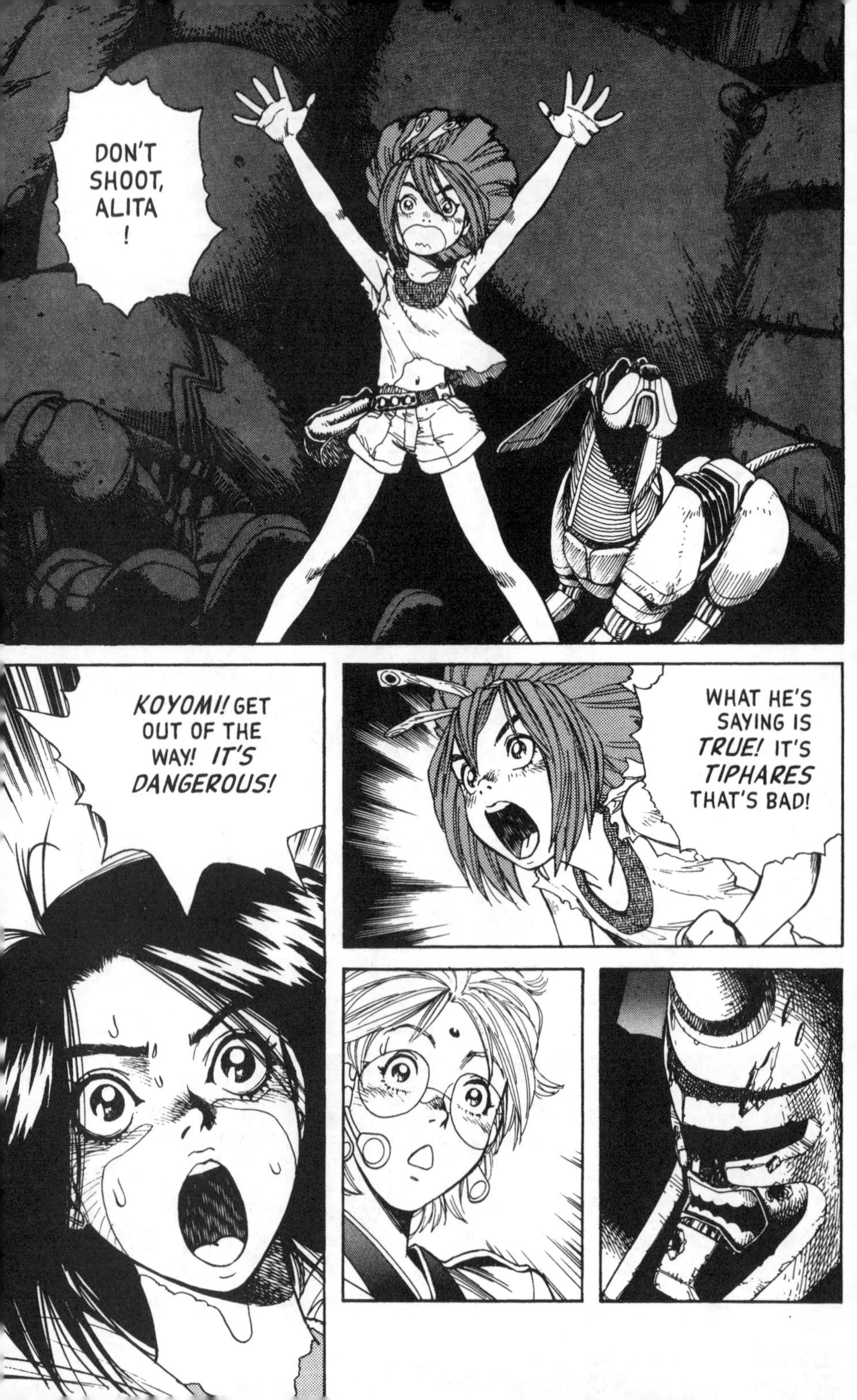
DON'T SHOOT, ALITA!
KOYOMI! GET OUT OF THE WAY! IT'S DANGEROUS!
WHAT HE'S SAYING IS TRUE! IT'S TIPHARES THAT'S BAD!

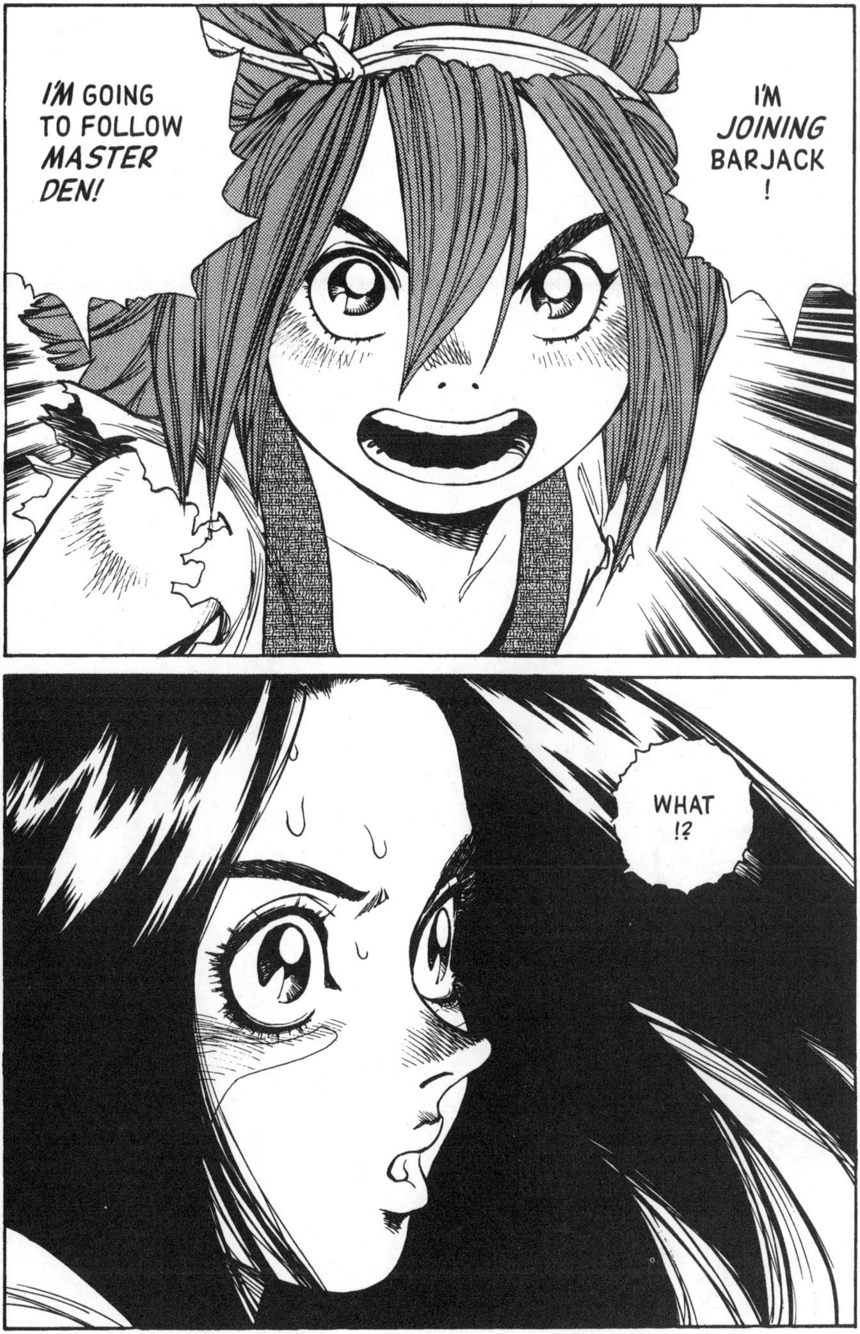
I'M GOING TO FOLLOW MASTER DEN!
I'M JOINING BARJACK!
WHAT!?

FORK IN THE ROAD
Mission 5: Choices

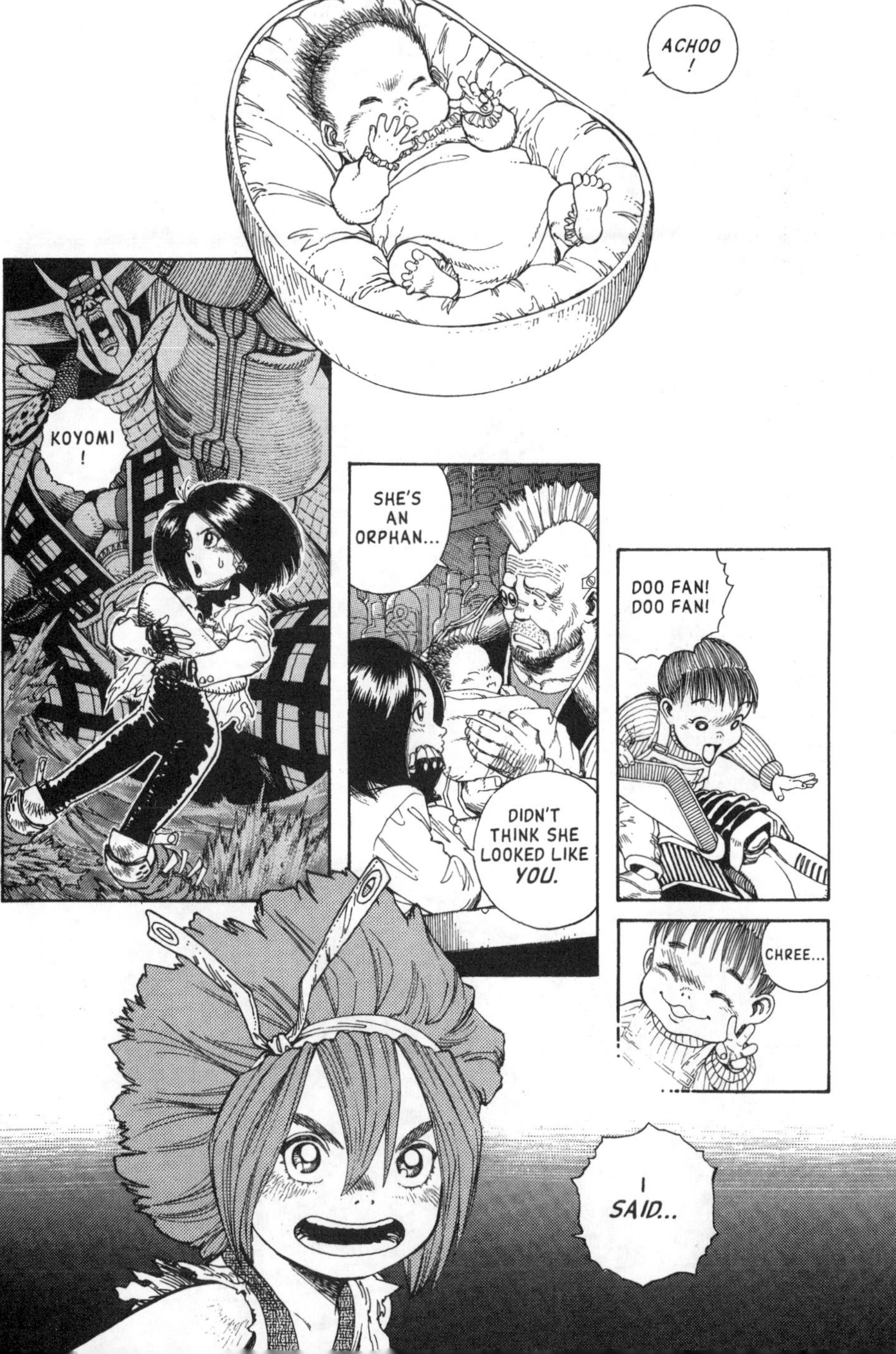
ACHOO!
KOYOMI!
SHE'S AN ORPHAN...
DIDN'T THINK SHE LOOKED LIKE *YOU.*
DOO FAN! DOO FAN!
CHREE...
I *SAID...*

FORK IN THE ROAD
Mission 5: Choices

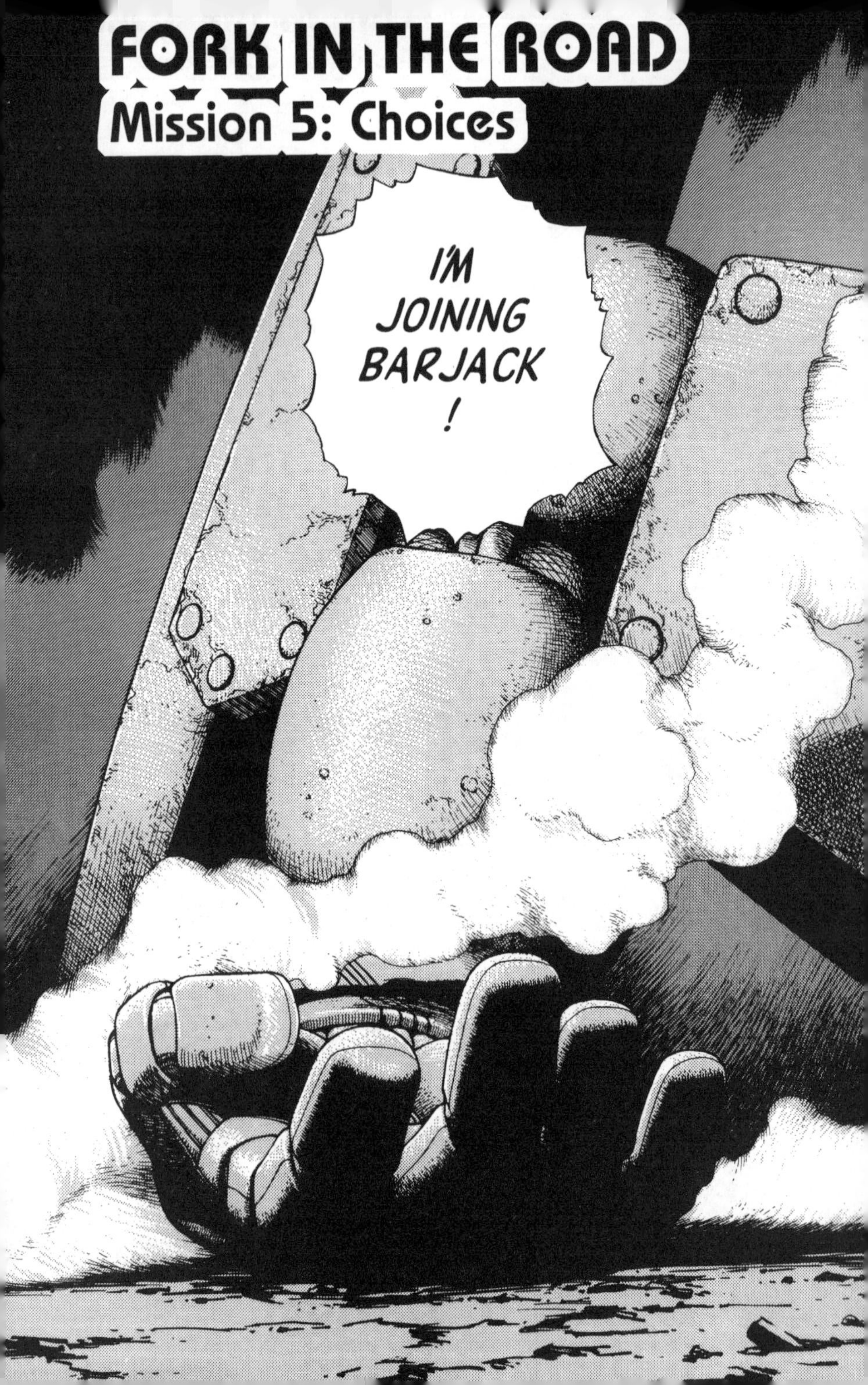
I'M JOINING BARJACK !

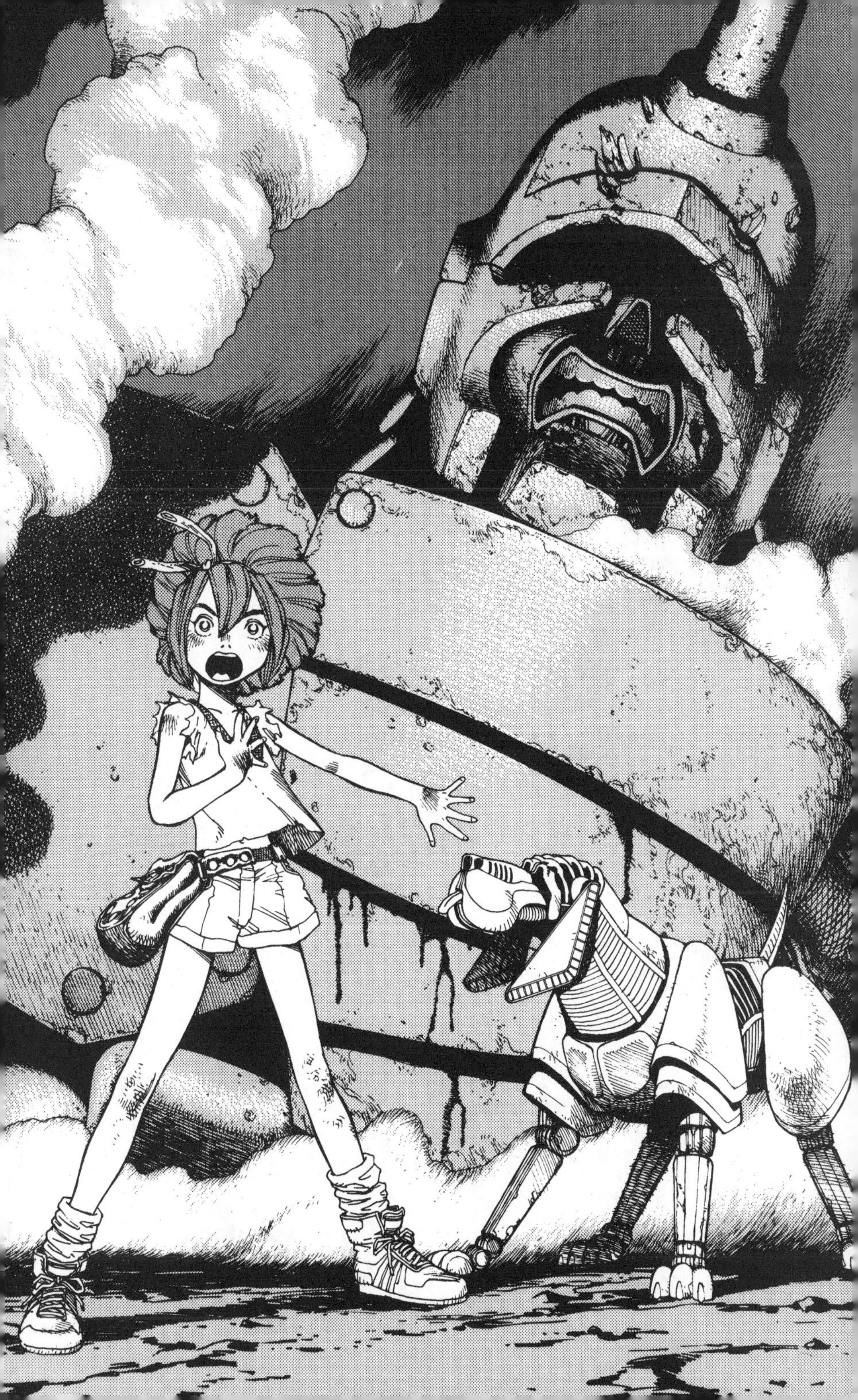

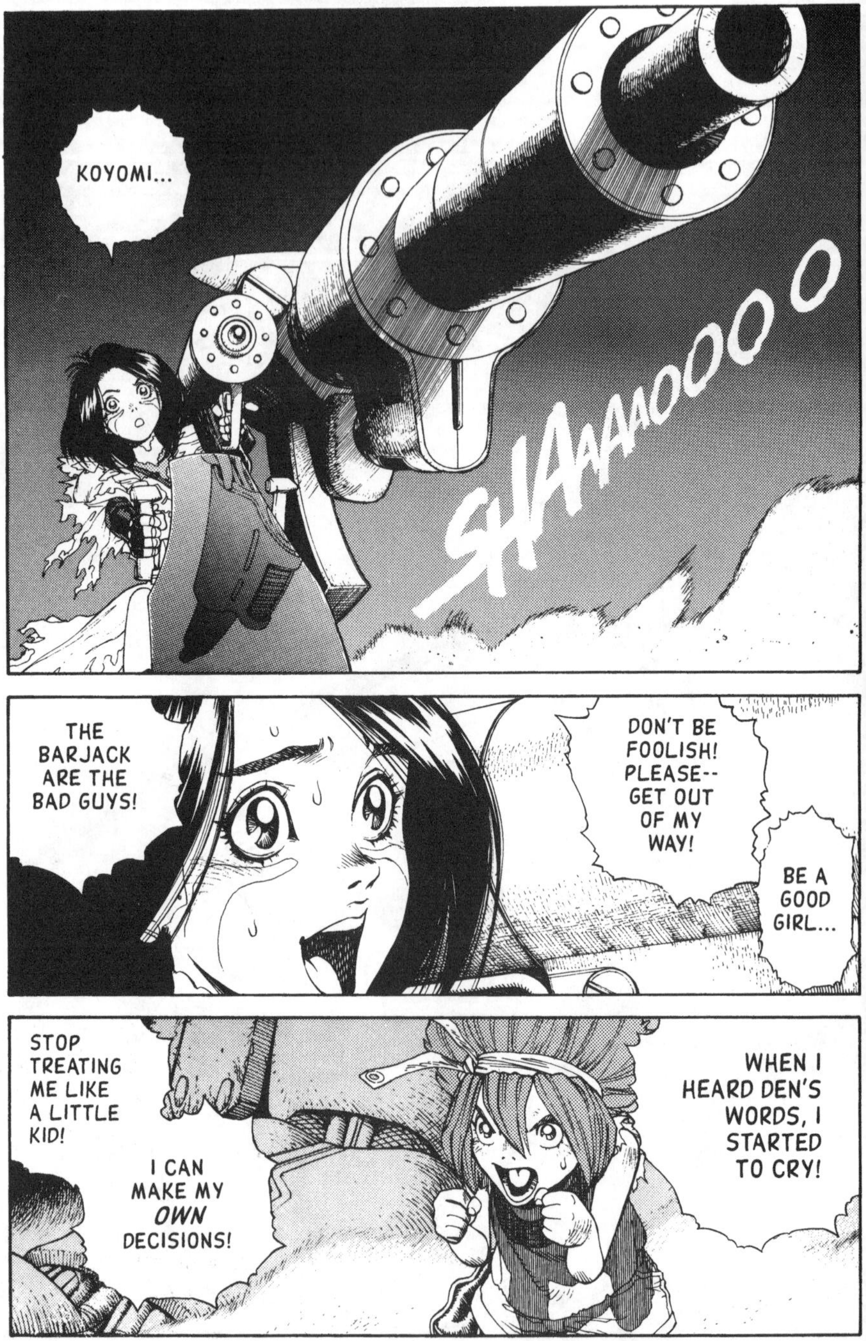
KOYOMI...
SHAAAAOOOO O
THE BARJACK ARE THE BAD GUYS!
DON'T BE FOOLISH! PLEASE-- GET OUT OF MY WAY!
BE A GOOD GIRL...
STOP TREATING ME LIKE A LITTLE KID!
I CAN MAKE MY *OWN* DECISIONS!
WHEN I HEARD DEN'S WORDS, I STARTED TO CRY!

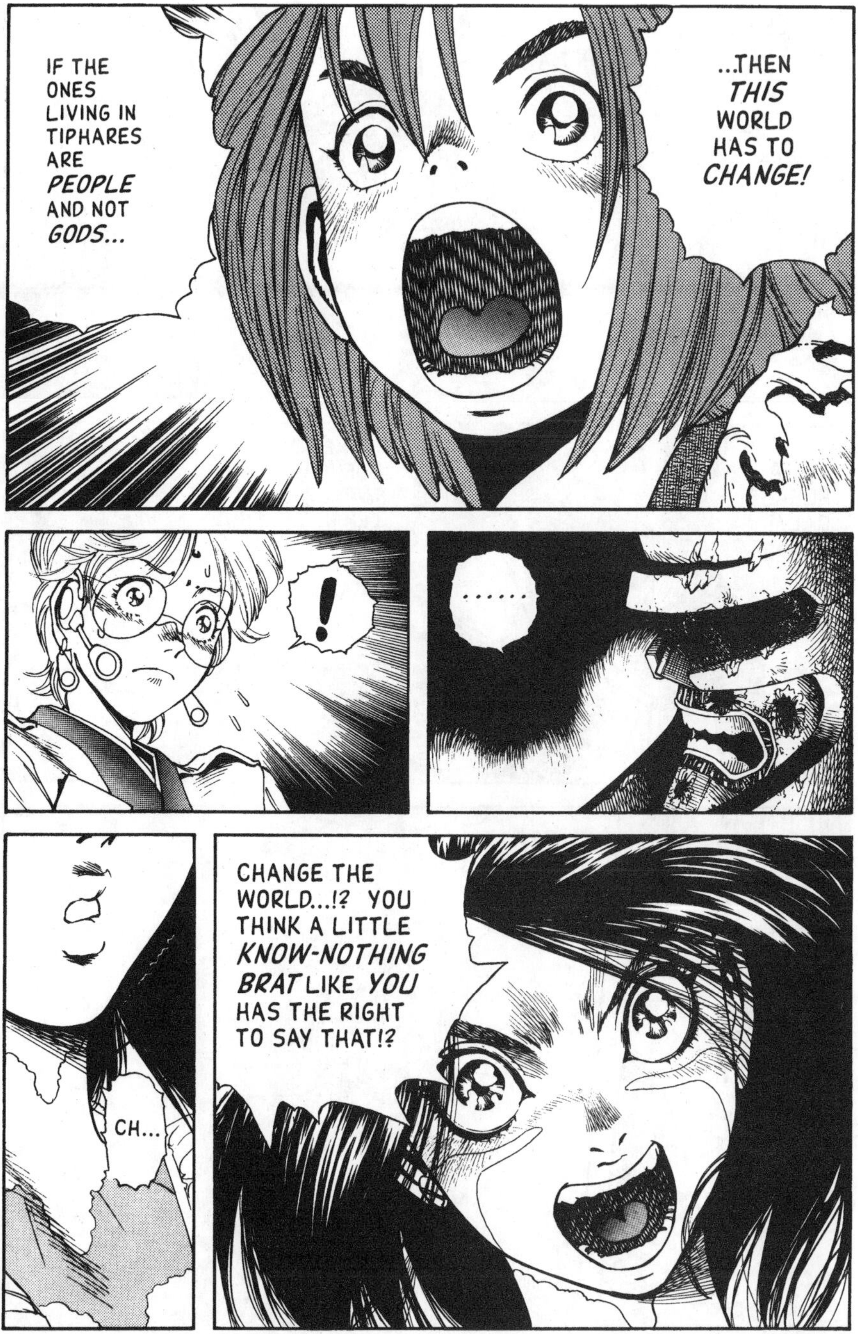
IF THE ONES LIVING IN TIPHARES ARE *PEOPLE* AND NOT *GODS...*
...THEN *THIS* WORLD HAS TO *CHANGE!*
!
......
CH...
CHANGE THE WORLD...!? YOU THINK A LITTLE *KNOW-NOTHING BRAT* LIKE *YOU* HAS THE RIGHT TO SAY THAT!?

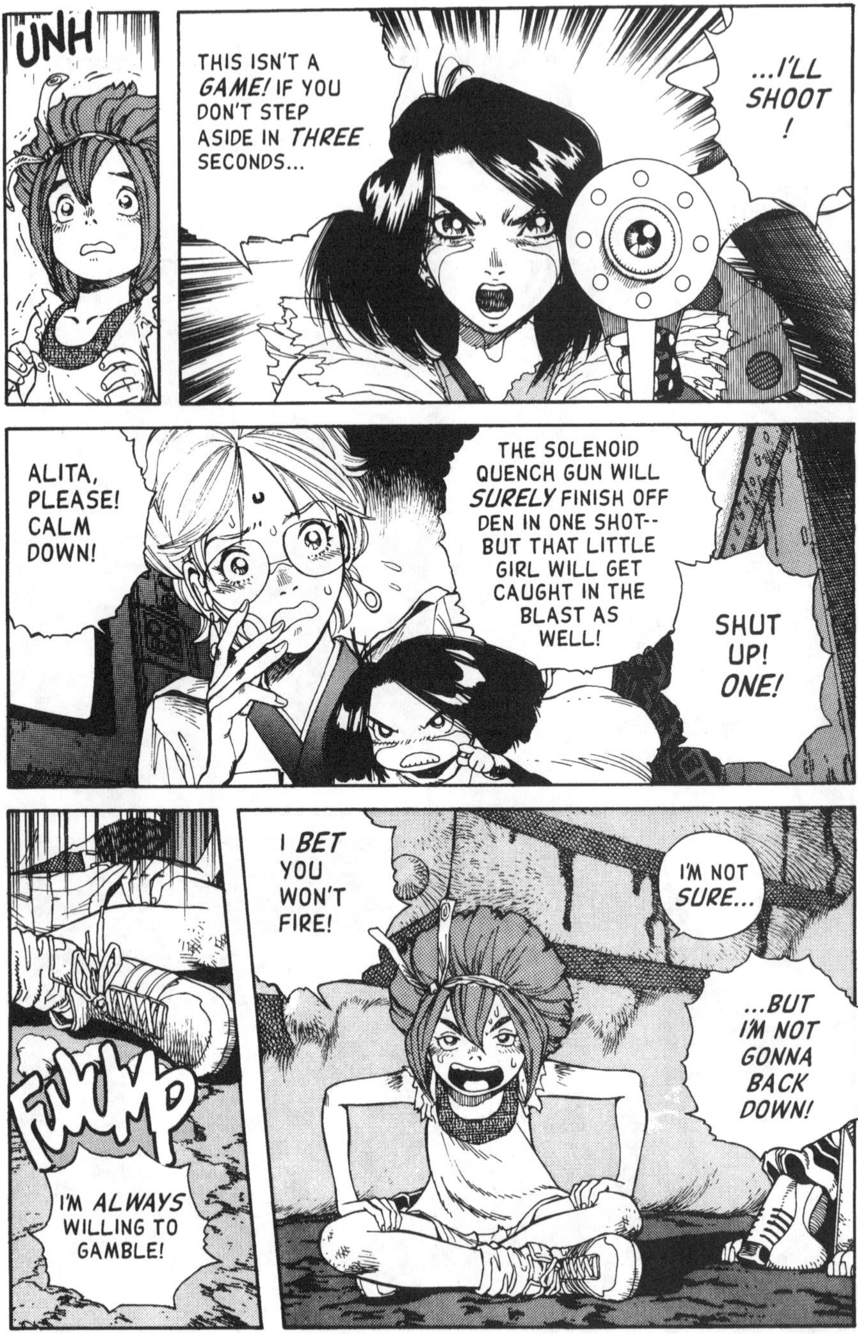
UNH
THIS ISN'T A GAME! IF YOU DON'T STEP ASIDE IN THREE SECONDS...
...I'LL SHOOT!
ALITA, PLEASE! CALM DOWN!
THE SOLENOID QUENCH GUN WILL SURELY FINISH OFF DEN IN ONE SHOT-- BUT THAT LITTLE GIRL WILL GET CAUGHT IN THE BLAST AS WELL!
SHUT UP! ONE!
FWUMP
I'M ALWAYS WILLING TO GAMBLE!
I BET YOU WON'T FIRE!
I'M NOT SURE...
...BUT I'M NOT GONNA BACK DOWN!

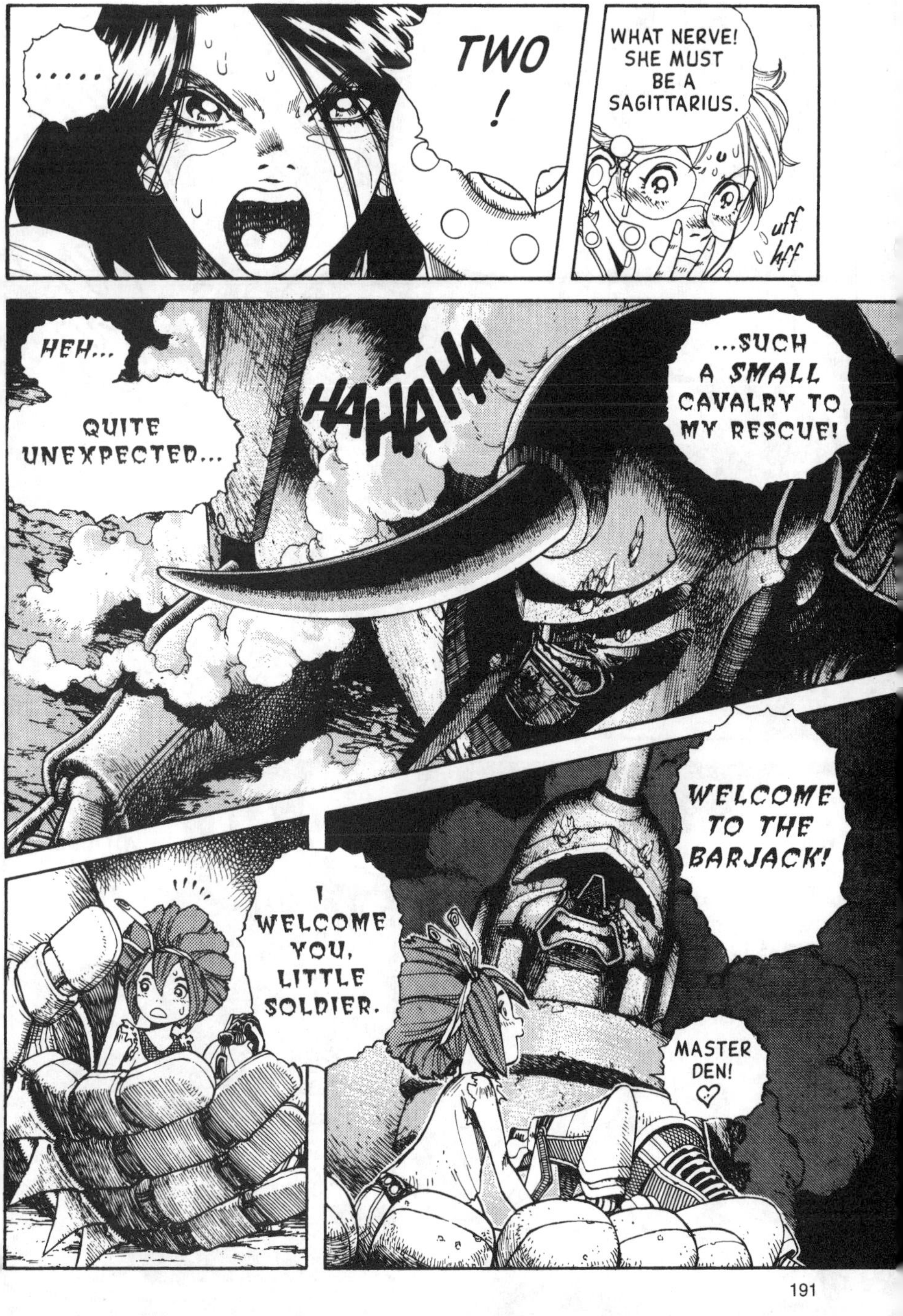
.....
TWO !
WHAT NERVE! SHE MUST BE A SAGITTARIUS.
uff hff
HEH...
QUITE UNEXPECTED...
HAHAHA
...SUCH A SMALL CAVALRY TO MY RESCUE!
WELCOME TO THE BARJACK!
I WELCOME YOU, LITTLE SOLDIER.
MASTER DEN!

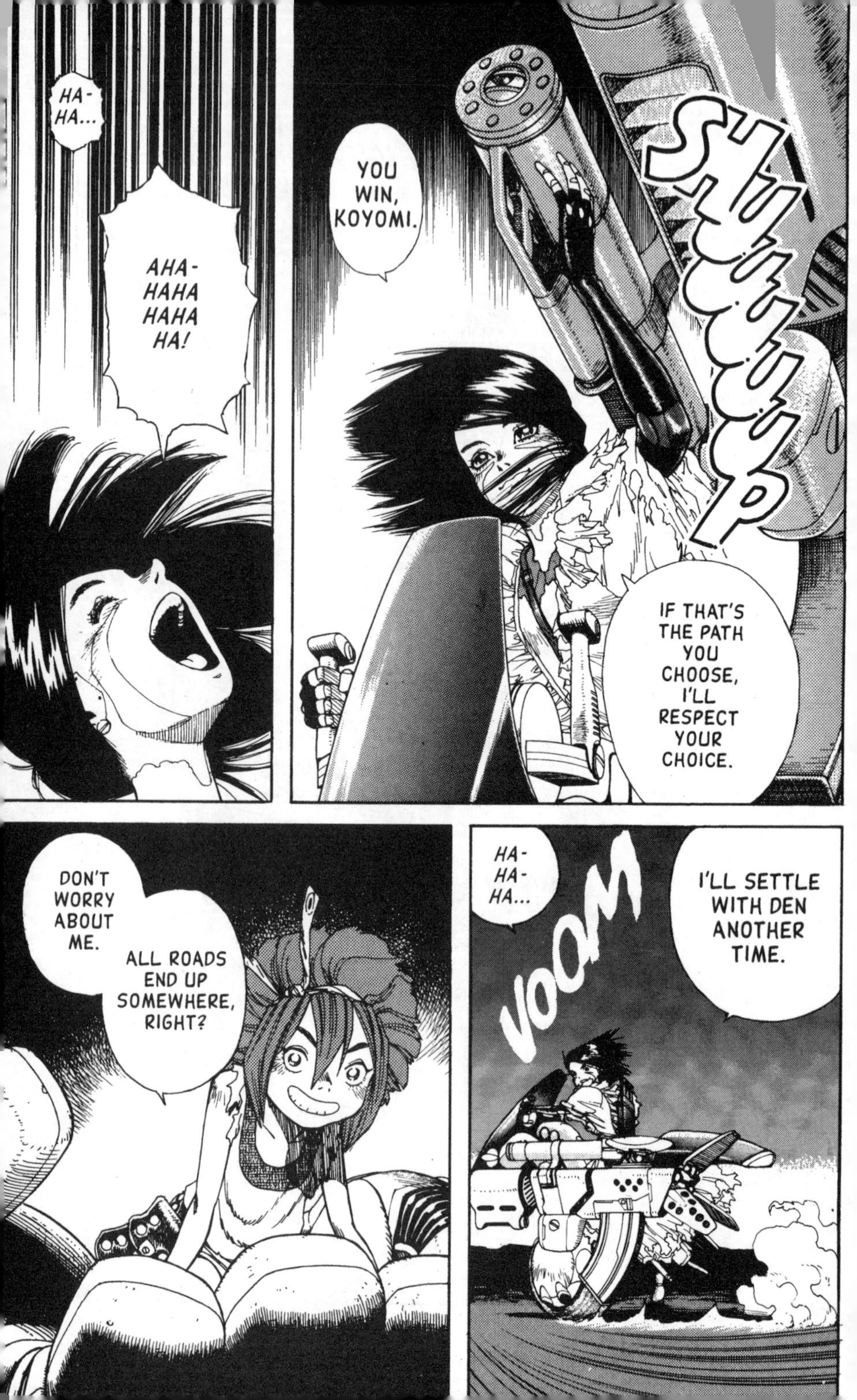
HA-
HA...
AHA-
HAHA
HAHA
HA!
YOU WIN, KOYOMI.
SHUUUUUP
IF THAT'S THE PATH YOU CHOOSE, I'LL RESPECT YOUR CHOICE.
DON'T WORRY ABOUT ME.
ALL ROADS END UP SOMEWHERE, RIGHT?
HA-
HA-
HA...
VOOM
I'LL SETTLE WITH DEN ANOTHER TIME.

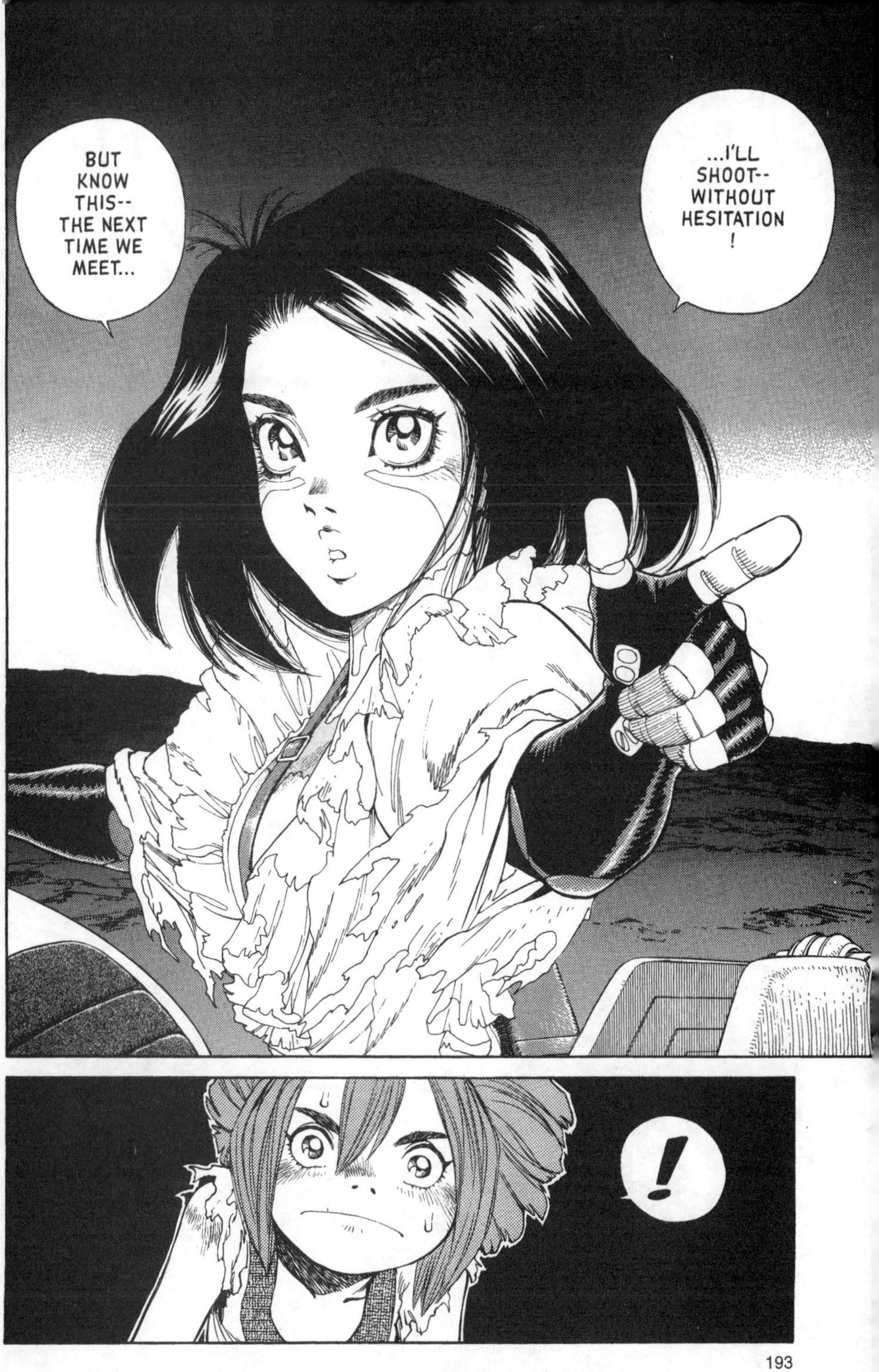
BUT KNOW THIS-- THE NEXT TIME WE MEET...
...I'LL SHOOT-- WITHOUT HESITATION !
!

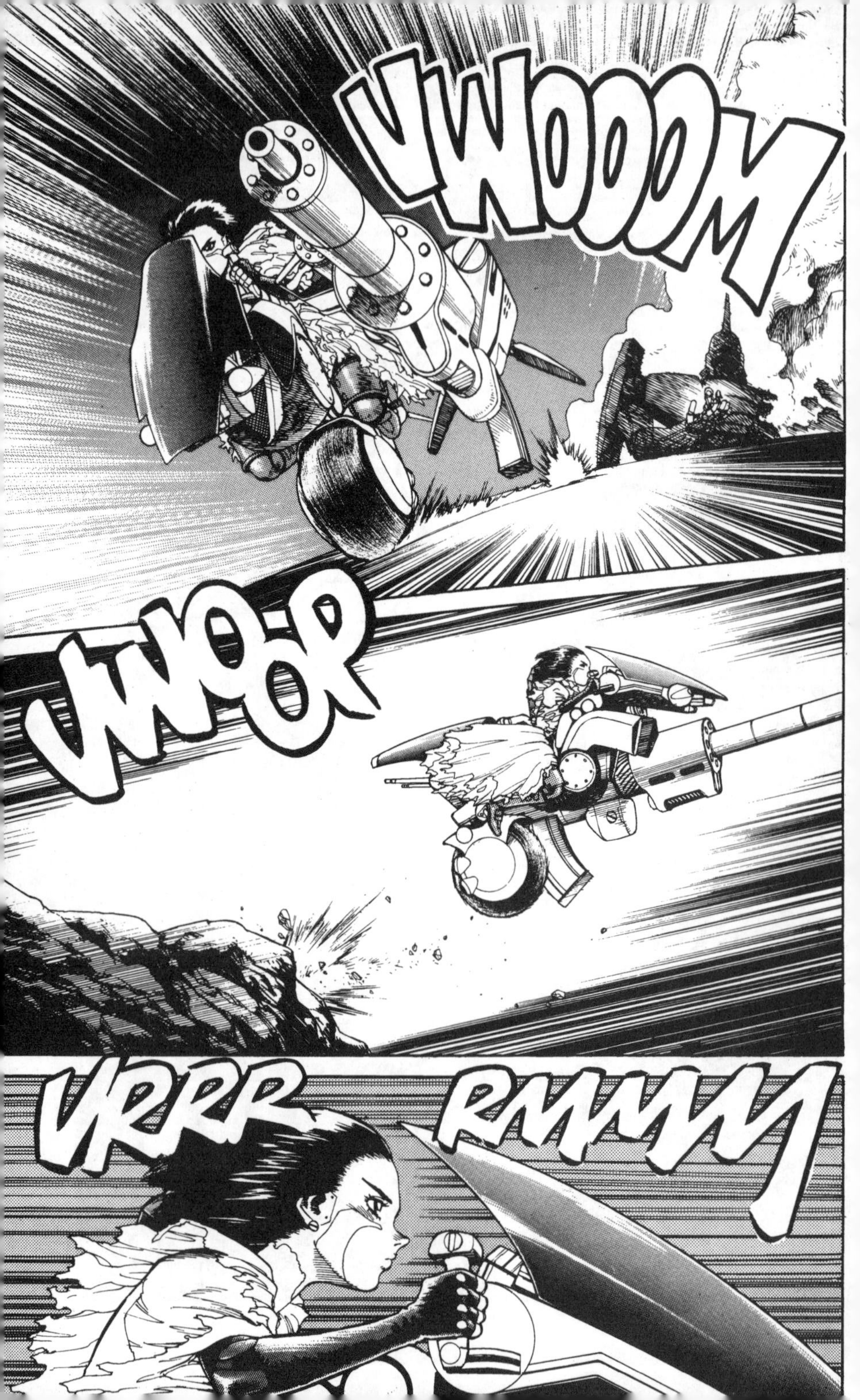
VWOOOM
VWOO-OP
VRRR
RMMMM

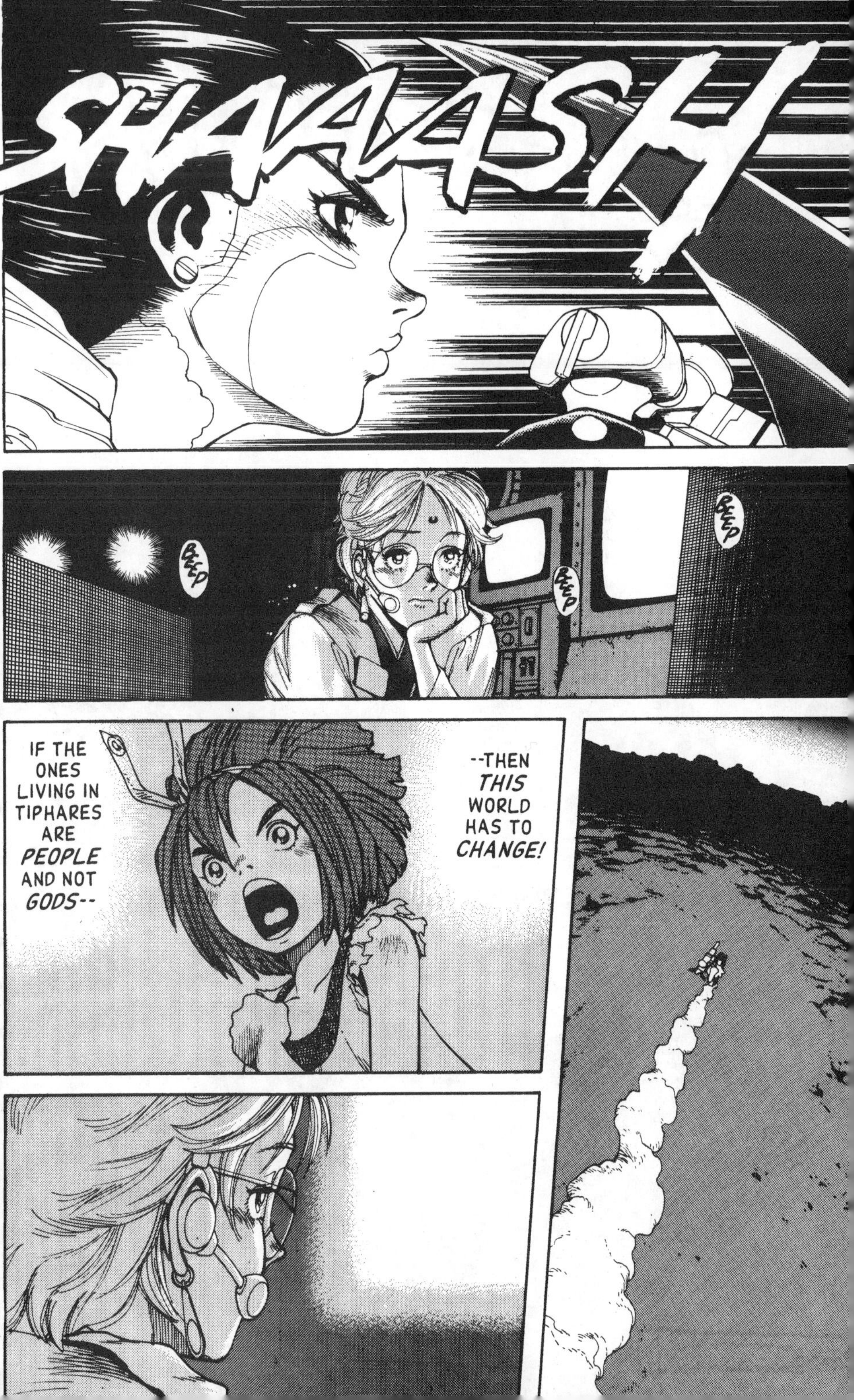
SHAAAASH
BEEP
BEEP
BEEP
IF THE ONES LIVING IN TIPHARES ARE *PEOPLE* AND NOT *GODS*--
--THEN *THIS* WORLD HAS TO *CHANGE!*

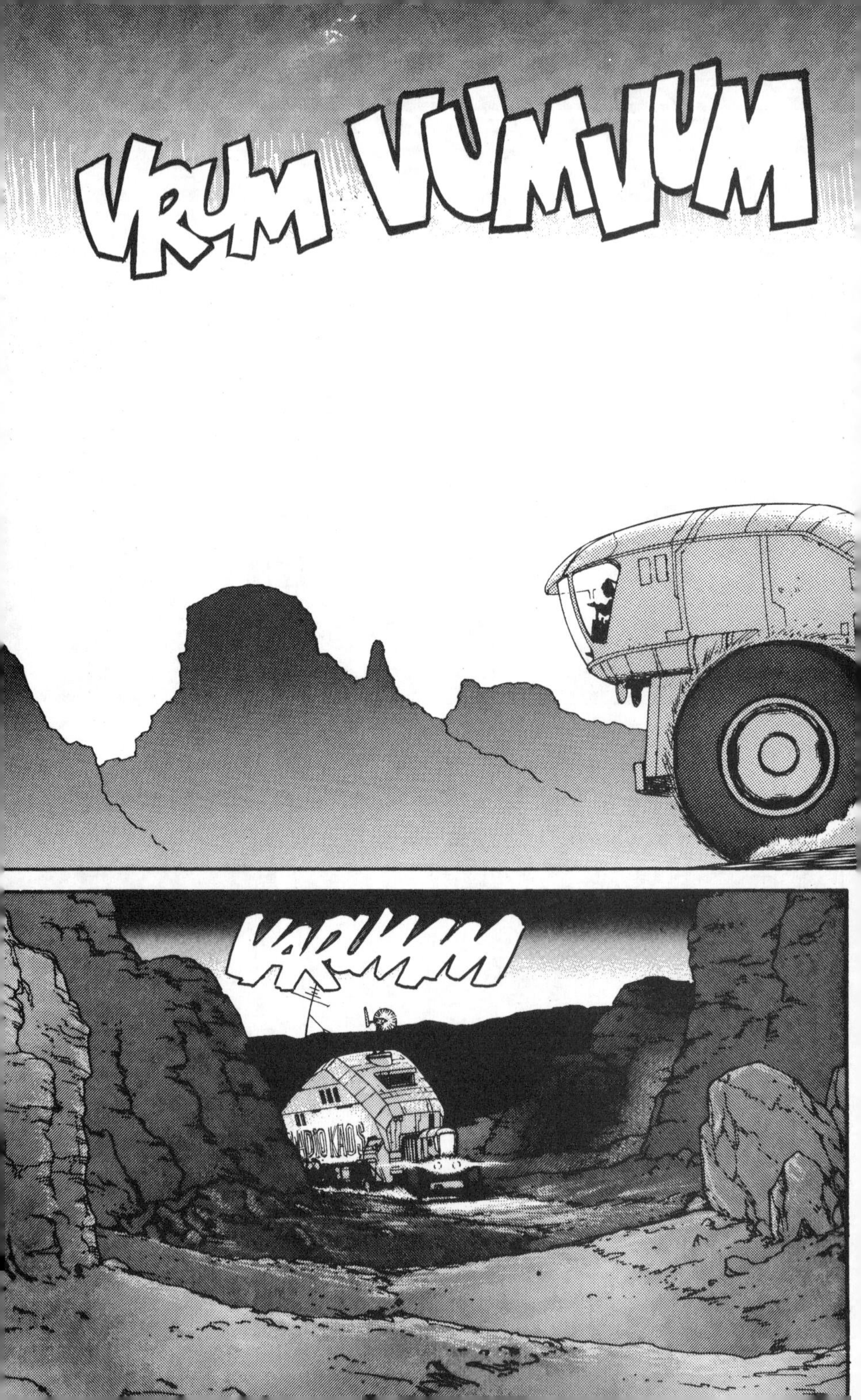
VRUM VUMVUM
VARUMM
ADIO KAOS

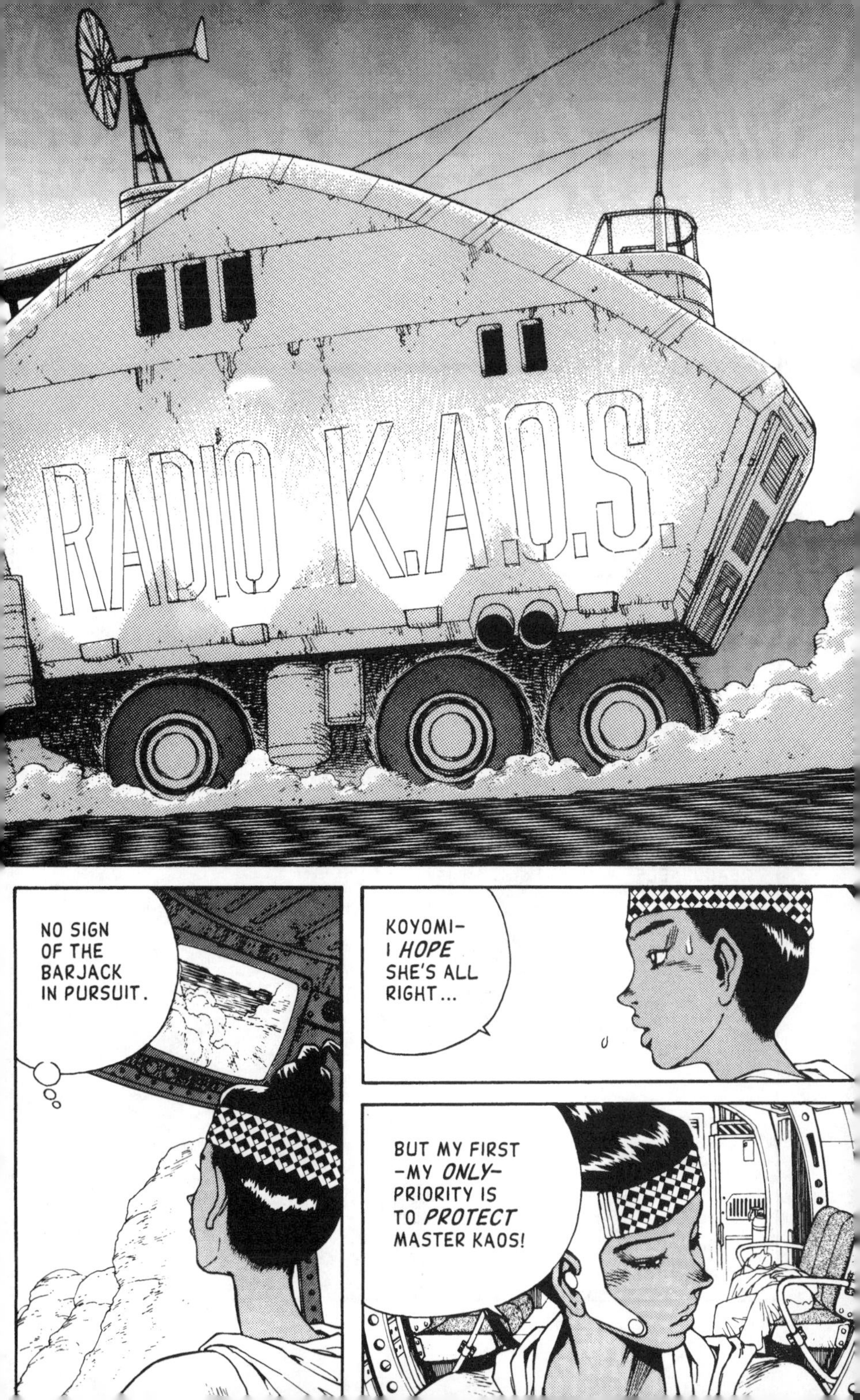
RADIO K.A.O.S.
NO SIGN OF THE BARJACK IN PURSUIT.
KOYOMI— I *HOPE* SHE'S ALL RIGHT...
BUT MY FIRST —MY *ONLY*— PRIORITY IS TO *PROTECT* MASTER KAOS!

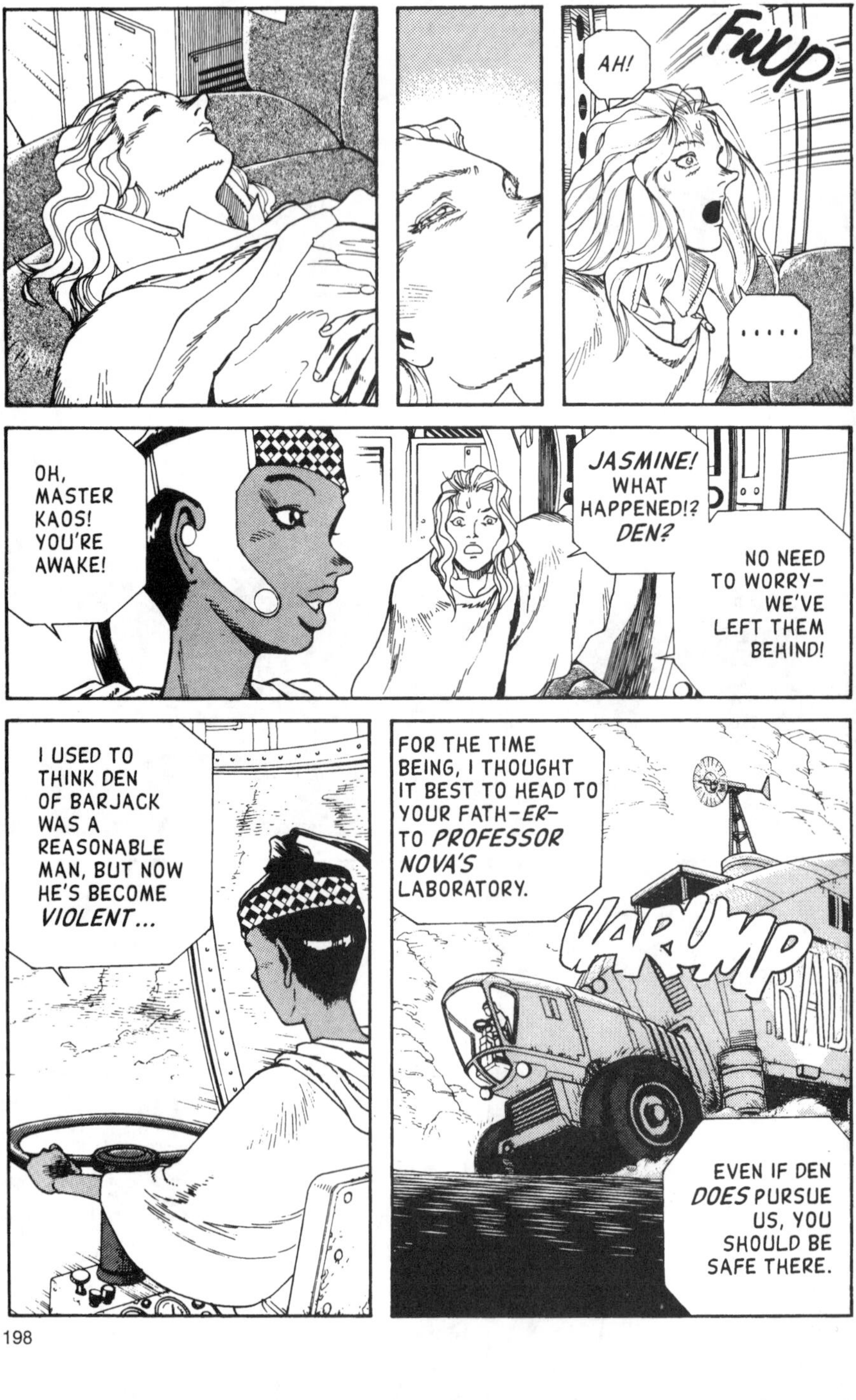
FWUP
AH!
.....
OH, MASTER KAOS! YOU'RE AWAKE!
JASMINE! WHAT HAPPENED!? DEN?
NO NEED TO WORRY— WE'VE LEFT THEM BEHIND!
I USED TO THINK DEN OF BARJACK WAS A REASONABLE MAN, BUT NOW HE'S BECOME VIOLENT...
FOR THE TIME BEING, I THOUGHT IT BEST TO HEAD TO YOUR FATH-ER— TO PROFESSOR NOVA'S LABORATORY.
VARUMP
RAD
EVEN IF DEN DOES PURSUE US, YOU SHOULD BE SAFE THERE.

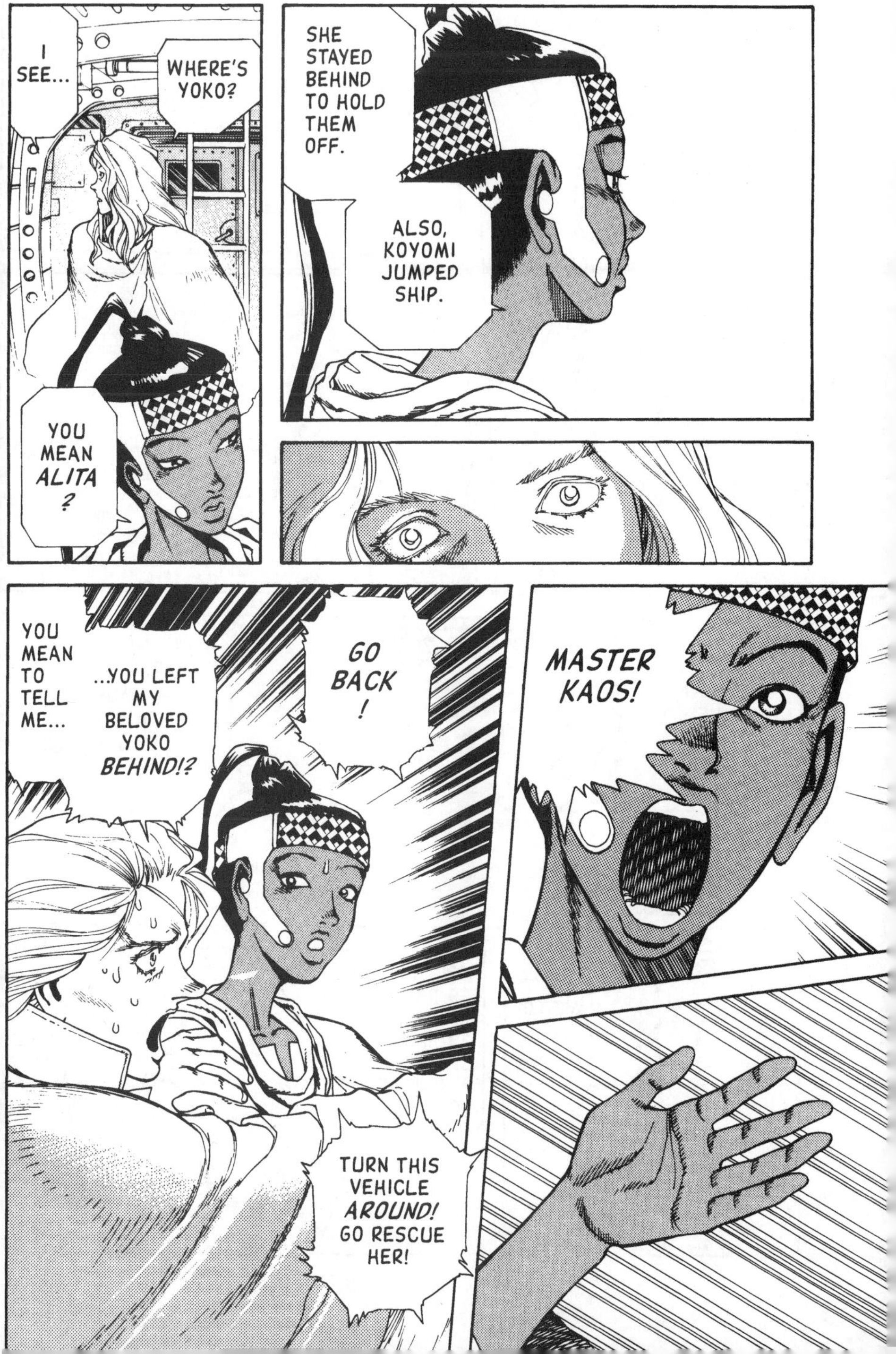
I SEE...
WHERE'S YOKO?
YOU MEAN ALITA?
SHE STAYED BEHIND TO HOLD THEM OFF.
ALSO, KOYOMI JUMPED SHIP.
YOU MEAN TO TELL ME...
...YOU LEFT MY BELOVED YOKO BEHIND!?
GO BACK!
TURN THIS VEHICLE AROUND! GO RESCUE HER!
MASTER KAOS!

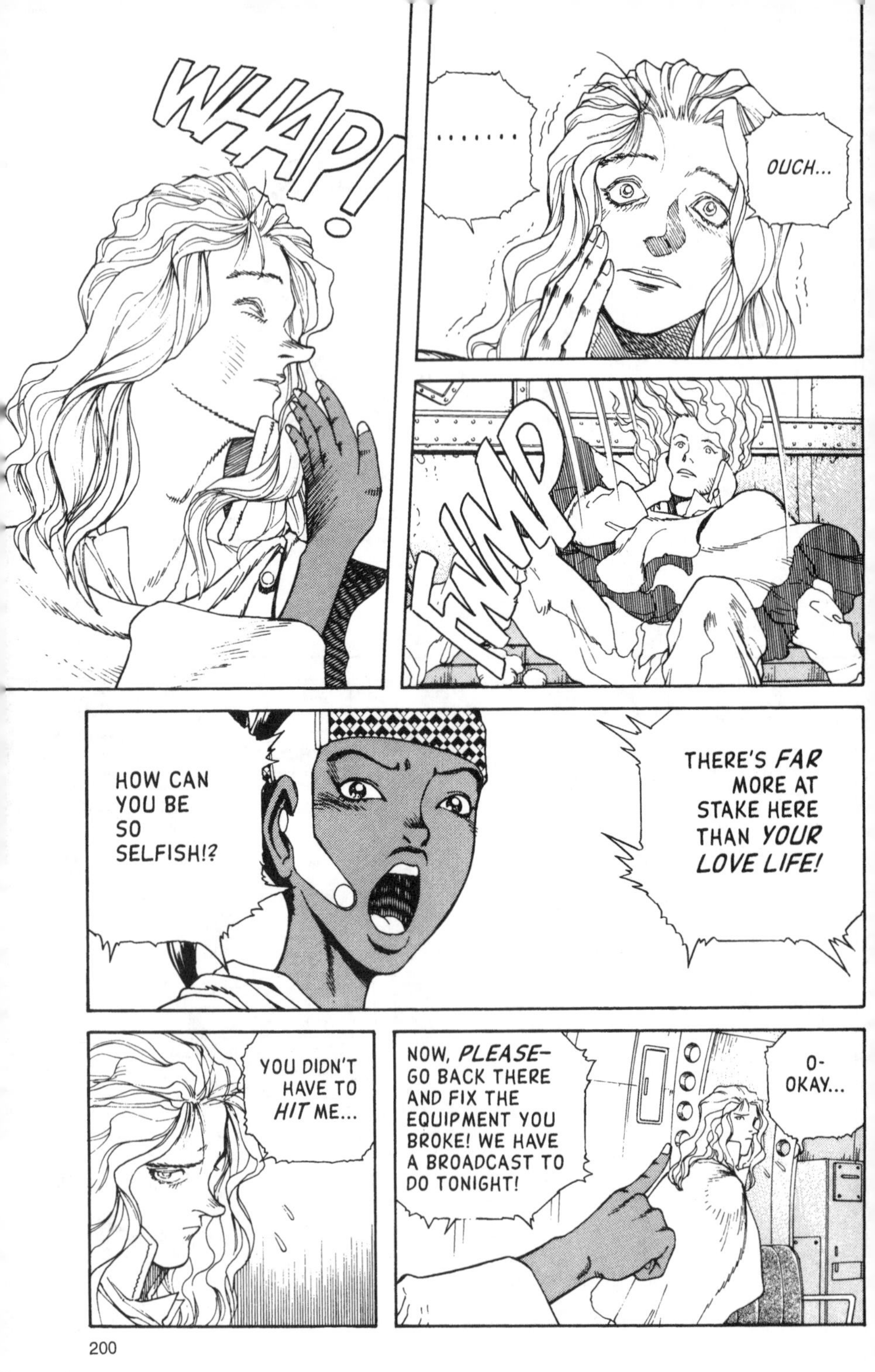
WHAP!
....
OUCH...
FWMP
HOW CAN YOU BE SO SELFISH!?
THERE'S *FAR* MORE AT STAKE HERE THAN *YOUR LOVE LIFE!*
YOU DIDN'T HAVE TO *HIT* ME...
NOW, *PLEASE*— GO BACK THERE AND FIX THE EQUIPMENT YOU BROKE! WE HAVE A BROADCAST TO DO TONIGHT!
O-OKAY...

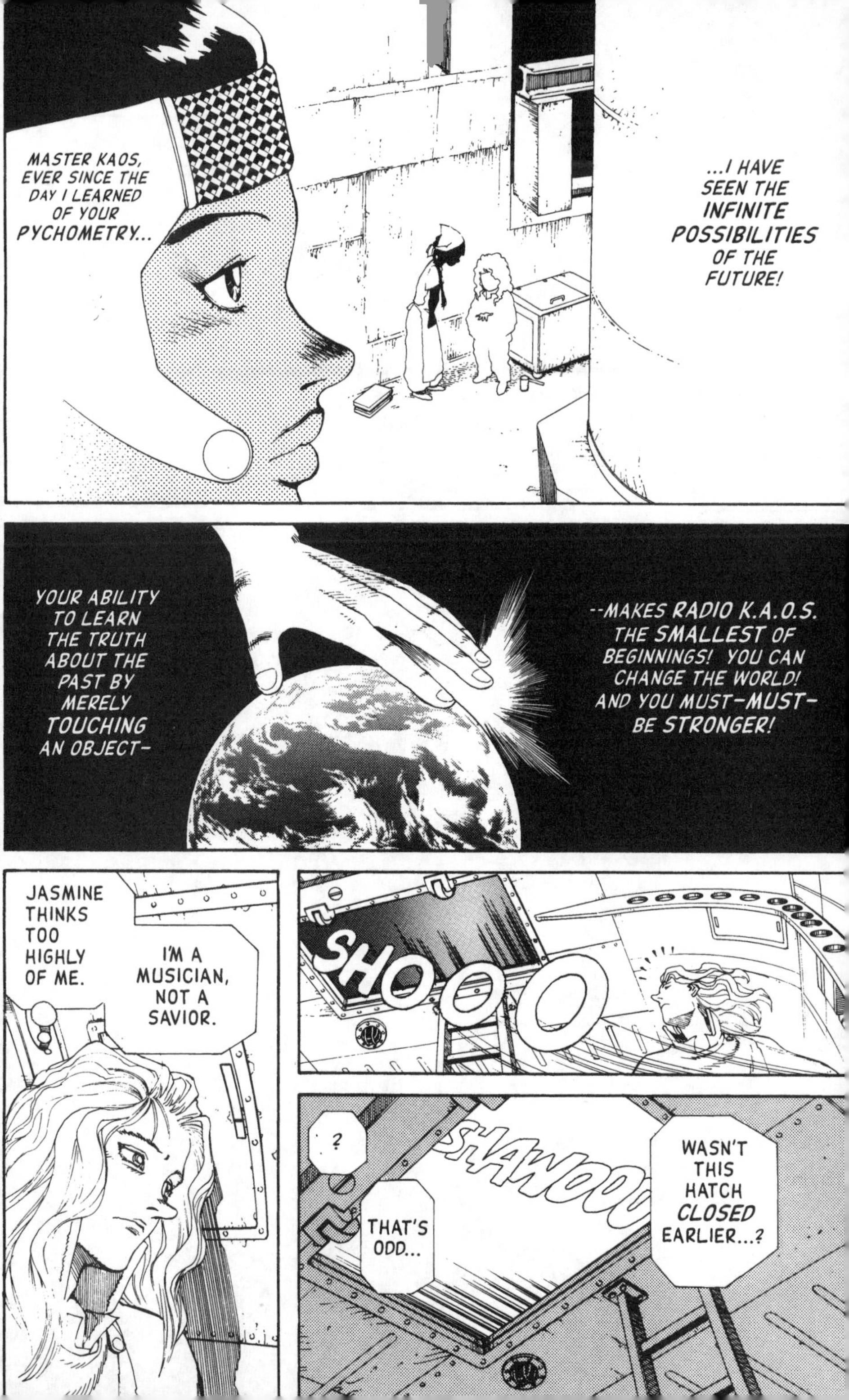
MASTER KAOS, EVER SINCE THE DAY I LEARNED OF YOUR PYCHOMETRY...
...I HAVE SEEN THE INFINITE POSSIBILITIES OF THE FUTURE!
YOUR ABILITY TO LEARN THE TRUTH ABOUT THE PAST BY MERELY TOUCHING AN OBJECT-
--MAKES RADIO K.A.O.S. THE SMALLEST OF BEGINNINGS! YOU CAN CHANGE THE WORLD! AND YOU MUST-MUST-BE STRONGER!
JASMINE THINKS TOO HIGHLY OF ME.
I'M A MUSICIAN, NOT A SAVIOR.
SHOOO
?
SHAWOO
THAT'S ODD...
WASN'T THIS HATCH CLOSED EARLIER...?

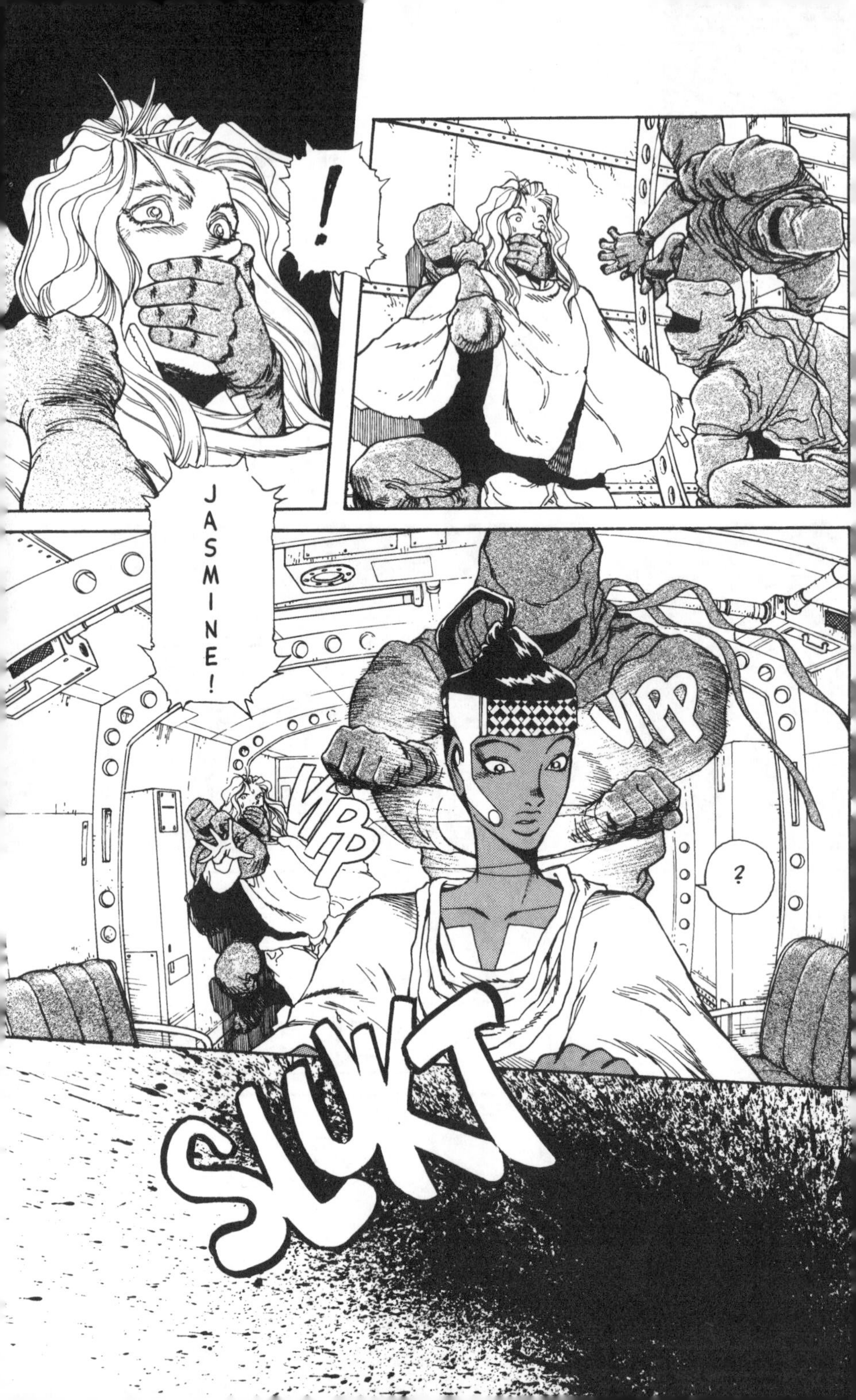
!
JASMINE!
VIPP
VIPP
?
SLUKT

SWEET FRUIT OF LIFE

Mission 6: Duality

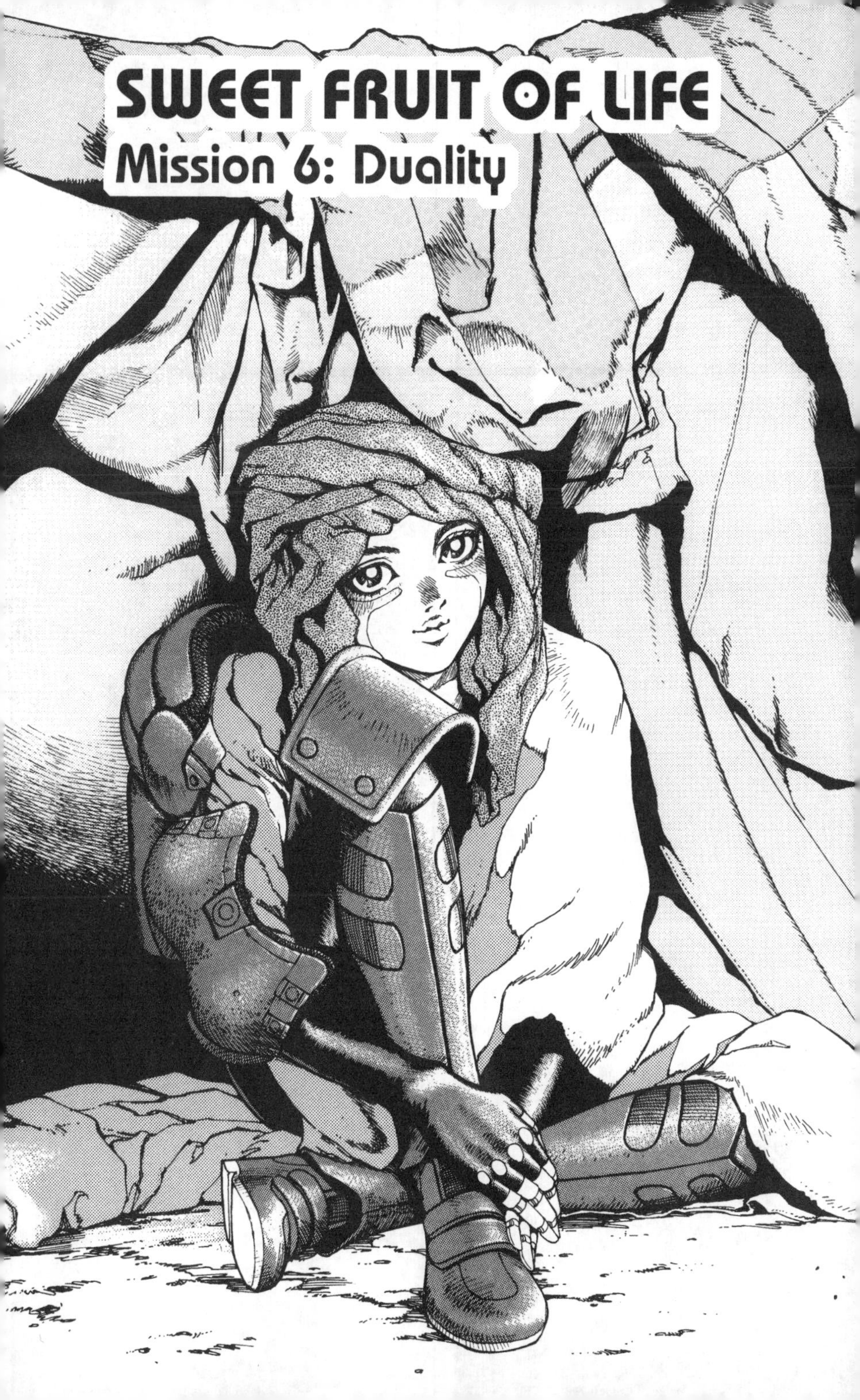

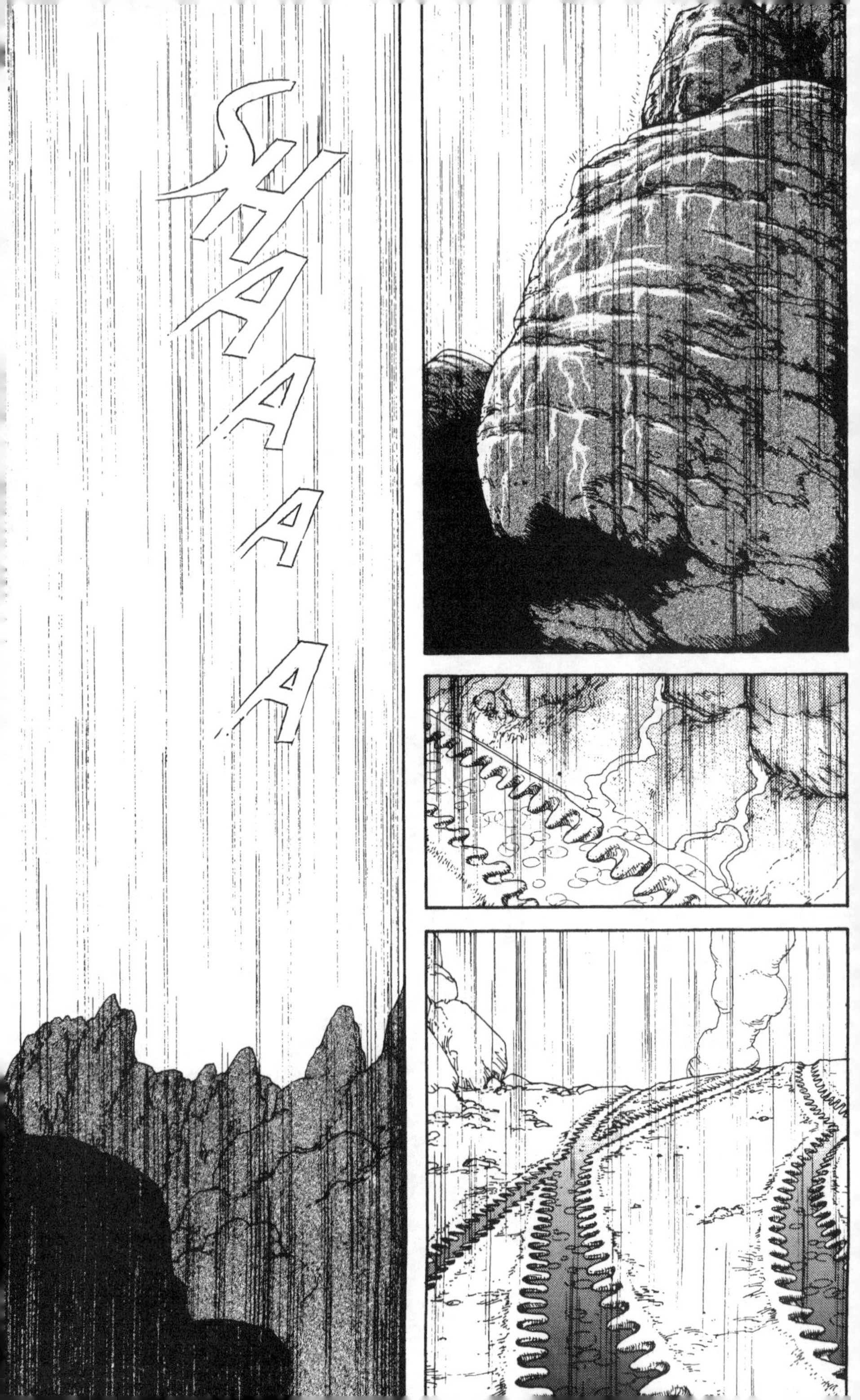
SHAAAA

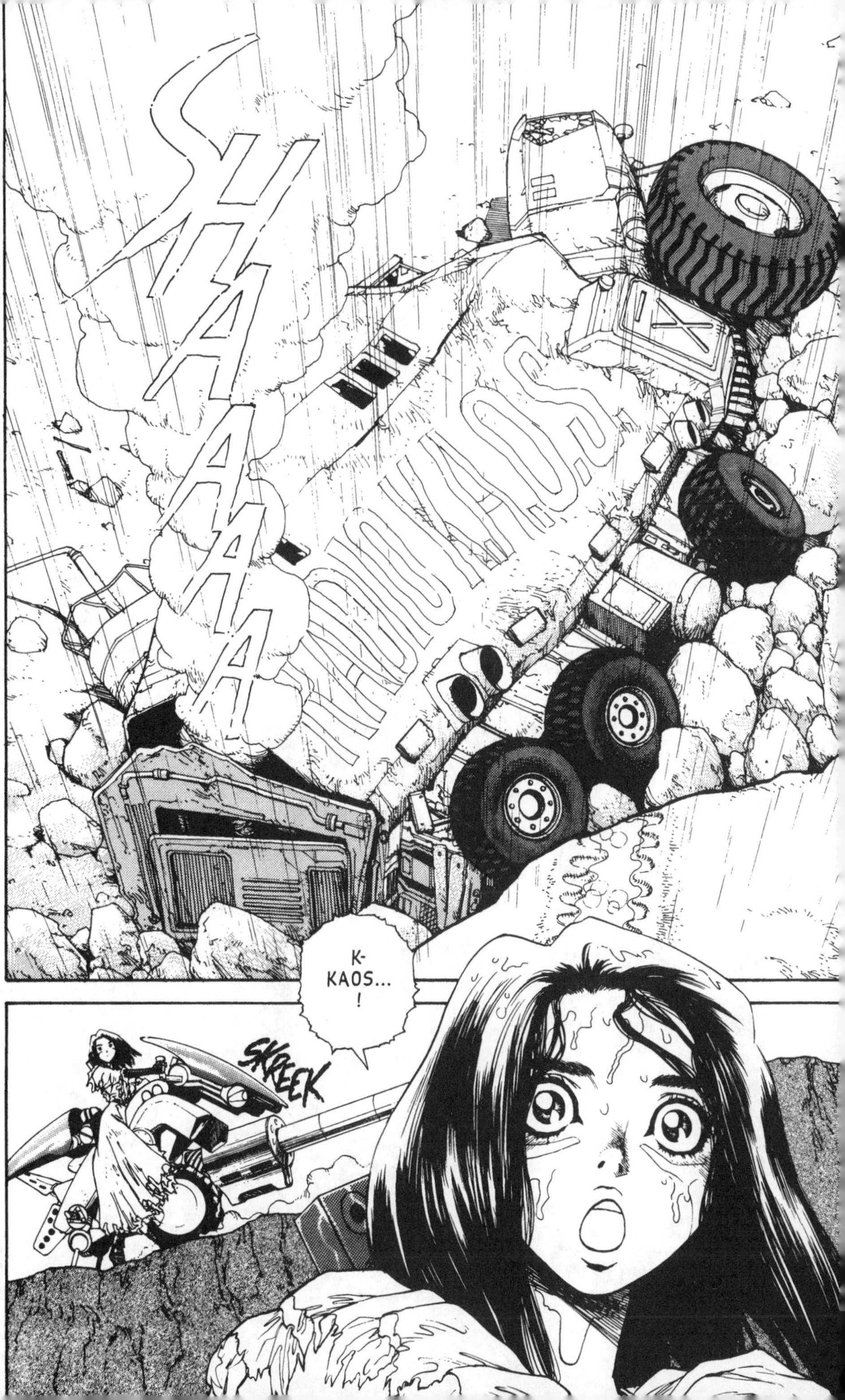
SHAAAAA
K-KAOS...!
SKREEK

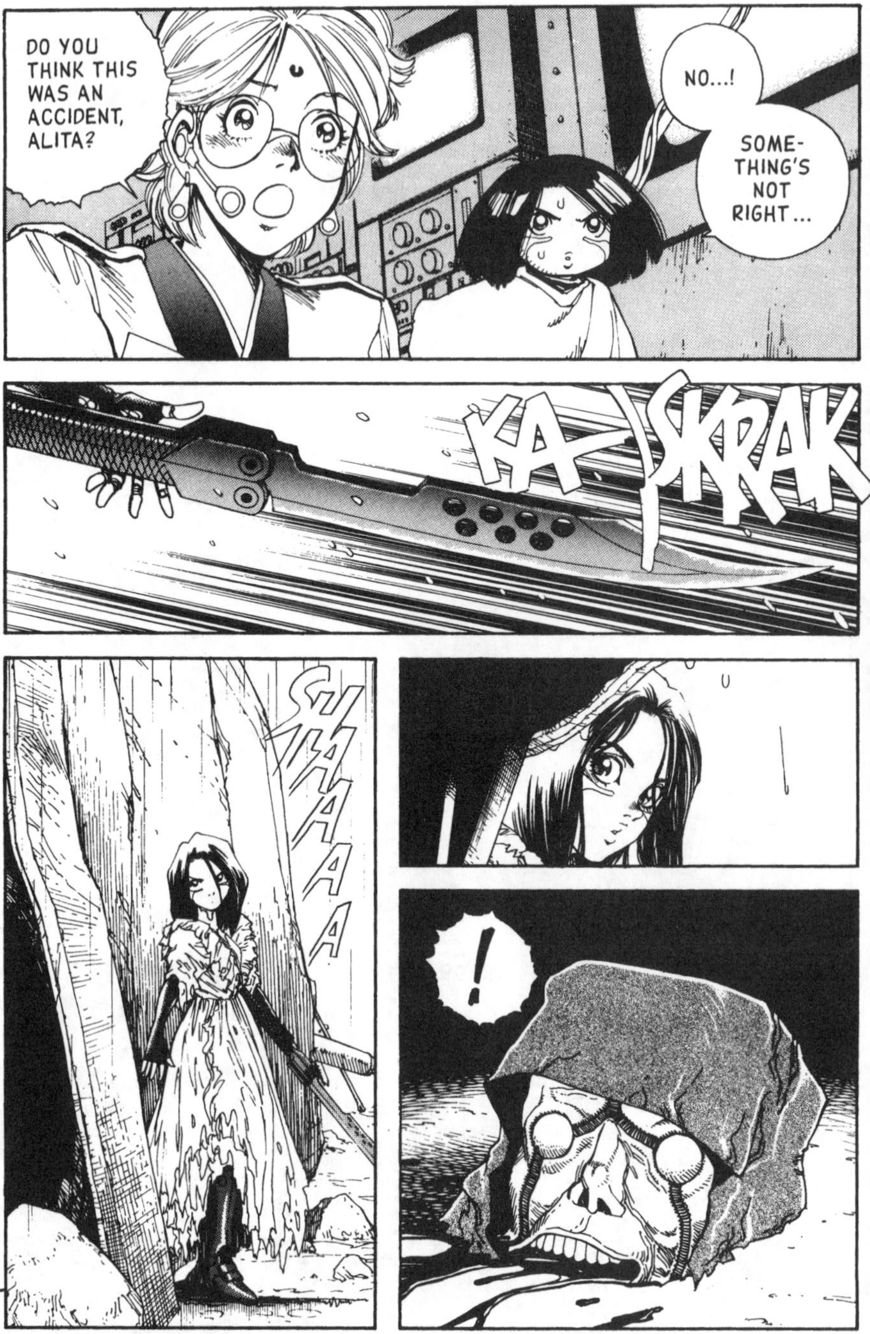
DO YOU THINK THIS WAS AN ACCIDENT, ALITA?
NO...!
SOME-THING'S NOT RIGHT...
KA-SKRAK
SHAAAAAA
!

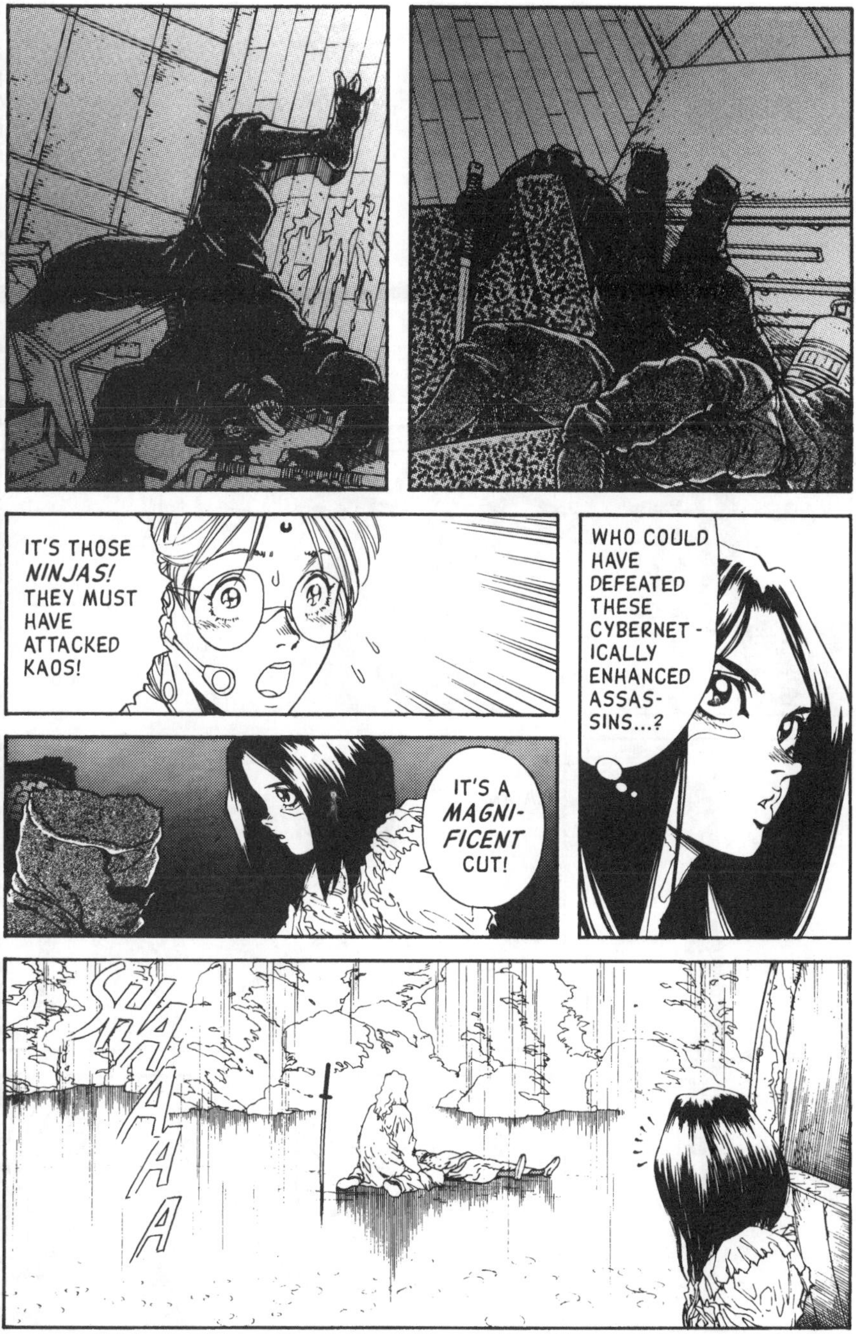
IT'S THOSE NINJAS! THEY MUST HAVE ATTACKED KAOS!
IT'S A MAGNIFICENT CUT!
WHO COULD HAVE DEFEATED THESE CYBERNETICALLY ENHANCED ASSASSINS...?
SHAAAAA

KAOS
!

HE'S
ALIVE...

THANK
GOD...

THIS
KATANA...

DID *YOU*
DEFEAT
THOSE
NINJAS?

JASMINE...

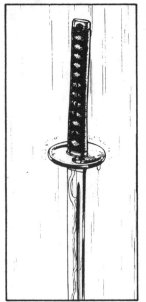

...SHE-
SHE'S
DEAD...

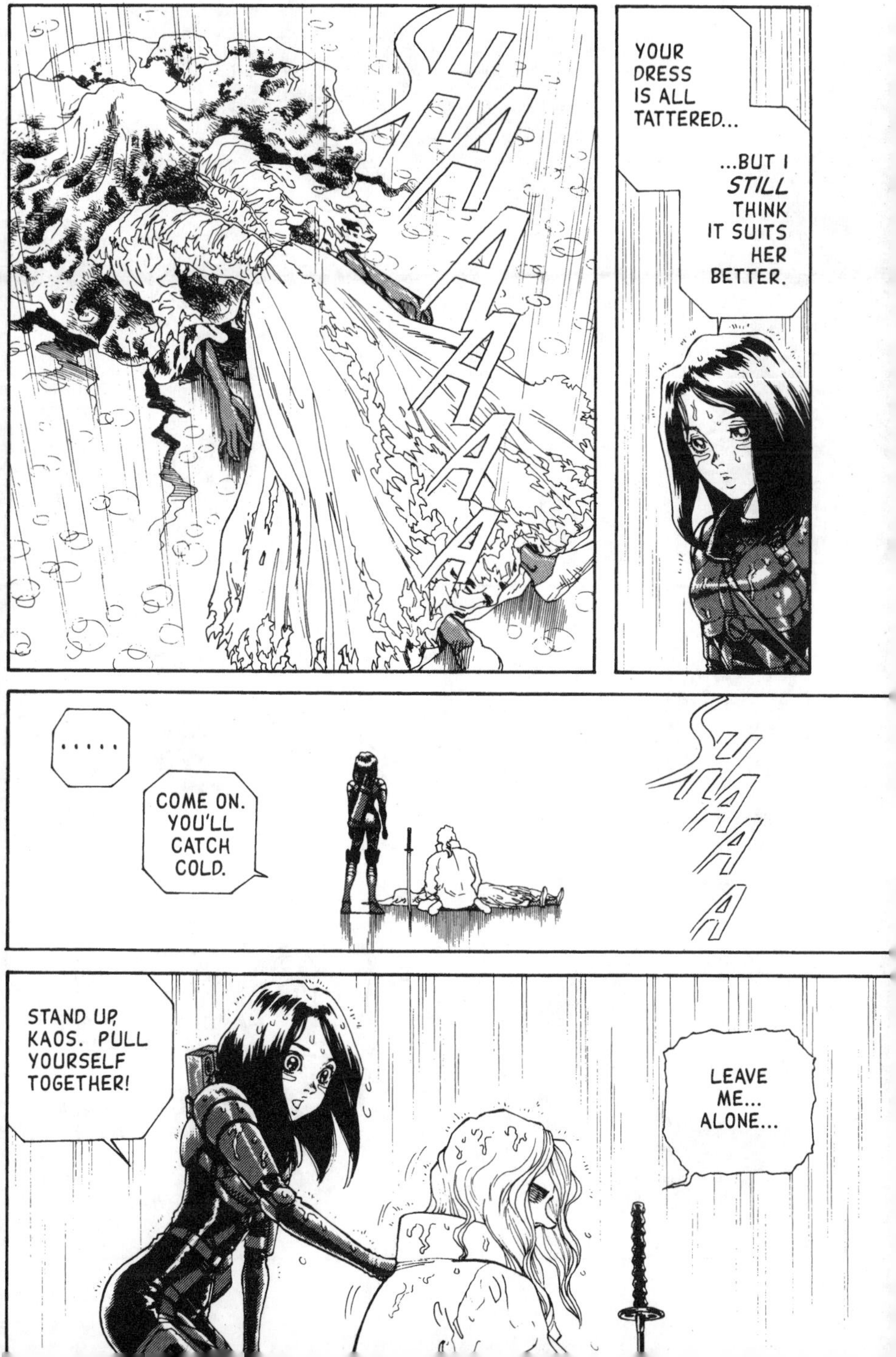
SHAAAAAA
YOUR DRESS IS ALL TATTERED...
...BUT I STILL THINK IT SUITS HER BETTER.
.....
COME ON. YOU'LL CATCH COLD.
SHAAAA
STAND UP, KAOS. PULL YOURSELF TOGETHER!
LEAVE ME... ALONE...

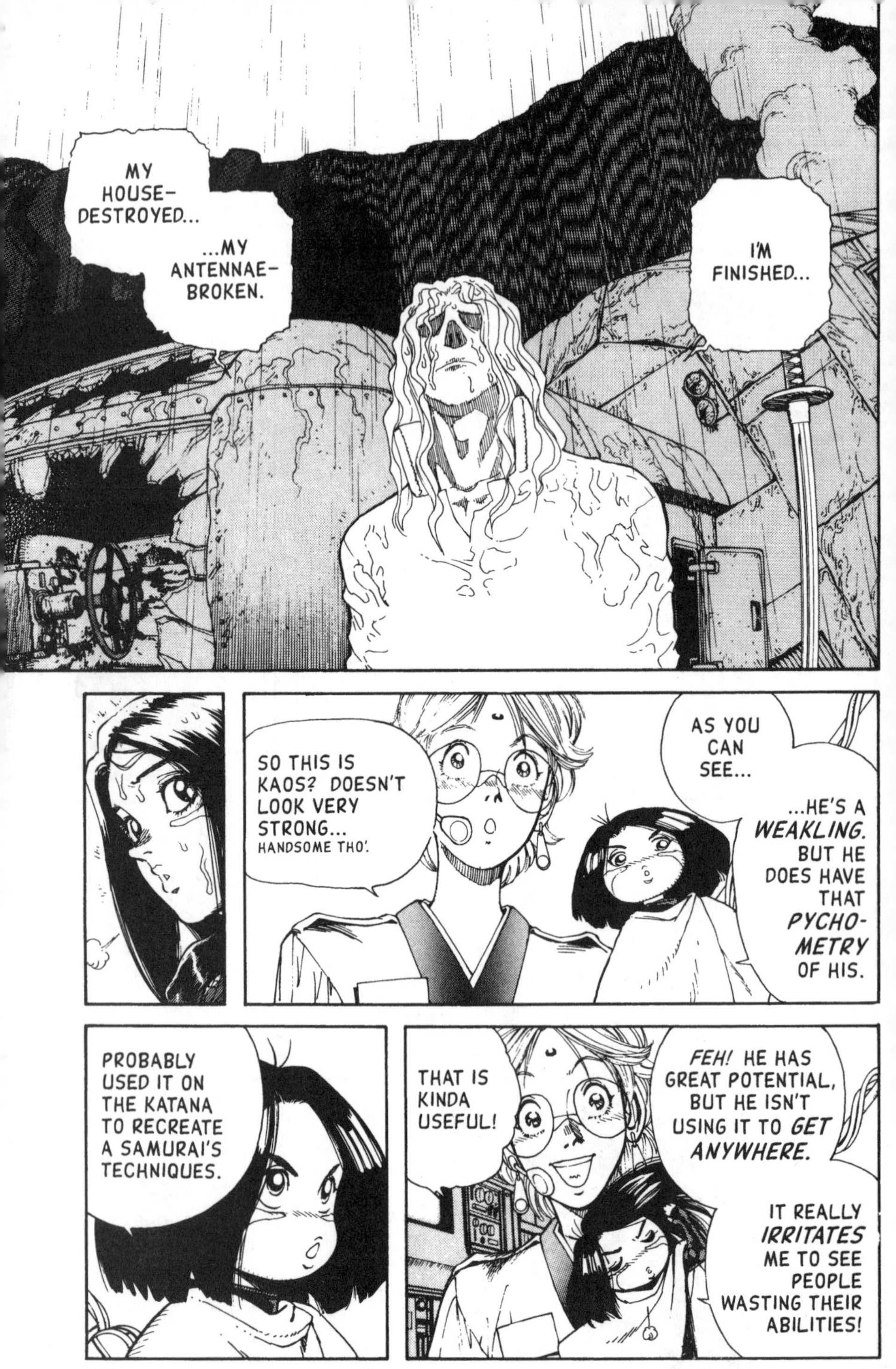
MY HOUSE- DESTROYED...
...MY ANTENNAE- BROKEN.
I'M FINISHED...
SO THIS IS KAOS? DOESN'T LOOK VERY STRONG... HANDSOME THO'.
AS YOU CAN SEE...
...HE'S A *WEAKLING.* BUT HE DOES HAVE THAT *PYCHO-METRY* OF HIS.
PROBABLY USED IT ON THE KATANA TO RECREATE A SAMURAI'S TECHNIQUES.
THAT IS KINDA USEFUL!
FEH! HE HAS GREAT POTENTIAL, BUT HE ISN'T USING IT TO *GET ANYWHERE.*
IT REALLY *IRRITATES* ME TO SEE PEOPLE WASTING THEIR ABILITIES!

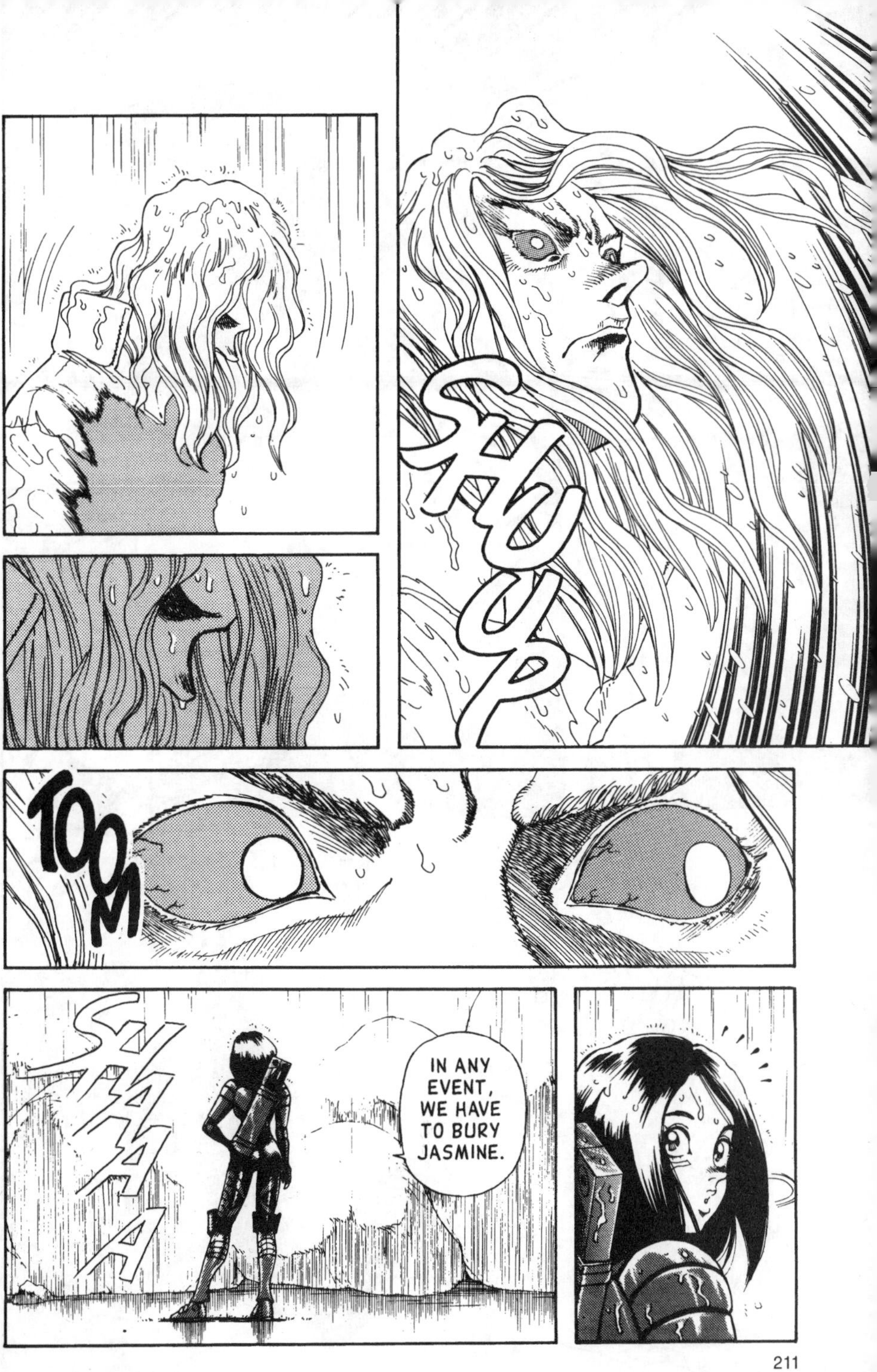
SHUP
TOOM
SHAAA
IN ANY EVENT, WE HAVE TO BURY JASMINE.

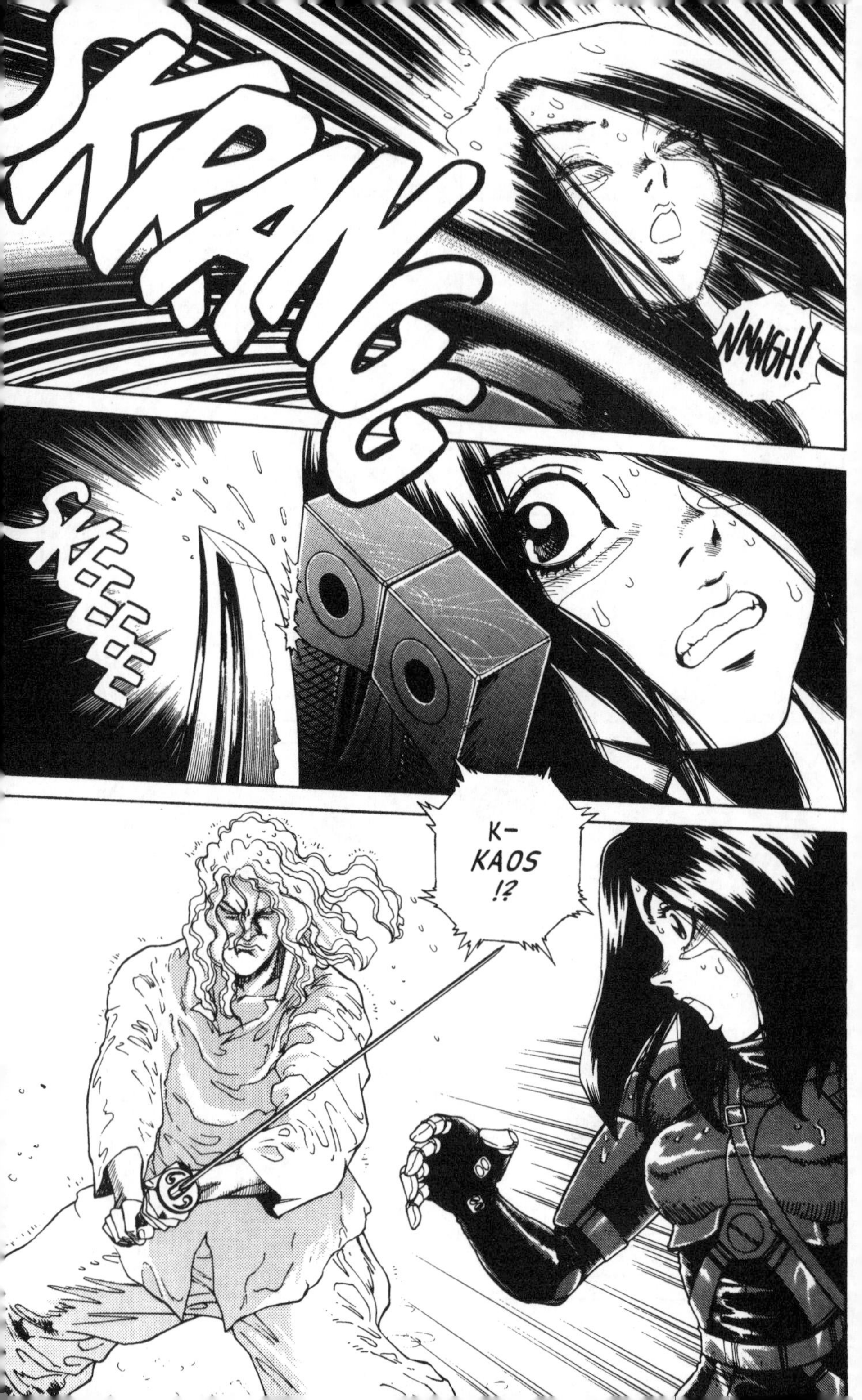
SKRANG
NNNGH!
SKEEEE
K-
KAOS
!?

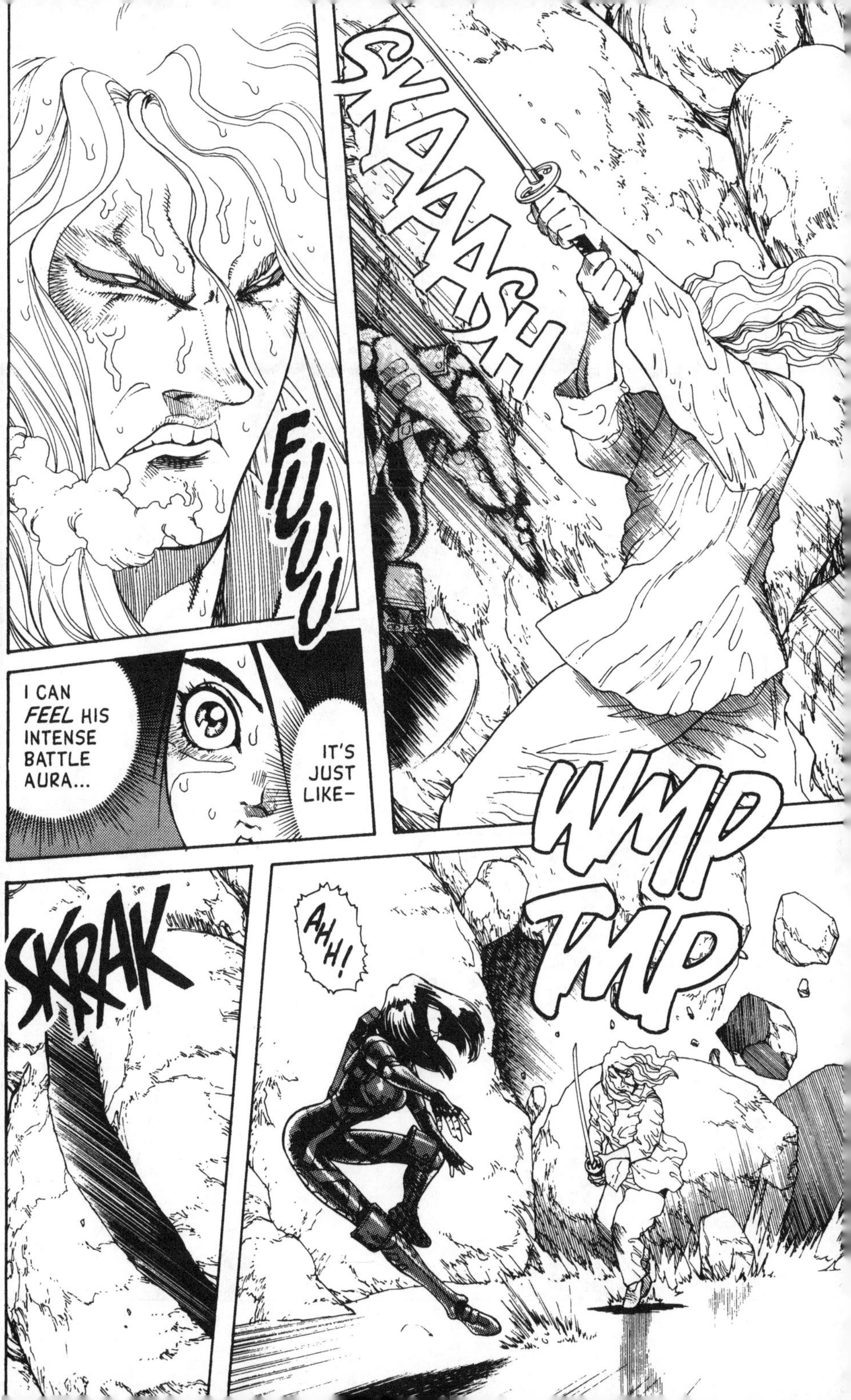
FUUUU
I CAN *FEEL* HIS INTENSE BATTLE AURA...
IT'S JUST LIKE–
SKAAASH
SKRAK
AHH!
WMP
TMP

EEK!

THIS IS A NORMAL MAN'S ATTACK!

W-WAIT! KAOS, WHAT'S GOING ON!?

KAOS IS...

...ASLEEP IN HERE.

D-DID YOU...

...JUST USE A *REAL* VOICE!?

HEH, HEH...

I SUPPOSE IT'S *POINTLESS* TO HIDE IT ANY LONGER.

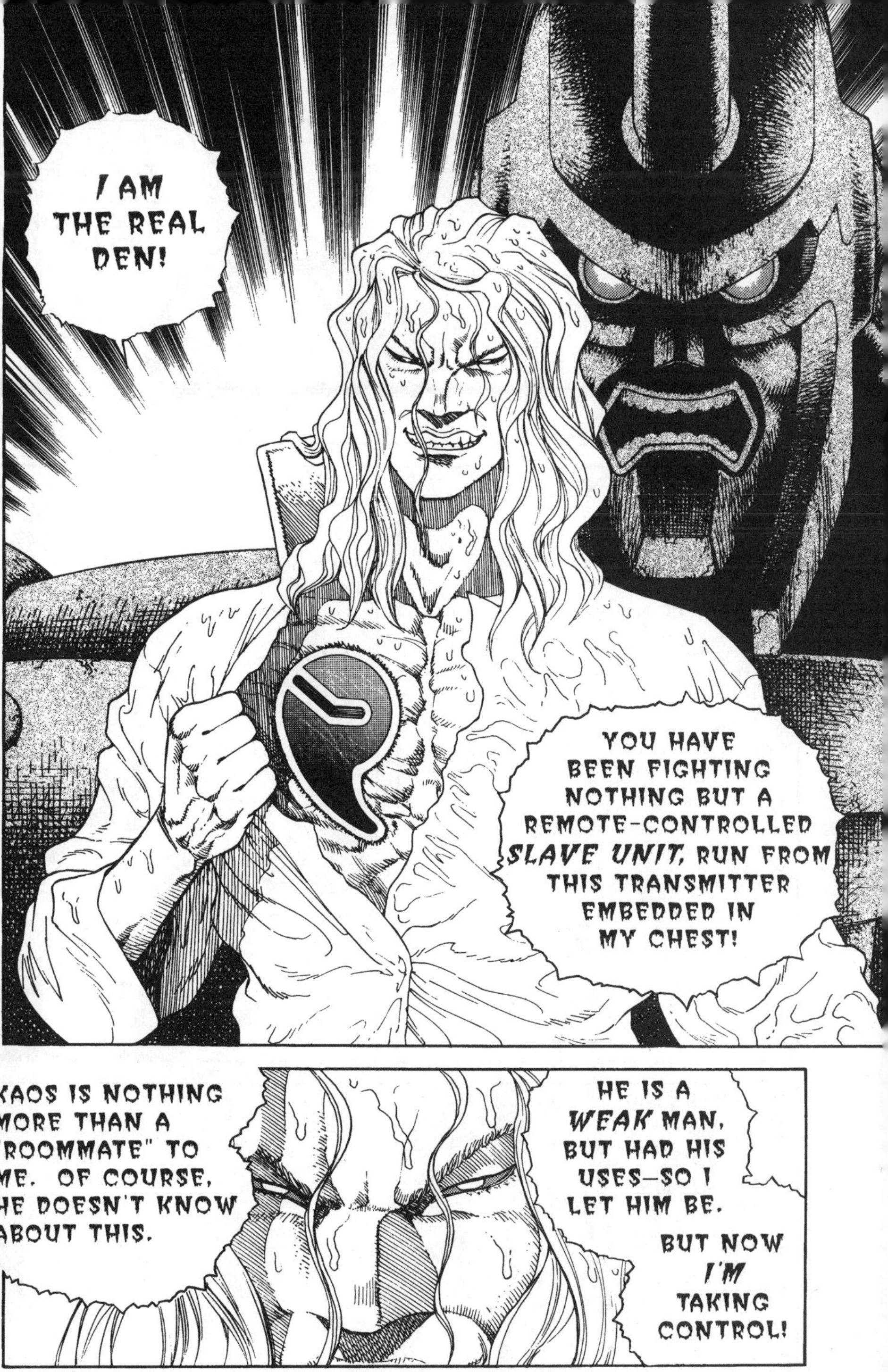
I AM THE REAL DEN!
YOU HAVE BEEN FIGHTING NOTHING BUT A REMOTE-CONTROLLED *SLAVE UNIT,* RUN FROM THIS TRANSMITTER EMBEDDED IN MY CHEST!
KAOS IS NOTHING MORE THAN A "ROOMMATE" TO ME. OF COURSE, HE DOESN'T KNOW ABOUT THIS.
HE IS A *WEAK* MAN, BUT HAD HIS USES—SO I LET HIM BE.
BUT NOW *I'M* TAKING CONTROL!

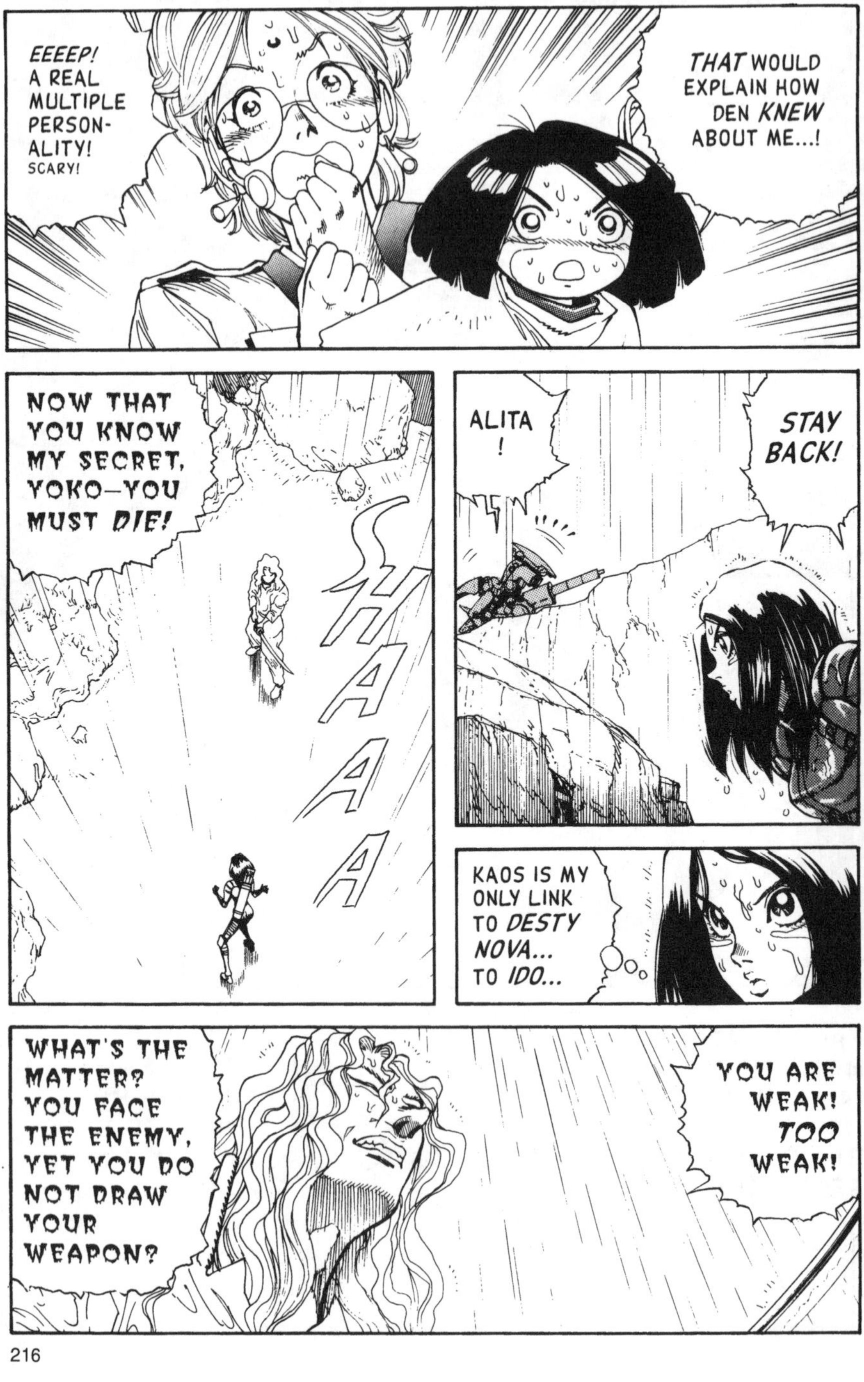
EEEEP! A REAL MULTIPLE PERSON-ALITY!
SCARY!
THAT WOULD EXPLAIN HOW DEN KNEW ABOUT ME...!
NOW THAT YOU KNOW MY SECRET, YOKO—YOU MUST DIE!
SHAAAAA
ALITA!
STAY BACK!
KAOS IS MY ONLY LINK TO DESTY NOVA... TO IDO...
WHAT'S THE MATTER? YOU FACE THE ENEMY, YET YOU DO NOT DRAW YOUR WEAPON?
YOU ARE WEAK! TOO WEAK!

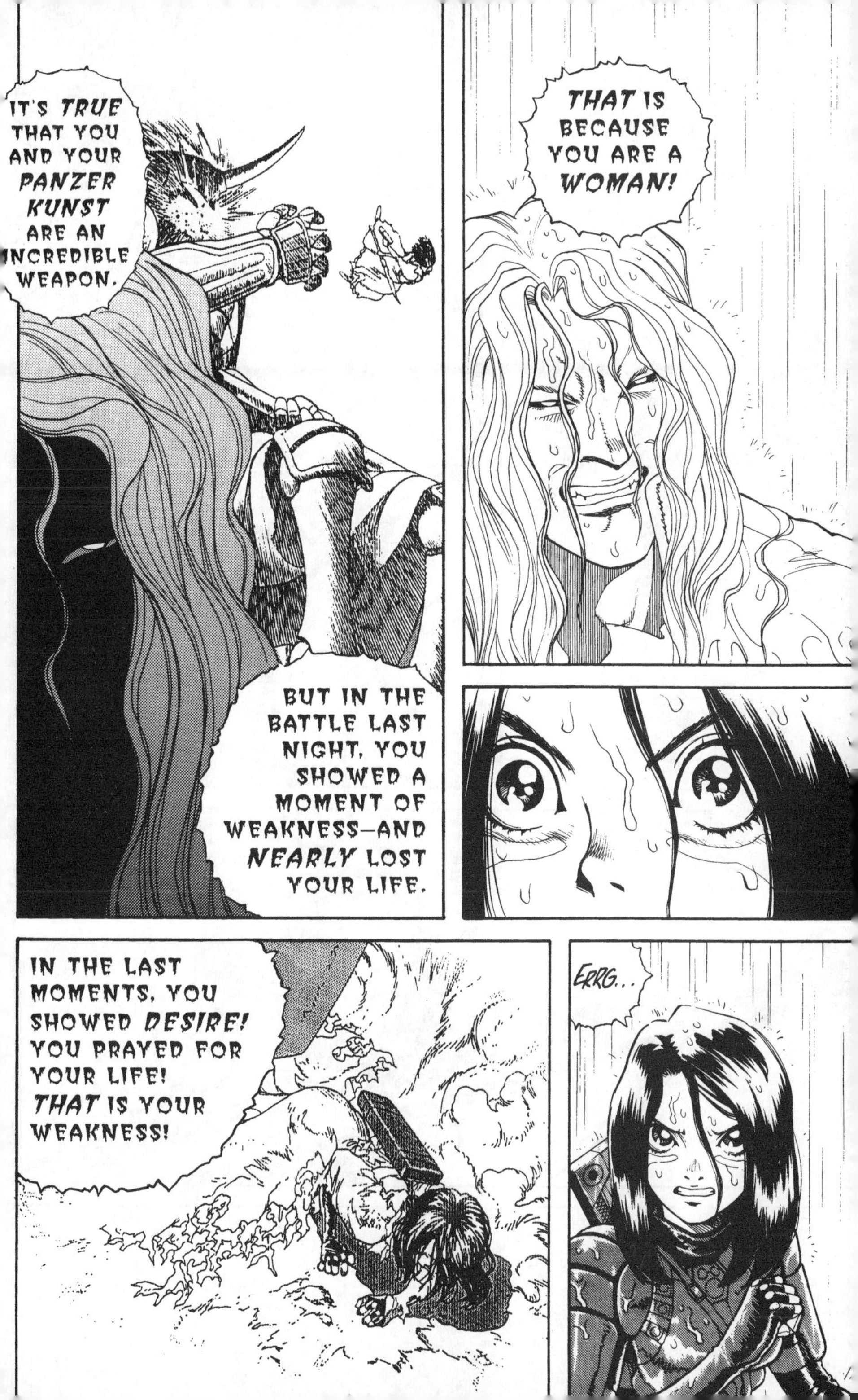
IT'S TRUE THAT YOU AND YOUR PANZER KUNST ARE AN INCREDIBLE WEAPON.
BUT IN THE BATTLE LAST NIGHT, YOU SHOWED A MOMENT OF WEAKNESS—AND NEARLY LOST YOUR LIFE.
THAT IS BECAUSE YOU ARE A WOMAN!
IN THE LAST MOMENTS, YOU SHOWED DESIRE! YOU PRAYED FOR YOUR LIFE! THAT IS YOUR WEAKNESS!
ERRG...

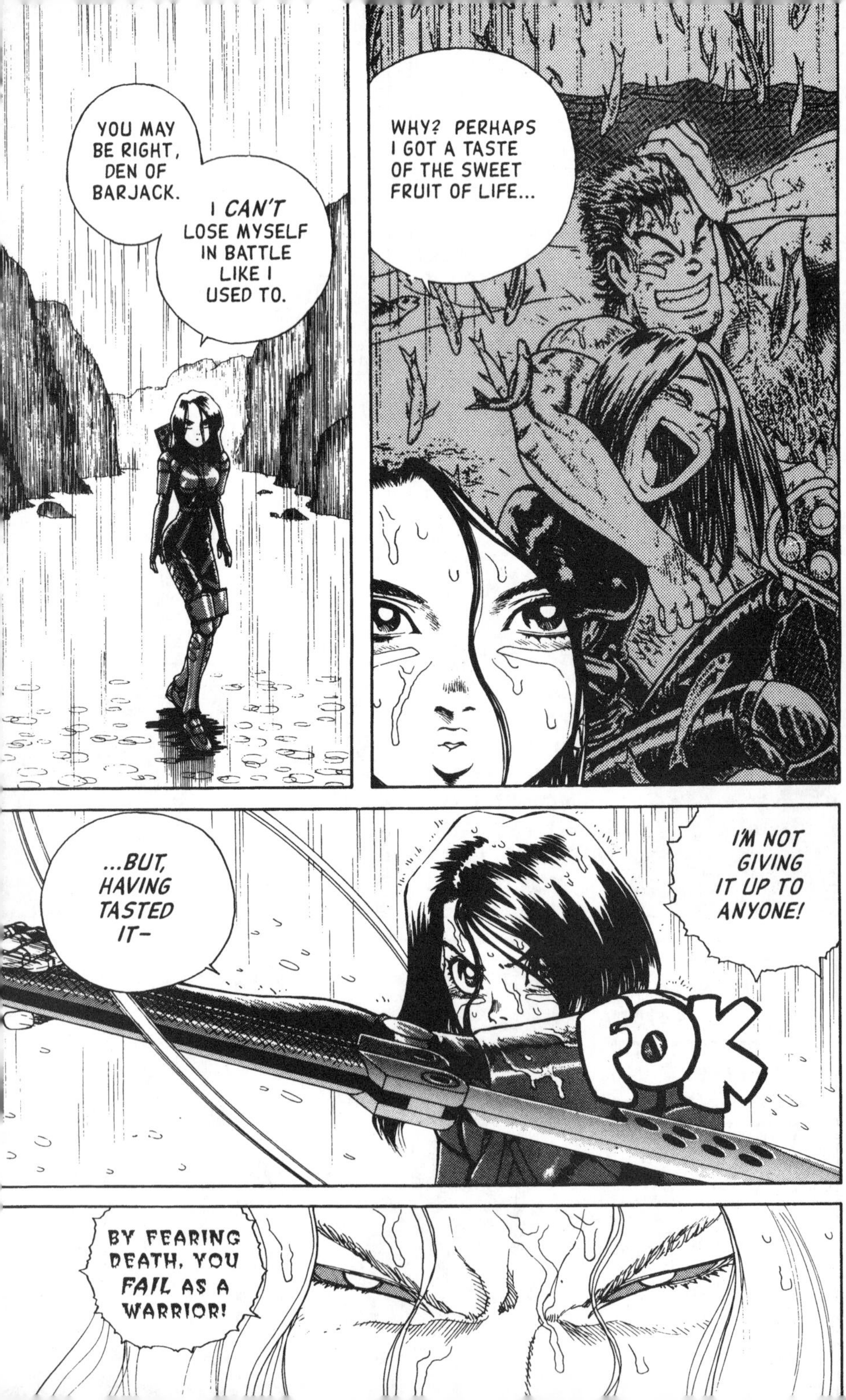
YOU MAY BE RIGHT, DEN OF BARJACK.
I *CAN'T* LOSE MYSELF IN BATTLE LIKE I USED TO.
WHY? PERHAPS I GOT A TASTE OF THE SWEET FRUIT OF LIFE...
...BUT, HAVING TASTED IT–
I'M NOT GIVING IT UP TO ANYONE!
FOK
BY FEARING DEATH, YOU *FAIL* AS A WARRIOR!

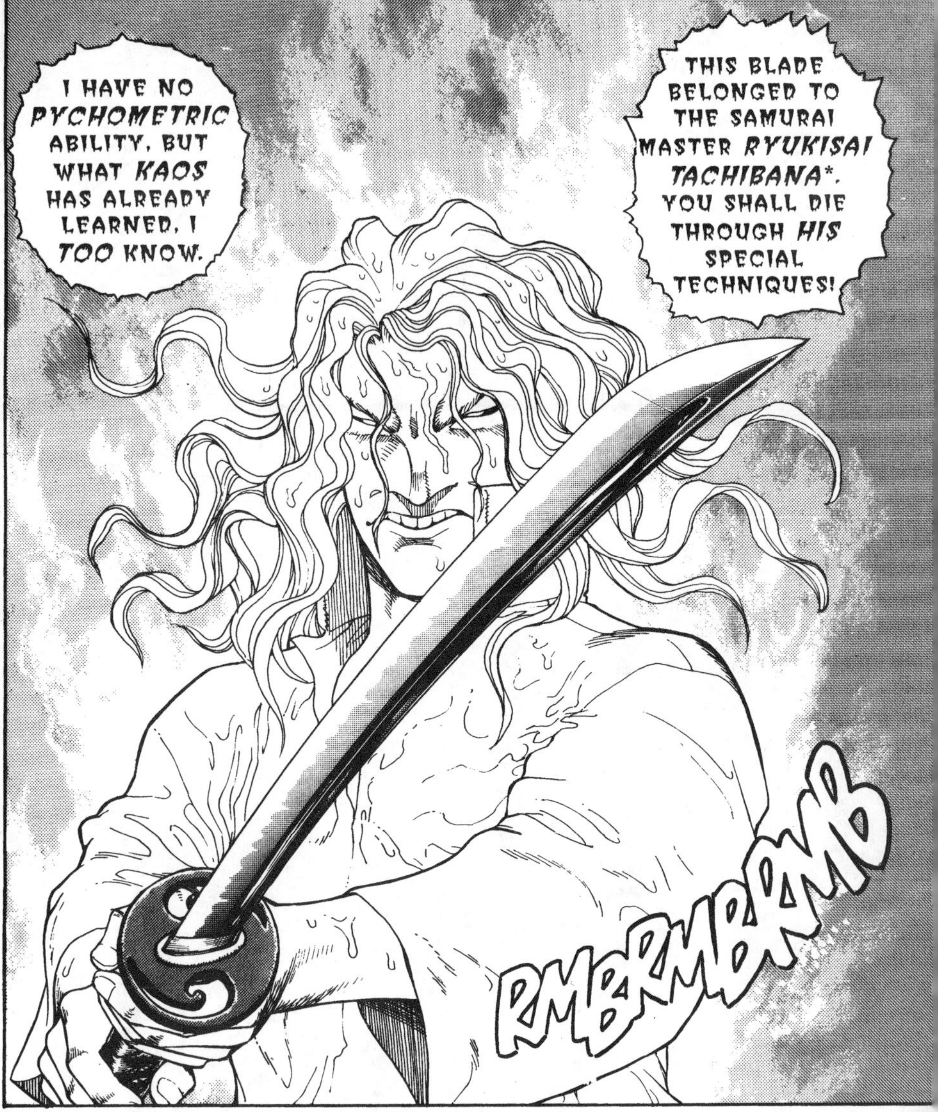
I HAVE NO PYCHOMETRIC ABILITY, BUT WHAT KAOS HAS ALREADY LEARNED, I TOO KNOW.
THIS BLADE BELONGED TO THE SAMURAI MASTER RYUKISAI TACHIBANA*. YOU SHALL DIE THROUGH HIS SPECIAL TECHNIQUES!
RMBRMBRMB
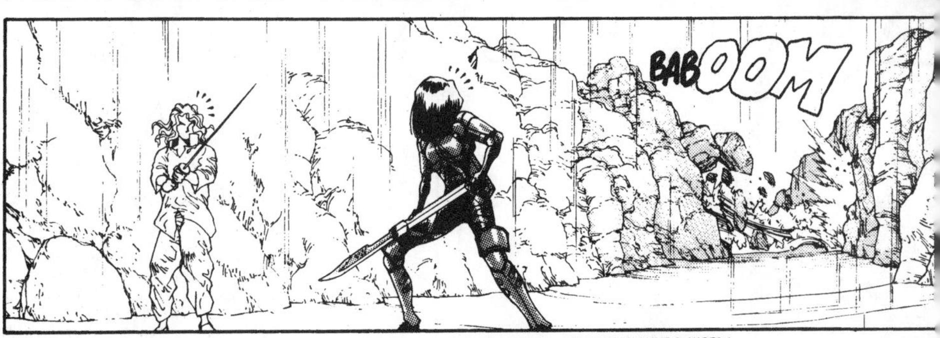
BABOOM

*RYUKISAI TACHIBANA: A MASTER AT AGE NINETEEN, WHO LIVED DURING JAPAN'S FEUDAL ERA. HE IS SAID TO HAVE CLIMBED A HIGH MOUNTAIN TO LEARN HIS ULTIMATE TECHNIQUE FROM A THUNDER GOD. EVENTUALLY, HE WAS KILLED BY LIGHTNING.

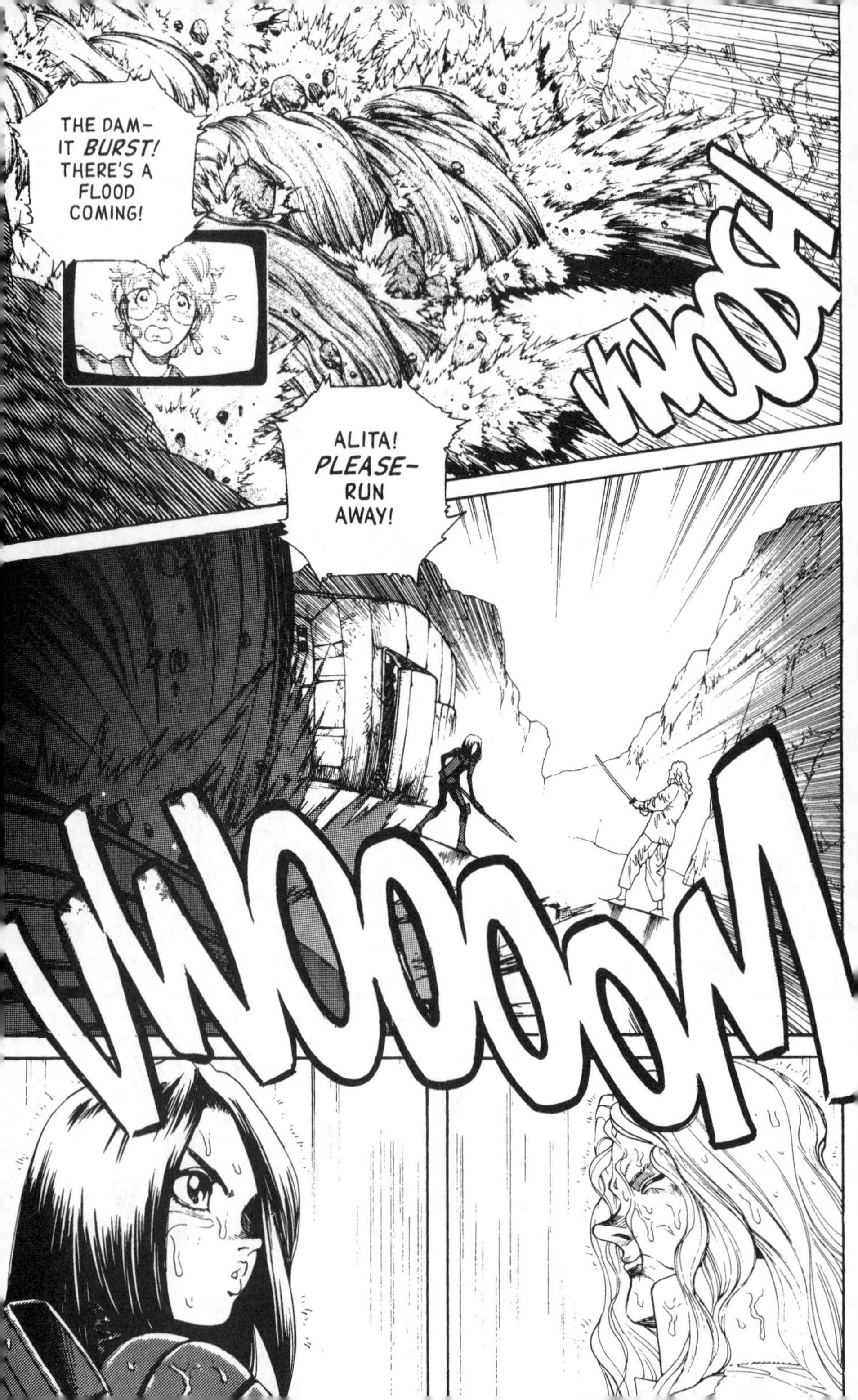
THE DAM- IT *BURST!* THERE'S A FLOOD COMING!
VWOOSH
ALITA! *PLEASE-* RUN AWAY!
VWOOOOM

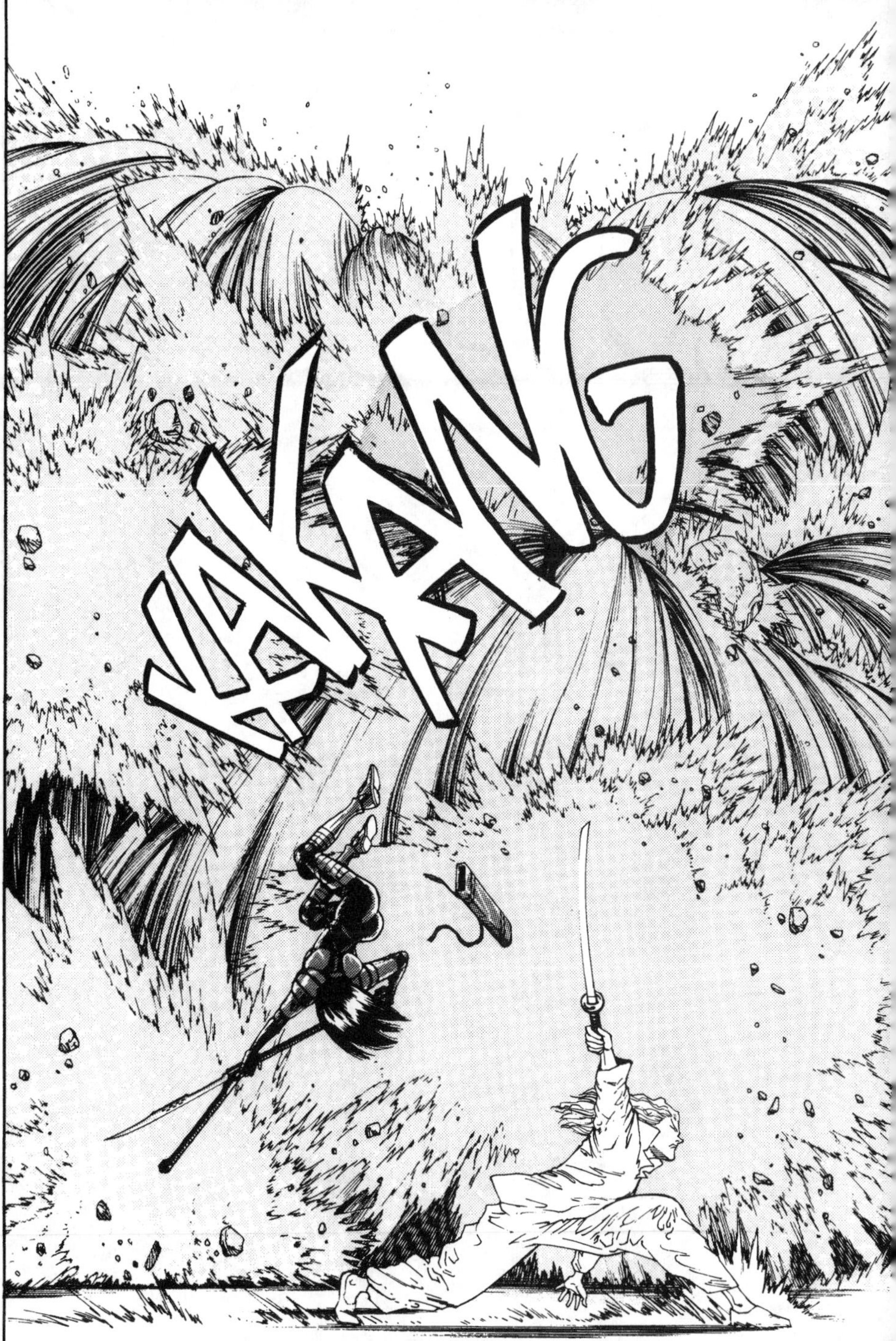
KAKANG

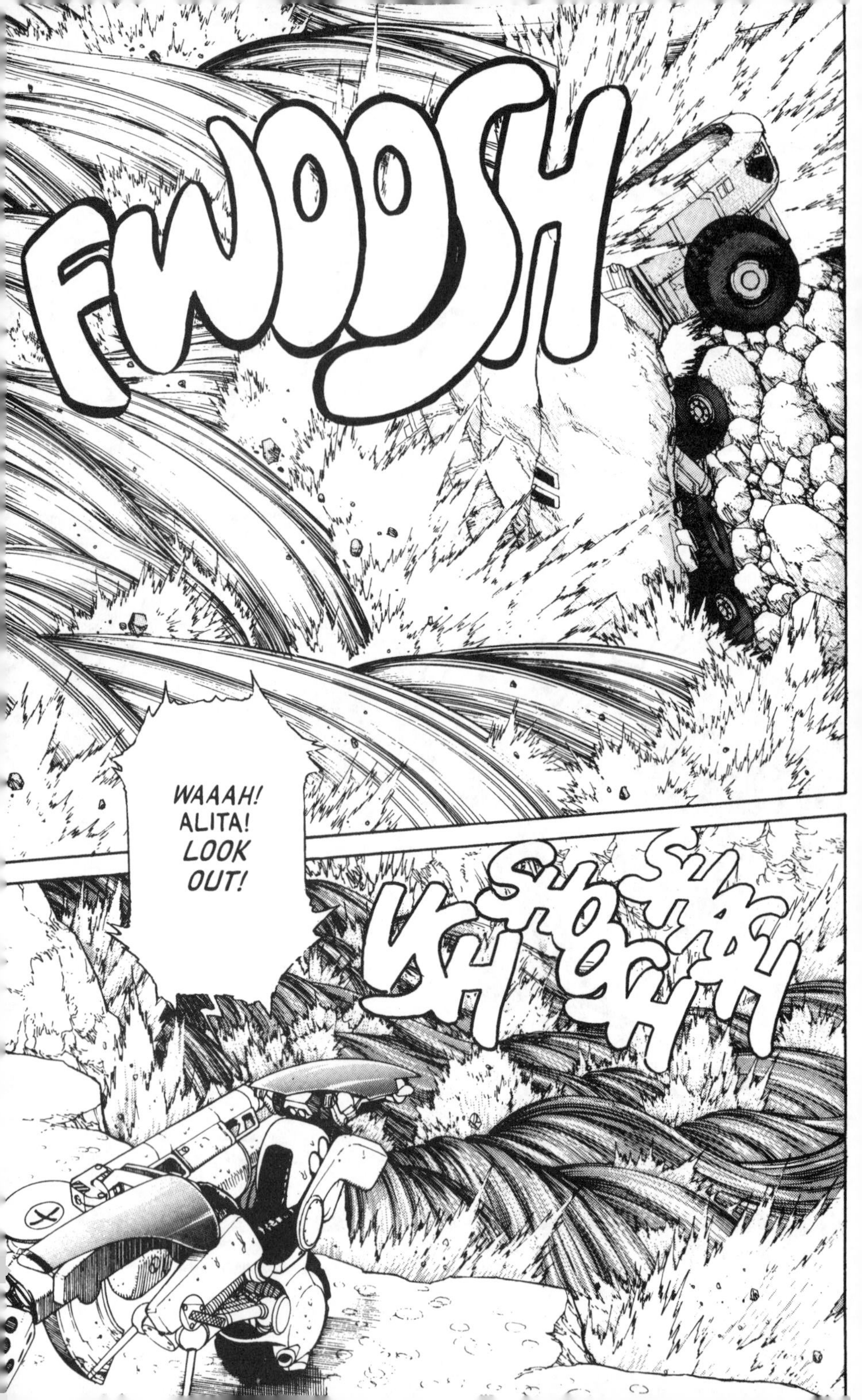
FWOOSH
WAAAH! ALITA! LOOK OUT!

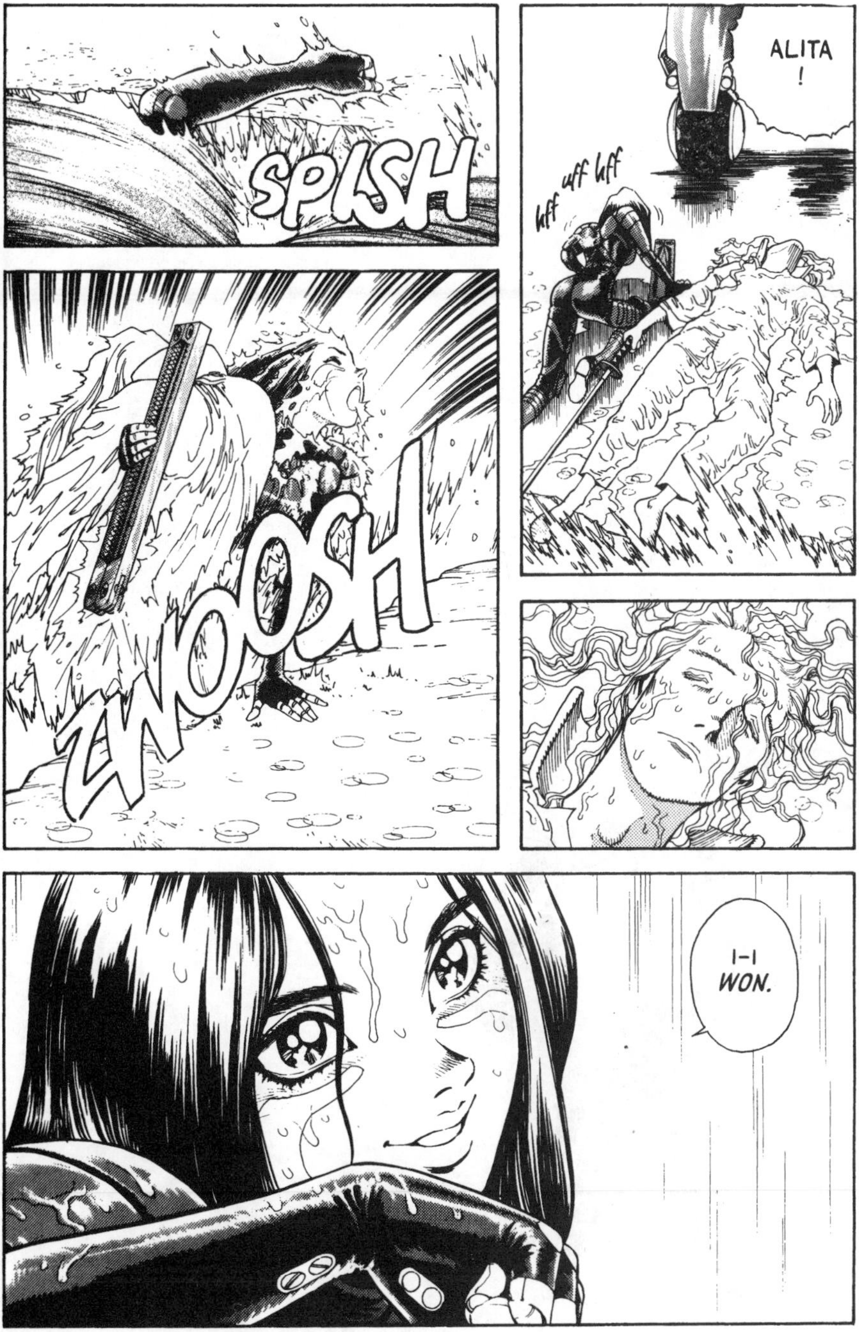
SPISH
ZWOOSH
ALITA !
hff uff hff
I-I WON.

End of BATTLE ANGEL ALITA:
ANGEL OF CHAOS graphic novel.